DATE DUE

FEB 2 9 2016

ALSO BY JONATHAN ALTER

The Promise:
President Obama, Year One

The Defining Moment:
FDR's Hundred Days and the Triumph of Hope

Between the Lines:
A View Inside American Politics, People, and Culture

THE
CENTER HOLDS

Obama and His Enemies

JONATHAN ALTER

SIMON & SCHUSTER
NEW YORK   LONDON   TORONTO   SYDNEY   NEW DELHI

Simon & Schuster
1230 Avenue of the Americas
New York, NY 10020

First Simon & Schuster hardcover edition June 2013

SIMON & SCHUSTER and colophon are registered
trademarks of Simon & Schuster, Inc.

For information about special discounts for bulk purchases,
please contact Simon & Schuster Special Sales at
1-866-506-1949 or business@simonandschuster.com.

The Simon & Schuster Speakers Bureau can bring authors to your live event.
For more information or to book an event contact the Simon & Schuster Speakers
Bureau at 1-866-248-3049 or visit our website at www.simonspeakers.com.

Designed by Akasha Archer

Manufactured in the United States of America

10   9   8   7   6   5   4   3   2   1

Library of Congress Cataloging-in-Publication Data is available.

ISBN 978-1-4516-4607-8
ISBN 978-1-4516-4610-8 (ebook)

For Emily, Charlotte, Tommy, and Molly

Things fall apart; the centre cannot hold;
Mere anarchy is loosed upon the world,
The blood-dimmed tide is loosed, and everywhere
The ceremony of innocence is drowned;
The best lack all conviction, while the worst
Are full of passionate intensity.

William Butler Yeats, from "The Second Coming," 1919

Contents

Author's Note

Since graduating from college in 1979, I've covered nine presidential elections, which may qualify me as a masochist. Every four years, at least one candidate piously claims that *this* election is the most important of our lifetimes. It was never true—until 2012. The last election wasn't the closest contest of recent times but it may have been the most consequential, a hinge of history.

The 2012 campaign featured trivial moments, of course, but it struck me at its core as a titanic ideological struggle over the way Americans see themselves and their obligations to one another. The social contract established during the New Deal era was on the line. Barack Obama's vision was, as he put it, "I am my brother's keeper" and "We're all in this together"; Mitt Romney's faith lay in low taxes and a shrunken government as the handmaiden of business. They agreed on one thing— that the stakes were immense.

With its themes of big money and "the top 1 percent," the election was a throwback to the class-based arguments that had once been a central part of our politics. Romney rejected criticism of Wall Street or calls for higher taxes on the wealthy as "class warfare." Warren Buffett, hardly a left-wing bomb-thrower, summarized what had become the mainstream view: "There's class warfare, all right, but it's my class, the rich class, that's making war, and we're winning." Had Romney prevailed, the win would have become a rout.

I can't pretend to know for sure how Romney would have governed. But it's fair to say that he wouldn't have been president of Massachusetts, with an overwhelmingly liberal legislature that had to be appeased. Romney would have arrived in office on the tide of a resurgent red state America, with a conservative Republican Congress claiming that its sweeping agenda had been validated by the voters. Emboldened movement conservatives would have given Romney little room to maneuver on issues ranging from the budget to Supreme Court nominations. He hadn't stood up to the base during the campaign and would have had a hard time doing so in office without becoming a president without a party.

Amid the cut and thrust of the campaign, I tried to keep the true stakes in mind. Had he won, Romney would likely have had the votes to repeal Obamacare* as promised on Day One (under the same Senate rules requiring only fifty-one votes that led to its enactment). During the campaign he pledged to cut federal spending so deeply that it would, as his running mate Paul Ryan put it, constitute "a fundamentally different vision" of government. Ryan, whom the Romney transition team had already designated to supervise the budget in a new administration, said that he viewed the social safety net, especially food stamps, as a "hammock" for the needy that was harming the "national character." The Romney-Ryan budget would have taken a machete to vital investments in the future, from college loans to medical and scientific research, while eliminating federal funding for other programs (Planned Parenthood, PBS, Amtrak) entirely.

Even if Democrats blocked some of Romney's bills, his election would have vindicated the Bush years and everyone associated with booting Obama, from Karl Rove to the Tea Party. It would have given comfort (and jobs) to those who considered climate change a hoax and the war in Iraq a noble cause. With Obamacare and his other achievements reversed, Obama's presidency might well have been seen by many historians as a fluke, an aberration occasioned in 2008 by a financial crisis and a weak opponent, John McCain.

As I learned when writing a book about Franklin D. Roosevelt and Herbert Hoover, history is usually written by the winners. If today's recovery continued or strengthened, it would have allowed a President Romney to argue that slashing taxes on the wealthy, slashing environmental regulation, slashing programs for the poor, increasing defense spending, and voucherizing Medicare were what led to economic growth. History would have recorded that Barack Obama (like Jimmy Carter) had failed to rescue the economy and Mitt Romney (like Ronald Reagan) had succeeded.

After an election, voters sometimes take the outcome for granted or say it was preordained. *See! I was right! I always knew Obama was going to win!* Anyone tempted to think this should note that Bill Clinton believed Obama would lose all the way up to the arrival of Hurricane Sandy, or so Romney said Clinton told him when the former president called him after the election. With a sluggish economy and

---

* After the president embraced the term in 2012, "Obamacare" ceased to be a pejorative. I've used it for convenience throughout.

a Republican Party backed by billionaires making unlimited campaign contributions, Obama could easily have been a one-term president.

The Center Holds is more than a campaign book and less than a complete history of the second two years of Obama's first term. My aim is to explain how the president's enemies sought to wrench the country rightward, how Obama built a potent new Chicago political machine to fight back, and how his, and Romney's, performance in the 2012 campaign played out against a backdrop of hyperpartisanship and renewed class politics.

All presidents face intense opposition, but Obama's race and "otherness"—not to mention his longstanding determination to "change the trajectory of American politics"—put him in a different category. He embodies a demographic future that frightens people on the other side. I've charted the progression of the malady known as Obama Derangement Syndrome and tried to explain the roots of the antitax and Tea Party uprisings. And I've devoted a chapter to what I call "the Voter Suppression Project," a concerted GOP effort in nineteen states to change the rules of the game to discourage Democrats from voting. Toward the end I explain how the backlash against voter suppression contributed to Obama's victory.

I'm also fascinated by what I see as a strange role reversal at the heart of the campaign. Romney, the self-described "numbers guy," rejected Big Data and ran a *Mad Men* campaign based on a vague and unscientific "hope and change" theme. Obama ran a state-of-the art "Bain campaign," using some of the same analytics pioneered in the corporate world to redefine voter contact and build the most sophisticated political organization in American history.

The 2012 cycle will likely be seen as the first "data campaign." Just as Franklin Roosevelt and John F. Kennedy have been viewed by historians as the first presidents to master radio and television, respectively, Barack Obama will likely be seen as the president who pioneered the use of digital technology that, in various forms, will now be a permanent part of politics around the world.

Like my 2010 book, *The Promise: President Obama, Year One,* this account draws on my Chicago roots. I met Obama there when he was an Illinois state senator who had recently lost a bid for Congress. In the years since, I haven't lost my fascination with the paradox of a man succeeding so spectacularly at a profession that he often dislikes. He is missing the schmooze gene that is standard equipment for people in politics. In the Washington chapters, I try to assess the consequences of this for his presidency.

The Promise was focused on Obama's governing, the part of the presidency that he likes best. *The Center Holds* has some of that (e.g., new details about the killing of Osama bin Laden and the Supreme Court battle over Obamacare), but it is mostly about politics. Obama knew as early as mid-2010 that almost nothing substantive would get done for the next two years as the country chose its path.

I'm focused here on detailing the backstory of the big events of 2011 and 2012. This is a work of reporting, chronicling everything from Roger Ailes's paranoid behavior to the geeks in the secret Chicago "Cave" who built crucial models for the Obama campaign to the car accident in the Everglades that helped motivate a South Florida bartender named Scott Prouty to videotape Romney talking about the "47 percent." While I'm not sure I agree with David Axelrod that campaigns are "MRIs of the soul," I hope to provide a few X-rays.

"Contemporary history" is a genre fraught with peril. Some events will shrink in significance over time, while others I underplay or miss entirely may end up looming large. Passions have not yet cooled, and the story of Obama contending with his enemies remains unfinished. It would be dishonest for me to pretend to be neutral in this contest. But all good history has a point of view. The important thing is that it be written under the sovereignty of facts, wherever they may lead.

In 2011, when it looked as if Obama might lose the presidency, a friend asked me to explain how such a thing could happen. Where did Grover Norquist come from? I told her I wasn't sure Obama would lose—that it could go either way—but I would try to tell a story of this moment in our national life that didn't neglect the historical context. So I write in the past tense and stud the narrative with bits of relevant history that are integrated into the text rather than relegated to footnotes. Franklin Roosevelt ordered the killing of a single enemy combatant; John F. Kennedy confronted right-wing haters; and Richard Nixon ran a TV ad mentioning "the 47 percent." As Mark Twain (supposedly) said, "History doesn't repeat itself, but it does rhyme."

The arguments of 2012 go back to the dawn of the republic, when Thomas Jefferson stressed limited government and Alexander Hamilton championed a strong nation investing in its people and future. Obama's themes are those of the great twentieth-century progressive presidents, from Theodore Roosevelt to Lyndon Johnson. Romney and the conservatives in Congress are ideological descendants of those who opposed the New Deal and the Great Society and saw the business of America as business. I've used my reporter's notebook to update these historical cleavages.

If the 2012 campaign had merely contained the natural tension in American history between individualism and community, it would not have been so extraordinary. Something more profound was at stake. E. J. Dionne wrote in his book *Our Divided Political Heart,* "At the heart of the American idea—common to Jefferson and Hamilton, to Clay and Jackson, to Lincoln and both Roosevelts—is the view that in a democracy government is not the realm of 'them' but of 'us.'" The radical right that would have been vindicated and emboldened by a sweeping Republican victory sees the government as "them." I make no apologies for suggesting that the United States dodged a bullet in 2012 by rejecting this extremist view of our 225-year experiment in democracy. We are a centrist nation and will remain so.

Writing history in real time has its advantages. What's lost in perspective is gained in finding stories and insights in their messy original state, before time and selective memories turn them neatly into pleasing myth. But in some respects, as the U2 song played at Obama campaign rallies goes, "The more you see, the less you know." I remain in what the Harvard historian and president Drew Gilpin Faust calls "the grip of the myopic present." I hope to have broadened my vision enough to see a few things that others missed. Where I haven't, there is no one to blame but me.

Jonathan Alter
Montclair, New Jersey
April 2013

THE
CENTER HOLDS

1

The Shellacking

President Obama sat hunched over in the second-floor Treaty Room of the White House. It was Election Night 2010, and he was doing his best to offer some solace in a time of loss. The president spent that night and most of the next day on the telephone—hour after hour, call after call, a cortege of funereal conversations with defeated members of Congress.

Reaching out didn't come naturally to this president, who normally preferred spending his evenings having dinner with his family and reading policy memos (with ESPN on in the background) to chatting with a bunch of politicians he barely knew. His detached and self-contained nature had hampered his presidency, though accounts differed over how much. Obama knew abstractly that he needed to establish what he repeatedly called an "inclusive" White House, but he much preferred the company of friends, his staff, and the extraordinary people he met in his travels to schmoozing in Washington. While *The Godfather* was one of his favorite movies, he sometimes seemed to have forgotten Hyman Roth's famous line, "This is the business we've chosen." This business, on this Election Night, was mostly about condolence calls. His personal secretary, Katie Johnson, stayed at her desk until 2 a.m. emailing him the phone numbers of every defeated Democrat on Capitol Hill and several who survived—nearly a hundred calls in all. He was gracious on the phone and between calls remarked to aides how sad it was to lose this member or that in the political earthquake they had just experienced.

The president felt personal affection for early 2008 supporters such as Tom Perriello, Patrick Murphy, and Steve Kagen, who went down in the House, and he reached out to defeated Democrats Russ Feingold and Blanche Lincoln in the Senate. He knew many of the others less well but was genuinely sorry about their fates. A large collection of smart young political leaders saw their careers crash and burn because they voted for health care reform or for the climate change bill that passed the House but died in the Senate, or simply because they were depicted as Obama Democrats. "I really wish I could have done more for those guys," he told Pete Rouse, his interim chief of staff.

Obama also placed a couple of congratulatory calls to important politicians he knew only from a few meetings. Mitch McConnell, the owlish minority leader of the Senate, had never in two years been to the White House for a one-on-one session with the president. John Boehner, the incoming Speaker of the House, caught the attention of young Obama aides mostly for drinking too much at a White House reception in early 2009 and asking if there was any place to smoke; he was so far off the Obama team's radar on Election Night that Katie Johnson searched unsuccessfully for his cell phone number before finally getting it from someone at the Democratic National Committee. The snubs went both ways: Neither Republican leader had accepted the president's invitations to attend state dinners, where politics traditionally gave way to the national interest, and they insisted that a small dinner for the congressional leadership hosted by the president after the midterms be changed to a lower-profile lunch. Obama aides thought that Boehner in particular paid a price with his Obama-despising caucus every time he met with Obama. Boehner said that was bull.

Now McConnell and Boehner could no longer be ignored. When the returns were complete, the GOP had won in a rout. Democrats held a narrow three-seat margin in the Senate, but Republicans had captured sixty-three House seats—the most that had changed hands since 1948. That chamber would soon be controlled by men and women who could not accurately be called members of the Grand Old Party. Boehner may have been an old-fashioned Republican, but he was outflanked by shock troops of the American right—activists elected in opposition to the party establishment that would now seek to corral their votes. The freshmen joined veteran lawmakers who had watched Boehner and company lose the Congress in 2006 and suffer further reversals in 2008.* They too owed little allegiance to the new speaker. Whether or not they identified with the Tea Party (and even most freshman declined to join the Tea Party caucus), these Republicans were impatient with the old guard and hell-bent on radical and immediate reductions in the size of government.

Boehner was so spooked by the freshmen that he felt forced to re-

---

* Many Republicans attributed their huge losses in 2006 and 2008 to the Iraq War. They argued that without that war there would have been no Democratic majority, no President Obama, and no Obamacare.

treat from a word that lay at the center of the entire experiment in self-government envisioned by the founders. A month after the midterms, the soon-to-be-speaker sat down with Lesley Stahl of *60 Minutes*, who asked him why he rejected the idea of compromise. "When you say the word 'compromise,' a lot of Americans look up and go, 'Uh oh, they're gonna sell me out,'" Boehner said. "And so finding common ground, I think, makes more sense."

Beyond Congress, Republicans also won a landslide in the states, where they took eleven governorships, including five in battleground states won by Obama in 2008. It could have been even worse: In five other blue states, the Democratic candidate for governor won by fewer than ten thousand votes. All told, the GOP now had control of twenty-nine of the fifty statehouses. Less noticed but perhaps more significant, Republicans picked up 680 state legislative seats, giving them control of more than half of state legislative chambers, the most since 1928. Not a single analyst on Election Night predicted what this might mean for election rules that could shape the outcome of the presidential race in 2012.

Democrats had the misfortune of getting clobbered in a census year, which meant a painful loss was potentially catastrophic. The loss of twenty state legislative chambers to Republicans meant that new congressional maps—drawn in state capitals every decade—would almost certainly lock in GOP control of the House for the foreseeable future. In the month ahead, the Republicans' master plan, called the Redistricting Majority Project (REDMAP), worked beautifully. In the seventy congressional districts labeled "competitive" in 2010, Republicans in 2011 were able to gerrymander forty-seven, compared to only fifteen for Democrats, with the remainder redrawn on a nonpartisan basis.* The result would be about fifty fewer competitive seats in the House of Representatives in 2012, which would mean more Republicans and fewer moderates in either party and thus fewer opportunities for compromise.

Meanwhile Florida, Ohio, Pennsylvania, Michigan, Wisconsin, and Iowa—all states easily carried by Obama in 2008—would now be in the hands of Republican governors and state legislatures with plenty of tools to hurt the other party, the most potent of which would be a series of measures making it harder to vote. These blue states would soon have House delegations that were as much as two-thirds red, an

---

* The word *gerrymander* dates back to 1812. It came from the redistricting map drawn by Massachusetts governor Elbridge Gerry, which included a district drawn roughly in the shape of a salamander.

undemocratic result locked in by redistricting. If Republicans could meet expectations by winning the Senate and the presidency, the conservative base—even if out of step with young and minority voters—would have control of all three branches of the federal government.

———

THE 2010 REBUKE to Obama reflected a powerful message from the voters who bothered to go to the polls: Two years is enough time to get the country back on track. They didn't want to hear how the recession was officially over, how much worse it could have been, or how impressive it was that Obama pushed more major legislation through Congress in his first two years than any president since Lyndon Johnson. Democrats bore a large share of blame for their own predicament. They chose to hold the president to a standard of perfection instead of working to hold a Democratic Congress.

Obama's response to his circumstances had been a belated effort to blame the other party, as Franklin Roosevelt had blamed Herbert Hoover's Republicans and Reagan had blamed Carter's Democrats during their first midterms. "They [Republicans] drove us into the ditch," Obama shouted at 2010 campaign rallies. "Don't give 'em back the keys!" The line was necessary but not sufficient. Reminding voters of the failed past wasn't enough without offering a coherent message for the future. A pragmatic absence of ideology was no shield against the other side's passionate ideology. Even in heavily blue New York City, the president couldn't fill the small ballroom of the Roosevelt Hotel when the tickets were only $100. If the still popular Michelle hadn't hit the campaign trail at the end, the damage would likely have been even worse.

When David Axelrod talked to the president on the day after the election, they agreed they had gotten their butts kicked. He tried to lift Obama's spirits by predicting that the GOP would overreach, thus setting up his reelection in 2012. But then Axelrod thought of Winston Churchill's comment after he was defeated for reelection as prime minister in 1945: "If this is a blessing, it is certainly well-disguised."

Publicly Axelrod tried to put the best face possible on the results, noting that Democrats had managed to defy expectations and hold the Senate. Of course, that was no thanks to the White House. Colorado, Nevada, and Delaware stayed in the Democratic column because of weak Tea Party challengers, including one who was forced to deny she was a witch. The Democrats' turnout explanations were more convincing. Only 80 million Americans voted in 2010, compared to 130 million in 2008. Even accounting for the normal drop-off in midterm elections, that difference was staggering. Where were those missing 50 million voters? They would have to be lured back to the polls if Obama was to have any chance of reelection.

Even before the 2010 votes were fully counted, attention was already shifting to 2012, when Democrats would defend twenty Senate seats to the Republicans' thirteen. It was hard to find anyone in Washington who would give the Democrats odds on holding the Senate. This view would persist. In November of 2011, a year before the 2012 election, Charlie Cook, a well-regarded Washington prognosticator, wrote that in the "best-case scenario" Democrats would lose only three seats, enough to give Republicans control if a Republican vice president broke the tie. (Cook's projections of a Republican Senate continued well into 2012). If Obama was defeated for reelection—and the odds now favored that too—conservative Republicans would control the presidency, the Congress, and the Supreme Court. They would repeal almost everything Obama had achieved and push the nation sharply to the right.

Less than two years after arriving in Washington as a historic figure heralding a new era, Barack Obama was a wounded president fighting for his political life. The bloggers and cable blowhards who hyped his rise now outdid themselves chronicling his fall. Many confidently invoked statistics about the effect of pocketbook issues on incumbency: Unemployment in October 2010 was a grim 10.2 percent, up 2.5 points from the day Obama took office twenty-two months before. No president had been reelected with an unemployment rate above 7.2 percent since FDR amid the Great Depression in 1936, and that was after the rate fell by a quarter. The consensus in the media was that anything above 8 percent or so would mean the end of the Obama presidency.

Obama despised the noisy cable culture and tried to ignore the manic-depressive fever charts of political fortunes that had come to define public life in the capital. But the car in the ditch was his now, and no one knew if he could haul it out.

———

THE ONLY COMPARABLE midterm experience was in 1994, when voters thought a young president had "overshot the runway" on health care and other issues and delivered a stinging repudiation at the polls. That year Democrats lost eight Senate seats, costing them their majority, and fifty-four seats in the House, which meant Republican control of that chamber for the first time since 1954. In the aftermath, President Clinton blamed angry white voters upset with the Democrats on "guns, God and gays." He claimed in public to be accountable for the result but snapped in private at his staff, fired several political advisers, and began spending hours in secret conversations with Dick Morris, a Republican strategist who had worked for him in Arkansas. One aide thought the president seemed foggy, as if he were on medication. He rarely went to the Oval Office, preferring to plot his future in the residence.

The new House speaker was Newt Gingrich, who brought a style of slash-and-burn politics to the Capitol not seen since the McCarthy era. Flush with victory, House Republicans at first rejected the idea of compromise altogether. But many of the new members owed their elections to Gingrich, so they followed him when he compromised with the president on the budget and other issues. Liberal Democrats meanwhile were disappointed with Clinton and what they saw as his modest, small-bore view of the presidency, but they mounted no primary opposition in 1996. The economy strengthened that year, with unemployment declining to 5.4 percent, and Clinton's reluctant signing of welfare reform legislation made him seem centrist. Two years after the humiliation in the midterms, Clinton handily beat former Senate majority leader Bob Dole for reelection, a comeback that seasoned Democrats kept in mind fifteen years later.

———

UNFORTUNATELY FOR OBAMA, 2012 wasn't 1996. The Obama "reelect" (as campaigns involving incumbents are known in the trade) wouldn't play out against 1990s-style peace and prosperity, a political culture with stakes so low that the country would soon have the luxury to obsess for months about stains on a blue dress. This president took office in 2009 amid two wars and an economy in free fall. Revised estimates showed the gross domestic product (GDP) had shrunk by an astonishing 8.9 percent in the fourth quarter of 2008, a steeper drop than during any single quarter of the Great Depression. Economists agreed that recovery would take at least a few years, as it always does after economic crises that begin in the financial sector.

Unlike Clinton in 1994, Obama didn't brood or lash out in the weeks following the election. He was in what Rouse described as "a little denial" about the returns. He knew the results looked bad and that he would have to retool, but he never internalized the magnitude of the defeat. This reflected either a worrying level of disengagement or commendable resiliency and solid mental health. Obama told his best friend, Marty Nesbitt, who ran a Chicago-based airport parking company, "In spite of what you're hearing, we're really handling it well." Nesbitt, who visited the White House often, didn't see anything to indicate otherwise.

Obama figured he had been elected not just to solve problems but to change Washington, and he had failed at the latter because of the circumstances under which he took office. He saw his debut in the presidency as a "triage moment" that pushed everything else aside. To stop the bleeding, he and his team had to play the Capitol Hill inside game proficiently. They had fallen into the habit of working the Washington levers of power, and it cost them.

"We were so busy and so focused on getting a bunch of stuff done that we stopped paying attention to the fact [that] leadership isn't just legislation," Obama told Steve Kroft of *60 Minutes* shortly after the midterms, "that it's a matter of persuading people. And giving them confidence. And bringing them together. And setting a tone. And making an argument that people can understand." This was a startling confession that he had failed at what is practically the sine qua non of a successful presidency.

Obama saw the results as a product of national impatience. "People are frustrated—they're deeply frustrated—with the pace of the recovery," he told a news conference on the day after the election. But he acknowledged that the voters apparently did not see the government as the way to quicken it. They "felt as if government was getting more and more intrusive into people's lives than they were accustomed to." If true, everything the president stood for—the investments in education, scientific research, clean energy, manufacturing, and the rest—would now be on the chopping block.

The president knew that he had to listen to the verdict of the voters, or at least seem to do so. Yet in the East Room that day there was no point in hiding the pain of a personal repudiation. "I'm not recommending for every future president that they take a shellacking like I did last night," he said, with as much drollery as the occasion allowed.

Obama left it to his political aides to admit that they had blown the basic blocking and tackling of politics. Looking back, they felt they hadn't gone negative early enough or strongly enough. "The one thing we could never solve was to create enough sense of risk about voting Republican," Axelrod said. It was a mistake they vowed to fix.

––––––

MITCH MCCONNELL WAS crystal clear about the stakes over the next two years. Just before the midterms, he famously told the *National Journal*, "The single most important thing we want to achieve is for President Obama to be a one-term president." Two days after the election, he doubled down, saying he didn't regret the comment and adding, "The fact is, if our primary legislative goals are to replace the health spending bill; to end the bailouts; cut spending and shrink the size and scope of government, the only way to do all these things is to put someone in the White House who won't veto all these things." Over time McConnell's "single most important thing" would come to symbolize how disconnected the political games in Washington were from the concerns of ordinary Americans. *Their* number one priority was a better life for themselves and their kids, which required a better economy, which in turn required the politicians to work together.

McConnell's Senate colleagues knew that in truth neither beating Obama nor helping the economy was his true priority. The minority leader's number one goal was retaking the Senate for Republicans so that he could be majority leader again. The biggest threat over the next two years to McConnell's dream wouldn't be Democrats but his more dangerous adversaries: House Republicans. If they messed with Medicare, he might not pick up the three Senate seats that he needed to take power.*

When he heard McConnell's statement, Senate Majority Leader Harry Reid told his spokesman, Jim Manley, "*My* number one priority for the next two years is to reelect Obama." Even if Reid didn't mean it literally—he managed a legislative calendar that would not be dictated by the White House's political calculations—the private comment made its way down Pennsylvania Avenue to Pete Rouse and to the president. Naturally it bound Obama more closely to the majority leader.

If reelection was the central goal, Obama would have to do something to reengage and reenergize his base. In 2010 the proportion of young voters fell by a third from 2008; the proportion of older voters (who favored Republicans) grew by a third; and the proportion of white voters grew by a third. Had turnout been the same in 2008 as it was in 2010, McCain would have won.

The big problem moving forward was the long-range outlook for the economy. What kept him up at night, the president told aides, was that he didn't know where the jobs for the long-term unemployed were going to come from. The economy didn't have a "next big thing" to employ people with no college education and few skills. He knew that the green jobs he had touted so hard in 2009 were a chimera. He mused that the factory workers laid off after the collapse of the manu-

---

* If a Republican won the presidency, McConnell needed just three seats because a Republican vice president would break the tie in favor of Republican control. If President Obama won, Vice President Joe Biden would break the tie in favor of the Democrats, which meant that McConnell would need four new Republican senators in order to take over.

facturing sector in the 1980s had in many cases been absorbed into construction trades during the housing bubble of the 1990s. But now they had been laid off again, and there was nothing else for them on the horizon. These folks, he feared, were spiraling downward. He was struck by an article in the March 2010 *Atlantic* describing how the social dysfunction in white working-class areas was beginning to mirror that of black neighborhoods. He felt that the answer, to the extent that there was one, lay in infrastructure, a multiyear "paid for" agenda to rebuild sewage systems, retro-fit schools and hospitals, and do a lot more on job creation that the GOP had long supported. Big projects, from the railroads to the interstate, had always been championed by Republicans. But those days were over. For 2011 at least, he would have to play defense while they carried the ball on austerity.

At the same time, the president would have to mute any message of progress on the economy. People just weren't buying it. The political commentator James Carville had laid out the challenges: "The hardest thing to do in all of political communications is deal with a bad but somewhat improving economy." Doing so required "threading the needle"—convincing people that things were getting better when they didn't yet feel it. Carville confessed that Clinton's White House had also failed at that early on: "It is not like someone has the holy grail of how to do this."

But even when he was in deep trouble politically, Clinton always loved the game. This wasn't true of Obama. His long list of policy achievements in his first two years occurred in spite of an aversion to the normal requirements of politics: dealing with legislators, building coalitions, selling relentlessly with a message repeated ad nauseam. The uncomfortable truth was that he didn't much like politics and didn't enjoy the company of other politicians; in fact he didn't even consider himself to be one, at least not at heart. Most of those around the president didn't think of him as a politician and marveled that he had come so far without the usual political equipment. Sure, he spent plenty of time calculating the political angles, but this engagement was usually from a distance, as if he had to prevent the grubby realities of his business from soiling his image of himself.

It was sometimes said that he didn't like people; this was wrong. It was needy and shortsighted politicians, entitled donors, and useless grandstanders who tried his patience. He liked people, including children, who could satisfy his curiosity, make him laugh, and tell him things he didn't know. He didn't like people who wanted a piece of him, failed to do their jobs, or who thought their wealth and position made their advice by definition superior to that of the less powerful.

Obama's rise had been so rapid that his natural political skills were never deepened by experience. So, for instance, he misconstrued a piece of old Chicago political lore. The first Mayor Daley had famously said in the 1950s that "good government is good politics," by which he meant that if you ran a smart and reasonably effective government that delivered services to people, they would vote for you. This was true as far as it went. But as Obama knew perfectly well, Daley's legendary "machine" was also built on an obsession with the machinations of politics for its own sake. It wasn't until January 2010, a year after taking office, when Republican Scott Brown won a special election to fill Ted Kennedy's seat in Massachusetts, that the president saw the shortcomings of his faith in just doing the right thing and expecting political rewards to follow.

And yet the events of his first year set up a perfect test of Daley's maxim. Obama had moved ahead with the auto bailouts even though they were unpopular even in the industrial Midwest, and with the Affordable Care Act despite being told by all of his top advisers that it was a loser with voters. He was betting on the ebbs and flows of fortune in politics, where time can change anything. The 2012 presidential election would resolve whether doing unpopular things to help the country could end up as crowd-pleasers down the road.

———

AGAINST ALL ODDS, the lame duck session of the 111th Congress proved to be one of the most productive of all time. Both McConnell and Boehner knew it would get worse for them in 2011, when the Tea Party would be flexing its muscles, so it made more sense to do business with the outgoing Congress in late 2010, before the freshmen radicals got to town. But at first it didn't look as if much would happen.

The new START Treaty that Obama had signed the previous April in Prague with President Dmitry Medvedev of Russia was languishing in the Senate, where sixty-seven votes were needed for ratification. The treaty cut in half the number of nuclear warheads on both sides, bringing the stockpiles (around 1,500 nuclear weapons) down two-thirds since START was initiated in the 1990s. That was still enough to blow up the world but moving significantly in the right direction. Three Senate Republicans came out in favor of the treaty, but the rest deferred to Jon Kyl, the savvy Republican whip who didn't have much use for arms control of any kind. In mid-November Kyl said there was "not enough time" to renew the treaty before the new Congress began. That was code for saying the GOP would not just stop START, but kill it.

The president decided to fight hard for the treaty, even at the expense of other priorities. "We said, 'Holy shit! We can't lose START,' and doubled down," recalled Ben Rhodes, the deputy director of the National Security Council. Obama saw START as the linchpin of much of the rest of his foreign policy, from resetting relations with Russia to handling China, getting North Korea "below the fold" (out of the headlines), and confronting Iran. The hard-line view, exemplified by Senator James Inhofe's claim that "Russia cheats in every arms control treaty we have," caused consternation in Moscow. Rejection of the treaty would have meant no cooperation on anything from the Russians. "We would not have gotten sanctions against Iran without START," Rhodes said.

Obama and Biden went into overdrive building elite public opinion for the treaty, enlisting in the cause NATO, German chancellor Angela Merkel, former president George H. W. Bush, Mitt Romney (already a likely 2012 presidential candidate), and all six living former secretaries of state. The key was winning over John McCain, who was lobbied by everyone from Henry Kissinger to the neoconservative writer Robert Kagan. When McCain came out for the treaty, he brought other Republican senators along and, to the surprise of almost everyone, isolated Kyl thoroughly enough to win ratification.

Obama was also skillful in winning a change in the Don't Ask Don't Tell policy on gays in the military. The key was the favorable testimony of Admiral Mike Mullen, chairman of the Joint Chiefs of Staff. Defense Secretary Bob Gates had been opposed to a new policy but grew convinced that the Pentagon's hand would be forced by the courts. And Gates was impressed by a report prepared by Jeh Johnson, general counsel to the Pentagon, and army general Carter Ham, that said the military could absorb the change without harm. By letting the Pentagon take the lead on Capitol Hill in 2010 instead of pushing hard from the White House for a reversal of DADT, Obama might have been leading from behind, as an anonymous insider charged, but he was leading.

———

AFTER THE MIDTERMS, the pressure to allow expiration of the 2001 Bush tax cuts grew more intense. The leader of the charge was Senator Chuck Schumer, who thought the best idea was to let all of the tax cuts expire, then vote in February 2011 to restore those for the middle class, but not for those making more than a million dollars a year. He said this loudly and publicly, which enraged the White House. Axelrod swore oaths against Schumer to anyone who would listen, and Pete Rouse and Deputy Chief of Staff Jim Messina told Schumer that the president wanted him to put a sock in it.

Obama's view at the time was that letting middle-class tax rates go up for even a couple of months in early 2011 would violate a campaign promise and validate the GOP victory. Democrats would take the blame and be in a poor negotiating position with the new Congress in February. He preferred using the Bush tax cuts to win all kinds of other concessions. This was shrewd poker by a player with only one good card in his hand.

Biden and McConnell did most of the negotiating in early December, but the president got involved when necessary. At one point, the Republicans wanted to scale back refundable tax credits—checks for a few thousand dollars from the government to families that made under about $30,000 a year. Obama said he would walk away from the table if that happened, telling Boehner and McConnell that he couldn't sign a bill with continued tax breaks for the wealthy and let breaks for working-class families expire.

In the middle of the talks, the president made a surprise holiday season visit to the troops in Afghanistan. He stayed on the ground for only six hours of a thirty-six-hour trip. After *Marine One* landed back on the South Lawn on Saturday, December 4, he went directly to the Oval Office, where he called Reid, Pelosi, McConnell, and Boehner with his bottom line: He would veto any bill that contained just the extension of the tax cuts anxiously sought by Republicans and an extension of unemployment insurance anxiously sought by Democrats. The deal had to be much bigger. For the next several hours, the haggling continued, with Biden, at home at the Naval Observatory, turning to the new budget director, Jack Lew, for fresh ideas. By the following week, the outlines of one of the most productive deals ever cooked up by a lame duck Congress were coming into view.

By the time Congress adjourned for the 2010 holidays, Obama had won a victory unimaginable just six weeks before. In exchange for extending the tax cuts—the GOP's true bottom line—Obama won approval of the START Treaty, an end to Don't Ask Don't Tell, extension of unemployment benefits, a payroll tax holiday, the first expansion of the school lunch program in four decades, a continuation of the Recovery Act's expansion of the Earned Income Tax Credit (the most successful antipoverty program in a generation, which boosted the incomes of the working poor), and increased medical care for 9/11 rescue workers at Ground Zero. The result of the fiscal parts of the compromise was a "stealth stimulus" of nearly a trillion dollars—a much-needed boost to the economy. All in all, not bad for a president depicted as politically weak.

Everything in the lame duck session was interconnected, and even seemingly unrelated external events were critical. The decision of Rich

Daley not to run for reelection as mayor of Chicago turned out to have a big impact. Had Daley run, Rahm Emanuel would have stayed past the election as chief of staff. And if he was handling negotiations with the Hill during the lame duck session, Emanuel would likely have traded repeal of the ban on gays in the military for the START Treaty instead of holding out for both. As one of his White House colleagues pointed out, it was simply in Rahm's nature to jump at such deals. Instead the key negotiator in this period was Rouse, who had replaced Emanuel as interim chief of staff. Rouse had been the top aide to Senators Dick Durbin, Tom Daschle, and Barack Obama. Over the course of three decades on the Hill, he had earned the nickname "the 101st Senator." On the DADT-START deal, he didn't take the bait. He and the president held out for a bigger deal, and they got it—a significant win.

The historical consequences of this lame duck deal were much greater than recognized at the time. When the repeal of DADT went smoothly, it created more political space for gay marriage. Had the old Pentagon policy remained in place longer, it's hard to imagine the climate of opinion on same-sex unions shifting as quickly as it did. Only a year later, the president endorsed gay marriage, and the military's years of discrimination already seemed a distant memory.

A key moment in the aftermath of the midterms came on December 12, when Bill Clinton went in to talk with the president. Their relationship was still fraught, but Clinton for the first time showed that he could be of genuine help to Obama. He calmed liberals who were concerned that Obama's big concession in exchange for all these achievements—letting the Bush tax cuts for the wealthy continue past the end of the year—was a sellout. For seventy minutes in the White House press room, long after the president had left, Clinton was back in his element, doing what he now did best: explaining Obama. He made the case for the president's year-end strategy better than the president did himself. Talk of insurrection in the Democratic ranks died down.

Just six weeks after the shellacking, Obama was back in the game, with caveats. Congress was still habitually unable to agree on a budget. The government would have to operate, yet again, on a "continuing resolution" or be forced to shut down in April 2011. Otherwise Congress failed to act on only two major items, both of which would have big consequences through 2012 and beyond. The first was the DREAM Act, which offered a path to citizenship to immigrants who arrived in the country as children and had kept out of trouble and stayed in school. The second was an obscure measure that most of the public knew little or nothing about: a vote to raise the debt ceiling so that the government could pay bills for expenses it had already incurred. Nancy Pelosi, the lame duck speaker, knew that the Republicans would use the debt ceiling as a weapon to hurt the president, and she urged the White House to make it an issue. Obama raised it several times. He asked his advisers, "Could we roll that into this deal?" They said no, that it was, as Axelrod later put it, "one brick more than the load could take." Boehner's staff said the biggest shock of the whole year was that Obama didn't stress confronting the debt ceiling in the lame duck session. "We were floored by that," Brett Loper, the top policy aide to the speaker, said the following summer.

The president miscalculated. He and Biden were working under the assumption that Republicans would threaten a government shutdown in early 2011, but it would be over the continuing resolution, which came before the debt ceiling had to be raised. It was hard to imagine Republicans would risk a government shutdown (which had gone badly for them in 1995) *and* a default on the national debt. A president respected by his team for thinking a few steps ahead failed to do so, with major consequences for his presidency.

Obama understood that the upcoming 2011 legislative calendar would require bipartisan cooperation to avoid a catastrophe. In December he invited Ken Duberstein to the White House for a chat. Despite the lame duck deal, Duberstein, a wise Republican who had been Reagan's last chief of staff, thought the president hadn't done enough relationship-building with Republicans. He suggested that Obama and Boehner get together and smoke cigarettes over a bottle of wine. The president laughed and said nothing. He'd just kept his promise to Michelle and given up smoking for good. The incoming House speaker, a proud smoker, would later snort with disdain to his staff that Obama always seemed to be chewing Nicorette gum.

NOT LONG AFTER the midterms, Obama and Rouse undertook a rigorous assessment of what had gone wrong over the previous two years. The president expressed great frustration over his failure to communicate better with the public but he also concluded that the policymaking process had failed, especially on the economy though also on breaking his promise to close the prison that held suspected terrorists at Guantánamo, where the administration had dithered until its hand was forced by Congress.

It was time for some personnel changes. The two biggest presences in the White House in the first two years, Rahm Emanuel and Larry Summers, director of the National Economic Council, had (along with

Secretary of the Treasury Tim Geithner) helped Obama put out fires that could have consumed the U.S. economy. While this was taken for granted by Wall Street and much of the public, an appreciative president had not forgotten. But Emanuel was tired of being undermined by Valerie Jarrett, and he was anxious to run for mayor of Chicago. Summers, for all of his brilliance and value as what one senior aide called Obama's "security blanket," had proven high-handed in his interactions with other administration officials, which impeded nimble policymaking. In 2009 and 2010 Summers slow-walked small business initiatives that were relevant both to recovery and to the president's political fortunes, and he blocked requests from Governor Ed Rendell of Pennsylvania and Transportation Secretary Ray LaHood to include more money for high-speed rail and other infrastructure in the Recovery Act. He felt it wouldn't jolt the economy quickly enough because so few projects were "shovel-ready." So in 2009 only $87 billion out of the $787 billion stimulus had gone for water and transportation infrastructure. This became one of the president's major regrets.

With the message failures of 2010 fresh in his mind, the president decided to change the public face of his administration. He wanted fresh blood, but there was a cosmetic dimension too: The first lady and Jarrett, the Obamas' closest confidante, weren't thrilled with the way David Axelrod came across on TV. Axelrod had vaguely planned to leave in the spring of 2011; now the president moved up his departure date to February. He told an exhausted Axelrod that he wanted him to go back to Chicago to rest and gear up for the 2012 campaign.

Press secretary Robert Gibbs hoped to become Axelrod's replacement as senior adviser, though he knew the job had long since been reserved for David Plouffe, the 2008 Obama campaign manager who had stayed out of the White House for the first two years. It didn't help that Gibbs had also run afoul of Jarrett, cursing her out in a meeting for misrepresenting the first lady's views on a minor matter. Once he indicated that he didn't want to stay through 2012, there was no job for him except possibly head of the Democratic National Committee, which he wasn't interested in. Obama, knowing that Gibbs wouldn't accept a job without portfolio, offered him one, a sign that the president was a little more manipulative than he appeared. The press secretary left shortly thereafter to write and give speeches, and he later became an especially effective Obama surrogate in 2012.

Everyone else, even Jarrett, got the once-over in the president's mind. She was just a hair below Chicago buddies Marty Nesbitt and Eric Whitaker as best friend of Barack, but she was not immune. We have to put personal feelings aside as we retool, he told Rouse. "I'd look at myself too if I wasn't president, but I can't remove myself." This was part of Obama's way of breaking the news to Rouse that he wouldn't be promoted from interim to permanent chief of staff, a decision that caused disappointment within the White House, where Rouse was seen as the unprepossessing and kindly uncle who looked out for younger staffers. Rouse and Jarrett would stay as senior counselors, but the president's new top team inside the White House would also consist of Plouffe, his 2008 campaign manager, and Bill Daley, hired as the new White House chief of staff on the strong recommendation of fellow Chicagoans Emanuel and Axelrod, who thought Daley would help the president get reelected.

Plouffe found working in the White House as stifling as "life on a submarine." But the man Obama most credited with his historic 2008 victory slipped seamlessly into his new role as inscrutable consigliore. "You know when people play cards close to the vest?" Daley said later of Plouffe. "He's got his cards [facedown] on the table and he doesn't even look at them. So how are *you* gonna figure what his cards are?"

Daley took over as chief of staff without having ever been close to Obama, who had a distant relationship with the Daley family going back two decades. Chicago Mayor Richard Daley never forgot that Obama had taken a vacation instead of casting a key vote in Springfield when he was in the Illinois State Senate. He wasn't amused by the story, repeated in several books, of Obama as a young law school graduate accompanying Michelle to meet Jarrett for the first time for the purpose of deciding whether Daley's City Hall was good enough for his junior lawyer girlfriend.

Bill Daley, the mayor's younger brother and a former commerce secretary under Bill Clinton, took a risk in late 2006 by becoming the first major Democrat to endorse Obama over Hillary Clinton. But even that was complicated. While Obama's campaign was pleased, Axelrod called Bill Daley and begged him to make it clear to the *Chicago Tribune* that he wouldn't be in the inner circle. Obama and his team were worried that he would look like a tool of the Machine. In mid-2007, when Obama trailed Clinton by 30 points in the polls, Daley figured Obama's campaign was a lost cause and said so a little too loudly. He was offered nothing when Obama became president and was rarely consulted in the first two years.

The Daleys also had an uneasy relationship with Jarrett, who had worked in Chicago government in various capacities. The mayor found her indecisive as city planning commissioner and refused to make her his City Hall chief of staff. Bill Daley thought he had a decent relationship with her, but she was unhappy when the president chose him

2

Tea Party Tempest

Significant political change in the United States is usually the result of social movements that work their way into the political realm. The years 2009–12 saw the emergence of an angry reactionary movement that will be best remembered for the part it played in the 2010 midterms and for the severe political dysfunction that flowed from that election. Its racial and ethnic undertones were subordinated to a brilliant marketing pitch: the old whines of even older white conservatives bottled as a refreshing new tonic for anxious voters.

At bottom, the Tea Party—the fastest growing political brand of the modern era—was more a temperament than a specific agenda for change. Its unifying idea was visceral opposition to the left in general and to Barack Obama in particular, especially to Obamacare and what conservatives considered the "socialistic" expansion of government. The movement was animated by a sense of foreboding that the survival of the nation was on the line, with opposition to immigration and Islam bringing together disparate elements of the coalition. Obama's "otherness," his not-from-here quality, became a euphemism for race and fueled absurd conspiracy theories.

At first it seemed as if the Tea Party was a godsend to the GOP. The energy it brought to the conservative movement helped its five preexisting wings get along. The economic establishment wing (deficit hawks), the neoconservative wing (foreign policy hawks), the antigovernment libertarian wing, and the Christian right wing all worked together with the help of the Murdoch-owned media wing: Fox News, the *Wall Street Journal* editorial page, and the *New York Post*.

One of the achievements of the Tea Party was to convince social conservatives to embrace an economic agenda. To Rob Stein, one of the founders of the liberal Democracy Alliance, this was an important moment in recent political history. Stein figured the billionaires subsidizing the conservative infrastructure must have experienced "orgiastic joy" when they found out the Tea Party could be the arms and legs of over Rouse as White House chief of staff and worried that it would affect her role as liaison to the business world.

Jarrett always appeared calm and self-possessed in public, but on learning that the president was poised to hire Daley she was in an agitated state. She went to Axelrod's office, just steps from the president's private study. She had crossed swords with Axelrod in the 2008 campaign and in the first two years in the White House; she surely knew that Axelrod had pushed strongly for Daley's hiring. But she sat on his little couch and opened up to him anyway, confessing to her fellow Chicagoan her anxiety about the road ahead.

Obama headed into the third and most dismal year of his presidency with a staff in turmoil and a family that had lost its appetite for living in the White House. "Michelle would be happy if I quit, but I can't turn this over to Palin," he said, only half joking.

In the period after the shellacking it often seemed that Obama didn't like being president all that much. More than one friend said that he'd be a happy guy in 2017, when his second term was over. That was assuming, of course, that there was a second term. Voters, he would learn, have a way of sensing who really wants the job.

libertarianism and turn it into a grassroots movement. The result was that one strain of conservatism, an ideology of enlightened selfishness, took center stage.

It wasn't clear if the energy behind the movement would translate into genuine power on the ground, where the Republican gap with Democrats seemed to be shrinking. Unions, once the backbone of the Democratic Party, had slid from representing 35 percent of American workers in 1954 to 11 percent in 2012 (and only 7 percent in the private sector). Labor still had plenty of bite, especially when it came to the use of union dues for political campaigns. But the left trailed the right in building party infrastructure. It had no comparable network of closely linked organizations and no feeder system for the young. The progressives' best training ground and alumni association was the 2008 Obama campaign.

———

THE TEA PARTY was born three weeks after Obama took office, when a libertarian business reporter for CNBC, Rick Santelli, lit into the new administration on the floor of the Chicago Board of Trade for making Americans "pay for [their] neighbor's mortgage [when he has] an extra bathroom and can't pay the bills." In fact Obama had unveiled a modest foreclosure relief bill that week but never endorsed a full housing bailout; he and his advisers thought it would have been political suicide to rescue every homeowner facing foreclosure. But Santelli's call for a "Chicago tea party" resonated, and within hours twenty conservative activists using the Twitter hash tag #TCOT (Top Conservatives on Twitter) held a conference call to build on the idea. Greta van Susteren's Fox News Channel show picked up the story, and by tax day on April 15, 2009—less than three months after Obama took office—tea parties had spread to 850 communities, fueled by round-the-clock coverage on Fox, where four anchors went so far as to cobrand with the movement by reporting, and cheerleading, on scene from "FNC Tea Parties."

It was hard to discern what lay behind the sense of outrage. Amy Kremer, a former flight attendant and real estate broker who helped organize Tea Party Patriots and later Tea Party Express, believed that the million or so people who took part that first spring were "united by anger over Washington not listening." But listening about what? The bank and auto bailouts were rarely mentioned by Tea Party members asked about their grievances. Despite some grumbling, no one had organized street protests on the right when President Bush pushed through huge bailouts, not to mention trillions in new spending on wars and a prescription drug benefit that wasn't paid for.

In late 2009 Obama said that he thought it was the debate over the stimulus that led to the Tea Party. (At the time, he was paying so little attention to the protesters that he inadvertently called them "teabaggers.") But when he saw the "Take Our Country Back" placards on television, he was under no illusions about the racial subtext. " 'Take back the country'?" he said one night to a couple of friends gathered in the Treaty Room in the residence. "Take it back from . . . ?" He didn't need to finish the sentence.

In twenty-first-century America, race was hard to talk about beyond a small circle of intimates. Even the most ardent Tea Party members went to pains, at least on the surface, to point out that they had black friends and acquaintances. While only 8 percent of self-described Tea Party adherents were nonwhite (compared to 11 percent of the GOP), members liked to brag that the movement sent two African Americans to Congress, Allen West of Florida and Tim Scott of South Carolina, and provided most of the money and staff for the presidential campaign of Herman Cain, a black man and former CEO of Godfather's Pizza.

Joel Benenson, the president's pollster, was convinced the Tea Party was a bunch of hype. He believed that those who self-identified as Tea Party members were no different from older white, very conservative Republicans. Democrats further comforted themselves that the Tea Party was the product of "Astro-turfing"—fake grassroots planted from Washington.

It was true that a few Tea Party groups received financial backing from FreedomWorks, an outfit run by former House majority leader–turned-lobbyist Dick Armey (and backed by major corporations), and from Americans for Prosperity, funded by the billionaire brothers Charles and David Koch. AFP suggested its true orientation when its Texas branch gave its Blogger of the Year award to one Sibyl West, who called Obama the "cokehead in chief" and said he was suffering from "demonic possession." By organizing training sessions and providing help with publicity, FreedomWorks and AFP watered the grassroots.

But the movement, made possible by the new social media world, was not a creature of billionaires. The Tea Party was propelled by the same forces that had brought Obama to power: disgust with government and a bad economy. It was best understood as a loosely organized collection of several hundred tiny groups connected mostly by websites and social media. Even Tea Party Patriots, the biggest group, was linked to only about half of the sites claiming to be Tea Party–affiliated. Only about a quarter of the small Tea Party websites even linked to FreedomWorks and Americans for Prosperity, suggesting that most of the movement was organic as well as Astro-turfed.

The scores of different tea parties had no leader, but Mark Meck-ler and Jenny Beth Martin of Tea Party Patriots probably came closest. Once a distributor and recruiter with Herbalife, a multilevel marketer of controversial nutritional supplements, Meckler believed in keeping the Tea Party independent of the GOP. Another group, Tea Party Express, disagreed. With the help of Sal Russo, a seasoned conservative political operative who had worked for Senator Orrin Hatch and former hous-ing secretary Jack Kemp, Tea Party Express organized bus tours around the country and PACs that poured money into Republican campaigns in 2010, starting with Scott Brown's campaign in Massachusetts. Tea Party Express came of age on September 12, 2009, which Russo described as a "holy day for the Tea Party crowd." Between 600,000 and 1.2 million people rallied at scores of events across the country, underwritten in part by money from the conservative Scaife Foundation, the tobacco giant Philip Morris, and other corporations.

The willful misuse of history was inevitably part of the Tea Party story. Harvard professor Jill Lepore argued that Tea Party activists prac-ticed "anti-history," a form of retroactive reasoning that allowed them to say with a straight face that "the founders are very distressed over Obamacare." They also practiced "historical fundamentalism," in which the Constitution and the Declaration were applied as if they were reli-gious doctrines.

Whatever the Tea Party's shortcomings, something big and uncontrol-lable had been loosed upon the political system, at least for a time. In the 2010 midterms, according to preelection surveys and exit polling, self-described supporters of the Tea Party made up 20 percent of the American population and 41 percent of those who voted. The name was so appealing, so redolent of the Founders and American ideals, that more than two-thirds of Republicans wanted to be connected to it in 2010.

As Tea Party activists looked to the Founders, progressives found more to learn from the New Deal. But sometimes they didn't learn enough. With millions of homes facing foreclosure at the depths of the Great Depression, Franklin Roosevelt brushed aside objections and pressured Congress to act. He launched the Home Owners Loan Cor-poration, a government agency that insured private lending and bought underwater mortgages from banks in exchange for safe government bonds. The agency sent special government representatives door-to-door to explain its housing programs, evaluate loans on a case-by-case basis, and help strapped homeowners find jobs, rent empty units, and even apply for public assistance.

All told, "the Incredible HOLC," as Bill Clinton's favorite economist, Alan Blinder, called it, saved more than a million homes—or 10 percent of nonfarm households—between 1933 and 1936. This would be roughly equivalent to 12 million households today, the approximate number of mortgages still underwater in 2012. A 20 percent national default rate in the 1930s did little to derail the program. By the time the HOLC closed in 1951, its mortgages were all paid off and the houses resold at a tidy profit for the government. By then a whole generation of Americans recalled that it was Franklin Roosevelt who helped them keep their homes and farms.

The same would not be said of Barack Obama, although on health care reform, he did resemble FDR; over the objections of Biden, Emanuel, Axelrod, and most of his other advisers, he pushed forward on reform that even Roosevelt wasn't capable of achieving. But housing was a different story. By 2012 the housing crisis that began in 2007 showed no signs of easing, as the number of foreclosures hit four million, not including the millions who sold their homes at a loss. In swing states like Nevada, Colorado, Ohio, and New Hampshire, more than a quarter of all homeowners were underwater, meaning their homes were worth less than what they owed on their mortgages; in Florida the figure was more than half.

Through most of 2009 the White House failed to grasp the import of the Tea Party movement, except when it came to housing. Within days of Santelli's rant on the extra bathroom, Obama's political advisers decided they didn't want to get on the wrong side of homeowners who had faithfully paid their mortgages and were in no mood to help those who had not, even if it helped stanch the decline of property values in the neighborhood. Joel Benenson's polls found that even underwater homeowners didn't want to see bailouts of irresponsible borrowers. The Tea Party was the majority party on that one.

But this left a lot of innocent homeowners in the lurch. Obama's new programs to address the issue, the Home Affordable Modification Program and the Home Affordable Refinance Program (HAMP and HARP), helped only about a million homeowners, less than one-tenth of the total who were in trouble. Without the stick wielded by bankruptcy judges—a stick withheld when the Senate rejected so-called cramdown measures in 2009—the banks simply dragged their feet on renegotiating mortgages, neglecting or even abusing thousands of homeowners with good credit histories. Obama called many White House meetings on housing and posed barbed questions. "What does it take to actually get a loan modified?" he'd ask with great frustration in his voice. He immersed himself in the details, pushing for steeper discounts in

HARP loans and adjustments in the incentives offered loan servicers. But every action entailed a complex trade-off. The president had to settle for merely nicking the problem.

The Santelli outburst and general fatigue with bailouts would have major downstream consequences. Had Obama borrowed more from Roosevelt and fashioned a successful housing program in 2009 or 2010, the economy would likely have revived faster. That, in turn, might have forestalled the Republican takeover of the House and all that followed.

––––––

THE TEA PARTY was a grassroots organization, but it wouldn't have amounted to much without lots of money behind it. While Democrats kept pace for most of the 2010 midterms, they were outspent down the stretch thanks to an explosion of new contributions from outside the campaigns themselves. Much of this new spending was the product of the Supreme Court's decision in the case of *Citizens United v. Federal Election Commission*, announced on January 21, 2010. *Citizens United* promised to be one of those rare cases, like *Dred Scott* (1857), *Plessy v. Ferguson* (1896), and *Roe v. Wade* (1973), that left a legacy of bitterness. In upholding the right of a nonprofit group called Citizens United to air a film critical of Hillary Clinton during the 2008 election, the Court invalidated much of the 2002 campaign finance reform bill known as McCain-Feingold. This opened the door to unlimited corporate and union money in campaigns.

As it happened, such contributions from corporations and unions didn't grow much after the decision. Publicly traded corporations were worried about a backlash from customers if they grew too partisan, and unions had long figured out how to use their diminishing muscle in politics. It was the so-called IE—independent expenditure—efforts, which were allowed long before *Citizens United*, that grew hugely in 2010, especially on the Republican side. The publicity from the case, generated largely by liberals, had the ironic effect of energizing already legal super PACs that included not just the Kochs' Americans for Prosperity and FreedomWorks (which underwrote Glenn Beck rallies in addition to Tea Party events) but Restore our Future (Mitt Romney's super PAC), the Club for Growth, the Faith and Freedom Coalition (the successor to the Christian Coalition), the Chamber of Commerce (which pumped $75 million into congressional races), and the National Rifle Association, among others.

Republican-affiliated organizations kicked in around a half-billion dollars to the 2010 campaign on behalf of Republicans, more than twice what Democratic unions and other progressive groups spent.

In off-year elections, to which few people pay much attention, this money made the difference in race after race, especially as young people, blacks, Latinos, and others who voted in 2008 stayed home. Super PAC ads charging Obamacare with taking "$500 billion from Medicare" were especially effective, even if they weren't, strictly speaking, true. (Obamacare cut nothing from Medicare benefits, only from bloated reimbursements to providers.)

A shadowy group called 60 Plus, which billed itself as a conservative rival to the American Association of Retired Persons, suddenly became a potent force. After AARP supported Obamacare, 60 Plus, whose donors are largely unidentified, shouted betrayal and poured tens of millions into ads in 2010 featuring the retired singer Pat Boone, who claimed that Obamacare cut Medicare. The subtext of Boone's message to seniors wasn't hard to figure out: Obama planned to take away their medical coverage and peace of mind and give the payroll tax money they had paid into the system during their working lives to poor uninsured blacks.

Seniors were the only age cohort to favor McCain in 2008, and they usually turned out heavily, especially in midterms. Many had grown so accustomed to government programs that they didn't recognize them as such. The cognitive dissonance imperiling Democrats was neatly summarized by a South Carolina man at a town meeting during the 2009 health care debate. "Keep the government's hands off my Medicare!" he told his congressman. When they weren't slamming Obama for his failures on the economy, Republican IE ads in 2010 were largely devoted to exploiting that confusion.

The most powerful of the IEs was a newcomer in 2010, American Crossroads, which was founded by Karl Rove, known for the past decade as "Bush's brain"; Ed Gillespie, a savvy lobbyist and former chair of the Republican National Committee; and Steven Law, a former top aide to Mitch McConnell. Impressed by the success in the 2006 cycle of a liberal consortium called Americans Coming Together, MoveOn .org, and of course the 2008 Obama campaign, they aimed to convince donors they would spend money wisely. The Virginia offices were stripped down, with no art or even plants. Rove, who earned his income from fat lecture fees and TV gigs, insisted he was "a volunteer" who didn't see a dime from his political activity, which may have been strictly true but didn't account for the large travel, scheduling, and research expenses that Crossroads picked up. All told, Crossroads spent more than $70 million in 2010, an amount that would look like a pittance when compared to 2012.

Crossroads boasted both a super PAC that gave directly to campaigns, and a C-4—short for section 501(c)4 of the tax code—called Crossroads GPS that didn't expressly advocate for candidates but told the government in filings that it was simply engaged in "social advocacy." This offered a legal fig leaf that allowed donors to remain anonymous, though of course the ads made by Crossroads GPS and other "dark money" C-4s in both parties weren't subtle; in 2010 they were usually the most vicious of an already virulent strain of ads, launched under the cover of darkness. To the problem of unlimited contributions—a lava of cash cascading into the process—dark money added a new threat to democracy: a complete lack of transparency and accountability.

The power of super PACs extended down to the state level. When Gillespie wasn't busy at American Crossroads, he chaired a little-known organization called the Republican State Leadership Committee. Backed by Walmart and the tobacco companies, among other corporate interests, Gillespie's super PAC pumped more than $40 million into key state legislative races in 2010 with the intention of bolstering Republicans who could gerrymander new GOP congressional districts. That was enough for an extra $50,000 or even $100,000 per state legislative campaign, which went a long way in most districts. Gillespie told donors that investing $5 million in 2010 was the equivalent of $25 million in 2012 in terms of electing Republicans and changing the country's electoral map.

———

IF THE TEA PARTY'S emergence had coincided with a strong recovery, it would have remained a mere historical footnote, no matter how well-funded. But the nostalgic conservative appeals fell on the soil of economic discontent. Americans wanted jobs, and they told pollsters they would demand a president who shared that single-minded focus.

The origins of the president's political problems lay in his failure to show voters that he was relentlessly focused on the same things they were. Such relentlessness had not been as necessary back in 2009, when the Recovery Act was new and the government was waiting for it to kick in. In that sense, the "opportunity costs" (economist-talk for consequences) of obsessing over health care for a year were negligible because there was no appetite for another stimulus so soon. It wasn't as if Congress was distracted from jobs while arguing about things like health insurance regulation and preexisting conditions.

But 2010 was a different story. When the Affordable Care Act became law in March 2010, the president failed to pivot immediately to a jobs agenda. Had the infrastructure proposals he included in the American Jobs Act in September 2011—when Republicans controlled the House—been rushed through the Democratic Congress in 2010, the president would have laid a more solid foundation for recovery. Instead he waited nearly eighteen months from the signing of health care reform to the introduction of his jobs package. This made him seem detached from what Americans considered Job One.

The White House offered plenty of excuses for failing to execute this pivot, some more convincing than others. From April 20, 2010, when BP's Deepwater Horizon drilling rig exploded in the Gulf of Mexico, to July 15, when the well was finally capped, the president and his team worked endless hours confronting a crisis that would soon be forgotten. Every time they tried to talk about anything else, critics, including Democrats like Louisianan James Carville, hammered them publicly. So it wasn't until midsummer that Obama could even talk about jobs, much less go out campaigning for Democrats.

White House officials said later that polls showed the public already had a bellyful of government programs. It wasn't just bank bailouts that stuck in the craw. The bailouts of Chrysler and General Motors were unpopular even in Michigan and Ohio, mostly because they hadn't worked yet. The Democratic Congress had no appetite for more stimulus, and the White House policy shop wasn't producing ideas for job creation. It didn't help that their hopes for economic improvement over the summer were short-circuited by the Japanese tsunami and the collapse of the Greek economy, both of which affected global markets more seriously than many realized at the time.

The president was torn over what tone to strike. While he campaigned hard against Republicans through the latter part of 2010, he continued to cling to a notion of bipartisanship that made him look out of touch. He stuck with it under the old Chicago political tradition "You dance with the one who brung ya." Since his 2004 Democratic National Convention speech, which made him a national figure, he had preached a politics that moved beyond red and blue, and he felt it would have betrayed his entire political identity to give up on that message. At a minimum, he had to be seen by the public as at least trying to be bipartisan. Or so they thought in the White House.

Bill Clinton felt strongly that Democrats should develop a national campaign in 2010 to combat the Tea Party. It wasn't enough for every member of Congress to run his or her own campaign without being in harness to a national message. He called Joe Biden, who agreed, and they worked on a one-page Democratic agenda, loosely based on the "Contract with America" that Gingrich's Republicans had used so successfully to take control of Congress in 1994. But after a couple of good conversations with Biden, Clinton heard nothing from the president, who had apparently decided that he didn't need Clinton's advice. In early August 2010 he assembled his political team for the first big meeting on politics since just after Obamacare became law in March. He started the meeting by saying, according to contemporaneous notes, "For the last 20 months I have not been political, not played politics. I've got three months before the election. What do I have to do? What's the best use of my time?" This was late in the game to be starting from scratch.

His advisers talked about how to motivate the base for the midterms, especially middle-age suburban voters, whose support for Obama was slipping in their internal polls. They disagreed on basic strategy, in part because the policy team was split over whether to let the Bush tax cuts expire. The research showed that voters were sophisticated enough to know that no one man could fix all the problems. But voters complained of a power grab from Washington and linked their economic condition to the deficit; rightly or wrongly, they thought it was an obstacle to creating jobs. How to deal with that? No consensus emerged.

It was likely too late anyway. Three months wasn't enough time to construct a strategy to overcome what they already knew was a strong Republican tide, though Clinton's ideas for nationalizing the midterms would likely have helped.

————

TEA PARTY ACTIVISTS did more than grab the attention of the media and generate volunteers for rejuvenating the GOP. They disrupted Obama's strategy for the early part of his presidency. The president and his people were operating under the long-standing assumption that success built on success, that health care would create momentum for a new clean energy policy, which would enhance the prospects of financial reform, which in turn would make immigration reform easier. When Rahm Emanuel was named chief of staff just after the 2008 election, he told the president it would work that way on the Hill. He was wrong. Each issue had its unique complexities unrelated to what came before. And each was vulnerable to a right-wing attack given extra juice by the Tea Party.

But none of this explains why the president went into the 2010 midterms without a bold and clear jobs agenda to help minimize the expected losses. In retrospect, Democrats should have used their strong control of the House and sixty-vote filibuster-proof Senate to take out insurance on the stimulus—to pass a bill saying that if unemployment didn't come down by a certain amount, more stimulus (in the form of spending on infrastructure and other spending on jobs) would automatically take effect. Larry Summers kept pointing out that future Congresses could not be bound by these actions, but they were worth trying anyway.

Peter Orszag, the president's first budget director, was a deficit hawk, and Jared Bernstein, the vice president's top economic adviser, was a progressive. Despite their philosophical differences, they agreed that not buying such insurance against a downturn was the major mistake of Obama's first two years. Had he thought it through more deeply, Obama could have told the country that full recovery would take five years and then introduced a multistage stimulus linked to the unemployment rate and matched by long-term deficit reduction, effective after the crisis passed. With the markets reassured by deficit-reduction commitments (as they had been, to great effect, in the Clinton era), the recovery would likely have been stronger.

But instead of buying such insurance, Obama bought into Summers's bet that the economy would come back fairly quickly. This led to rationalizations and "punting on housing," as Orszag put it, under the assumption that the economy would bounce back faster than it did. In fact housing cratered.

The internal debates in 2009 featured a sharp clash between V-shape economists and L-shape economists. The V guys thought the economy would plummet, then shoot back up; the L guys thought the line on the graph would drop sharply, then flatten out without rising much for years. The White House, Federal Reserve, and Congressional Budget Office economists were Vs, while the Nobelists Joseph Stiglitz and Paul Krugman were Ls, with an important assist from Kenneth Rogoff and Carmen Reinhart, whose 2009 book, *This Time Is Different: Eight Centuries of Financial Folly*, demonstrated conclusively that recessions originating in the financial sector always take several years to recover from.

"V" was for Victory for Barack Obama in 2012, an economic result that could lead to a landslide reelection like Reagan's in 1984. "L" meant a long, lethargic lapse into a Lost Decade like that of Japan and certain defeat at the polls. As it turned out, the recovery over the next three years was somewhere between the two, an unreliable "U," with all that implied for the president's political fortunes.

———

EVEN AS RECRUITMENT flagged and public attention turned elsewhere, the Tea Party retained real influence over American politics. Because they had burst forth in a census year, Tea Party activists gave Republicans a big edge in redrawing congressional maps that were already tilted toward their party. By securing rural districts largely unaffected by rapid demographic change, they enhanced their chances of locking in control of the House of Representatives for at least a decade. Democrats would have to run several million votes ahead in the overall balloting for House candidates even to come close to retaking control.

In the meantime, the Tea Party got to work tossing Barack Obama overboard.

3

Obama Derangement Syndrome

On November 22, 1963, President John F. Kennedy's motorcade in Dallas was headed for the Trade Mart, where the president was scheduled to give a luncheon address. Kennedy didn't live to deliver the speech, but the text suggests that he had become preoccupied with the rise of right-wing conservatism. He planned to assail "voices preaching doctrines wholly unrelated to reality, wholly unsuited to the Sixties, doctrines which apparently assume that . . . vituperation is as good as victory."

The forces arrayed against Barack Obama a half-century later were interested in vituperation *and* victory. Their aim was not just to fling invective but to block everything the president stood for and eventually drive him from office. These goals were shared by all of the GOP, but the fringe elements within the party, the ones often described even by some other Republicans as "wing nuts" or "crazies," had more power in 2011 and 2012 than ever before. Their outlandish views were once articulated mostly by crackpot writers and perennial also-rans and relegated to pamphlets full of exclamation points published in Kennedy's day by the extremist members of the John Birch Society, a far-right organization that was denounced by mainstream Republicans like William F. Buckley. Now the John Birch Society, though much reduced in influence, was a cosponsor of the 2011 Conservative Political Action Convention (CPAC), a mini–GOP convention attended by all of the Republican presidential candidates. And the smears were often part of that mainstream, regurgitated by members of Congress and titans of industry and always welcome at the top-rated cable news network.

During the Bush administration, left-wing critics were sometimes described as suffering from Bush Derangement Syndrome. A few demented individuals, described as "truthers," even convinced themselves that Bush had known in advance about the attacks of 9/11. But the number of blogs, tweets, and books devoted to "birthers"—those who

believed Obama wasn't born in the United States—far exceeded anything on the left. And the left-wing conspiracy theories around 9/11
never went anywhere in Congress or the media or among major constituencies of the Democratic Party. Birtherism, by contrast, was a staple
of talk radio, cable TV, and even the once-august Sunday shows. The
depiction of the president as a dangerous interloper could be heard almost anywhere Republicans gathered.

Soon Obama Derangement Syndrome became so widespread that
a large chunk of the Republican Party seemed to suffer from the affliction. More than 50 percent of Republicans surveyed in August 2010
thought it was "definitely true" or "probably true" that Obama "sympa-
thizes with the goals of fundamentalists who want to impose Islamic
law around the world." Nearly 25 percent of Republicans said that they
thought the president was a Muslim, up from 13 percent in 2008, and
more than 33 percent believed he wasn't born in the United States.

It's not true that racism lay at the root of all opposition to Obama.
Millions opposed him or even despised him for reasons entirely unrelated to race. But for plenty of others, racial feelings infected their
views of the president in ways they often could not express. Many ag-
grieved whites fell back on the same line: "I can't explain it. I'm just not
comfortable with him." This view was a product of the country's tortured
racial history. For some whites of a certain age and background, it was
impossible to square the man with the office he held, no matter how he
filled it. In hundreds of all-white rural counties, Obama's 2008 and 2012
totals were far below those of losing Democratic candidates Michael Dukakis and John Kerry, not to mention Bill Clinton and Al Gore.

The question of electing an African American president had, on
the surface, been resolved in 2008. Pollsters were no longer interested
in sampling racial attitudes. But beyond Obama's weakened support
among whites, there was anecdotal evidence that the level of racism
was up over 2008, when a black man in power was merely an abstraction. Sabrina Tavernise of the *New York Times* interviewed voters in Lo-
rain County, Ohio, and found that 16 percent of the people she talked
to said explicitly that they wouldn't vote for Obama in part because
he was black. She found similar sentiment the following month in Jefferson County, Ohio, a Democratic county where Kerry, who lost Ohio
in 2004, far outpolled Obama. About 10 percent of voters there raised
race directly (and on their own accord) as a reason they wouldn't vote
for Obama. It was hard to calculate how many more people felt that
way but would not share it with a reporter.

Ron Fournier, a reporter for the *National Journal*, returned to his
hometown of Detroit and was appalled by the level of racism he found

among white voters. To Fournier, the code used by a Detroit firefighter and his friend, a contractor, wasn't hard to decipher:

"Subsidization" = Welfare
"Generational Apathy" = Lazy
"They Slept All Day" = Blacks Sleep All Day
"I Feel Like a Fool" = I'm Mad as Hell

The same people defending Ann Romney's dressage horse found it outrageous that Michelle Obama took her daughters skiing. When Glenn Beck asked, "Why can't we call her uppity?," Megyn Kelly, Michelle Malkin, and Sean Hannity were among those on Fox News agreeing it was a legitimate semantic question.

The smearing of Obama was greater than anything experienced by presidents in the recent past but hardly a departure from an ugly tradition in American history. Obama haters were the splenetic descendants of the partisans who depicted John Adams as a "hideous hermaphroditical character" in the election of 1800, Abraham Lincoln as an African dictator and hairy baboon in the early 1860s, Franklin Roosevelt as a Jewish bloodsucker (the name conjoined from "Rosen" and "Felt") in the 1930s, Dwight Eisenhower and John F. Kennedy as communists (courtesy of the Birchers) in the 1950s and 1960s, and Bill Clinton as a murderer dealing drugs out of an airport in Mena, Arkansas, in the 1990s. Most of these calumnies were part of what the historian Richard Hofstadter called "the paranoid style in American politics," though plenty of others, like commentator Ann Coulter branding the president a "retard," were simply the product of an entertainment industrial complex that profited off insults.

Whatever the source, Obama's name, race, and exotic background lent urgency to the usual vitriol directed at presidents—a sense that this alien must be removed from the seat of power. You didn't have to be a fanatic racist drawing the president as an Afro-Leninist savage with a bone in his nose to believe the lies. Many less extreme Americans were unusually open to fringe arguments, even if unaware that their fears were increasing their belief in nonsense. Time and again, Obama's enemies used the same words to describe him: "Socialist," "Muslim," "not really American." Had he been a full African American with an Anglo-Saxon name, he might not have been as subjected to the same untruths, though undoubtedly other lies would have arisen from the muck. Instead the president's "otherness" took the old racial fears to a new and more confusing place.

———

THE SMEARING BEGAN in earnest in early 2007, when Steve Doocy, a former weatherman turned morning talk show host on *Fox & Friends*, reported as fact a collection of bogus blog rumors charging that Senator Obama, a newly announced candidate for president, had been educated in a radical Muslim madrassa in Indonesia. A CNN reporter dispatched to Jakarta debunked the story, but not before it spread widely.

By then Hillary Clinton's campaign was giving it a boost. Just as Al Gore's campaign for the Democratic nomination in 1988 used the Willie Horton story against Michael Dukakis before it was picked up by George H. W. Bush's backers, so the conservative criticism of Obama as "the other" had its origins in the 2008 Democratic primary.* Mark Penn, Hillary Clinton's chief strategist, wrote to Clinton in a March 2007 memo, "All of these articles about his boyhood in Indonesia and his life in Hawaii are geared toward showing his background is diverse, multicultural and putting it in a new light. Save it for 2050. It also exposes a very strong weakness for him—his roots to basic American values and culture are at best limited. I cannot imagine America electing a president during a time of war who is not at his center fundamentally American in his thinking and his values."

Of course, there were limits to how much one Democrat would trash another. The "voices of vituperation" on the right had no such boundaries. They began to spread lies—many of which contradicted each other—that Obama was a communist, a fascist, an atheist, a homosexual, the bastard son of Malcolm X, or the bastard son of Frank Marshall Davis, an African American leftist poet living in Honolulu. The most infamous of these crackpot stories was that Obama had not been born in the United States and thus was ineligible under the U.S. Constitution to be president. By most accounts, the bizarre birther story was born in August 2008 in a lawsuit filed by a former deputy attorney general of Pennsylvania, Philip Berg, later described by a judge as an "agent provocateur." After Obama was elected, more than a dozen people filed lawsuits. To argue that litigants had standing in court, they enlisted the support of a retired air force colonel, Gregory Hollister (who argued that Obama wasn't his legal commander in chief), and Alan Keyes, the Harvard PhD, Reagan-era ambassador, and perennial can-

---

* Willie Horton was a black murderer Dukakis had furloughed, who then went on a crime spree.

didate whom Obama had beaten for the Senate in 2004. Keyes called
Obama a "radical communist" and "usurper." His suit, like all the others,
went nowhere.

By early 2009 the tale of the forged birth certificate was circulating
widely on right-wing websites. The story was implausible if not insane.
To be true, it required that clairvoyant conspirators in 1961 had planted
fake birth announcements in two Honolulu newspapers to cover up
for the fact that the infant son of an obscure mixed-race couple at the
University of Hawaii had in truth been born in Kenya; that Barack
Obama Sr., whose visa didn't allow him to return to the United States
after he left, would somehow risk a quick trip home to Kenya and be
readmitted to the United States without incident; that talented criminals would go to work forging a birth certificate to pave the way for a
"Manchurian candidate" to seize power half a century later; that doctors
and nurses at the hospital who remembered laughing over a patient
named Stanley (Obama's mother, Stanley Ann Dunham) having a baby
were lying; and on and on. When confronted with any of this, birthers
would retreat into the familiar dodge that they were merely "raising
questions."

And the haters had a convenient loophole: Obama's exotic background and strange name allowed them to avoid the stigma associated with outright racism. Enlisting blacks like Keyes and immigrants
like Orly Taitz, a loud right-winger who elbowed her way into regular
cable TV bookings, made the whole birther thing seem more ridiculous
than rancid. The sideshows in the media circus attracted viewers in
part because they worked on an ironic level; they appealed to a new
generation that saw politics as a source of entertainment from revered
comedians like Jon Stewart, Stephen Colbert, and Bill Maher.

The birther story also penetrated because it was given credence by
respectable politicians. When the racist Gerald L. K. Smith charged in
1937 that Franklin Roosevelt was a secret Jew (he later called Eisenhower a "Swedish Jew"), no one could have imagined that the Senate
minority leader at the time would be asked about it, much less tacitly
endorse the claim. But there was Mitch McConnell in 2011 saying "I
take the president at his word" when he said he wasn't a Muslim—a
passive-aggressive way of keeping the story alive. Mitt Romney paid
no political price for spreading innuendos about Obama's birthplace.
"I love being home, in this place where Ann and I were raised, where
the both of us were born," he said on a trip to Michigan. "No one's ever
asked to see my birth certificate."

With such high-level backing, it was no surprise that so many in the
GOP thought Obama represented a dangerous threat. These suspicious

yet credulous conservatives came to believe that a mild-mannered and moderate (by any historical standard) president who refused to nationalize the banks, embraced a GOP health care plan from the 1990s, and made $300 billion in tax cuts a centerpiece of his economic recovery program was in fact a dangerous radical bent on hijacking the nation and trampling on the Constitution.

THE GODFATHER OF Obama haters was arguably Joseph Farah, an author and former editor of the *Sacramento Union*. Farah first emerged as an influential conspiracy theorist in 1993, when he was among those claiming that the suicide of Vincent Foster, the deputy White House counsel under Clinton, was actually a murder covered up by the U.S. Park Police in Washington. He collaborated with Rush Limbaugh on a book before moving on in 1997 to found WorldNetDaily, which became a highly successful purveyor of right-wing dirt and the first repository of anti-Obama stories.

WorldNetDaily's best-known writer was Jerome Corsi, who went from earning his PhD from Harvard in 1972 under the tutelage of liberal professors Laurence Tribe and Michael Walzer to peddling conspiracy theories about 9/11 and Democratic politicians being on the take from Iranian mullahs. Corsi was immensely popular. Both *Unfit for Command*, his 2004 book using a few conservative Swift Boat veterans to savage John Kerry as a coward under fire, and *The Obama Nation*, his 2008 catalog of concocted Obama outrages, went to number one on the *New York Times* bestsellers list, though independent assessments of Corsi's books found them riddled with fabrications.

Edward Klein's bestseller, *The Amateur,* was received more respectfully because Klein had been a *New York Times* editor, but the book was so scurrilous and unsubstantiated that, except for a scathing review, his former colleagues at the paper ignored it. While it was plausible, even likely, that Bill Clinton called Obama an "amateur," Klein's sourcing was sketchy. And Caroline Kennedy said in private that both his assertion that Obama had alienated her and his claim to have been a friend of her late mother were false.

The columnist John Avlon toted up eighty-nine titles in what he called the Obama Haters Book Club, nearly twice as many as were written about George W. Bush during his first term. The titles ranged from *The Communist* and *The Manchurian President* to *Gangster Government* and *The Great Destroyer*. Avlon's personal favorite was *Whiny Little Bitch: The Excuse Filled Presidency of Barack Obama*.

For those who preferred a more academic tone, the conservative author Dinesh D'Souza wrote a bestseller called *The Roots of Obama's Rage* that claimed that Obama's obvious (to D'Souza) hostility toward the United States and desire to destroy the U.S. economy were somehow shaped by the anticolonial impulses of a father he never knew. The peculiar book, a favorite of Newt Gingrich, was catnip for those with Obama Derangement Syndrome, who quickly took D'Souza's argument to its logical conclusion. Robert Weissberg, a retired professor of political science at the University of Illinois, wrote a widely circulated article entitled "A Stranger in Our Midst" that reflected the mind-set of the afflicted. Weissberg wrote that "countless conservatives despised Bill Clinton but nobody ever, ever doubted his good-ole-boy American bona fides." By contrast, he argued, Obama and his "collaborators" resembled "a foreign occupying force" bent on "alien rule."

It wasn't hard to find "evidence" to bolster the point. For instance, Obama was photographed carrying a book by Fareed Zakaria, a columnist for *Time* and an anchor on CNN. The viral email that followed was typical of the genre:

> *THIS WILL CURDLE YOUR BLOOD AND CURL YOUR HAIR!!!!!!*
> *The name of the book Obama is reading is called:* The Post-American World, *and it was written by a fellow Muslim.*
> *"Post" America means the world After America! Please forward this picture to everyone you know, conservative or liberal. We must expose Obama's radical ideas and his intent to bring down our beloved America!*
> *If each person sends this to a minimum of 20 people on their address list, in three or four days, all people in The United States of America would have the message.*
> *The new "OMG" is Obama Must Go!!!!!!!!!!!!*

Scores of myths about the president went viral. Gun owners claimed that Obama was intent on banning all weapons in the United States by signing international treaties that bypassed Congress. Anti-Muslims circulated a photo of the president bowing "too deeply" to the king of Saudi Arabia (whose hand George W. Bush had held at his ranch in Crawford, Texas, without much comment) as proof that he was a jihadist selling out the country to the Arabs. A retired local judge in Marble Falls, Texas, interpreted health care reform proposals to include not just the nonexistent "death panels" made famous by Sarah Palin but provisions giving free insurance to all illegal immigrants and allowing the government to loot an individual's bank account. A lie circulated that

Craig Robinson, the president's brother-in-law, kept his job as the University of Oregon's basketball coach only because of stimulus money received by the university. One movie theater owner in Florida even put "Limited Engagement: The Obama Lying Sack of Shit Tour" on his marquee.

Some of the attacks took on a more sinister cast. A group called the American Family Association alleged that the president was using the Department of Homeland Security to create his own fascist brownshirt army to wage war on Americans. The organization's best-known face, Bryan Fischer, a right-wing talk radio host, warned that DHS had riot gear and nearly a half-billion rounds of ammunition that "they're going to use . . . on Americans." He added that if Obama was reelected, Americans would "hear some serious talk about secession in any number of places around America." (An accurate prediction, as it turned out.) Alex Jones, who hosted Ron Paul several times on his radio show, insisted that both the 2011 shooting of Representative Gabby Giffords outside a Tucson shopping center and the 2012 Aurora, Colorado, cineplex shootings were Obama administration plots aimed at letting the United Nations confiscate guns.

The haters were imaginative. In the summer of 2010, talk show host Glenn Beck held what he called a "Restoring Honor" rally in Washington. Beck, always a sucker for crackpot history that reinforced his preference for theocracy, explained to the crowd that he wanted to form a "black-robed regiment" in homage to the clergymen he wrongly placed at the center of the American Revolution. (Contrary to Beck's claim, most historians view it as a secular not theocratic event.) His later "Restoring Love" rallies ladled out heaping portions of piety. Sensing public unhappiness with the bitterness of the debate, Beck claimed to want to lower the temperature of the Tea Party rallies. But many of those who spoke at the event couldn't help themselves. Aryeh Spero of Caucus for America compared Obama to Ahab, who, along with his wife Jezebel, worshipped false gods. Members of the political left, Spero said, were descended ideologically from Ahab, a leader committed to "transforming the nation" and "subjugating the people." Those in the audience, by contrast, were like the revered prophet Elijah, committed to fighting paganism. Spero urged the crowd to "make sure a President does not crown himself Caesar."

Calling Obama a Roman was a compliment, relatively speaking. More often, of course, he was called a Muslim, an untruth that took as evidence the fact that his middle name was Hussein and kept spreading even as Americans got to know him better. One viral email described a man at a Blockbuster Video who learned from a pair of Arab customers that, unlike Laura Bush, Michelle Obama didn't accompany her husband to Saudi Arabia and Turkey because "Obama is a Muslim, and by Muslim law he would not be allowed to bring his wife into countries that accept Sharia Law."

This post let the first lady off easy. More often, she was depicted by right-wing crackpots in the most vile racist terms—so disgusting that the emails were almost impossible to read without flinching. Many were accompanied by threats of bodily harm to the first family that were referred to the Secret Service. All told, the Obamas were subjected to more death threats than all of their recent predecessors combined.

———

IT DIDN'T TAKE long for Obama Derangement Syndrome to move beyond anonymous bloggers to public officials. U.S. District Court Judge Richard Cebull, a George W. Bush appointee in Montana, admitted that he forwarded an email suggesting that the president's late mother had sex with a dog. Dean Grose, the mayor of Los Alamitos, California, resigned because of his email showing the White House lawn as a watermelon patch. On Capitol Hill, Representative Joe Wilson's 2009 "You lie!" outburst when the president was addressing a joint session of Congress on health care was only the most public example of members of Congress denigrating the president and his program in terms far outside the mainstream. Representative Allen West of Florida, a self-described "radical and extremist" best known for saying that the number of communists in Congress was somewhere between "seventy-eight and eighty-one," called Obama not just "a low level socialist agitator" but "probably the dumbest person walking around in America right now." Like Alan Keyes, West's African American heritage may have lent a special venom to his attacks. "[Obama] does not want you to have the self-esteem of getting up and earning and having that title of American," West told constituents. "He'd rather you be his slave." Such apocalyptic rhetoric was common. Representative Mike Kelly of Pennsylvania compared August 1, 2012, the effective date on which most insurers were required under Obamacare to offer coverage for contraception, to Pearl Harbor Day and 9/11: "I want you to remember August 1, 2012— the attack on our religious freedom. That is a date that will live in infamy, along with those other dates."

Sarah Palin could always be counted on to share creatively extreme ideas with Fox viewers. She told host Sean Hannity that Obama's "philosophy of radicalism" was a throwback to "the days before the Civil War." Obama, she said, was moving the country backward to "those days when we were in different classes based on income, based on color of skin." Glenn Beck won notice in 2009 for saying that Obama had a "deep-seated hatred of white people," but this was merely business as usual for him. His popular Fox News program (later switched to his own TV network) featured disjointed monologues in which he routinely depicted Woodrow Wilson as a socialist Satan. "The president is a Marxist," Beck said, and "the government is a heroin pusher using smiley-faced fascism to grow the nanny state." David Frum, a conservative writer worried that his party was headed over the cliff, wrote that Beck's appeal represented "the collapse of conservatism as an organized political force, and the rise of conservatism as an alienated cultural sensibility." For a time it seemed as if Obama's alienated enemies could punch him again and again and he would never respond. Then one day he did.

———

JEROME CORSI WAS sure that he had another bestseller about Barack Obama. This one tackled the big white whale: the president's place of birth. Corsi's book *Where's the Birth Certificate?* was scheduled for publication in April 2011. It brought together in one handy place all the lies about a forged short-form birth certificate and a missing long-form birth certificate and all of the conspirators involved. Three weeks before the book's publication, Obama decided to release his birth certificate. This was a response not to Corsi but to the real estate billionaire Donald Trump, who had transformed himself into a birther as part of his flirtation with running for president. The highly public toe-in-the-water never seemed serious; Trump was believed to have already quietly signed a contract to continue his NBC show. But taking his clown act into the political realm ("The blacks love me") helped feed The Donald's addiction to publicity.

In 2009 Obama had been bemused by the birther rumor, and in 2010 he was not yet willing to dignify the stupid story with a response. But now, in 2011, he was increasingly frustrated with the oxygen that it was consuming. John Boehner was asked on *Meet the Press* about Trump's claims that Obama wasn't born in the United States. George Stephanopoulos asked Obama directly about it. The story was getting in the way of the White House assault on the budget plan put forward by Representative Paul Ryan. Studies showed the two stories roughly tied in the amount of media coverage they received.

On April 14 Obama went to Chicago for a fundraiser and decided to rummage around in his late mother's possessions, which were stored at his Kenwood home. There he found his short-form birth certificate, which he'd never seen before. He told his advisers that politically it was better for him to have the birth certificate story play out for a while and let the Republicans make fools of themselves. It would build up Trump, which would hurt the other side. But, he said, it was bad for the country; everyone had better things to talk about, and he was planning to go into the press room and say so.

Of course, releasing the short-form birth certificate he found in Chicago wouldn't solve the problem; the press had seen copies of it already. So before Obama went public, White House Counsel Bob Bauer worked with the attorney general of Hawaii to obtain a waiver allowing the long-form birth certificate to be released. Copies wouldn't do, which meant that Judy Corley, the president's personal attorney at the law firm of Perkins Coie, had to fly to Hawaii to pick it up. When she returned with the document, the president told his staff that this could be a "teachable moment" about silly politics interfering with important matters of state.

The original idea was that Bauer and Dan Pfeiffer, the White House communications director, would release the birth certificate and the president would answer a question about it on *Oprah*, where he had a scheduled interview. But Obama didn't want to reflect on the smallness of American politics on *Oprah*, a venue he saw as more appropriate for uplifting themes. He wanted to disclose the document in the briefing room because he saw the press as bearing a share of the blame for spreading the bogus story in the first place. David Plouffe asked if they needed the speechwriter Jon Favreau to draft a statement, but Obama said he would speak from handwritten notes, though he did give Bauer, Press Secretary Jay Carney, and other staffers a heads-up on what he would say. Pfeiffer hadn't seen him feel so strongly about a communications issue since his speech on Jeremiah Wright and race during the 2008 campaign.

When the birth certificate was handed out at 8:45 a.m., the press went crazy with the story. In public, the president seemed angry about the distraction from serious issues by "sideshows and carnival barkers." But in private he also saw the humor in it—and the potential for rallying his base. "Where are the mugs?" he asked a couple of weeks later, when it took a little longer than expected for the Obama-Biden online souvenir store—a significant source of revenue for the campaign—to produce coffee mugs with the birth certificate emblazoned on the side. "I want my mugs."

————

DONALD TRUMP GAVE himself a pat on the back: "I'm very proud of myself, because I've accomplished something that no one else has been able to accomplish." Just to be sure that his message was received, he added, "I really did a great job." But it went without saying that the crazies wouldn't be satisfied by the release of the long-form birth certificate. Not a single birther apologized or admitted error. Instead a talk show host named Eric Bolling, auditioning on Fox to replace Glenn Beck, hosted Pam Geller, who had championed opposition to the placement in lower Manhattan of a mosque sponsored by moderate Muslims. Bolling and Geller began claiming the long-form birth certificate was a forgery.

Obama's release didn't impress Joe Arpaio either. Arpaio, the demagogic sheriff of Maricopa County, Arizona, used his office as a platform for keeping the birther story alive. He spent $10,000 in taxpayer money sending investigators to Hawaii, where, of course, they came up with nothing. In July he held a press conference that was not well-received. "Show us the microfilm," Arpaio demanded. "Show us the microfilm!" Arpaio demanded to puzzlement all around. Jerome Corsi's *Where's the Birth Certificate?* went to number six on the bestseller list even after Obama answered the question and produced it. Corsi claimed that even if Obama was born in the U.S. he still was not a "natural born citizen" under the Fourteenth Amendment because his father was not—a slur against all Americans who are the children of immigrants.

Obama occasionally tried to joke about the fictions, which his friends thought would be almost funny if they weren't so sick. "Some folks say, 'Well, you know, he's not as cool as he was, when they had all the posters around and everything,'" Obama told a small group of supporters in California. "Now I've got a Hitler mustache on the posters. That's quite a change."

———

THE CRAZIES WERE plenty racist, with their talk about the president's laziness and the first lady's big bottom, but most Republicans had learned long ago to take explicit references to race out of the discussion. Instead they adopted euphemisms. In 1968 Richard Nixon, implementing his Southern Strategy, used the phrases *law and order* and *forced busing* to signal to white voters that he shared their fears. Ronald Reagan, who never mentioned race as such, began his 1980 campaign in Philadelphia, Mississippi, of all places, the site where the civil rights workers Mickey Schwerner, James Cheney, and Andrew Goodman were murdered in 1964. Reagan spoke of states' rights and "welfare queens" in ways that contained an obvious racial subtext. The Willie Horton ad made on behalf of George H. W. Bush's campaign against Michael Dukakis had the same effect. Bush's chief political strategist,

Lee Atwater, explained the evolution of the code in a 1981 audiotape made public by the dogged researcher James Carter (Jimmy Carter's grandson) in 2012:

> You start out in 1954 by saying, "Nigger, nigger, nigger." By 1968 you can't say "nigger"—that hurts you, backfires. So you say stuff like, uh, "forced busing," "states' rights," and all that stuff, and you're getting so abstract. Now, you're talking about cutting taxes, and all these things you're talking about are totally economic things and a byproduct of them is, blacks get hurt worse than whites. . . . "We want to cut this" is much more abstract than even the busing thing, uh, and a hell of a lot more abstract than "Nigger, nigger."

As fear of blacks became more "abstract" at the turn of the new century, the strategy was expanded to include fear of Arabs. George W. Bush didn't play racial politics and tried outreach to Muslims. But by the time Obama was president, code words and "dog whistles" (language understood only by the intended recipients) were once again part of the dialogue, as Obama's race and Muslim middle name made him a twofer in the minds of the fringe. The contradiction between Obama's being a Muslim and being in thrall to Reverend Jeremiah Wright, a Christian minister, didn't faze zealots who believed both to be true.

As the fear moved from Tea Party rallies to the campaign trail, the code wasn't hard to decipher. The president embodied not just the intolerable present but the terrifying future, when hordes of dark-skinned people would make whites a minority in the United States within less than thirty years. The 2008 election had shown it was possible to elect a president who didn't receive the most white votes. And this was terrifying to some Americans.

This fear of losing control was matched by at least some measure of guilt. Even if they hadn't been personally responsible for subjugating blacks, white Americans knew somewhere deep in their psyches that the country had been conceived at least partly in sin and built with the help of blacks who might have some reason for revenge. That racial fear and guilt was not directly connected to Obama; assuming as much would be an oversimplification of tangled social psychology. But it was unmistakably present, as it had been throughout American history.

The tactical brilliance of dog whistles was that these dogs knew exactly how to respond to their commands. When blacks or their white liberal allies complained about the coded racial messages, conservatives (the dogs in the metaphor) would loudly accuse them of playing the race card. Both sides could then be counted on to play out their tiresome racial psychodramas.

But a strange thing happened to those who believed they could easily destroy the new black president. He was unflappable, even cold, and when they couldn't rattle him, it was the critics who came unglued. Tom Burrell, founder of the nation's first large black-owned advertising agency, made a study of how Obama interrupted the familiar cycle of racial recrimination. By refusing to react to their taunts, Burrell noticed, the president was depriving the other side of its usual opening. He was smart, a family man, ethically clean, and, in his first two years, successful at getting his program through Congress. This meant that the target on his back was much smaller than his enemies expected. Where Bill Clinton gave his critics plenty of ammunition, Obama offered little more than some pot smoking in high school and a couple of so-called scandals (Solyndra and Fast and Furious*) that were more about bureaucratic bungling and partisan wrangling than genuine wrongdoing in the White House.

So those bent on destroying Obama had to lie and disrespect the president, which made them suspicious to a public less suggestible and more sophisticated than they imagined. Representative Barney Frank, a Democrat from Massachusetts, put a bumper sticker on his car that declared, "We're Not Perfect. But They're Nuts." Bit by bit many Republicans were not just losing contact with the country beyond their echo chamber; they were entering a fantasyland of self-delusion. Obama Derangement Syndrome was a symptom of a deeper disturbance on the American right that would eventually help, not hurt, the president.

---

* Solyndra was a solar panel manufacturer that received a $535 million loan guarantee from the Department of Energy before declaring bankruptcy. Operation Fast and Furious was a gun-tracking program run out of the Phoenix office of the Bureau of Alcohol, Tobacco and Firearms that was badly managed and led inadvertently to the death of a border patrol agent.

4

Strangled in the Bathtub

It was Obama's historical misfortune to serve as president during the most partisan era in modern American history. For generations Democrats and Republicans included both conservative and liberal (or at least moderate) wings; now, in a period defined by what political scientists called "asymmetrical polarization," this was true only of the Democrats. Republicans had only one wing, a malformation that would affect the party's flight pattern as far as the eye could see.

As an Illinois state senator, Obama worked well with Republicans in Springfield. After his speech at the 2004 Democratic National Convention, devoted to looking beyond blue states and red states, the first magazine cover he ever appeared on bore the headline "Seeing Purple." In 2007 a Republican state senator, Kirk Dillard, was so convinced of Obama's bipartisan sincerity that he appeared in an ad for him to use in the Iowa caucuses.

As president, Obama continued to take bipartisanship seriously, not because he was naïve but because he believed it was the most productive approach to governing. Moreover, he calculated that it wouldn't be politically smart to abandon a theme that had helped bring him so far. He routinely described himself in private as "not your classic party animal" and made a point of stressing that two of his four favorite presidents, Lincoln and Theodore Roosevelt, were Republicans. (The other two were FDR and Truman.)

But by the summer of 2010, a few months before Democrats lost the House, the president was deeply worried about the direction of the GOP. He told visitors that he thought the other party was shot through with hypocrisy, full of members saying, "We love fiscal discipline unless it's our stuff." He longed for the party of George H. W. Bush, Bob Dole, and Howard Baker and the "fact-based conversations" they held with Democrats. "All I want for Christmas is a smart, loyal opposition," Obama said, mentioning how great it would be to negotiate with David

Cameron, then the head of the Tory opposition in Great Britain. "We'd make music together."

The president, of course, was dreaming. The Bush-Dole-Baker world was as far removed from the current GOP as Lincoln's Republican Party. Obama was famously Lincoln-obsessed, but a lesser-known part of his interest in the sixteenth president revolved around Lincoln as a believer in the federal government's investing in people and infrastructure. Lincoln was a former Whig still devoted to that party's platform of "internal improvements"—in other words, spending that would be anathema to the GOP of 2012. At the bicentennial celebration of the Great Emancipator's birth in February 2009, Obama went out of his way to note that beyond winning the Civil War and freeing the slaves, Lincoln also subsidized railroads and launched the Homestead Act, the first land-grant colleges, the National Academy of Sciences, and a national currency. Obama didn't mention that his hero also instituted the first American income tax, which was revived with a constitutional amendment in 1913. Until the late twentieth century Republicans routinely supported not just critical infrastructure but raising income taxes in the interest of fiscal responsibility. Now they opposed all of that.

ONE EVENING IN 1974, the economist Arthur Laffer was having drinks in the bar of the Two Continents restaurant in Washington with Donald Rumsfeld, who was Gerald Ford's White House chief of staff, and Rumsfeld's deputy, Dick Cheney. Laffer sketched what was to become the famous "Laffer curve" on a cocktail napkin. It purported to show that tax revenues would actually go up when tax rates went down, and vice versa. Laffer was right that confiscatory taxes at a certain level— say, the 70 to 90 percent top rates of the Eisenhower era—were often counterproductive; they forced the wealthy to figure out convoluted ways to avoid paying them. In 1978 Representative William Steiger, a Republican from Wisconsin, succeeded in cutting the capital gains rate from 49 to 28 percent, kicking off an investment boom. But Steiger, an environmentalist who had helped establish the Occupational Safety and Health Administration, died that year at forty, leaving Republicans who were fiscally conservative but otherwise moderate without a champion.

The principle behind supply-side economics took a beating in the 1980s. After slashing marginal tax rates in 1981, Reagan ended up presiding over a soaring deficit—just the opposite of what Laffer and other supply-siders predicted. Buffeted by a recession, he signed two budget deals in the early 1980s in which tax hikes accounted for 80 percent of the deficit reductions. The much praised bipartisan tax reform of 1986, brokered by Democratic Senator Bill Bradley, sharply lowered rates and closed loopholes but helped make the deficit worse.

In 1990 George H. W. Bush signed off on a budget deal with a 2:1 ratio of spending cuts to tax increases. The members of Congress who backed their president were the last congressional Republicans for the next two decades to vote for an income tax increase. When Clinton proposed raising the top bracket from 31 to 39.6 percent in 1993, he received no support from any Republicans. Senate Minority Leader Robert Dole and his colleagues went to the floor and argued en masse that Clinton's tax increases would sap incentives to save and invest and send the economy into a recession. The bill was approved on a party-line vote and the country had a clear test: Would tax hikes on the wealthy hurt job creation? The answer was an emphatic no. The combined effect of the Bush and Clinton budget deals—and a later deal between Clinton and House Speaker Newt Gingrich—helped balance the budget in 1999 and did nothing to dampen what soon became the greatest economic boom of modern times, with 22 million new jobs and a soaring stock market.

In 2012 the Congressional Research Service, a nonpartisan agency of Congress, looked back over decades of economic studies and concluded, "The reduction in the top tax rates appears to be uncorrelated with saving, investment and productivity growth." Shortly before the 2012 election, Senate Republicans pressured CRS to squelch the report.

The verdict of history had no effect on Republican thinking. Admitting they had erred on the magic of tax cuts would mean repudiating the core of the party's identity. Instead smarter Republicans conceded that cutting taxes wouldn't miraculously lower deficits, but they claimed that this was fine with them. Large deficits would offer the excuse they needed to shrink government. Starting in the late 1980s they used the limitations of supply-side economics to fashion a fresh argument. The new glue holding together the GOP was no longer fiscal discipline, as it had been from William McKinley through George H. W. Bush, but tax cuts.

"Deficits don't matter," Dick Cheney told a newly inaugurated George W. Bush in 2001 as Bush weighed whether to follow through on a 2000 campaign promise of sweeping tax cuts. Bush had made that promise in order to siphon off supporters of Steve Forbes, a self-financed candidate who was threatening him in the New Hampshire primary. While Bush was a true believer in ending what conservatives had cleverly rebranded "the death tax," he winced at the idea of cutting the top income tax bracket so sharply, wondering aloud whether the cuts were too tilted toward the top end. But he went ahead under the theory that it was time, as old Reaganites put it, to "starve the beast": reduce the federal Leviathan through tax cuts that would deprive Washington of the revenues necessary to run a large government.

How to dispose of the beast was summarized by a Reagan acolyte and talented political operator who gave Bush crucial support in the 2000 primaries and would play an important role in the unfolding drama of the 2010–12 period. "I'm not in favor of abolishing the government," Grover Norquist famously said. "I just want to shrink it down to the size where we can drown it in the bathtub."

––––––

NORQUIST PERSONIFIED THE rise of the American right inside Washington. Raised in a well-to-do household in Weston, Massachusetts, the son of a Polaroid executive, he arrived at Harvard in 1974 already an arresting combination of implacable libertarian and fierce anticommunist. At the *Harvard Crimson*, still a far-left newspaper in the mid-1970s, Norquist was a geeky yet unself-conscious dissenter whose calm and friendly arguments even then were delivered with an eerie confidence that he had figured out exactly how the world works.* "When I became twenty-one, I decided that nobody learned anything about politics after the age of twenty-one," he said later. Consuming political tracts from all perspectives, he quietly adapted Lenin's idea of a "vanguard of the proletariat," by which a small group of zealous intellectuals would master power politics and execute choke holds on the old order. Norquist simply substituted "freedom" for "the proletariat" and moved to Washington to build his conservative vanguard during the "Reagan Revolution." He later denied this was his goal but suggested that Straussians (disciples of Leo Strauss, a conservative political philosopher who celebrated elitism), neocons, and others on the right may have borrowed tactics from the left.

In the mid-1980s Norquist traveled several times to Angola, where, donning the uniform of rebel leader Jonas Savimbi's UNITA Army, he instructed the anticommunist guerrilla leader in free market principles. He ghostwrote articles under Savimbi's byline in the *Wall Street Journal* and elsewhere that suggest the Leninist influence on his own thinking about political struggle. "We are using Communist military and propaganda principles in order to defeat the Soviets and their political ideology," Savimbi/Norquist wrote in *Policy Review*. Savimbi, whose

---

* The author first got to know Norquist in the late 1970s when they worked together on the *Harvard Crimson*.

movement had originally been backed by Mao, was described by Don
Steinberg, President Clinton's ambassador to Angola, as "the most ar-
ticulate, charismatic homicidal maniac I ever met."*

By this time Norquist had emerged as a right-wing antihero, holding
raucous parties on Capitol Hill for other young conservative thinkers
and activists. When Gingrich became speaker of the House in 1995,
Norquist all but moved into his friend's office as a close adviser, though
he preferred the movement cred that came from staying on the outside.
The conservative humorist P. J. O'Rourke described him as "Tom Paine
crossed with Lee Atwater plus just a soupçon of Madame Defarge."

While building his organization, Americans for Tax Reform, Norquist
always had time to play the provocateur in politics. At the 1988 Republican Convention in New Orleans, he printed cards with pictures
of Michael Dukakis and Willie Horton on one side and the Monopoly
legend "Get Out of Jail Free!" on the other. When Norquist convinced
two network anchors to show the faux Monopoly card on air, it was
the first time the story went national. (Floyd Brown's infamous ad on
Horton didn't debut until the following month.)

Eager to stop President Clinton's health care plan, Norquist began
hosting meetings in Washington every Wednesday for elected officials,
the heads of all major conservative organizations, lobbyists, and other
elements of the GOP coalition. After the Republican takeover of the
House in 1994, the Wednesday Meeting became an important Washington institution; when George W. Bush was president, Karl Rove
made sure to show up several times a year; later someone senior from
Boehner's office was almost always in attendance. The Wednesday
Meeting was not a debating society; Norquist's rules required that attendees make only positive nuts-and-bolts comments about how to advance conservative ideas and candidates, with no doctrinal arguments
allowed. In the late 1990s he began to replicate the meetings in all fifty
states. The idea wasn't complicated. "We are trying to change the tones
in the state capitals—and turn them toward bitter nastiness and partisanship," Norquist said in 2003, only half-kidding.

Norquist, also an important member of the board of the NRA,
worked closely with House Majority Leader Tom DeLay, the godfather
of modern hyperpartisanship. Tea Party obstruction and Boehner's fear
of the word *compromise* grew directly out of DeLay's long intransigence, which led to the impeachment of Clinton, among other victories.

---

* In 1996, "*after* the Cold War was over, *after* Savimbi's true self had been revealed," as the
conservative writer Matthew Continetti pointed out, Norquist registered as a paid lobbyist for
UNITA.

When DeLay resigned the House under fire in 2006, he went out with a blast: "It is not the principled partisan, however obnoxious he may seem to his opponents, who degrades the public debate, but the preening, self-styled statesman who elevates compromise to a first principle."

Norquist added historical sweep to the rigid ideology. He thought the country had been off on a statist, un-American track ever since American progressives imported centralization and regimentation from Bismarck's Germany at the turn of the twentieth century. He saw his movement as dismantling the legacy of Theodore Roosevelt's Square Deal, Franklin Roosevelt's New Deal, Harry Truman's Fair Deal, Lyndon Johnson's Great Society, and all the other "encroachments" on freedom over the years. He figured that government spending should be about 8 percent of GDP, as it was during much of the nineteenth century, instead of more than 20 percent.

As the beast shrank, of course, Norquist, like DeLay, would extract his own pound of flesh. His lobbying firm, Janus-Merritt Strategies, prospered but also became enmeshed in scandal. Congressional investigators accused the firm of lobbying on behalf of a Saudi national and Hamas supporter later convicted of plotting the assassination of Crown Prince Abdullah of Saudi Arabia. Norquist denied that association but admitted to representing a Saudi businessman whose "charity" was connected to financing terrorism. For years Norquist, who is married to a Palestinian Muslim, had sought to bring American Muslims into the GOP, a project that, especially after 9/11, met with less success than his antitax efforts.

Norquist had been friends with the lobbyist Jack Abramoff since they were young conservative activists together. He knew all about "Casino Jack" bilking his American Indian clients of millions to pay for lavish overseas trips and to finance the efforts of Ralph Reed's Christian Coalition to stop a rival casino. In 2000 Abramoff used his old friend Norquist as what a congressional committee later called "a conduit" for some of the money ("Call Ralph re Grover doing pass through," Abramoff wrote in an email reminder to himself in 1999), and Americans for Tax Reform got a cut of Abramoff's take from clients. Abramoff went to jail and Reed's reputation was tarnished, but Norquist emerged largely unscathed.

Although Reagan had occasionally raised taxes, Norquist worked tirelessly to memorialize him. He spearheaded efforts to name Washington National Airport and nearly two hundred bridges, highways, and schools after the former president. With a Republican president and Congress in 2013, he was confident he would have the votes to push Alexander Hamilton off the ten-dollar bill and Franklin Roosevelt off the dime in favor of Reagan—a symbolic nail in the coffin of both Hamiltonian centralized power and the New Deal.

Norquist launched his "Taxpayers Protection Pledge" in 1986; it was quickly signed by one hundred House members and twenty senators, with hundreds more legislators at the federal and state levels on the way. Vice President George H. W. Bush signed the pledge in 1988, which helped him win the nomination and, by Norquist's account, the election. Thanks in part to Norquist, the story of the pledge and the 1988 election would wear heavily on every Republican politician who came of age in that era.

That year Bob Dole won the GOP Iowa caucuses handily and was the strong favorite in the New Hampshire primary less than a week later. Bush, the sitting vice president, finished third in Iowa behind the televangelist Pat Robertson and faced political oblivion. To turn it around, Bush's team created an ad called "Straddle" that attacked Dole for not being clear in his opposition to new taxes. Dole was the only GOP presidential candidate that year—or any year afterward—who didn't sign the pledge. Normally WMUR, the premier station in New Hampshire, would be closed for the weekend, which would have meant no time for Bush's ad to air. But because the vice president—at the prodding of New Hampshire's governor John Sununu—had done the station a favor the year before by coming down from his vacation home in Kennebunkport, Maine, to take part in a local forum, the station manager agreed to make an exception and broadcast the Bush spot. The ad began to turn the tide. Then, in a televised debate two days before the primary, another candidate, former Delaware governor Pierre "Pete" du Pont, thrust Norquist's pledge in Dole's face. When Dole said blandly that he would have to read it first, his fate was sealed. Bush won the primary by 10 points and cruised to the nomination.

At the Republican convention in New Orleans that summer, Bush, reading an especially effective Peggy Noonan speech, famously said, "Read my lips: no new taxes." Earlier a senior Bush aide, Richard Darman, had crossed out the line; he thought it "stupid and dangerous" to tie the next president's hands when the country faced a huge deficit. But another adviser, Roger Ailes, argued strongly to keep it in. When Bush went back on the pledge and agreed to tax hikes in 1990, conservatives—led by Norquist—were furious. Norquist argued long and hard that this cost Bush the 1992 election against Clinton. Ignore that history at your peril, he threatened other candidates. (Most analysts argue that Bush's anemic 37 percent that year was more the result of Ross Perot being in the race and the economic downturn.) A myth was born. By 1996 Dole, belittled by Gingrich as "the tax collector for the welfare state," found himself back in New Hampshire, under attack again on the pledge, this time from Pat Buchanan. Dole lost the presidential primary there once more, though he went on to win the nomination.

Norquist never tired of pointing out that the pledge meant no *net* tax increases, so that any deduction that was eliminated had to be compensated by a tax cut somewhere else. In other words, only spending cuts, not the tax code, could be used to reduce the deficit. This had been Norquist's position for years, and it would continue to be, even when the deficit passed a trillion dollars. As the Obama years began, Norquist was confident that Republican members of Congress would keep their pledges. After all, he said with sweet reason, those pledges weren't made to Grover Norquist or Americans for Tax Reform, but to the people in their states and districts who sent them to Washington in the first place.

ON THE NIGHT of the Obama Inauguration, January 20, 2009, the GOP public opinion impresario Frank Luntz hosted a four-hour dinner for conservative lawmakers at the Caucus Room, a Washington steak house. Minority Leaders McConnell and Boehner, neither of whom had much use for Luntz, were no-shows, but almost every other important Republican on Capitol Hill was present. Those in attendance agreed that it was necessary to oppose the new president at every turn, and when the author Robert Draper reported on the evening three years later, no one denied this goal. Obstructionism was their only way back to power, and they pursued this strategy relentlessly.

The core of the party—represented at the dinner—felt that working with a Democratic president would be folly. The takeaway point was made by Paul Ryan, a sad-eyed thirty-eight-year-old congressman from Wisconsin who knew the budget numbers better than the others. "The only way we'll succeed is if we're united," Ryan said. "If we tear ourselves apart, we're finished."

"United" meant one thing: implacable opposition to whatever Obama proposed. Joining with the immensely popular president might be patriotic and make them look good to their constituents in the short term, but it wouldn't do anything for the party in the long term. They felt they had already compromised too much on their conservative principles under President Bush.

So beginning in the first week of Obama's presidency, Republicans agreed on the broad outlines of a strategy to win back power. They would immediately start hammering vulnerable Democrats (paid attack ads would begin within six weeks) and stand united against Obama's economic plan. Boehner instructed his caucus that Republicans were opposing the Recovery Act no matter what was in it. He said explicitly that any effort by the president to amend the stimulus to meet their concerns should be rebuffed. And there would be no equivalent of the Boll Weevils (Southern Democrats who peeled off from the party and backed President Reagan's economic recovery in 1981). Unity demanded total party discipline.

On the Senate side, McConnell said much the same, telling his caucus that GOP senators must stand together to survive. He decided from the start to make everything a chore for the Democrats, using the threat of a filibuster to prevent dozens of routine bills from coming to the floor. Majority Leader Harry Reid first realized what was up when a national parks bill that had enjoyed strong bipartisan support in the past came to the floor. Normally it would have passed in a day or two, but now it took three weeks, as Republicans introduced amendment after amendment to allow more guns in national parks. Later a transportation bill took weeks because of amendments allowing passengers to carry weapons when they got on Amtrak.

Obama, trying to dig the nation out of a deep hole, harbored hopes that he could make good on his campaign promise to bring the country together. Part of him knew, as he admitted a few weeks later, that the GOP didn't see it as their duty to pitch in during the crisis. But he still felt it would have been wrong for him to strike a partisan tone right out of the gate. So during his first week, the new president did something unprecedented: He traveled to Capitol Hill not to talk to fellow Democrats but to meet just with House Republicans. He had already put $300 billion in tax cuts into his stimulus plan, a preemptive effort to win bipartisan support, even if all the economists were telling him that tax cuts were the slowest way to pump money into the economy. (He later admitted this was "bad poker" and one of his biggest mistakes.)

No one expected a true compromise. Elections have consequences, and the big Democratic victory the previous November meant that Republicans would not get their core agenda: lower marginal tax rates and less regulation. "We won," Obama said flatly to Republican Minority Whip Eric Cantor when Cantor held out for this. But short of letting the losers dominate the rescue plan, maybe they could agree on targeted tax relief or other bipartisan elements of a stimulus. Or so he had hoped. When he was in the limo en route to Capitol Hill, the president learned that the Republican caucus had been instructed by its leadership, Boehner and Cantor, not to be seduced. They were to listen politely but not take part in trying to save the economy.

In the first three weeks of his presidency, amid a flurry of cable news attacks, only one House Republican and three Senate Republicans voted for the Recovery Act. Later none voted for Obamacare and only a tiny handful for any of the president's other legislation.

———

ANYTIME REPUBLICANS THOUGHT of trying to be even a smidgen more moderate, they worried about being *primaried*, the new verb on the lips of the incumbents. Senators were reminded of the fate of Senator Bob Bennett of Utah, who served in the GOP Senate leadership and, according to scorecards published by conservative groups, amassed a nearly perfect conservative record. A former top lieutenant to billionaire Howard Hughes, Bennett was Mormon royalty, the son of a senator and grandson of a president of the LDS Church. He was the only senator in either party to vote against domestic partner benefits for federal employees. He was well-liked personally in both Utah and Washington and considered a shoo-in for a fourth term.

Then Bennett made a horrible political mistake: He was caught working with a Democrat. Bennett joined with Democratic Senator Ron Wyden of Oregon on a more market-based health care reform idea that got no traction in the capital (except with experts and editorial writers). The Utah Tea Party erupted, and at the May 2010 state party convention, Bennett, still leading comfortably in polls of Republicans, finished a shocking third in the balloting. Upon returning to Washington to serve out the remaining seven months of his term, Bennett became a walking advertisement for the power of the Tea Party.

Bennett's leader, Mitch McConnell, also learned a hard lesson in 2010, when his candidate for Kentucky's other Senate seat, Trey Grayson, lost badly in the primary to libertarian Rand Paul. McConnell believed his best route to becoming majority leader was iron-fisted control over his caucus. Usually McConnell didn't have to say much beyond expressing his "disappointment"; fearful GOP members were fully aware of his leverage over them in doling out committee assignments and cosponsorship of their favorite bills. Senator Olympia Snowe, for instance, was an original cosponsor of a bill to create a consumer financial protection bureau. But when Obama nominated Richard Cordray to head it, she voted to filibuster the nomination at McConnell's instruction.

Over on the House side, John Boehner didn't have anywhere close to that degree of control. Consider the House Republican caucus meeting of July 11, 2011: The members had positive feelings about the GOP's plan to cut $5 trillion from the deficit, but several freshmen wanted to know why it had to be over ten years. Why not cut $5 trillion over two years? No one dared mention the most basic of facts: that with a federal budget of $3.6 trillion a year, such a move would mean cutting nearly three-quarters of the entire federal budget.

Representative Michael Burgess of Texas was a good example of what Boehner was up against. Burgess, an amiable ob-gyn first elected in 2002, was more conservative than most of the Tea Party freshmen. He thought Boehner should have been thrown out of the leadership after losing a combined total of fifty-four seats in 2006 and 2008, and he regretted voting with him on issues such as extending unemployment insurance, which Burgess said people in his low-unemployment district in East Texas called "FUNemployment insurance" because it subsidized good times while recipients made money off the books. He recalled more than two thousand people at a town meeting in Denton, Texas, hollering at him over Obamacare for no other reason than that he wasn't angry enough in his opposition to it. "It's impossible to exaggerate how conservative my district is," Burgess said. "They're even against a payroll tax holiday," in part because Fox and talk radio had convinced his constituents that it was an Obama gimmick worth opposing even if it meant more money in their pocket. Boehner had to deal with more than a hundred or so Michael Burgesses every day.

The natural leader of these and other Republicans wasn't Boehner or even Eric Cantor, who never enjoyed the popularity in the caucus that the press assumed. It was Paul Ryan, the new chairman of the House Budget Committee. His startling rise to power—eighteen months from backbencher to GOP vice presidential candidate—began in 2010, when the president traveled to Baltimore to take part in the House Republican Conference retreat. Obama's televised back-and-forth with members of the House minority left the White House ecstatic. He had shown such mastery over the event that the Republicans never invited him to engage in televised dialogue again. But one member of the minority party was also delighted. Obama not only called Ryan by his first name but showed evidence that he had actually read his preliminary budget plan. When had a president ever paid the slightest attention to a powerless backbencher's budget? Ryan's stature rose.

The key to Ryan's influence was the support he built among the House freshmen. Late in 2011 pollster Frank Luntz surveyed freshmen on which colleague they would seek guidance from if they arrived on the floor without knowing what was being voted on—a common enough occurrence. Most said they would look up on the electronic board for two names: Paul Ryan and Allen West.

Nearly every week Ryan held what were called "listening sessions" for members in the Capitol conference room of House Whip Kevin McCarthy. These PowerPoint presentations combined mastery of the details with a winning explanatory style. His influence within the caucus was arrived at honestly, through persuasion, not horse trading or earmarks or any of the other traditional tools of the inside game that often cost taxpayers billions. It helped that he was drawing the public spotlight, which reinforced his clout, but by renouncing any claims on a leadership post he never posed a direct threat to Boehner or Cantor. Within a few months no self-respecting member of the Republican caucus, freshman or otherwise, would be caught admitting he or she had never heard the Ryan PowerPoint. His budget blueprint became the GOP agenda, and when he revised it, the new revisions became the new agenda.

Not surprisingly Ryan was an enthusiastic backer of the Norquist pledge. In the 112th Congress, sworn in on January 5, 2011, a total of 236 out of 242 Republicans serving in the House and forty out of forty-seven in the Senate had signed the pledge at some point in their careers. (Senator Ben Nelson of Nebraska and Representatives Rob Andrews of New Jersey and Ben Chandler of Kentucky were the only three Democrats to do so.) When a Republican was tempted to stray, Norquist, comparing himself to a shepherd and his flock, would get on the phone and gently nudge him back in line.

Sometimes the man David Plouffe called "the modern puppeteer of the Republican Party" wasn't so gentle. Norquist warned Mitt Romney not to renege on the pledge and then took off after his old enemies in the Bush family. When Jeb Bush in 2012 described the pledge as "outsourcing your principles," Norquist, an admirer of George W., said on CNN that Jeb had "stepped in it." He threatened Jeb Bush by invoking the infamous (to him) 1990 budget deal: "There's a guy who watched his father throw away his presidency on a 2:1 [ratio of spending cuts to tax increases] promise. . . . And he thinks he's sophisticated by saying that he'd take a 10:1 promise. He doesn't understand—he's just agreed to walk down the same alley his dad did with the same gang. And he thinks he's smart. You walk down that alley, you don't come out."

From Kennebunkport a peeved George H. W. Bush asked, "Who the hell is Grover Norquist, anyway?" The contempt of a former president carried no weight. Retired politicians and two or three senators with safe seats might scoff at the importance of the pledge, but it was the only glue that held together the GOP. Everything else (except abortion) was the subject of fierce debate within the party. The simplicity of rejecting any tax increases under any circumstances gave Norquist as much power on fiscal matters as anyone in Washington.

———

IN THE BUSINESS community, the solution to the nation's budget woes seemed obvious: Simpson-Bowles, an elixir that, like a fine wine, seemed to get better with age. It referred to the advisory report of a bipartisan deficit-reduction commission that the president created in 2010. While Simpson-Bowles wasn't an issue for the electorate at large, many American elites cited the president's failure to endorse his own commission's recommendations as their main reason for opposing him for reelection. This analysis—widespread among the business class—is accurate as far as it goes, but it fails to account for how radical Republicans sabotaged the balanced approach at the heart of Simpson-Bowles both before and after the cochairs announced their recommendations on December 1, 2010.

The idea for a deficit-reduction commission to put everything on the table began in 2009, when Senators Kent Conrad and Judd Gregg—one Democrat, one Republican—proposed an eighteen-person panel modeled on the successful base-closing commission of the 1990s. The point was to fast-track a bill to the Senate floor for a straight up-or-down vote, no amendments. As with shuttering popular military installations, lawmakers knew this was the best way—maybe the only way—to accomplish something big and politically ugly. In this case, the ugly thing was simultaneously raising taxes and cutting entitlements in order to restore fiscal sanity.

The Conrad-Gregg commission drew more support from Republicans than Democrats, so when Obama surprised official Washington and endorsed it at the beginning of 2010, deficit hawks celebrated. But then McConnell decided that if Obama was for it, he was against it. Seven original GOP cosponsors of the Conrad-Gregg bill, including John McCain, bowed to their leader and now opposed what they had created, fearing they would lose their seats or at least their standing with McConnell if they supported their own commission. This was astonishing and perhaps unprecedented—an effort, Alan Simpson later said, "to stick it to the president." For nonpartisan political scientists like Norman Ornstein and Thomas Mann, the move symbolized the utter failure of the Republican Party to put the interests of the country above its own.

Some Republicans said the president bore some blame too. Obama let his understandable anger prevent him from calling the minority leader for a little chat. In fact they had no contact beyond big meetings. "If the president had passed that bill, this commission report with $4 trillion in savings would have had an automatic vote in the Senate," Republican Senator Lamar Alexander said later. "That's what the lack of relations with the Republican leader cost Obama and the country."

After the Senate rejected the idea of a deficit-reduction commission with teeth, Obama established an advisory National Commission on Fiscal Responsibility and Reform to make nonbinding recommendations. He named Alan Simpson, a former Republican senator, and Erskine Bowles, White House chief of staff under Clinton, to head it. The bipartisan commission met often during 2010 and made surprising progress, with Democratic members like Senator Dick Durbin agreeing to entitlement cuts and Republican members like Senator Tom Coburn agreeing to tax hikes.

To make formal a recommendation, fourteen of the eighteen Simpson-Bowles members had to agree on it. After the midterms, this became impossible. The three GOP congressmen on the panel—Paul Ryan, Jeb Hensarling, and Dave Camp—had been reasonable and productive members of the commission all year long but now decided to play to the new Republican House. They went from "maybe you can get our votes" to "no way," as a Republican member of Simpson-Bowles remembered.

Simpson, who described his commission as "the stink bomb at the garden party," paid a visit to the Republican House members of the panel. "I want to tell you if you voted against this because you're afraid of Grover Norquist, I have no respect for you—none," Simpson told them. (Simpson had earlier called Norquist "the most powerful man in America—including the president of the United States.") Ryan assured Simpson that the real reason was Obamacare, which the commission had not voted to repeal. This excuse for not embracing several trillion dollars in deficit reduction seemed to mollify Simpson. When four Democrats on the panel saw that the House Republicans wouldn't even vote for revenue increases that came from closing loopholes and ending deductions, they too voted no. The final tally, eleven to seven, fell three votes short.

Lacking formal backing from their panel, Simpson and Bowles nonetheless unveiled the defeated plan on December 1, 2010. It slashed discretionary spending by $1.6 trillion; saved about $800 billion from Medicare, Social Security, and other entitlement programs; and raised close to $1 trillion in new revenue—a 3:1 ratio of spending cuts to revenue increases. With the savings from lower interest payments, the total deficit reduction over ten years was an impressive $4 trillion. That aggregate figure and many of the commission's specifics, from "chaining" cost-of-living adjustments to a different Consumer Price Index and capping government outlays at 21 percent of GDP, would become important debating points in the budget battles to come. But the plan itself went nowhere.

Obama's failure to embrace Simpson-Bowles in 2011 didn't doom its recommendations, which had little chance of being adopted by Congress anyway. But if he had supported Simpson-Bowles, or at least used it as a basis to put forward his own plan, he might have positioned himself better for 2012. At a minimum, he would have seemed less tactical and reactive through much of 2011. If Obama and the Democrats had been braver in reforming unsustainable entitlement programs in some fashion, they might have won credit for confronting budget problems squarely instead of kicking the can down the road yet again.

With 20/20 hindsight, it was obvious to Pete Rouse that the president should have embraced Simpson-Bowles as a starting point for his own plan, which would have laid down a marker of how to protect the needy while achieving long-term deficit reduction. But it hadn't been obvious at the time. Obama knew that the moment he supported the commission's recommendations, the chances of passage would drop to zero, just as they had on Conrad-Gregg and several other measures that had received bipartisan support in the past but were now DOA in the Republican House.

Even without the president's backing, more politicians touted Simpson-Bowles than actually supported it. When a bipartisan version of it reached the House floor in March 2012, it lost 382 to 38, with just sixteen Republicans in support. Only a few more Democrats, twenty-two, backed it, but Democrats had never been the party of deficit reduction. The conservative rejection was more instructive. It proved once and for all that tax cuts were more important to the GOP than fiscal responsibility.

Nobody understood this better than Senator Tom Coburn, a true deficit hawk who was friendly with Obama but soon feuding with Norquist.* After Coburn revealed that he voted in favor of Simpson-

---

* In 2005 and 2006 the Obamas and the Coburns enjoyed going out to dinner together a couple of times. The two senators would tease each other on the floor, with Obama showing that he could muss Coburn's hair but Coburn couldn't muss his. After Obama became president, he welcomed Coburn's ideas on cutting spending and incorporated some of them in his budget.

Bowles, Norquist's staff leaked word that Coburn had been two-faced during the commission's deliberations. Coburn called Norquist and confronted him. Norquist denied responsibility for the slurs. So when Ryan Ellis, the policy director of Norquist's Americans for Tax Reform, later posted a column entitled "The Two Faces of Tom Coburn" on the ATR website, Coburn was enraged. He photocopied the column, scrawled "You lied" on it, and mailed it to Norquist.

The fight between the two men continued throughout the year. "Don't tell me getting rid of useless $5 billion ethanol subsidies is raising taxes," Coburn said in response to Norquist's interpretation of the pledge. Calling tax favors "tax expenditures," Norquist replied, is like saying that "when a mugger walks down the street and doesn't steal your wallet, he's giving you your wallet. It's your wallet, not the mugger's." Norquist had no problem comparing the U.S. government to a mugger.

If Norquist's bathtub would never be big enough to drown the beast, at least he could look forward confidently to a Republican president and a Republican Congress to keep the United States "from becoming Europe." At the Conservative Political Action Conference annual meeting in February 2012, he made it clear that he didn't think the identity of the new Republican president was especially important. The bills to slash taxes, repeal Obamacare, and radically reduce the size of government were what mattered. "Pick a Republican with enough working digits to handle a pen," he said, to laughs and cheers from the CPAC audience.

5

Fox Nation

Around 125 million Americans would end up voting in 2012, but only 10 to 20 million of them paid much attention to politics until shortly before the election. That was the aggregate number of all cable news viewers, readers of political coverage in major newspapers and magazines, talk radio listeners, visitors to political websites, and fans of fake news programs like *The Daily Show* and *The Colbert Report*. Everyone else was visiting popular sites for other kinds of information (mostly about entertainment) and getting on with their lives just fine without Bill O'Reilly or Rachel Maddow.

Fox News, the cable news leader in ratings, drew about a million viewers during the day and two million in prime time, which, combined, was less than 3 percent of the electorate. But ideas and stories that started on cable often leached into the rest of the culture, where positions hardened. Before the rise of Newt Gingrich, Fox News, and the new smash-mouth politics, analysts worried about the death of political parties. (David Broder wrote a book titled *The Party's Over*, arguing for more partisanship.) Now all the tut-tutting from the graybeards was about the decline of civility and the demise of moderates—especially moderate Republicans—who could work across the aisle.

Engaged voters increasingly inhabited parallel universes—separate political realms hermetically sealed off from one another and, too often, from the outside world. Viewers became ideological extensions of their favorite commentators, tuning in less to learn something that challenged their assumptions than to cackle at the comeuppance of their enemies and luxuriate in the warm validation of the worldview they already held. Those on the left gravitated to MSNBC, the *Huffington Post*, and NPR. The right watched Fox News, read the Drudge Report, and listened to talk radio. Each side included too many people who talked too much to themselves inside their respective echo chambers. By egging each other on, they made compromise seem like capitulation.

There was some equivalence here, but the right was much farther to the right than the left was to the left, and was further cut off from the social and demographic changes reshaping the country. The same was true in media, where the right moved further away from reason and disinterested reporting. This flight from facts was intensified by institutional arrogance. After so many years feeling marginalized by what Sarah Palin called "the lamestream media," conservatives established their own hyperpartisan media colossus, suffused with righteousness and unburdened by conventional ideas of rationality.

But it did have conventional ideas of ratings. For Fox News, it was all business. Critics often misunderstood how its management operated. They assumed that Roger Ailes or some other senior-level conservative gave marching orders on what the line of the day would be. It didn't work that way. Instead Fox became the repository of nearly every story conjured by different outlets of the conservative media. An article might first appear on Newsmax, WorldNetDaily, the Washington Examiner, the Daily Caller, Red State, or a hundred other blogs and end up on Drudge, the most reliable indicator of the stories that viewers would see Fox anchors and their guests hyperventilating about that evening or the next day. If Ailes noticed that an issue played well, he would push for more coverage, though producers, consulting the ratings, usually didn't have to wait for him to do so. Fox thus became the validator of the conservative media entertainment complex. Its New York–based producers, most of whom were political centrists or even liberals, knew which way the wind was blowing at their workplace.

For instance, in 2009, when Obama nominated Judge Sonia Sotomayor to the Supreme Court, a Fox producer (whose colleagues believed him to be nonpolitical) sent out an email saying that of the two still photos the network had of Sotomayor, the unsmiling, less attractive picture should be used on the air. Every day, producers highlighted some piece of "news" about the Obama Justice Department or sketchy terrorist threats or an obscure dopey liberal, not because it was important or necessarily true but because it advanced the conservative argument or played to the insecurities of the Fox audience. Anything emotional involving race, class, gender politics (especially strident, young, sexually active women), lazy "takers," mindless professors, and the biased liberal media elite was likely to be a crowd-pleaser. The best stories of all involved anything that reflected badly on the president of the United States.

Ironically Fox and Obama had one motivation in common: an eagerness to mobilize their respective bases. In Fox's case, the base consisted of viewers, not voters. Convincing viewers to cast their ballots for Republicans was not part of the network's core mission; the aim instead was to get viewers into the tent the old-fashioned way: with conflict (the essence of any kind of journalism) and high production values. That meant skewered liberals, pretty women, and fancy graphics that went whoosh. "I hired Sarah Palin because she was hot and got ratings," Ailes said on the occasion of Fox's fifteenth anniversary.

The Fox base rejected juicy tabloid stories if the subtext was wrong. One Fox producer had assumed that sex always sold on TV, until the story about Republican Senator Larry Craig, who was arrested in 2007 for solicitation in the men's room of the Minneapolis airport. The story turned out to be of little interest to Fox viewers, who had no taste for watching Republicans exposed as hypocrites. Once management noticed that viewers were changing channels during news segments on the Craig story, they stopped covering it. Fox's unscientific viewer polls were also important in determining coverage. When 2011 polls showed, for instance, that many viewers thought Wisconsin state workers received pensions they didn't deserve, subsequent coverage came through that lens.

Fox believed in payback. In 2008 John Edwards used several primary debates to work in digs at the network. Later, after Edwards had a child with his mistress, Fox ran many more segments than the competition combined on the tell-all memoir by Edwards's aide, Andrew Young. "Roger wanted to make sure Edwards paid a heavy price for opposing Fox and for boycotting the Fox debate that year," an Ailes friend recalled. "He was sending a message to anyone with skeletons to lay off Fox."

RUPERT MURDOCH, CHAIRMAN of News Corp., which owned Fox, had met every president since Harry Truman and enjoyed meddling in politics. He liked to pick winners and was willing to back progressives when necessary, as he had Tony Blair in Great Britain. In 2008 he believed Obama was going to win and began trying to ingratiate himself with him. At first Obama rebuffed the overtures, but he finally relented and agreed to see Murdoch at the Waldorf-Astoria in New York. It was to be the next president's first and so far only meeting with the Fox high command.

Murdoch and Obama chatted amiably, but when Ailes joined them, the conversation turned tense. Obama demanded to know why he was accused of being a terrorist on Fox every night. Not true, Ailes responded. "Sean Hannity does it every night," Obama repeated, referring to Hannity's obsession with Obama's former neighbor in Chicago, the onetime radical William Ayres. Ailes tried to explain that evening shows were more like op-ed articles than news shows and that Hannity's viewers wouldn't be voting for him anyway. Ailes said bluntly that his biggest concern was that he wasn't sure Obama would defend the sovereignty of the United States. "That's ridiculous," Obama replied. When the candidate left, Murdoch told Ailes, "Boy, you were tough on him."

A couple of months later, after Murdoch pushed him to moderate Fox's coverage of Obama, Ailes threatened to quit. A panicked Murdoch gave Ailes a lucrative five-year contract and promptly endorsed McCain, though he privately told several liberals he knew that he had voted for Obama. None was sure that was true.

If Murdoch was agnostic about Obama, Ailes and his subordinates helped popularize the idea that he was a threat to the republic. In March 2009 Ailes read the executive summary of the president's first budget, entitled *A New Era of Responsibility: Renewing America's Promise.* He told his colleagues at News Corp. that it was a socialist manifesto for the redistribution of wealth and that Obama was the most liberal president in history. Neither of these things was remotely true: Obama's Democratic predecessors, including Clinton, favored higher levels of taxation and more progressive health care reform. But this was what Ailes believed, and it made its way into the conservative bloodstream for good.

For the next three years Fox News pummeled the president relentlessly, trying to turn every flap into a major scandal. From the bogus 2009 stories of White House "czars" (every president has aides assigned to oversee policy areas) to the outrageous 2012 claims that Obama administration officials had intentionally left Americans to die in Benghazi, the network was committed to ripping down the president. Many Fox producers, reporters, and anchors were able journalists trying—and frequently succeeding—to perform professionally. Unfortunately the questions they asked and stories they pursued were too often in the context of their employer's bias. Republicans responded by saying that the *New York Times* and the big broadcast networks were biased too, but the inapt comparison never resonated beyond the conservative base.

The question Fox faced as the 2012 election approached was whether to ratchet the anti-Obama tilt of the network up or down. Murdoch was clearly worried that the phone-hacking scandal embarrassing him in Great Britain could spread to the United States. To lower the temperature (and possibly dissuade Obama-appointed prosecutors who might be looking into phone hacking in the United States), Murdoch once again told Ailes to lighten up a bit on Obama. When the morning program *Fox & Friends* aired a video about Obama's record that was depicted by an often friendly critic as "resembling propaganda films from 1930s Europe," the network publicly disavowed the work of the young staff producers. Romney still got five or ten minutes whenever he wanted to deliver his message on *Fox & Friends* without having to worry about even a slightly challenging question. But some of the most egregious stunts faded.

THROUGHOUT 2011 NEITHER Murdoch nor Ailes was enthusiastic about any of the Republican candidates. Their secret first choice was General David Petraeus, who was running the war in Afghanistan and in line to be Obama's CIA director. In the spring of 2011, Ailes gave K. T. McFarland, a Fox national security analyst, a message for Petraeus when she interviewed him in Kabul. According to an audio recording obtained by Bob Woodward, McFarland said that Ailes advised Petraeus that if he wasn't named chairman of the Joint Chiefs of Staff he should run for president in 2012. Ailes would resign as chairman of Fox to run his campaign and Murdoch would bankroll it. Ailes confirmed the story to Woodward, but characteristically trashed McFarland in the process, disclosing her "less than $75,000" part-time salary. McFarland was right that a Petraeus campaign was feared in the White House, though less so than in 2009 and 2010, when David Axelrod spoke openly of his concern about it.

Ailes, McFarland, and other Republicans assumed that military officers were safely in the Republican camp, and, if past preferences were any indication, most were. But according to Colonel Jack Jacobs, a retired Medal of Honor winner who taught Petraeus at West Point, the highest-ranking officers, especially those with direct contact with the president, generally backed Obama for reelection. They found him supportive of the military and much more knowledgeable than any of the Republican challengers. Petraeus didn't reveal his preference, but he accepted the president's offer to run the CIA and enjoyed an increasingly close relationship with him right up to the time he resigned in November 2012 after the disclosure of his extramarital affair.

Murdoch meanwhile couldn't find anyone else to get excited about. By this time he had discovered Twitter and begun sniping at Romney: "Met Romney last week. Tough O Chicago pros will be hard to beat unless he drops old friends from team and hires some real pros. Doubtful." Ailes agreed, and he didn't contact Romney's senior aides directly with advice, as he had with the Bush team. He still despised Obama but knew that his presidency was good for Fox. Since launching the network in 1996, Ailes had created at least a billion dollars in value for News Corp., and he was anxious that the profits keep rolling in.

That would be easier with a Democrat in the White House to continue using as a punching bag. The network had first begun to thrive during the impeachment of Bill Clinton in the late 1990s. Under Obama, the aim was to ignite a Watergate-level blaze that would both consume the president and draw a bigger audience. A Romney presidency, everyone agreed, would bring at least marginally worse ratings for Fox, which was more popular as attack dog than cheerleader.

EVEN AS HE moved up to a bigger corporate job as chairman of the Fox Television Stations Group, Ailes remained obsessed with Fox News, which had been in his head in various forms forever. While working in the Nixon White House, he had circulated a memo entitled "A Plan for Putting the GOP on TV" that read like a prototype of the channel he would create. The idea—never adopted by Nixon—was to build a White House–run TV network that would circumvent the "liberal media" that he and Nixon detested and deliver pro-Nixon broadcasts directly to conservative-owned local stations.

Four decades later Ailes was a brilliantly successful entrepreneur surrounded by fiercely loyal acolytes to whom he was generous. But Ailes was also a merciless bully, tormented by inner demons that went back to a childhood of long, lonely hospital stays as he battled hemophilia. Tales of his paranoia had circulated for years, like the time he tried to order bombproof glass for his office because he thought homosexuals outside News Corp. headquarters on Sixth Avenue might shoot at him (he settled for drawing the blinds instead), or when he demanded that security throw a "Muslim-looking" man out of the building and the man turned out to be a janitor.

Other stories about Ailes's mental torment had gone untold. Two former News Corp. senior executives said that Murdoch routinely called Ailes "cuckoo," "bonkers," "nuts," and "crazy," but he also found Ailes's behavior amusing. For instance, one Monday, Murdoch snickered to senior staff that Ailes was convinced that the whole News Corp. building was bugged: "Roger came in over the weekend to work in the only room that he thought was secure—a supply closet." Ailes had a television monitor on his desk that showed video of the empty hall outside his office so that he would have warning if terrorists were coming to kill him. He posted round-the-clock security guards outside the locked gates of his Putnam County, New York, estate and insisted on entering News Corp.'s headquarters through a side door used by no other executives, not even Murdoch, who entered through the front. Where Ailes had two bodyguards escorting him into the building, Murdoch had one, who doubled as his driver and left him at the curb. Current and even former News Corp. employees were terrified of Ailes, whose apparatchiks monitored their email like the Stasi and wreaked vengeance at his command. Associates described Ailes as charming but unhinged and a little pathetic. More than once he told his colleagues, "They hate me because I'm fat."

––––––

AILES HAD REASON to be paranoid about the long-term future of Fox News. In April of 2009, after Glenn Beck, then a top-rated Fox News host, called the president "a racist" on *Fox & Friends,* a liberal advocacy group called colorofchange.org launched a boycott of Beck. ConAgra, Procter & Gamble, Geico, and a few other advertisers pulled their ads from Beck's show. At first, Apple was slow to respond to the boycott, but when Apple founder Steve Jobs found out what Beck said, he was furious. On a Saturday, Jobs, who hadn't known Apple advertised on Fox, fired off an email to a West Coast executive of Omnicom, the giant ad agency that spent hundreds of millions a year on Apple's behalf. Jobs's message was simple: I want all Apple ads off all Fox News shows immediately. And no, it couldn't wait until Monday. After much scrambling, an Omnicom executive and a technician from News Corp. had to drive to a News Corp. facility on Long Island that Sunday and remove the digital file containing the ads.

Even before the incident, Omnicom and other agencies were beginning to pull away from Fox News Channel because its demographics were the oldest in cable news. By 2010 only six of Omnicom's hundred biggest corporate clients advertised there. The audience was affluent but otherwise monochromatic and uninteresting to advertisers. Sean Hannity and Bill O'Reilly became unpopular with blue-chip advertisers, who in their package ad buys paid Fox News a small premium to skip over them in favor of other Fox programs with younger viewers. The ratings at Fox were still higher than those for CNN and MSNBC combined, but several shows slipped into second place in "the money demo," the demographic of twenty-five- to fifty-four-year-olds that advertisers crave.

The Fox News business model was still a money machine that pumped out hundreds of millions in profits, but the trend lines were ominous for Ailes. Cable subscriptions were declining as news and other content moved online. And the ad market had turned sour. Omnicom, the second largest ad agency in the world, bought more ads for corporate clients like Pepsico and GE on Jon Stewart alone than on all of Fox News. That left Ailes with "direct response" ads for gold coins, medical devices, and the like. "Long-term, there's no possibility for growth," one senior Omnicom executive said of Fox News. "Their audience is simply not getting replaced by younger viewers." He contrasted Fox News with Spanish-language TV, where Omnicom's revenues had doubled. Univision, the fourth largest broadcast network in the United States, had ratings three or four times as great as Fox News, a data point that would take on great significance in the 2012 campaign.

BILL O'REILLY AND Sean Hannity were the most prominent faces on the network. For fifteen years their tough-guy personas had defined not just Fox News but the entire aesthetic of the American right: The Clintons were scum, Obama was a dangerous socialist, and liberals were "pinheads" (O'Reilly's word) who hated America. When it served their purposes, they let up on the Clintons to pile onto Obama. To keep it interesting, O'Reilly occasionally gave Obama a break, only to trash him on something else the next night. Hannity was consistently ferocious and untruthful, from insisting that Reagan had "inherited a far worse economy than Obama" to claiming to "never hear" Obama praise America. When the Federal Reserve Board released statistics showing a 38.8 percent drop in the median net worth of Americans, Hannity, Karl Rove, and others at Fox blamed it all on Obama, without mentioning that the Fed's starting point was 2007, which meant that more than half of the decrease was on George W. Bush's watch.

O'Reilly was the anchor of the highest-rated cable news show and the author of bestsellers, but he was angry and depressed around the office. His childhood had been more affluent and less happy than he let on. (Despite claiming repeatedly that he was raised in a working-class family in Levittown, New York, he was in fact from the more affluent suburb of Westbury.) Because of alcoholism in his family, he vowed from the time he was a child never to touch a drop of alcohol or smoke a cigarette, and he never did. By all accounts, his success brought him no pleasure. He was loyal to his staff but terrorized them daily. The famous viral video of him screaming "Do it live!" at a hapless *Inside Edition* producer was, according to longtime staffers on *The O'Reilly Factor*, business as usual.

Hannity, who treated his staff kindly, loathed O'Reilly personally; the feeling was mutual. Their feud went back to a time shortly after the founding of Fox in 1996, when *Hannity & Colmes* was the top show on the network and O'Reilly's program (not yet called *The O'Reilly Factor*), had low ratings. Hannity, an ingratiating right-wing radio talk show host, was friendly toward O'Reilly, a journeyman TV reporter and anchor with no personal following. But after Ailes moved O'Reilly to 8 p.m. and his show took off, O'Reilly didn't return the favor. He saw himself as a speak-truth-to-power tribune of the working stiff, not an ideologue cheering for Republicans, and he was cold and snide toward his in-house rival.

Unlike his counterparts at MSNBC, Hannity was willing to jump in bed with any crackpot. He and his fellow radio talk show host Dennis Prager were on the advisory board of a Tea Party group called Brotherhood Organization of a New Destiny (BOND), headed by a right-wing activist and regular Hannity guest named Jesse Lee Peterson. "I think that one of the greatest mistakes that America made was to allow women the opportunity to vote. We should've never turned it over to women," Peterson said in a March speech. Peterson is African American, which Hannity felt gave him immunity from criticism for associating with him. Here was a clear case where the ratings bump for Fox by having someone like Peterson on the air was at odds with the GOP's obvious political interests.

––––––––

WHILE HE DIDN'T like to admit it, Obama kept tabs on the right-wing media. At a White House Christmas party for the news media in late 2011, he told Ailes when they were posing for a picture, "I saw on the cover of a magazine [*Newsmax*, a conservative publication] that you're the most powerful man in news." Ailes and his wife loved it. In private, Obama found this a sad commentary on the media culture. The president often said that he thought of Fox News, which he rarely watched, as nothing more than talk radio on television. That was an oversimplification. If Fox were the lungs of the conservative base, breathing life into the Tea Party and its other causes, Rush Limbaugh and his imitators were its spleen. The reach of talk radio in red states helped explain why the president was so unpopular in rural America at a time when the farm economy was doing so well. It was as if a viciously anti-Obama radio ad played on a loop all day and night to anyone in a car on the highway.

Limbaugh had been on the air so long that his racism had lost its ability to shock. But it was racism nonetheless, and not a particularly subtle strain of it. He had begun in 2007 by calling Obama an "affirmative action candidate" and playing a ditty entitled "Barack the Magic Negro" (to the tune of "Puff the Magic Dragon"). After the 2008 election, Limbaugh confronted his slipping ratings by going even harder on the theme. Although the benefits of food stamps, Medicaid, and other social programs went mostly to whites, Limbaugh insisted, "Obama's entire economic program is reparations."

Obama, an African American under the most literal definition of the term, couldn't even get that concession out of Limbaugh. The talk show host deemed him a "halfrican American," by which he meant that Obama wasn't black but Arab because "Kenya is an Arab region." (This would come as a surprise to any resident of Kenya, where Arabs make up less than 1 percent of the population.) Later Limbaugh changed his mind and said, "Obama is more African in his roots than he is American and is behaving like an African colonial despot."

For Limbaugh, anything that involved blacks anywhere in the country was somehow Obama's fault. In September 2009 video surfaced of a white kid being beaten up by black kids on a school bus. Even though all the children involved said the issue wasn't racial, Limbaugh disagreed, insisting, "We need segregated buses." Then he blamed the president: "You put your kids on a school bus you expect safety, but in Obama's America the white kids now get beat up with the black kids cheering 'Yeah, right on, right on, right on.'"

When the Occupy Wall Street movement coincided with Obama's unveiling his jobs bill, Limbaugh drew a sinister connection and added a racist twist: "There's rioting in the streets now! And there's going to be more rioting in the streets because that's part of the problem here. And next up there are going to be race riots, I guarantee it. Race riots are part of the plan that this regime has. That's next." Limbaugh's ads drove home that the broadcast thrived on stoking fear. He sold precious metals, threat protection, debt consolidation, and other services of special interest to white males who overextended themselves.

The insults spewed forth for three hours a day. Limbaugh repeatedly called the president "an angry black guy." Even if most listeners viewed Limbaugh as entertainment, the relentless message couldn't help but sink in: "Barack Obama hates this country" and appeals to "people with miserable, meaningless lives and people who don't count." When Limbaugh wasn't peddling fear, he switched effortlessly to belittlement: "If Obama weren't black he'd be a tour guide in Honolulu or teaching Saul Alinsky constitutional law in Chicago." Lest there be any doubt about his unalloyed racism, years earlier he had told an African American woman caller, "Take that bone out of your nose and call me back."

Limbaugh was only the most public face of racial animus toward Obama. When Neil Munro, a "reporter" for the Daily Caller, used a day pass at the White House to shout at the president in the Rose Garden while he was speaking, it offended the veteran reporter Sam Donaldson, who had famously shouted questions at the six presidents he covered but only after they finished their remarks. "Many on the political right believe this president ought not to be there—they oppose him not for his policies and political view but for who he is, an African American!" Donaldson emailed the *Huffington Post*. "These people and perhaps even certain news organizations (certainly the right wing talkers like Limbaugh) encourage disrespect for this president."

Grover Norquist thought Limbaugh had outlived his usefulness to the GOP: "In 1994, especially, Rush was very helpful, but now these guys are just talking to themselves. You can get rich as a talk show host with 10 percent of the market, but you can't get elected dog catcher with ten percent. It's a subculture only." Norquist failed to mention that even on its best days, Fox News was watched by less than 5 percent of the American electorate.

Fox Nation wasn't a nation after all. It wasn't the real America, the country's heart. It was a bubble, though the people inside didn't know that yet.

6

The Voter-Suppression Project

It was the biggest open secret in politics: To win and keep power, Republicans felt they had to hold down turnout among young people and minorities, who tended to vote Democratic. With demographic trends moving against them, the task took on a new urgency.

But the GOP had a problem in 2012. Many Americans saw voting as both a right and a rite, a core value and an almost sacred tradition. So Republicans needed a cover story. They embraced the convenient fiction that massive vote fraud threatened the integrity of the ballot box. This became writ within the party. Any Republicans admitting the truth—that fixing voter fraud was a solution in search of a problem—risked being ostracized. Their insecurity about attracting voters trumped their faith in democracy. Few stopped to think of the backlash should their obvious motive—voter suppression—become widely recognized among those whose rights they sought to violate.

Suppressing the vote was hardly a new feature of American political life. In the late nineteenth century and early twentieth, Southern Democrats imposed literacy tests, "grandfather clauses" (citizens could only vote if their grandfathers had, which was impossible for blacks), and poll taxes designed to disenfranchise African Americans. Many of these Jim Crow–era abuses survived past midcentury, well within the living memory of black voters.

Republicans, who thought of themselves as the party of Lincoln, didn't take up suppression tactics until after the 1960 election, when they charged that Mayor Daley had stolen votes for John F. Kennedy in the "river wards" of Chicago. (In fact Kennedy would have won even without Illinois's electoral votes.) In 1964 the Republican National Committee launched "Operation Eagle-Eye," ostensibly to guard against vote fraud. Volunteers were dispatched to inner-city precincts as poll watchers. Among them was William Rehnquist, a future Supreme Court justice, who was alleged to have taken part in efforts to discourage

African American voters in Phoenix in the early 1960s, though he later denied it.

Over the next two decades, a combination of the Voting Rights Act and the decline of big-city political machines led to much cleaner American elections. As reformers in both parties stamped out most genuine vote fraud, all that remained were scattered anecdotes that, even if true, amounted to less than 0.001 percent of ballots cast.

But the GOP was determined to use "ballot security" to suppress the black vote. Since 1982 the Republican National Committee has been operating under a federal consent decree (stemming from racist ballot suppression in New Jersey) that prevented the party from backing efforts by its activists to police the polls. When the RNC tried to get the consent decree lifted on the peculiar grounds that President Obama and Attorney General Eric Holder were black, a U.S. District Court judge called the argument "offensive" and the Supreme Court agreed.

By this time a new and more pervasive form of voter suppression was making headway. The twenty-first-century efforts to restrict the franchise came not from racists or grubby aldermen but from extremely wealthy men who saw a chance to bend the political system to their will.

———

THE MODERN ERA of corporate power in the political realm began in August 1971 with a thirty-four-page "confidential memorandum" to the Chamber of Commerce entitled "Attack on American Free Enterprise System." The author was Lewis F. Powell Jr., a prominent Richmond, Virginia, lawyer who two months later would be appointed by President Nixon to the Supreme Court. Powell began by arguing, "No thoughtful person can question that the American economic system is under broad attack." The attack from college campuses, the pulpit, the media, liberal politicians, and consumer advocates like Ralph Nader was "quite new in the history of America." Business, Powell wrote, had responded, if at all, by "appeasement, ineptitude and ignoring the problem."

Powell, who today would be characterized as a moderate Republican, was right that American liberal discourse in the early 1970s routinely denigrated business and ignored the importance of entrepreneurship. But it wasn't accurate even then that "few elements of American society today have as little influence in government as the American businessman [and] the corporation." Nowadays, thanks in part to the movement that Powell kicked off, the opposite is closer to the truth.

The memorandum's recommendation of a "more aggressive attitude" toward generating conservative books, articles, institutes, and television programs bore fruit beyond anything Powell could have imagined. It led, directly and indirectly, to the creation of more than a dozen conservative legal foundations and think tanks. William Simon, treasury secretary under Nixon, convinced the Coors, Scaife, and Olin families to establish the Heritage Foundation in 1973. This kicked off an effort to subsidize the spread of conservative ideas that dwarfed anything on the left. Within a decade of its founding in 1982 as a student organization at prestigious law schools, the Federalist Society and its impressive alumni had already moved the American legal system in a conservative direction. Two billionaire brothers, Charles and David Koch, alone funded 150 programs at colleges and universities to promote their libertarian ideas.

Over the years Heritage helped fuel conservative domination of the intellectual debate, with some significant ironies. It was at Heritage in the early 1990s that a health policy expert named Stuart Butler first popularized the idea of a "mandate" on employees, requiring them to buy health insurance. This was seen as a conservative alternative to a government-run health care system and a way of dealing with the "free riders" who received treatment at hospitals without paying for it. Politicians ranging from Hillary Clinton to Mitt Romney and Barack Obama would eventually adopt Heritage's proposal.

The transition of these institutions from right-leaning think tanks to political outfits was best exemplified by the case of the Cato Institute, founded in 1974 by Charles Koch and Edward Crane to spread libertarian ideas. After the death of Chairman Emeritus William Niskanen in 2011, a court fight erupted over control of the foundation, with Crane charging that Koch was trying to turn Cato into "some sort of auxiliary of the GOP."

It was a cofounder of Heritage, Paul Weyrich, who in 1980 first argued to Republicans that the long-term demographic trends of the country were moving against them. Weyrich addressed a conference in Dallas headlined by Republican presidential candidate Ronald Reagan. "I don't want everyone to vote," Weyrich told the crowd. "As a matter of fact, our leverage in elections quite candidly goes up as the voting populace goes down."

In the 1970s Weyrich was also a cofounder, with Representative Henry Hyde, of one of the most influential, and least known, of all conservative organizations: the American Legislative Exchange Council, a bland-sounding outfit originally called the Conservative Caucus of State Legislators. ALEC sponsored forums that brought together corporate lobbyists and state representatives to write model bills that could be used to advance conservative causes in state capitals. Jack Kemp, Jesse Helms, John Kasich, and many other prominent conservative politicians have been associated with ALEC, which worked closely with donors to state campaigns. The bylaws of ALEC's closed-door meetings gave corporate lobbyists an equal vote with legislators on which model bills to introduce, with the practical effect that Republican-controlled state legislatures were often rubber stamps for corporate interests. Thousands of cookie-cutter state laws on everything from tax cuts and deregulation to the "Stand Your Ground" legislation that figured in the 2012 case of Trayvon Martin (an unarmed teenager shot and killed in Florida) began as ALEC model bills. In 2002 ALEC began to explore ways of changing state election laws to help Republicans and their corporate backers.

AS REPUBLICANS SOUGHT to curtail turnout, Democrats were busy making the country's changing demographics work for them. In 1993, after Clinton was elected president with the help of first-time voters, Democrats passed the "Motor Voter" bill, which required states to offer voter registration at departments of motor vehicles. While the Democrats' partisan motive for expanding turnout was as plain as the Republicans' partisan motive for restricting it, the effect of Motor Voter and other such bills was to expand democracy without any discernible rise in corruption.

After *Bush v. Gore*, the U.S. Supreme Court decision that shut down the Florida recount of the 2000 election and assured Bush's victory, Democrats became convinced that Republicans had stolen the election. It took years of recounts and investigations, but proof finally arrived in 2004, when it turned out that a list of fifty thousand ex-convicts purged from voter rolls included about twenty thousand voters who weren't felons, half of them black in a state that was just 15 percent African American. The improperly purged names added up to more than enough votes to give Gore the presidency. The experience was seared into the psyche of Democrats—especially minority voters—in ways that would prove relevant in 2012.

The Florida recount put pressure on Washington to upgrade election procedures, but the 2002 Help America Vote Act did little more than banish punch-card ballots and the infamous chads that hung from them. Karl Rove, by then President Bush's chief political adviser, saw an opening. With attention focused on fixing the system, he gave speeches and interviews claiming that the real problem was vote fraud. Bush's new attorney general, John Ashcroft, placed the issue near the top of his agenda and hired a savvy conservative activist from the Florida recount, Hans A. von Spakovsky, to head the voting rights section of the Justice Department—an insult to civil rights activists who trusted Justice to guarantee voting rights, not restrict them. Several career staffers quit in protest after von Spakovsky, a member of the Federalist Society, overruled them in backing a photo ID law in Georgia (later invalidated by a judge as "akin to a Jim Crow–era poll tax") that became a national model for conservatives.

From the White House, Rove pushed career prosecutors to win convictions for vote fraud. When U.S. attorneys in New Mexico and Seattle appointed by Bush couldn't make cases, they were fired for disloyalty, a politicization of law enforcement so blatant that it led Rove to be subpoenaed by Congress.* After five years of investigations and prosecutions, the Bush Justice Department acknowledged in 2007 that no evidence existed of a widespread problem with vote fraud. In a nation of more than 200 million citizens of voting age, fewer than fifty people were convicted of voting illegally, almost all of whom offered convincing explanations that they had done so unintentionally. In the climate of prosecution created in Washington, however, several were rewarded for their confusion with prison or deportation.

This did nothing to dampen enthusiasm on the right. Von Spakovsky, whose nomination by President Bush to be a member of the Federal Election Commission was derailed in 2007 by Senator Barack Obama, cowrote a book with the conservative journalist John Fund that claimed vote fraud by convicted felons delivered Minnesota's Senate seat to Al Franken in 2008. Because Franken's race against Norm Coleman was so close, it was exhaustively investigated by authorities in Minnesota, who found "zero evidence of fraud." Nonetheless von Spakovsky helped spread the word among Republican state legislators in 2011 that they should introduce "election reform" bills that could take effect before the 2012 election.

Fox News helped. After the 2008 campaign, the network blew up small, isolated voting irregularities in Milwaukee and South Bend, Indiana, into national "scandals." When two members of the New Black Panther Party showed up at a polling place in Philadelphia, not a single actual voter there complained of intimidation. But the name of the group and the fears it conjured in viewers fueled weeks of the stories in the conservative media. Fox News reporter Eric Shawn launched a weekly "Voter Fraud" segment that publicized any random accusation,

---

* Rove ignored the subpoena issued by House Democrats but, unlike Attorney General Eric Holder in the Obama administration, was not held in contempt.

even if minor and unconfirmed. Stories of forged ballot access petitions, on which volunteers would list celebrities or phony obscene names as a goof, were covered on Fox as major crimes, even though no referenda made the ballot or ineligible persons voted as a result. The shenanigans of a media provocateur, James O'Keefe, brought down the left-wing ACORN organization for alleged offenses unrelated to vote fraud. But in 2008 ACORN had self-reported a few bogus registration forms it collected (with names of cartoon characters and NFL players put on the forms by petition passers), which added to the GOP's momentum.* So did Norquist's baseless claim that Obama campaign workers had promised Democrats they could get jobs in the post office if they voted for Obama in 2008.

Norquist, von Spakovsky, and Fund then began arguing with only minor anecdotal evidence that vote-by-mail systems adopted by thousands of counties across the country led to widespread vote fraud. Their examples of absentee vote fraud, which Fund called "the easiest and most pervasive kind," made their arguments seem to be backed by facts. But because absentee ballots in many states favor Republicans (who are more likely to travel out of town on Election Day on business), most of the hundreds of "election reform" bills introduced by Republicans in state legislatures in early 2011 did little to change the rules on them.

Without good evidence of vote fraud convictions to bolster their case, ALEC and the Republicans pushed hard on von Spakovsky's idea of requiring photo IDs. On the surface, showing ID before voting seemed reasonable; the idea enjoyed strong public support from voters required to provide proof of identity to cash checks or get on an airplane. But the only reason to move hastily to change the law would be if there were widespread evidence of voter fraud, which there wasn't. Lawyers for Republicans could come up with only nine anecdotal cases of in-person voter impersonation (the only crime that photo IDs guard against) in the entire country in the past quarter-century, none of which led to prosecution.

Nonetheless, in 2008 the Supreme Court in *Crawford v. Marion County Election Board* upheld Indiana's state photo ID requirements. The Court's reasoning was that because the IDs were free, they didn't constitute an unconstitutional poll tax. Although the state of Indiana

---

* These half dozen cases, including one during the Indiana presidential primary in 2008, took place in isolated counties, implicated only a handful of would-be registrants, and involved no pattern of fraud that might affect the ability to get on the ballot, much less the outcome of an election.

failed in its brief to produce a single case in the history of Indiana of in-person voter impersonation, ALEC and other backers of photo ID laws invoked the decision to advance their argument in state capitals. After *Crawford* the Democrats miscalculated. Instead of using their majorities in several battleground states to compromise on commonsense photo ID bills, Democrats dug in against any changes in those laws, a decision that almost sank them when so many states went Republican in 2010.

———

IN 1998 A quiet movement began that would change the way much of the country voted. That year Oregon, under a visionary secretary of state named Phil Keisling, became the first vote-by-mail state in the country, a move that boosted participation in presidential elections to more than 80 percent of registered voters. Whether citizens voted by mail or in person, the convenience of voting early spread quickly to hundreds of counties in dozens of states. After 2004, when John Kerry lost Ohio and thus the election at least in part because of extremely long lines at polling places, voting by mail and voting early became a priority for the Democratic Party, and many Republican election officials agreed that it was the right thing to do for harried voters who often couldn't get time off from work on Election Day. By 2008 nearly a third of the American electorate voted early. Because Democrats more often took advantage of the convenience of early voting, the change helped Obama in Ohio, Florida, and other states.

Then came the midterms. With so many statehouses and state legislatures suddenly in Republican hands, it wasn't hard to roll back the small *d* democratic victories of Democrats. Starting in early 2011, the GOP, often using ALEC model bills, launched quiet voter-suppression campaigns in forty-one states. It was the most systematic and pervasive effort to discourage voting in almost a century. GOP state legislators introduced 140 bills to restrict voting, and by mid-2012 sixteen states had approved legislation, including the battleground states of Ohio, Florida, Colorado, Virginia, Wisconsin, New Hampshire, and Pennsylvania. Through the beginning of 2012 there was little publicity about these suspiciously timed efforts, but Democrats were under no illusions about what was happening. The White House believed the GOP was trying to rig or at least tilt the election. Bob Bauer, the president's longtime attorney, called it "a remarkable piece of concerted execution."

Not every state enacted every provision in the ALEC model bills, but the similarities in many of the measures were striking. It was an open secret within the GOP that Republican governors were racing to see who could be the first to sign far-reaching election "reform." Republican secretaries of state, egging each other on at conservative conferences, recognized that their ticket to higher office was proving to donors and party officials that they would use their power to hold down Democratic turnout.

The GOP's goal was to require state-issued photo ID; to curtail voter-registration drives (which register minorities at twice the rate of nonminorities); to cut back on early in-person voting; to repeal "same-day" (Election Day) registration, used by many college students; and to intensify citizenship challenges against those suspected of being ineligible to vote. All of these changes were aimed at suppressing turnout by the minorities and young voters who make up the base of the Democratic Party. Almost all of the bills were effective in the 2012 cycle, which, as former RNC chairman Michael Steele later acknowledged, further confirmed that the goal was less to improve the system over time than to defeat the president and other Democrats.

If racism was involved in the GOP-backed bills, it was a secondary factor. The new laws also discriminated against students, the elderly, and anyone who didn't drive.

FLORIDA WAS TYPICAL of what happened behind closed Republican doors. On New Year's Day 2011, Emmett "Bucky" Mitchell IV, the attorney responsible for the notorious list of purged "felons" in 2000, called a meeting with several political consultants and state officials. Jim Greer, the state party chairman, soon to plead guilty in a corruption scandal, said later that Mitchell's meeting disturbed him. "I was upset because the political consultants and staff were talking about voter suppression and keeping blacks from voting," Greer testified in a deposition. Republicans charged that the accusations were concocted to bolster the defense in his case, but three other former GOP officials backed Greer up in interviews with the *Palm Beach Post* and the *Tampa Bay Times*.

At the New Year's Day meeting, Mitchell, who had been elevated to general counsel to the Florida GOP, took on the assignment of writing the vote fraud bill to be introduced in Tallahassee. Passed in May 2011, the radical overhaul of election laws cut early voting days from fourteen to eight, made it more difficult to change registration to a different county (affecting African Americans, who move more often than other voters), and placed crippling restrictions on voter-registration efforts. Florida's new law effectively ended all voter-registration drives, an activity the League of Women Voters had undertaken in the state for nearly a century. The statute required voter-registration volunteers to go to the county office and take an oath agreeing to be personally liable for thousands of dollars in fines if they didn't deliver completed forms without the slightest error within forty-eight hours, among other restrictions.

Republicans in Michigan went even further, requiring that voter-registration volunteers attend training sessions but providing no funds or other provisions for such training—a state-sanctioned Catch-22. The League of Women Voters had no choice but to suspend its operations in Florida and Michigan and join with Rock the Vote and other organizations to file suit.

In Ohio, where control of state government had also moved to the Republicans, the aim was to reverse the conditions that existed in 2008. That year John McCain polled 263,000 more votes on Election Day than Obama but lost the state by 4.6 points. The difference was early voting, which Obama won overwhelmingly. In a new tradition called "Souls to the Polls," more than 119,000 African American Obama supporters were bused directly from church to polling places on the Sunday before the 2008 election. Like the Florida statute, Ohio's new law, signed by Republican Governor John Kasich, ended that practice. The bill was so sweeping that the Obama campaign calculated it would put them at a crippling 400,000-vote disadvantage in 2012.

Fortunately for Obama, Ohio state law allowed for a petition campaign to place a repeal measure on the state ballot in November 2012. If such a repeal initiative were put before the voters, it would mean that the new election law would not be in effect for the presidential election. But the 231,000 signatures necessary for a ballot initiative wouldn't be easy to obtain, especially with Ohio unions and other Democratic allies busy trying to repeal Governor Kasich's union-busting bill. For much of 2011 it wasn't clear whether Ohio would even be in play for the Democrats in the presidential election.

Ohio's secretary of state, Jon Husted, a Republican and ALEC alumnus elected in 2010, used every lever he had to reduce turnout. Under Ohio law, county boards of elections are evenly divided between Democrats and Republicans, with the secretary of state empowered to break the tie on rules governing elections. In urban Democratic counties, Husted broke the tie in favor of shorter voting hours, even though he knew that this would lead to more long lines like those Ohio experienced in 2004. The racial disparities in Ohio were disturbing. In 2010, according to a lawsuit, 94 percent of new African American voters were challenged at the polls, compared to 16 percent of new white voters.

Normally the legislative process is excruciatingly slow. But not this time. It seemed as though every week in 2011 and early 2012 brought word of another Republican-controlled state moving to restrict voting. Iowa's new Republican governor, Terry Branstad, took executive action that made it difficult for anyone with a criminal record to have his or her voting rights restored. Wisconsin and New Hampshire passed restrictive voter ID laws that made it harder for students who didn't have a driver's license to vote. William O'Brien, New Hampshire's Republican speaker of the house, explained the logic of the bill to a Tea Party audience. "Voting as a liberal, that's what kids do," O'Brien said. "They just vote their feelings and they're taking away the town's ability to govern themselves, it's not fair."

Colorado's secretary of state, Scott Gessler, a Republican, was determined to outdo Katherine Harris, the Florida secretary of state who helped Bush win Florida in 2000. Gessler didn't have a Republican governor and legislature to help him suppress Democratic turnout, so he acted unilaterally by making a list of what he considered suspicious voters, then mailing threatening letters to thousands of Coloradans, most with Latino surnames, whom he wrongly accused of being noncitizens. He estimated that 11,805 noncitizens were registered to vote but later admitted that the number was less than two hundred and only thirty-five of them may have voted. Gessler also refused to send mail-in ballots to residents of the heavily Democratic Pueblo and Denver counties, whom he considered "inactive voters" because they hadn't voted in 2010—the midterm election that many 2008 Obama voters sat out.

In 2012, Gessler spoke on a panel at a CPAC where he accused Democrats of subjecting ineligible voters to the risk of criminal prosecution by registering them, a questionable appearance for a sitting secretary of state duty bound to be a neutral supervisor of state elections. Soon it came out that Gessler had billed the state for travel to a meeting of the National Republican Lawyers Association and to the Republican National Convention with the explanation that he was discussing Colorado voter fraud there.

Pennsylvania's bill had a bring-me-the-witch's-broomstick quality. It required state department of transportation photo IDs; photo IDs issued by counties, cities, or regional transportation authorities were not valid. As in several other states, the new law disallowed student IDs unless they contained an expiration date, which few of Pennsylvania's colleges provided on the cards; this meant that students must go to their school's bursar's office for a new card before they could vote, which would dramatically reduce youth turnout, as intended. Republicans claimed the law was aimed only at increasing efficiency and ballot security, but when it was signed in early 2012, the Pennsylvania house majority leader, Mike Turzai, let the cat out of the bag at a Republican

State Committee meeting about the party's legislative accomplishments. "Voter ID, which is going to allow Governor Romney to win the state of Pennsylvania: done," Turzai told the applauding crowd.

The Republican secretary of state assured the public that 99 percent of registered voters already had the proper state-issued photo ID. But it turned out that 750,000 registered voters lacked a driver's license and were thus in danger of losing their right to vote. Even if that number was inflated, as the Obama team thought, the new law made voting a hassle for between 5 and 10 percent of the Pennsylvania electorate. Obama eventually had two hundred paid staff on the ground in Pennsylvania, and the Obama campaign thought it could keep the state blue even if the new law stood. Some Pennsylvania Democrats weren't so sure.

By mid-2012 nineteen states had approved new legislation restricting voting, including seven of the nine battleground states in the general election. The total number of electoral votes potentially affected, 212, was more than three-quarters of the 270 electoral votes required to win the presidency.

––––––

FOR MONTHS THE GOP's effort to suppress the vote had the wind at its back. Opinion polls showed overwhelming public support for requiring photo IDs in order to cast ballots. It wasn't long before Tea Party activists in several states decided that they wanted in on voter-suppression efforts. A Texas Tea Party group called King Street Patriots, funded by the Koch-backed Americans for Prosperity, began in 2010 to use new software to check voter registration lists against driver's licenses and other records. In Houston they descended on African American precincts to challenge voters who had changed addresses or had typos in their voter files. In 2011 the group renamed itself True the Vote and launched chapters in thirty states. Republican secretaries of state from around the country attended their forums. In the recall election of Governor Scott Walker of Wisconsin, True the Vote volunteers used bogus identity checks to slow down student voting at Lawrence University in Appleton. The group's founder, Catherine Engelbrecht, promised that one million True the Vote activists would descend on polling places in the 2012 general election. At the group's 2012 summit in Boca Raton, Bill Ouren, the national elections coordinator, told recruits that their job was to make voters feel like they're "driving and seeing the police following [them]."

The months ahead would bring hand-to-hand legal combat, with every battleground state except Nevada embroiled in a struggle over voter eligibility. Lawyers for state parties with help from the Obama campaign and nonprofits like the NAACP and the Brennan Center for Justice handled most of the litigation for those challenging the new laws. Jim Messina, Obama's campaign manager, told the White House that the Republicans were "trying to steal the 2012 election in 2011." He needed Bob Bauer to leave his position as White House counsel to become the campaign's lawyer. Bauer found himself consumed by the legal threats to victory across several states. He felt as if he were fighting not just for his friend and longtime client Barack Obama, but for American democracy.

For years political operatives have understood that Democrats win by addition and Republicans by subtraction. Now the GOP, embracing Lewis Powell's "more aggressive attitude," was poised to subtract roughly five million votes from an American election. In a close contest, that would be enough to tip the balance against the president.

7

The New Chicago Machine

"Chicago," as the Obama campaign headquarters came to be known, always thought the 2012 election would be close. David Axelrod, back in his hometown to begin strategizing, predicted the game would be won in the last seconds by the field goal team.

On paper, the 2011 odds on Obama's reelection weren't good. Both public and private polls showed overwhelmingly that the economy was the number one issue for voters and that Americans consistently gave one GOP candidate, Mitt Romney, much higher marks than the president on handling it. Unemployment in 2011 was 8.9 percent. It would have to come down a point or so for Obama to be reelected.

Worse for Obama, the enthusiasm level just wasn't the same as in 2008. "You're only the 1965 Rolling Stones once," Steven Spielberg told Jim Messina, the campaign manager. "The second time, it's, 'You charge too much for your tickets.'" The president himself came up with a homier metaphor one day on *Air Force One*. The difference between 2008 and 2012, he said, was the difference between a hot romance and being married with two kids and a mortgage. "In 2008 it was 'cool' to vote for me," he told a gay and lesbian fundraiser in 2011. "Now I'm sorta old news."

Despite the falloff in enthusiasm, Obama thought "the reelect" was more pivotal than his original victory. "This election will probably have the biggest contrast that we've seen since the Johnson-Goldwater election [in 1964]—maybe before that," he said. He saw it less as a struggle between conservatives and liberals than a fight between right-wing extremism and pragmatic centrism.

If Obama and his campaign team faced a daunting economy in 2011, they also enjoyed a luxury: time. While the Republicans bloodied each other with devastating super PAC ads and embarrassing primary debates, Obama had no challengers in the Democratic primaries; no prominent Democrat would dare run against the first black president in a party with a large African American base. That and a proven record of raising prodigious amounts of money would give the Obama team many months to plan, build, and execute.

It was the way Chicago used that time that counted. For generations, all American campaigns had the same basic departments: fundraising, advertising, field, advance, press, operations, volunteers, and some kind of liaison with other party-affiliated organizations. Starting in 2004 with Vermont governor Howard Dean's presidential campaign, a new section, small at first, was added to a century-old campaign structure: digital. Dean's campaign chief, Joe Trippi, was the first major strategist who sensed how the new technologies would change politics. But he and his tech wizards were too early. Even the 2008 Obama campaign barely scratched the surface of what could be done online. By 2012 data and technology personnel would account for more than one-third of the Obama campaign's payroll—a huge bet with an uncertain outcome. In 1932 Franklin Roosevelt was the first presidential candidate to exploit radio and in 1960 Kennedy the first to make full use of TV. Now, if his big plans paid off, Obama would be the first to use sophisticated digital technology to transform campaigns.

The idea was to construct a new kind of political machine. The old machines, like Richard J. Daley's in Chicago, were run on patronage; Fraser Robinson, Michelle Obama's father, held a job in the city water department that was dependent on his work during elections in the 1960s and 1970s as a Daley-backed precinct captain in his South Side neighborhood. The grease for the new machine that Obama was building was money, of course, but also data—highly sophisticated analytics of what worked and what failed that could help field, fundraising, communications, and the other traditional elements of a campaign. "What we did was to merge the old and the new—shoe leather with technology," Axelrod said later. The aim was to erase the barriers between Chicago and the field and allow a presidential campaign to be run as a collection of ward races. "In 2008, you had two campaigns: a grassroots campaign on the ground and then an online campaign, which really didn't touch," Messina said. "Now we're busting down the walls." Old-fashioned intuition was still valuable, but elegant algorithms were much better. Like Billy Beane, the Oakland Athletics general manager portrayed in Michael Lewis's *Moneyball*, Obama and his team would try to reimagine an old game with new statistics.

Large corporations had already begun moving in this direction, with analytics departments that went beyond the plodding old analysis of sales patterns to sophisticated models integrating huge data sets. Bill Gates liked to say that "measurement" was the most powerful force in the world for improving the quality of life. After the failure to "connect the dots" on terrorists before 9/11, the concept of Big Data was slowly adopted by the government. New York Mayor Michael Bloomberg moved aggressively to measure everything, and other cities and states began following suit. Now Big Data would be applied to electing a president.

The focus on rigorous new metrics for performance was the product of a revolution in the business world in the 1980s and 1990s pioneered by advisory companies like Bain Consulting (where Romney then worked) and later advanced by private equity firms like Bain Capital, which Romney founded. The 2012 campaign would feature a former low-level community organizer beating a big-time "numbers guy" at his own Bain Game.

———

AS CHICAGO'S BAIN-STYLE PowerPoint presentations showed, the electoral map favored the president. Obama's campaign manager, Jim Messina, was forty-two, and he liked to say that he had forty-two different computer-generated scenarios for how to reach the magic 270 electoral votes. All combinations involved what both parties believed were a handful of battleground states. At first they were Ohio, Florida, Virginia, Colorado, Iowa, Nevada, New Hampshire, New Mexico, and North Carolina. (Later New Mexico became solidly blue and North Carolina likely red, and Romney tried to make Wisconsin, Minnesota, and Pennsylvania competitive.) Messina figured the map meant combat in a handful of states, all of which had different rhythms, issues, and convoluted local politics. He compared it to running nine or ten separate gubernatorial races, each analyzed down to the few thousand people who could be mobilized to register and vote for the president. If Obama held Ohio, Florida, and one more state, the Republicans would have to run the table with the rest. But Messina understood that was an awfully big "if."

The secret was to restore the president's support in the field. Messina had been a big believer in the ground game since he was a college student knocking on doors in a trailer park in Missoula, Montana. The tall, cherubic-faced Idaho native managed his first campaign, for the mayor of Missoula, at age twenty-one and had been a political operative ever since. Before laboring on the 2008 campaign and as Rahm Emanuel's deputy in the White House, Messina won his spurs turning mild-mannered Max Baucus into a brawler to save his Senate seat in 2002. This one would be a knife fight too. The two scariest weapons wielded by the other side, the things that kept Messina and his team up at night, were money and voter suppression.

The most logical move would have been to keep Messina in place in the White House, where he could serve as Obama's political adviser, and have David Plouffe reprise his role as campaign manager in Chicago. But in the Hawaii surf during Christmas in 2010, Obama told Messina, "I'm gonna get rid of you." The president waited a beat before adding, "I'd like you to move to Chicago." Plouffe had argued that if he went back to Chicago to manage the reelect he would run the same campaign he had the previous time, which wasn't what 2012 required. "You've got to run your own campaign," he instructed Messina. "You won't be wed to the same decisions I was." And Messina did have some autonomy; everyone agreed that placing campaign headquarters in Chicago, away from the distractions of Washington, was essential to its success. Even so, Messina was Plouffe's man, and they often talked several times a day.

David Axelrod, who had been close to Obama since he guided his 2004 campaign for the Senate, would be back in his 2008 job as chief strategist, though Messina was upset that Axelrod, who had sold his old consulting firm, felt it necessary to hire a lawyer to negotiate his compensation. The president told Messina he didn't want to cheat anyone, but he didn't want anyone getting rich either. This was an impossible requirement; the Democratic firm GMMB (owned by a dozen longtime operatives) would make a fortune off the ad buys alone. Eventually Messina and Axelrod came to terms and Chicago marveled at the profligacy of the Romney campaign, which was structured in a way that feathered many more nests.

It didn't take long before Messina told everyone he saw, "If we run the same campaign, we will lose. We will lose badly." He liked to point out that Twitter didn't even exist until June 2008 and that Facebook was so small then that only one campaign staffer had been assigned to handle it. This time a whole section of the campaign would be devoted to exploiting Facebook. Even the layout of the new fifty-thousand-square-foot headquarters in the Prudential Building was different. Everyone was on the same floor—mostly in the same vast open space—for easier interaction. "The Floor" took on a Silicon Valley vibe. It was full of young, supersmart Obamaniacs, who often sat on large rubber balls for chairs, played Ping-Pong on breaks, and rang a bell every time the campaign raised a million dollars. Department heads took their employees on team-building retreats in the woods. A large sign near the sixth-floor entrance read, "Respect. Empower. Include. Win."

The campaign infrastructure was new. In 2008 the departments weren't linked; that meant that a supporter who gave money in New Jersey, knocked on doors in neighboring Pennsylvania, and placed telephone calls to Virginia would be in at least three different databases. Now he or she would be in one. The idea this time was that Finance would tell Field about the contribution, and Field could then try to recruit the donor as a volunteer. Or it might work the other way around, with Field telling Finance that a newly registered voter should be hit up for a donation. The key to victory wouldn't be a single department but an often subtle interaction among all of them: Analytics helping Field with sophisticated modeling of voters and giving Paid (the TV and radio ad makers) algorithms for efficient media buys, or Digital helping Finance with elaborately tested fundraising emails, or Comm (the communications shop) offering a nicely executed rapid response to Digital for social media distribution. This process sounded intuitive, but it had been followed rarely if at all in American campaigns, which were usually jerry-built contraptions that sped through the fog of combat to Election Day.

SHORTLY BEFORE THE 2008 election, Jeremy Bird got a call from Jon Carson, who had organized Obama's historic victory in the Iowa caucuses. Bird was a young field director who started in 2004 with Howard Dean's presidential campaign, then worked to secure better pay and benefits at Walmart. He entered Obama lore for his efforts in the 2008 South Carolina primary. Carson asked Bird to come to Chicago after Obama won and head up a special project. Bird's job was twofold: to make sure all the data from 2008 were preserved and updated, especially the storied Email List (which contained about 10 million email addresses of Obama supporters) and to prepare a five-hundred-page "What We Learned" document. The preparation and analysis of that document led to the development in 2012 of the largest and most sophisticated field organization ever.

It was also one of the first such grassroots operations at a national level. For generations, Democratic presidential campaigns usually subcontracted much of their canvassing and GOTV (get out the vote) to local organizations and unions. Political machines like the one the Daleys ran for a half-century in Chicago were mostly focused on electing local candidates, not presidents. Precinct captains might personally prefer, say, Richard Nixon to George McGovern, but their jobs at City Hall were dependent on winning votes for their Democratic bosses and other local politicians. To carry their precincts, they might offer tickets to a big parade, some homemade brownies, or, most important, the promise of help if the reliable voter had some problem with his garbage pickup or other city service. Unions meanwhile worked the

rank and file, and liberal groups canvassed in liberal areas. That was
about it in the field, and these GOTV structures atrophied greatly over
time. Candidates like Jimmy Carter in 1976 and Bill Clinton in 1992
built good field organizations in primary states but relied more on paid
and free media for their general election campaigns. From the 1960s
through the 1990s voters grew accustomed to aerial bombardments of
TV ads but infrequently encountered door knockers on behalf of presidential candidates, even in highly contested states.

That began to change in 2004, when a coalition of Democratic
groups formed Americans Coming Together, a field organization funded
largely by the billionaire George Soros. In Ohio, the pivotal state that
year, ACT did well for John Kerry but got beat by Karl Rove's 72-Hour
Project, which mobilized evangelicals and others for a big push on
the ground in the three days before the election. ACT suffered in part
because voters at the doorstep respond less well to canvassers representing groups than to those making a pitch for specific candidates,
a problem the Koch brothers would encounter in 2012 as their super
PAC–funded organizations tried fieldwork.

When he first weighed running for president, Senator Obama told
Axelrod that he would jump in only if they built a new type of grassroots campaign. Obama had personal experience with this kind of
work; in 1992 he had spearheaded an effort called Project Vote that
registered more than 150,000 black Chicagoans and helped make Carol
Moseley Braun the first African American woman elected to the U.S.
Senate. By 2008 he was taking the ideas he developed on Project Vote
and applying them in a much larger and more complex effort called
Obama for America, which exceeded anything tried before in grassroots organizing on a presidential campaign. The results were spectacular but not permanent. Obama's political organization, renamed
Organizing for America (OFA), helped rally support for health care reform but proved no match on the ground for all the new Tea Party
groups.

In 2009 and 2010 the White House, distracted by national crises,
let OFA wither. But Jen O'Malley Dillon, the executive director of the
Democratic National Committee, and Mitch Stewart made a decision
in this period that would have big ramifications for the 2012 campaign
and the future of the party. They convinced party chairman Tim Kaine
to invest heavily in analytics at a time when most people had barely
heard the word. It gave the Democrats a head start on developing Big
Data products that could turbocharge field organizing, media buying,
and other functions of a campaign.

The 2010 midterms were a disaster for OFA, as tens of millions of

Democrats they had shepherded to the polls in 2008 decided to sit out this election. The no-show Democrats weren't generally angry at Obama; in fact it was his absence from the ticket that caused many to stay home. The thousands of OFA volunteers and dozens of paid staff still on the ground after 2008 felt crushed by the results, but there were compensations. "Our people learned how to lose," Bird said later. "It gave them humility. They were so much better after 2010 because they *had* to be better." The same was true of Bird himself and a couple dozen other young but senior staffers who had suffered through 2010 at the DNC and now brought their combat experience back to Chicago. This continuity from 2008 would prove essential.

In Washington, the White House finally began to work in harness with the Democratic Party. Taking a leaf from Grover Norquist's Wednesday Meeting, Democrats organized a "Common Purpose Project" that held meetings every Tuesday at 5 p.m. at the Capital Hilton, where leaders of more than one hundred progressive organizations could share their policy ideas with senior White House aides. Unlike Norquist's meetings, the Democrats' weekly "Big Table" confabs were secret. After an early leak, officials like David Plouffe wouldn't return until total confidentiality was restored. Eventually, the Big Table, under the leadership of Jon Carson, became a little known but critical link between the White House and the liberal base.

In Chicago, the focus was more prosaic. The first task was to bring back those who had unsubscribed from the Email List and to register the millions of kids who had turned eighteen since 2008. In the early going, the door knocks and other voter contact would be targeted on hard-core Obama supporters who might become committed volunteers again. Then came the establishment of neighborhood team leaders, with eight to ten precincts apiece under local, regional, and state directors. Eventually more than thirty thousand of them became full-time volunteers. Finally, there would be "persuasion" of undecideds and a massive GOTV campaign for early voting and on Election Day. The whole thing would be much better organized than in 2008, which had already been the best organized presidential campaign in history.

The heart of the field operation was a small office off the Floor that Bird shared with Mitch Stewart, a South Dakotan whose work running Virginia for Obama in 2008 put that state in the Democratic column for the first time in a generation. By now the two were old roommates, having shared an office at OFA inside Democratic Party headquarters in Washington, and they developed various Oscar-and-Felix routines. Stewart liked to dip tobacco and was a Diet Coke fiend, which left Bird (and sometimes Stewart) confused over which old Coke cans contained soda and which tobacco juice. They had the walls repainted with an erasable surface so they could constantly diagram their complex field maneuvers, like Eisenhower and Patton planning the invasion of North Africa.

The two were relentless about keeping the focus on the old interactions, not the new technologies that were helping them sharpen their focus on the voters they needed to contact. "All roads lead to the face-to-face conversation," Stewart said. "It's not about the math; it's about helping those relationships."

———

AT THE VERY first all-staff meeting in June 2011, Messina poured it on thick. In a Montana version of Rahm Emanuel famously losing part of a finger while working as a kid at Arby's, he told the story of how he was so eager to work for pathetic pay on an early campaign that he took a night job to support himself at a corn-processing facility. One night, he got his pinkie mangled in a corn machine. "It reminds me every single day of how badly I wanted to work in that campaign and how I resolved to be the first in every morning and the last out and that you do whatever the fuck it takes to win," he told the staff. He explained that he wanted the campaign to be a family, but he hated complainers. Success was the only option; they had to be all-in, all the time, at any cost as they built "the largest grassroots campaign in American history." Then he held up his pinkie and said that anything other than that kind of commitment was unacceptable.

Messina had a tough act to follow. David Plouffe was not just respected in 2008; he was revered as the beau ideal of campaign managers, a disciplinarian who spoke with the voice of God. Messina couldn't win that degree of loyalty, but he picked up many of Plouffe's tightwad qualities. A billion-dollar campaign rationed staples and pens. Unlike in 2008, almost no one was granted a TV in his or her workspace, which meant lower cable bills and less distraction from work. (Big TV events were projected on white walls.) Travel and lodging expenses were strictly rationed, and it wasn't unusual to see people sleeping in the conference room before shipping out the next day for battleground states.

Messina could be brutal; under Emanuel, he had learned from the master how to tell people off. At other times, he was malleable. Senior staffers used him to deliver messages to rivals whom they feared confronting themselves. The result was that it could be hard to tell if Messina actually wanted you to do something or was merely the instrument of someone else. Early on, the manipulation was too transparent.

"If Jim says, 'I'm not mad at you, Axelrod is,' then Jim gets to play the good guy, though you don't actually trust that he is," said one senior staffer. Over time Messina won the respect of his team for his entrepreneurial skills in building and running such a complex organization.

Messina claimed to have read around twenty books about campaigns before accepting the job, and he took two things away from them: Presidential campaigns always revolve around which candidate builds a bridge to the future, and they are always, at bottom, choices. Above all, Chicago had to keep 2012 from being an up-or-down referendum on Obama's performance. The unofficial motto, repeated endlessly by Joe Biden, came from the reelection campaigns of the late Boston mayor Kevin White: "Don't compare me to the Almighty, compare me to the alternative." In early 2011 Messina and Patrick Gaspard, who had left the White House to become executive director of the DNC, spread that message on what they called "the Apology Tour." They visited big donors and progressive interest groups around the country with the message that they understood their disappointment with the president, but he would do better in a second term.

The campaign knew that journalists visiting the Floor needed simple analogies to shape their stories. So from the start, Chicago made no secret of its theory that 2012 was most similar to 2004, when Bush held off Kerry despite widespread unhappiness about the Iraq War. This time, in Chicago's view, Obama was Bush, and Mitt Romney, the man they assumed all along would win the GOP nomination, was Kerry, the out-of-touch Massachusetts elitist and flip-flopper. For "Boston," as Romney's team was called (his headquarters were in a nondescript office building on Commercial Street near Boston's North End), the analogous year was 1980, when the challenger, former California governor Ronald Reagan, was running neck and neck with President Jimmy Carter amid an awful economy until their only debate, held the last week of the campaign, helped change the dynamic and Reagan won in a landslide.

Axelrod didn't want to take the 2004 analogy too far, and not just because he thought Obama was a great president and Bush a horrible one. He felt that "Romney makes Kerry look like Benjamin Disraeli," a reference to the distinguished nineteenth-century British prime minister. Unlike Kerry, Romney wasn't merely in favor of one policy idea (in Kerry's case, funding the war in Iraq) before he was against it. He was for dozens of things before he was against them, and vice versa. It was more than could be explained by the usual flip-flops of politicians, Axelrod thought. From the beginning of 2011, he argued that Romney's behavior was "almost pathological." In more charitable moods, he ascribed it to Romney's role in business as the guy who came in at the end of negotiations and said anything to close the deal.

Chicago was worried all along about Romney's background in business. It was enormously appealing in focus groups of undecided voters. But just as Rove had attacked Kerry in 2004 on his greatest strength (his heroism in Vietnam), Axelrod knew from the outset that he would take a leaf from Ted Kennedy's 1994 campaign against Romney and go straight at his storied business record. Even before Romney opened his mouth, Chicago had plenty of material, starting with the notorious photograph of a young Romney and his partners at Bain Capital gleefully holding dollar bills.

If it did nothing else, the Occupy Wall Street movement that erupted in 2011 popularized the concept of the top 1 percent. Romney called the protesters occupying a park in Lower Manhattan "dangerous," but the real danger was to his campaign. He immediately became the poster boy for the 1-percenters, the embodiment of the Wall Street multimillionaires so many Americans had once revered and now resented. But that resentment burned the president too. Chicago winced as it watched focus group after focus group blast Obama for the bank bailouts.

Axelrod didn't like to admit he was playing class politics, but he did so early and often. He divided the Republicans into the Tea Party and the "Martini Party," the right-wing anti-Washington social conservatives and the traditional corporate country club Republicans who cared mostly about their taxes. "When Romney says, 'Elect me, I know how to fix the economy,'" Axelrod said in mid-2011, "I think every voter is going to say, 'Fix it for who? Who are you fixing the economy for?'"

Obama had been skittish about sounding populist notes in 2009, when the banks teetered on collapse. But now he didn't hesitate to sign off on class-based attacks on Romney. He had respected McCain in 2008 even as he concluded that he was clueless about how to rescue the economy. At least McCain was a war hero and (usually) a stand-up guy. The president had no such feelings toward Romney, whom he considered an empty suit, a man with "no core," as Plouffe, echoing the president, said on TV. This wasn't a new view. As early as the 2009 economic crisis Obama would mutter to old friends that he'd be damned if he'd "let Mitt Romney step in and get credit for the good stuff that happens after we've been through all this crap."

———

AFTER GENDER, ON which the Democrats held an advantage with women and meant to keep it, the most basic way to analyze the American electorate was along racial lines. In 2008 Obama won 95 percent of the black vote, 66 percent of the Latino vote, and 43 percent of the white vote. Those figures were seen as the high-water mark, and the defining question for Chicago was how much slippage from there was survivable.

For Messina, holding the Latino vote was the most important part of the equation. He calculated that if Obama fell below 56 percent there, he was finished. Remembering that Hillary Clinton had beaten Obama in every primary where Latinos were a major factor, Messina figured there were more Latinos they could get who hadn't been enthusiastic for Obama in 2008. And the registration possibilities were immense. Florida alone had 150,000 unregistered Puerto Ricans, an exploding Mexican American population, and young Cuban Americans who weren't as conservative as their parents.

Messina told the president he wanted to hire a Latina, Katherine Archuleta, as his political director, and Obama said fine. He was thinking along the same lines. Later, at Valerie Jarrett's urging, the president had passed over better-known candidates like Cass Sunstein, Walter Isaacson, and Patty Stonesifer for Cecelia Muñoz, a midlevel White House aide, to replace Melody Barnes as the new director of the Domestic Policy Council, his top domestic policy adviser. This infuriated Bill Daley, who wanted someone from the outside who would bring fresh ideas into the White House. But the president liked Muñoz and was determined to do whatever it took to show Latinos that he was on their side, even if few knew who Muñoz was.

The true inner circle of the campaign to reelect Obama remained tiny, but at some point the troops would need their marching orders. So in September 2011 a series of White House political meetings, usually held on Saturdays, commenced with about two dozen people, roughly half from the White House staff and half from the campaign. The first meeting was held in the State Dining Room, where the president made two fundamental points about why he had to win. First, he said, they were doing the right thing for the country. Second, the stakes were higher than in 2008. Defeat would not only reverse what they had accomplished; it would hurt a lot of Americans who were already suffering enough.

After David Binder, the focus group expert, explained why voters were disheartened over the economy, Joel Benenson made a poll presentation outlining how the campaign intended to draw a contrast with Romney over who was better on creating economic growth. Later Saturday meetings, usually held in the Roosevelt Room, included lengthy discussions of how to mesh policy and the campaign and sequence the rollout of various initiatives. Everyone agreed that the fight that fall over the extension of the payroll tax holiday was the least appreciated big event of the whole election cycle. Congressional Republicans were arguing against tax cuts for ordinary Americans. Chicago couldn't have scripted it better as a way to tee up the election year.

If Obama's instruction on policy was often "Don't relitigate," on politics it was more often "Tighten it up," an expression favored by Romney too. As a former political organizer himself, the president knew campaigns could lose focus. In the weekend meetings that followed, he was fully engaged in the details of his campaign. In retrospect, the biggest decision to come out of those meetings was to go early and hard at Romney—$50 or $60 million in ad buys in the early summer of 2012, when Boston had little on the air.

———

AS RECENTLY AS 2004, incumbent presidents could run for reelection with what was known as a "Rose Garden strategy." This meant that they could use the power of the presidency to shape the news and rarely had to campaign until after Labor Day. Facebook, YouTube, and the rest of the new media order changed that forever. Even if the economy had been better, Obama could never have gotten away with a Rose Garden strategy.

Jimmy Carter attended only four fundraisers when running for reelection in 1980 and Ronald Reagan none in 1984, when wealthy friends and the RNC could handle everything. It helped that every president from Carter to George W. Bush accepted public financing for the fall campaign. Having rejected public financing in both the 2008 and 2012 cycles, Obama had to fundraise like crazy. He attended seventy-two fundraisers in 2011 alone, an average of one every five days before 2012 even began. These under-the-radar political events were no fun for him, and they crowded out presidential duties, but campaigns had become so expensive that he had little choice.

In Chicago, where Finance was headed by Julianna Smoot and Rufus Gifford, some traditional sources of Democratic donations were drying up. At first, Gifford, a gay man who produced the film *Daddy Day Care* before getting involved in politics, despaired of getting others in the LGBT community to contribute more. They were still upset about the administration's not fighting harder against the Defense of Marriage Act and they misunderstood the politics of the government's Don't Ask Don't Tell policy on gays in the military. Obama had finally convinced Congress to end the policy in late 2010, but by then many of his gay and lesbian supporters had turned lukewarm on the president.

The fence-mending wasn't easy with any constituency. Large numbers of Obama's 2008 supporters felt they hadn't been kept in the fold. It wasn't that they expected an invitation to a state dinner, but they wanted to be armed with facts so that they could at least defend the man they had once been so passionate about. At a 2010 fundraiser Gifford was bombarded with sharp questions, a dramatically different tone than in 2007 and 2008. "Kind of hostile," an old colleague from 2008 said to him afterward. "That's what they're all like now," Gifford replied.

Fundraising through 2011 remained disappointing. It was both easier and harder financially to have no primary opposition: easier because the burn rate would be reduced and money could be hoarded until the general election; harder because for months it seemed as if there was no contest to get excited about, which made it tougher to put the squeeze on donors. On balance, of course, incumbents do much better when they run unopposed and unite their party early. Ted Kennedy did terrible damage to Carter in 1980 by challenging him for the nomination. The advantage of being renominated without opposition was taken for granted by voters, but not by the Obama campaign.

———

DAVID BINDER'S FOCUS groups showed that voters liked Obama personally and saw him as different in a good way. They were rooting for him. But they had what Larry Grisolano, the director of Paid Media, who was usually on the other side of the two-way mirror, described as "performance qualms." They generally thought the president knew what they were going through, but he didn't talk about their struggles in a way that lit it up for them. And they had no patience for claims that it was "morning in America." Most respondents in both focus groups and polls remained convinced the country was on the wrong track, a finding that in the past had doomed incumbent presidents.

Stan Greenberg, a former Clinton pollster unaffiliated with the campaign, angered Chicago by publishing the findings of his focus groups, which sent shivers through the Democratic Party. Messina unloaded on him, and he became persona non grata in the Obama camp. But Greenberg, who thought the White House had a "disastrous" message in 2010 that the economy was coming back, was picking up something important. "The Obama campaign kept saying that the 'foundation' of its positive message was to talk about job growth," Greenberg said. "But the more you talk about job growth, the more you piss people [in the focus groups] off. They attack the moderator and say with a lot of heat, 'You don't get what's happening in the economy!'" Hearing that,

Greenberg thought it was amazing that the president wasn't trailing by double digits.

For all the defensiveness about Greenberg and his sometime partner, James Carville, Chicago got the point that the president had to talk less about macroeconomic policy and more about real people. In one meeting of the high command, Grisolano described the macro approach as the president "looking out over a mass of people and seeing them yearning for 3.5 percent GDP growth." Everyone laughed and agreed it was a problem.

But improving presentation wouldn't be enough. The biggest thing that voters in polls and focus groups wanted was more concrete action, and this was beyond the president's control. Americans thought Obama was well-intentioned but couldn't get Congress to move, and that doing so was a big part of his job. The irony of this finding didn't ease the pain. In all of the focus groups of 2009 and 2010, the complaint had been the opposite: that the president was doing too much. Now the problem was that he was doing too little.

When that message reached the White House in late 2011, Obama launched his "We Can't Wait" campaign of executive orders and other action he could take unilaterally. He had done some of this all along, but not enough to leave an impression of continuous activity on behalf of struggling Americans. Whether because he was inexperienced in the mechanics of governing or just leery of exceeding his constitutional authority, he had left a critical policy and political tool on the ground.

CHICAGO'S BASIC TAKE on Mitt Romney was that in one respect he was the same man he'd always been: He would say or do anything to advance himself. This may have been the right take on Romney, but it led Chicago into a cul-de-sac. Depicting him as a flip-flopper was accurate but of limited effectiveness.

The person who reinforced this point for the Obama team was Bill Clinton, himself a virtuoso trimmer in his day. At a meeting in his Harlem office in November 2011, he told Axelrod, Messina, and Gaspard that making Romney seem "severely conservative" (as he had awkwardly described himself at CPAC) was more potent early on than going after him as a weather vane. Clinton wasn't rejecting the idea of depicting Romney as a flip-flopper, only suggesting that Chicago hold off until after he wrapped up the nomination and galloped to the center. Clinton also thought that hitting Romney as a right-winger would help open the wallets of wealthy Democrats. Clinton was contemptuous of Obama's poor donor-maintenance skills. The least he could do, he figured, was give the campaign the right argument to separate a few of Clinton's friends from their cash.

Chicago got Clinton's point about how to go negative but was still having problems articulating the positive. "You rarely get credit for the crisis you avert," Grisolano said early on. "So this has to be a fight about the future." But there was danger in ignoring the present. Only a couple of months after Obama unveiled the slogan "Winning the Future" in his 2011 State of the Union Address, the campaign chucked it. The "proof points" (ad-speak for being able to back up the slogan with facts) were right, but it was too optimistic when so many people believed they had yet to win the present.

Axelrod and Grisolano thought campaign slogans were like vice presidential picks: Each could be either really good or really bad but in most cases would make little difference. And slogans carried a special threat to Obama's particular brand, which was grounded in avoiding anything phony. A slogan that sounded too much like a slogan would erode the authenticity that his acolytes thought critical to his success.

But if a slogan was dispensable, a message was not. Money, analytics, field organizers, beautiful ads—the shiny new machine would not function properly without the right message. It would be a while before Chicago found it.

8

The Cave

Obama's reelection campaign was like running for Chicago alderman over and over with the help of nerdy kids who spoke a math language no one else understood. The key was microtargeting, which had first been used in direct-mail campaigns by Karl Rove and others. That word had been in bad odor in recent years thanks to the marketing industry. Microtargeting sounded intrusive, even a little creepy, but it had the potential to return politics to the most local level of all: the individual voter.

After a quarter-century of viewing voters as gross ratings points, target demographics, or plain old constituency groups, the best minds in politics were trying to see them again as ordinary people with their own specific interactions with the American political process. Like the ward heelers of old who knew a lot about their neighbors when they rang their doorbells, Obama field organizers, armed with the fruits of Big Data, could bring a presidential campaign to the front porch as never before. OFA's aim was to use algorithms to enhance the human (and thus more persuasive) part of politics: face-to-face, friend-to-friend, or at least Facebook friend–to–Facebook friend.

Befitting an intellectual president, the microtargeting revolution in politics began in academia. In 1998 Yale professors Alan Gerber and Don Green performed the first randomized tests that measured which voters responded best to which get-out-the-vote techniques: mail, phone banks, or door knocks from canvassers. Suddenly randomized tests like those used in medical research, complete with control groups and other rigorous empirical standards, were being applied to street-level politicking.

Soon consortiums like the Analyst Institute (which embedded three analysts in the Chicago headquarters) expanded A/B testing from get-out-the-vote efforts to voter registration.* The new analysts did

---

* A/B testing, used often in web design, tests different versions of the same information to see which gets the better response.

something unheard of by profiling and targeting *unlikely* voters. That transformed registration from a passive activity—sitting at a folding table in a supermarket parking lot—into something active and much more efficient. In 2012 Chicago sought to extend the modeling to the third and most difficult form of voter contact: persuasion.

Doing so required a big digital upgrade. By 2011 the technology of the 2008 campaign was long obsolete—so old that the original website for volunteers, called MyBO (short for My Barack Obama), had been named after the long-forgotten social network Myspace. In early 2011 Messina set out for the West Coast, where Eric Schmidt, chairman of Google, and executives from Apple, Facebook, Zynga, Microsoft, DreamWorks, and Salesforce all told him he should not just view the campaign as a start-up—he already knew that—but hire much of his digital crew from start-ups that were outside of politics. The digital team assembled in Chicago was in fact three teams—Digital, Tech, and Analytics—with interrelated and often competitive functions. All were headed by soon-to-be-legendary characters within the campaign.

Digital was the domain of Teddy Goff, a boyish twenty-six-year-old gay New Yorker who joined the 2008 campaign fresh out of Yale before landing at Blue State Digital, the pioneering "online engagement" company. Goff, with help from Blue State Digital founder Joe Rospars (who got the whole digital thing going in Howard Dean's 2004 presidential campaign), managed a staff of two hundred that pumped out thousands of videos, emails, texts, tweets, reddit posts, Facebook messages, and other online offerings, not to mention managing a $109 million digital advertising budget (one-fifth of the campaign's overall media budget). In early 2011 Goff told his staff that whatever they sent out had better be damn clever or it wouldn't stand a chance of breaking through the online clutter. Later, when the campaign hung in the balance, he would learn how wrong he'd been on that point.

Tech was the haven for eccentric code writers and product developers. It was supervised by Michael Slaby and the campaign's chief technology officer, Harper Reed, a thirty-three-year-old hipster who topped off the usual black rectangular glasses with product-heavy high hair and ear gauges big enough to push a broomstick through. Reed's ideas on crowdsourcing and cloud computing, respected in the tech world, had helped boost Threadless, a Chicago-based T-shirt design firm, into the web stratosphere. His personal website, which obsessively chronicled not just his exact food intake, weight, and minute-by-minute playlist but the number of steps he took each day, described his activities as "pretty awesome" and bore the legend "Harper Reed: Probably one of the coolest guys ever." It turned out that not everyone in Chicago thought so.

The third digital kingdom, Analytics, was run by Dan Wagner, twenty-eight, a nerdy University of Chicago econometrics student who had started in the 2008 campaign as a volunteer calling Latino voters. That year he created a "caucus math tool" that let Obama supporters at the Iowa caucuses negotiate with also-ran candidates to deny Hillary Clinton a larger share of delegates. While working at the DNC, his team's models predicted with uncanny precision just how badly Democrats would lose in 2010, which was one of the only pieces of good news for the party and bolstered the argument for a heavy investment in analytics in the 2012 cycle. Wagner then brought his core of fifteen statisticians with him to Chicago to model everything from how to reach persuadable older white males in southeastern Ohio to why placing ads on reruns of *The Andy Griffith Show* made sense on some cable systems but not on others. In 2008 Chicago's Analytics team consisted of six people; in 2012 it boasted fifty-four, with a budget of more than $25 million. That sounded like a lot, but it ended up being only a little more than 2 percent of the $1.2 billion Chicago raised. To build esprit de corps and protect what the campaign considered its nuclear codes, Wagner housed his team in a secret windowless room off the main floor, dubbed "the Cave."

Located behind an unmarked door, the Cave was off-limits to all noncampaign visitors, though Messina once brought Eric Schmidt in for a look. When Peggy Noonan attacked the campaign in the *Wall Street Journal* for sending out a hiring notice asking for expertise in "predictive modeling/data mining" that "read like politics as done by Martians" (part of a column accusing Obama and his team of bloodlessness), Wagner hung a thirty-foot banner of Mars across the back wall of the Cave.

The Cave was so small that it contained only one proper exit, which meant that the Secret Service wouldn't let the president inside during his occasional visits to the Chicago headquarters. With only three feet at a long table (and no drawers) allotted for each staffer to set up a laptop, the place could get claustrophobic. Every afternoon at 4:30, the Analytics team, only halfway through its sixteen-hour day, would take a break, close the door, and watch as the Cave was transformed with strobe lights and loud DJ beats into "Club Claster," named for Wagner's deputy, Andrew Claster, who voiced a parody of a campaign robo call remixed Gangnam-style. Every Friday at the same hour, Dan Porter, a statistician and professional poker player, held court with an analysis of an episode of *Seinfeld* and explained to staffers too young to remember the show how it related to something in the campaign. On Halloween, for instance, he wore a David Puddy "magic 8-ball jacket" that he bought on eBay and recounted Elaine's annoyance with the line "All signs point to yes."

IT WASN'T LONG before the loose strands of the Obama campaign were brought into a centralized database. Messina liked to say that in 2008 there were two campaigns—grassroots and Chicago—and they didn't touch. Now the wall was down and everything was entered into the system. With the Cave's better-integrated information, Jeremy Bird and Mitch Stewart created a new field structure for volunteers built on the concept of neighborhood teams. In Ohio, for instance, where several paid organizers on the ground never left after 2008, regional field directors quickly established a thousand neighborhood teams to handle eight thousand precincts—more than a year before the election. The campaign adhered to a familiar management principle, that once someone is managing more than ten people, underlings feel like cogs in a wheel. So the Field team created a pecking order of battleground state leadership that contained half a dozen levels of advancement, from "core team member" at the bottom to "state director," a conventional post, at the top. No one had more than ten people to supervise until the eve of the election, when the volunteers poured in.

The young paid OFA organizers and their neighborhood team leaders had discretion in handing out titles to volunteers. Many chose to call them "captains": data captain (in charge of entering voter information into the database), canvass captain (in charge of door-knockers), comfort captain (keeping everyone happy and well-fed). The campaign was creating hundreds of thousands of supporters performing some of the same electoral functions as Michelle Obama's late father; they were twenty-first-century precinct captains getting out the vote, though without the promise of a job after the election.

Each week the Obama army grew. In the summer of 2011 every battleground state hosted unpaid "summer fellows," 1,500 in all, who were given training, housing, and a special smartphone. By 2012 the campaign would boast more than three thousand bright and fiercely committed full-time paid organizers in battleground states, a huge advantage on the ground.

The management challenges of ramping up were immense. So when Mobius Executive Leadership, an executive coaching firm that supported Obama, offered each senior campaign official an hour a week of free executive coaching, Messina said yes, though he was worried it would look bad and made everyone sign confidentiality agreements promising they wouldn't disclose the deal. Some found it only slightly helpful, but Jeremy Bird swore by the secret coaching; he said it helped make his state directors into rational managers and "greatly reduced the number of assholes who often get hired in campaigns just because they've been on a winning campaign somewhere before."

For all the organizational advances, reenergizing the base was tough. For much of 2011, the campaign's biggest problem was complacency. Bird thought the weak GOP field was dampening enthusiasm among his organizers, who weren't worried enough about Obama losing. The good news for Chicago was that things were looking better on the left, which went from despair after the 2010 midterms to stronger support when Obama won concessions in the lame duck session. And the stories of union-busting by Governor Scott Walker in Wisconsin and Governor John Kasich in Ohio proved to be powerful motivators for the base.

In mid-2011 Ohio police, firefighters, and other state employees, angry about Kasich-backed law that stripped away collective bargaining rights, amassed enough signatures to get a repeal measure on the November 2011 ballot. Emboldened by that success, Chicago launched a large but low-key project to repeal the voter-suppression bill that had passed early in the year and threatened to make it impossible for Obama to win the state. Messina tried to avoid publicity about OFA's efforts, on the theory that knowing it was now harder to register voters and get them to vote might demoralize supporters. Sixteen months later, when a huge backlash against voter suppression erupted, he would learn that the reverse was true.

Bird quietly dispatched several field organizers to Ohio, where they worked with local Obama volunteers to collect more than 300,000 signatures under the radar—an impressive show of strength and useful spring training for the Ohio organization. With the repeal referendum slated to be on the ballot in November 2012, the new Ohio voter law, even if upheld by the voters, would not be in effect in time for the 2012 election.

Nobody noticed, but Chicago had won its first victory.

————

IN THE SUMMER of 2011 the Obama campaign fell into a funk. The core of the problem was the contrast to 2007, when everyone at the old headquarters (just a block up Michigan Avenue) worked together on a clear plan to win the Iowa caucuses. Even when Obama was running third in Iowa and 30 points behind Hillary Clinton in national polls, OFA that year was on task and confident of victory. This time the early work was equally critical. The refrain around the office was

"We can win 2012 in 2011." But, at first anyway, the atmosphere on the Floor was less feverish and fun than in 2008.

There was an upside to this. Teddy Goff noticed that because working for Obama was less cool this time, those who gravitated to the campaign came for the right reasons. "They were true believers but not Kool-Aid drinkers," he said later, "people who love Obama but have their heads screwed on straight."

Between them, the campaign's Data and Technology departments had to hire several hundred people, for which they received tens of thousands of applications. Goff said he wanted the young recruits in Digital to be so good they could be hired afterward by Nike or Coca-Cola and "not be seen as hippy dippys." Michael Slaby and Harper Reed hired geeky geniuses from top tech companies ranging from Google to craigslist.

The selection process for the Cave was especially rigorous. Dan Wagner and Andrew Claster began by searching Obama donor lists for those whose occupation included the word *data* or *analytics*. His finalists had to complete a four-hour online exam consisting of seven or eight fiendishly difficult analytical problems. In the final interview, Wagner informed applicants that starting in mid-2012 the job would be seven days a week until at least midnight every night. "The presidency is on the line and I don't care about your personal life," he told them. "We're not selling popsicles here." Analytics ended up with a motley crew of mostly under-thirty data scientists and financial analysts, plus a biophysicist, a former child prodigy, and three professional poker players.

The prodigy, David Shor, had gone to a local college in Miami at age thirteen. When his friends in the Cave asked him why he didn't go to MIT, he said that when you're thirteen, you go to college where your mother tells you. Now he was twenty and in charge of assembling the Golden Report, a summary of the sixty-two thousand simulations that Analytics ran every night to create a sophisticated picture of the state of the race. The Golden Report was sent at 2 p.m. every day to a tiny handful of senior aides, including David Plouffe, who often shared the highlights with the president.

———

THE BUILDING BLOCKS for both the Golden Report and Field were the Cave's "ID calls," the four thousand to nine thousand phone calls a night placed to voters in battleground states. The calls, which eventually numbered nearly one million, sampled ten times as many voters a night as a standard pollster surveyed in a week. While these short, four-question surveys provided less depth than regular polls, they offered more breadth, giving the campaign high command a 360-degree view of the state of the race. Most important, the ID calls allowed the Cave to build and update the models that Field and other departments used every day.

For decades, campaigns had assembled giant lists of voters, then tried to turn out those who they guessed were likely to vote for their candidate. Now the game was much more about predictive modeling and extrapolation. The modeling produced a "support score" that ranked every registered voter in the United States on a scale of 0 to 100 (100 being a certain Obama supporter) to make canvassing and other voter contact more efficient. Why direct a volunteer to ring the doorbell of a 33 who was most likely a Republican? Instead of wandering aimlessly around the neighborhood dropping off leaflets, canvassers would have maps that mysteriously prioritized visits to residents. Volunteers didn't know specifically that they were going to see those with the highest scores on different models, though they were vaguely aware that there was more logic than in the past behind their canvassing. The Cave dwellers figured that any new voters or voters with infrequent voting history above a 65 (having a 65 percent chance of supporting Obama) were worth contacting and those ranked 80 or above were must-see.

Support scores—accessible only to Chicago and certain paid organizers in the field—sounded arid and impersonal. In fact they reflected what was relevant about an individual in an election—not just age, ethnicity, and the other usual demographic categories, but whether the person voted in school board elections, had a spouse from a different party, wanted to volunteer, hated phone calls from politicians, owned a home, would pay for an Obama bumper sticker, and nearly a hundred other variables. The data were obtained mostly from publicly available sources like voter rolls.

Analytics also data-mined certain consumer preferences, but this was a small part of the model. The most critical data, obtained from the DNC, were door-to-door voter contact information going back to 1992, much of it from long-forgotten local elections. The voter file assembled over the years was the best resource available, especially when constantly updated with information from the field. It was much more useful for the Cave to learn that a thirty-five-year-old persuadable voter in Zanesville, Ohio, had volunteered in 2000 for the Democratic candidate for state senate than if she drove a Volvo, ate Brie, and listened to NPR.

Even so, no one in Chicago would ever say exactly what data went into the models. That would disclose the analysts' secret sauce, not to mention opening them up to charges that they were snooping on

Americans. Whatever they had was enough for the Cave to confidently extrapolate from the data to build support scores for the entire electorate, more than 180 million Americans, though the information on those outside battleground states was much less complete. The Cave calculated not just their likelihood of voting for Obama but also the chances they might donate or volunteer and—of critical importance—the odds that they would vote early. Building this support model took much of 2011.

Support scores were only the beginning, of course. The Cave also issued occasional "persuasion scores" that predicted on a scale of 0 to 10 the effectiveness of a volunteer in getting a voter to change his or her mind. Not surprisingly, those who scored as more persuadable received more voter contact. For the first time, canvassers were enlisted to test messages at the door and go through the awkward conversation necessary to gather data on why someone was not supporting the president. Wagner later said that the modeling on persuasion was perhaps the Cave's biggest contribution of the whole year.

When the Cave tested persuasion messages, most of the responses made intuitive sense and corresponded to public polls. But other findings took the campaign beyond mobilization of the base to picking off likely Republicans, especially otherwise conservative women who responded positively to Obama's positions on women's health. If the campaign's "youth track" was aimed at mobilization, the "women's track" was more about persuasion. Chicago was targeting a very small number of people in ten states who might change their minds—only a dozen or so, on average, per precinct.

———

FROM THE START, there was trouble in digital paradise—a culture clash between the engineers from tech companies and the more politically seasoned product managers and data analysts. Harper Reed's code writers, though lacking in campaign experience, were often paid $100,000 a year, twice as much as some of their colleagues in other sections of the campaign. Reed said Tech could afford the higher salaries because it held down head count by hiring fewer people than rival departments. But that didn't go down well in other departments. The pay gap was exacerbated by the Tech team's habit of routinely leaving the office at the ungodly hour of 6:30 p.m., five, six, even seven hours before Digital, Analytics, and other sections went home. This schedule was explained by the fact that they were older (meaning a few were in their mid-thirties) and, unlike most Chicago staffers, often had families.

A little humility would have gone a long way toward helping Tech blend in, but it wasn't forthcoming. "Instead of 'Listen and learn,' they [Tech people] came in with a 'Burn the place down' attitude—real arrogant," said one senior campaign official. "It was, 'Fuck the vendors—we'll build everything in-house.'" But the vendors, firms like NGP VAN that specialized in voter contact, knew politics, and Reed's department did not. Tech team members used their fluency in tech jargon to their advantage, but they were often illiterate in basic political language, with everything from SEIU (Service Employees International Union) to GOTV going over their heads. And they often took their mandate for "disruption" too far. Some Tech staffers even dismissed email as old-fashioned and uncool, without understanding how indispensable it would be in saving the campaign.

All of this would have been minor if the products Tech developed were working. But they were late and often useless, like an online fundraising tool that took six weeks of precious time to build and raised a pathetic $20,000. "It's not 2011 anymore!" Finance chair Julianna Smoot would complain in meetings, her frustration growing. The beta testing schedules the product designers were accustomed to in the private sector were much too slow for a political campaign.

Tech's great white whale, dubbed "Narwhal" (after a toothed whale), was to integrate the more than 13 million Obama supporters now on the Email List with many other databases. Instead of modeling and extrapolating, the dream was to match 25 million Facebook "likes" of Obama with county voter registration rolls, census data, 2008 voter contact information, contributor lists, and fresh information from door-to-door canvassers for a unified data platform on millions of voters in battleground states. Narwhal was supposed to be built on the fruits of the 2008 Houdini Project, the Election Day voter-tracking system that assigned Obama volunteers at thousands of polling places to record which Obama voters showed up and why. Much of Houdini crashed on Election Day 2008, but the data survived and became a vital part of the 2012 database. This time Chicago would name its Election Day voter-tracking system Gordon, in honor of J. Gordon Whitehead, a college student who punched Harry Houdini in the stomach in 1926, killing him.

In Tech's defense, the complexity of the Narwhal project was daunting. It was easy to give an Obama volunteer the names and emails of supporters in the same zip code. And making the DNC's massive voter file, called "Votebuilder," available to local field organizers was doable, though it hadn't been accomplished in 2008. By 2012 the campaign had "support scores"—usually based on rudimentary data such as party ID—on all 180 million American voters. But Chicago had originally envisioned something much more sophisticated. The hairiest challenge, the goal of Narwhal, was identifying which Obama backer served in Iraq and might be willing to send his buddies a video of the president talking about the VA, or which dieting donor might want to learn more about Michelle Obama's anti-obesity initiative, or which Obama supporter had once signed a petition for women's rights and might now be willing to send her whole mailbox something about Mitt Romney's attack on Planned Parenthood.

This was much harder than it sounded. Instead of waiting for Tech to build Narwhal, Analytics compensated by relying more heavily on software from a company called Vertica that helped produce enough new data sets to keep the Cave dwellers happy. And Chris Wegrzyn and Gabriel Burt of Analytics developed a tool dubbed "Stork" that allowed key vendors to transfer their data into campaign databases. Suddenly the fruits of door-to-door canvassing in a 1998 city council race in Youngstown, Ohio, could be used to help target voters with similar support scores in Littleton, Colorado. OFA ended up with pieces of Narwhal instead of the whole whale.

The best piece of all was Facebook, which was growing so fast that it might be able to accomplish some of what everyone had hoped for from Narwhal. The social networking site was ten times as big in 2012 as it had been in 2008, with more than half of the U.S. population now active users. In 2010 Facebook embedded new widgets in its system that gave users a bumper crop of fresh information. "It cookies ya," Teddy Goff said, using the slang for tracking software as a verb. Goff, four years out of college, joked that he was "a little too old to understand these things." Fortunately for Obama, the campaign was loaded with geeks who knew what Facebook could do before Facebook did. The Cave's Rayid Ghani, OFA's chief data scientist, led a team that began to customize a Facebook app into something called "targeted sharing." The idea was that if an Obama supporter had, say, one thousand Facebook friends, the campaign could determine that nine hundred of them were already for Obama, focus on one hundred who were persuadable, and ideally zero in on six or so who lived in battleground states and were in regular enough contact to be considered real friends, not just Facebook friends. When those potential Obama voters were identified, their friend (the active Obama supporter) would be notified. He or she could then send them Obama's position on issues and urge them to register and eventually to vote. Because the message came from a real friend, it would be much more credible and influential than if it came from a stranger representing the campaign. That was the theory, anyway.

All of this was much easier to envision than to execute. Common names meant thousands of cases of mistaken identity. Uncommon names were often misspelled and thus orphaned. Some voters used home addresses, others work addresses. Some states had clean, well-maintained voter rolls; others had what Digital called "hygiene" problems—messy, outdated lists that were of little use in cross-referencing with Facebook. This had been one of the reasons why the full Narwhal had been so hard to build. To succeed, OFA needed to develop a confidence level on the part of its supporters that "John Smith" was your friend John Smith and not someone else. Projects like Narwhal and targeted sharing were so complicated and secretive that beta testing was tough, which meant that the geeks would have to work out the bugs after it went live, if it ever did. Some of the people designing Narwhal thought it wouldn't be fully functional until 2016, by which time Barack Obama, if he won, would be getting ready to leave the White House.

A modified OFA product, designed for paid field staff and their most committed volunteers, aimed to help them keep track of all the money they raised, calls they made, and doors they knocked on. Originally called "the Wire" and later rechristened "Dashboard," it was also constantly behind schedule. Harper Reed promised it in November 2011, but—to the fury of Field—it wasn't delivered until the summer of 2012. The same went for the "Quick Donate" button, a one-click to allow supporters to text money without filling out credit card information each time. It was promised to Digital and Finance for June 2011, then September, and finally delivered (by Digital's own tech crew) in January 2012.

The delays and glitches could be terrifying for Chicago. Just five months before the election, a server crashed when a mere ninety-two people went on a site at one time after a campaign tweet. The Tech crew didn't fix the servers, and three weeks later the site was brought down by three hundred hits. Someone on the Floor heard Teddy Goff yell, "What if Lady Gaga tweeted!?!" Goff wasn't sure Tech would be ready for crunch time in the fall.

Could Narwhal be reeled in? Was targeted sharing a Facebook fantasy? Would the servers crash and Gordon meet Houdini's fate on Election Day? No one in Chicago knew.

———

WHATEVER THE TECH frustrations, the broad targeting of soccer moms and NASCAR dads was all in the past for OFA. Now it was about using "propensity models" and a hundred other analytical tools to mobilize and persuade voters. Whether a voter was an 85 on the support scale or a 6 on the persuasion scale was more important than if she was a young African American woman in Pittsburgh or he was an old Jewish man in Cleveland or vice versa. Obama had come to national prominence in 2004 by saying in his convention speech, "We pray to an awesome God in blue states and we don't like federal agents sniffing around our libraries in red states." While his 2012 campaign couldn't afford to target red states, it made a point of targeting outnumbered Democrats in bright-red precincts and otherwise moving beyond the crude stereotypes that had dominated voter contact in the past.

There was a hierarchy to what the campaign called "supporter mobilization." Friend-to-friend contact was best, which was why the campaign put so much energy into its Facebook strategy. Then came face-to-face contact with voters, aided by durable Votebuilder software that allowed canvassers to efficiently skip most houses and only knock on doors where supporters or potential supporters (ranked on a 1 to 5 scale by volunteers) lived. Door knocking was more effective than phone banking, which in turn was more persuasive (and brought higher call volume) when volunteers came into an office with automatic dialers and other callers rather than making the calls from home.

The least effective forms of voter contact were robo calls (except when they featured the Obamas or Bill Clinton reminding people to vote) and paid solicitors. The latter, avoided by Chicago, featured low-wage workers with no connection to the campaign reading scripts in a monotone, a turnoff on the phone or at the door, especially if the solicitor said he or she was from a super PAC–funded group nobody had heard of. The point was, the Koch brothers couldn't just buy a first-class field organization from afar; it had to be painstakingly built at the local level. That explained why OFA was so obsessed with building a million-plus corps of volunteers.

————

THE ANALYTICS THAT worked so well for Field also helped Obama's TV advertising. Larry Grisolano and Jim Margolis, the message mavens and Paid Media experts just below Axelrod, worked with the Cave to build a system they called "the Optimizer" that allowed them to target ads with a precision never before seen in politics.

The traditional approach was to advertise heavily during local news, the theory being that people who watch news are more likely to be voters. In recent elections, ad buyers grew more sophisticated and purchased local time on popular network and syndicated shows watched by different demographic groups. Cable, which is much cheaper, was often an afterthought to broadcast. This changed in 2012. Chicago decided that shows with small audiences could be efficient delivery systems for certain narrowcast messages. With a treasure trove of data newly available from set-top cable boxes, the Cave's algorithms could now match niche-viewing habits to the millions of support and persuasion scores of individual voters amassed by the campaign. This allowed Grisolano and Margolis to figure out exactly which undecided voters in which media markets were likely to watch which TV shows. Analytics estimated that it made the ad buys 15 percent more efficient.

Contrary to the fears of privacy advocates, OFA never linked names to viewing habits. Carol Davidsen, a Cave dweller with experience in TV ratings, supervised a contract with a company called Rentrak that received the Analytics list of undecided voters and cross-referenced it with the billing records of cable providers, which it was able to buy as long as no names were attached. To assure confidentiality, Rentrak used ID numbers instead of names and a third party instead of sending the set-top cable box data directly to Chicago.

The Optimizer could calculate that, say, less likely young voters in Madison, Wisconsin, watched college football, or undecided older voters in Toledo watched *Judge Judy*, or that persuadable veterans in Tallahassee watched the History Channel. An ABC show called *Don't Touch the B—— in Apartment 23* was headed for cancellation but in the meantime was especially good for targeting young women in certain media markets.

Messina invested heavily in Digital but tried to avoid coming fully under its spell. The idea was that everything that the geeks did should be a "force multiplier" for Field, Communications, Finance, and other departments, not an end in itself. And the measurements of performance had to be kept in perspective. The most important metric wasn't the size of the Email List but how many were converted into donors and volunteers. In 2008 nearly half of the 13 million names on the Email List were active in some way in the campaign—a ridiculously high number that no one expected could be matched in 2012.

In the meantime, OFA was doing well among small donors, but not well enough. Outgunned by GOP super PACs and sucking wind on Wall Street, the campaign needed to ramp up the take from small donors to have any chance of being financially competitive. In the months ahead, the twenty-seven-year-olds in Chicago would have to come through for the president.

9

Not So Great Communicator?

In the movie *Cool Hand Luke*, the warden famously says to the inmate played by Paul Newman, "What we've got here is a failure to communicate." Obama had confessed to his own failure in this area as early as 2009, but he never tried a new communications strategy or otherwise gave it more than episodic attention after 2010.

When Obama was good, he was outstanding, as he was when he spoke about the victims of gun violence in Tucson, in Newtown, and in his 2013 State of the Union Address. But much of the rest of the time his speeches failed to break through, partly because, from the start, the expectations had been too high and partly because of the fragmentation of the old media culture. As recently as the late 1990s (when the web, Fox, and MSNBC were brand new), the Clinton White House only had to worry about a few newspapers, newsmagazines, television networks, and talk radio. Now every president was confronted with a Balkanized, polarized, and ill-defined media where almost anyone could drop poison into the national bloodstream and make "news," whatever that meant anymore.

Obama was also much taken with an article in the *New Yorker* by Ezra Klein debunking the notion of the presidency as what Theodore Roosevelt called "a bully pulpit." The evidence proving that presidential speeches changed minds was scant. Klein cited work by the political scientist George Edwards showing that even Ronald Reagan's rhetoric had no effect on public opinion. While missing the enduring power of the presidency to set the agenda, the story made Obama into a fatalist about how his words would be received.

OBAMA BEGAN HIS presidency with a low-key inaugural address intentionally stripped of rhetorical flourishes. The aim was to lower expectations and get down to the business of governing. "It's as if Superman stepped out of a phone booth and became Clark Kent," Princeton professor Fred Greenstein said the week after Obama was sworn in, meaning it as a compliment. But toning down the high-flown speechmaking bought the new president nothing. Obama not only didn't have a honeymoon, he barely had a wedding night. Republican legions launched their onslaught on January 21, 2009, the president's first full day in office. That day the GOP talking points, distributed to any politician appearing on television, included complaints about plans to reseed the National Mall (unaffordable in a recession, according to Republicans), money for women's health that might go to contraception, and anything else they could cherry-pick from a nearly $1 trillion recovery plan that could conceivably make the president look bad. The steady cable barrage attacking what the GOP immediately dubbed "the stimulus" (which sounded worse than "Recovery Act") meant that Obama's opposition controlled much of the conversation from the start.

The question of why Republicans seemed better at messaging even when they had less popular ideas had bedeviled Democrats for years. Part of the problem was cultural. Democrats were more policy-oriented and vulnerable to jargon. Democratic Senator Byron Dorgan liked to say that while Democrats talked like twits about "renewable portfolio standards," Orwellian Republicans called their clear-cutting schemes "healthy forests."

David Axelrod, the man first assigned to marry policy and communications, was well-liked inside the White House and among reporters, but he had no experience in Washington or even in state government, and he was unprepared for the right-wing media attacks. Of course, no one wanted to hear complaints about Republican unfairness in early 2009, when the president enjoyed high approval numbers and a near-supermajority in Congress. The presumption was still that Obama had the power to dictate the terms of the debate. He told his people not to worry about winning the cable wars. Echoing the boss, Axelrod developed a mantra that in Washington every day is Election Day, but that's not so in the rest of the country.

It was true that the public wasn't keeping score of who was winning the day-to-day communications war in the capital. But in war and peace, the side that seizes the initiative often keeps it, especially when the opposition refuses to see the battle for what it is. Obama developed a habit of letting the dialogue deteriorate until he rode to the rescue like a one-man cavalry, solving all the problems with a big speech, large chunks of which he wrote himself at the last minute. The MO had worked spectacularly well during the 2008 campaign, and it could succeed in the White House for a news cycle or two, but the effect wore off quickly.

THE PRESIDENT DIDN'T cater to White House reporters other than to occasionally bring them cupcakes on their birthdays. He held only thirty-six news conferences in his first term, fewer than Reagan and Clinton and less than half the number held by George H. W. Bush. (The fact that this openness did nothing to help Bush win reelection in 1992 didn't escape attention in the Obama White House.) George W. Bush held only thirteen full news conferences during his first term, but he engaged in regular informal exchanges with reporters, whereas Obama deigned to answer shouted questions only a couple times a month. He preferred one-on-one interviews where he could be more contemplative and the journalists would have less incentive to show colleagues how tough their questions were.

The White House thought this approach protected the president, but it more likely hurt him. Ever since Franklin Roosevelt, who held two Oval Office press conferences a week for most of his presidency (with quote approval from his press secretary), presidents had understood that frequent interactions with the press helped them do their jobs better. To handle these press conferences well, especially the prime-time televised variety, presidents needed to go through what were once called "murder boards" with their staff—prep sessions in which hard questions from all quarters were flung at the president. The murder boards and the reporters' actual questions often gave him and his staff early warning about stories brewing inside his government. David Plouffe believed this was no longer the case, that reporters' questions were now so narrowly focused on political angles and the transitory "story of the day" that they taught the president nothing new. This was an excuse. More relevant was that press conferences, like debates, were part of the theatricality of the presidency that the president disliked. Later, in Denver, this distaste for performance would contribute to a disastrous outcome for Obama in the first presidential debate.

BECAUSE OBAMA DIDN'T much like the public parts of the presidency, he wanted them to be as easy, and easily controlled, as possible. From the start, his reliance on a teleprompter became an issue. Even liberals like former vice president Walter Mondale thought the "idiot boards," as Mondale called teleprompters, were shielding Obama's "brilliance" and inhibiting his connection with the American people.

Every president since Eisenhower had relied on a teleprompter; Johnson, reluctant to go off-script, called his "Mother." Obama used his more than Clinton and about the same as or less than George W. Bush. This didn't deter conservatives, beginning with Bill Sammon, Fox's Washington Bureau manager, from deciding to make Obama's reliance on the device a theme of their coverage. Taking their cues from Fox, the right went wild with the story. "Obama is helpless without a tele-prompter," a blogger named Andrew K. Dart wrote, in a vein repeated tens of thousands of times across the blogosphere over four years: "If Mr. Obama is so smart, and has even a loose grasp on all the impor-tant issues of the day, why does he need to rely on a teleprompter for *every word he speaks?*" This right-wing meme conveniently ignored that the president sat for many more off-the-cuff interviews than all of his recent predecessors.

The falsehood was connected to deep-seated hatreds. "Why is Obama a Slave of the Teleprompter?" asked the Texas Hill Country Blog, inadvertently illuminating the subtext of at least some of the attacks on Obama. The president could be rightly accused of many things, but inferior intelligence was not among them. The idea that he wasn't smart enough for the job—and was some speechwriter's puppet—grew out of pernicious racial stereotypes.

———

SOMEHOW, A COUPLE of years after assuming office, the president had allowed himself to be portrayed as in over his head, when in fact he had largely mastered foreign policy and pushed more major legislation through Congress in a shorter period than had any president in half a century.

The worst communications failure was on health care reform, where the messaging was bollixed up from the beginning. Ezekiel Emanuel, a physician and health policy adviser in 2009, gave the White House (including his brother, Rahm) an "F-minus" on it. Had they been better able to sell health care reform, the Democrats might not have lost the House in 2010 and put control of the White House in such jeopardy in 2012.

Progressive efforts to pass national health insurance had consistently fallen short since first proposed in the platform of Theodore Roo-sevelt's Bull Moose Party in 1912. Franklin Roosevelt, Truman, Johnson, Nixon, Carter, and Clinton all failed to overcome the various interests opposing reform. After a century of trying, Obama succeeded. It was, as Biden whispered at the signing ceremony, "a big fucking deal."

There was a reason it took so long. For years Democrats had mind-lessly framed the public debate as a struggle for "universal coverage," a technical term that meant nothing to the public. When Americans finally learned what it meant, they didn't much like it. Polls showed that more than 90 percent of people who vote already had health insurance; the 30 to 40 million uninsured were often younger singles and the unmarried poor who didn't vote. This meant that liberal politicians were asking voters to support benefits for someone else, not themselves, which is the hardest thing to do in politics. Explaining that taxpayers were paying more by subsidizing emergency room care for the uninsured was too complicated for the shorthand of modern communications.

In 2009 Obama dropped *universal coverage* from his lexicon and also stopped framing health care as a right, an approach Ted Kennedy and other liberals had tried without success for a generation. Instead he sold the bill on cost, affordability, and access. But this didn't work any better. The idea that insuring another 30 million Americans would be cheaper for the country and for individuals defied common sense, even if it passed muster with the Congressional Budget Office. And access wasn't much of an issue for those who already had insurance.

A bigger problem was that the president didn't campaign in 2008 on an individual mandate and didn't realize that a change that big required a sustained conversation with the American people. One senior White House aide compared the situation to the Bush administration's assumption that the invasion of Iraq would be quick and easy. The White House, he said, prepared for a three-month engagement over health care, but it lasted at least a year.

All along, the president's polling showed the best way to sell the idea was to make the whole thing an *insurance* bill instead of a *health care* bill. But the political reality, as Rahm Emanuel reminded everyone, was that beating up on the insurance companies too much early on would make it harder to get the legislation enacted, though doing so at the end, when it was too late for the industry to oppose the bill en masse, was helpful to passage.

It didn't help that no one was hired as a spokesperson for the bill, so the only face associated with it was the president's. On the few occasions when he did talk about the Affordable Care Act, he inadvertently reminded voters that he had more important things to do than hawk a bill that had already been passed.

Steve Kagen, a colorful doctor and congressman from Appleton, Wisconsin, met in the White House with Stephanie Cutter, the point person on health care communications, in mid-2010 and begged her to have the president stand up and claim credit for changing the country. Kagen argued that Obama should flip the bill right back on top of the Republicans by telling the public, "Don't let Republicans take away your new 'Five Freedoms'—freedom from discrimination due to pre-existing medical conditions; freedom from going broke and losing your home just because your child gets seriously ill; freedom to choose your own doctor; freedom to go to the nearest emergency room; and freedom from being dropped by insurance companies if you are sick." Maybe this wasn't the right frame, the congressman said, but the White House needed *something* to show pride in what had been accomplished for the American people. Cutter listened politely but said that the White House believed the more Americans heard about the Affordable Care Act, the more they would like it, and the White House was preparing a really good website to spread the word.

The website and other messaging failed, and along with fifty-three other Democrats, Kagen lost his House seat that fall. Finally, on Super Bowl Sunday, February 6, 2011, Obama, after rarely mentioning health care reform on the stump, crystallized the message in an interview with Bill O'Reilly. "In this country, there's no reason why, if you get sick you should go bankrupt," the president said. It was cogent and convincing and not too late to use in defense of his greatest achievement. But he rarely did.

———

EARLY ON, OBAMA thought he could do more to control how the White House communicated. But over time, he grew more philosophical, anthropological (studying the media almost as though it were a tribe), and cynical. The president chalked up much of his failure in this area to a media obsessed with politics and indifferent to policy. For instance, the era of classifying as national security something that was merely embarrassing was over—and the news media didn't notice. Nor did many reporters cover the major but slow-moving news that 100,000 fewer troops were in Iraq and that the war in Afghanistan was winding down, with the surge ending as promised in July 2011 and 100,000 troops on the way home from that country too. The same liberals who had confidently predicted that the United States would construct a string of permanent bases in Iraq were reluctant to give the administration credit when the troops withdrew. The president noticed.

A more adept performer in the presidency would have made a joke about the press missing big stories. Obama was enormously confident in most things but not about making jokes in public without going too far. He didn't trust himself to stay on the right side of the line if he tried spontaneous humor in public. This gave him one less tool for handling the press.

The most common critique of Obama in the liberal media was that he had found no "narrative" to his presidency (to use the cliché of the moment). The best explanation for why the president had dropped the ball rhetorically since the glory days of 2008 was his allergic reaction to sound bites. Ever since his Philadelphia speech in 2008 on Reverend Wright and race succeeded magnificently without snappy one-liners, Obama figured they were not only phony—a threat to his much-prized "authenticity"—but unnecessary for getting his message across. Whenever a speechwriter put in anything that sounded at all precooked, he'd bristle. Only Axelrod and later Plouffe could convince him to work in a line. Eventually the speechwriters, anxious to please the boss, came to see the art of the presidential speech the way he did. The president and his team somehow forgot that all great communicators, from Abraham Lincoln to Franklin Roosevelt to Ronald Reagan, used cogent one-liners. And while the bully pulpit might not change his standing in the polls, particular lines—"The only thing we have to fear is fear itself" (FDR); "And we, too, shall overcome" (LBJ); "Mr. Gorbachev, tear down this wall!" (Reagan)—had the power to shape a president's legacy.

Obama had disdained slogans in the 2008 campaign too. He had to be talked into "Change We Can Believe In" ("Do you really think it says enough?" he asked Plouffe) and even "Yes We Can," the line, originated by the late Cesar Chavez of the United Farm Workers union, that helped him come back from a devastating loss to Hillary Clinton in the New Hampshire primary. In the spring of 2009 Obama gave a major policy address at Georgetown University that laid out a "new foundation" for the country. But the press never picked up on the slogan and he stopped using it altogether after Doris Kearns Goodwin told him that "New Foundation" sounded like a girdle. He allowed "Winning the Future" into his 2011 State of the Union address but quickly abandoned it.

The lesson he took from these speeches was to do what came naturally—professorial explanations—and give tub-thumpers only in the right context. Obama was an author before he was a politician, and his medium was long-form nonfiction, which was hardly conducive to pithiness. Unfortunately for him, audiences no longer clung to his every word. They still liked him, but the magic was wearing off. So instead of a half-million downloads or more of a YouTube video of a speech, he would get under fifty thousand.

In his impromptu remarks, Obama had a verbal tic that spoke to his high expectations that the public would respond to reason. He often began sentences with the words, "Now keep in mind . . ." It was a professorial and no doubt unconscious way of trying to get the listener to use the mind—not the heart—to process sometimes contradictory information. Emotional appeals, which he learned by studying great speakers, were for getting votes, not for governing or persuading journalists or others with influence. Obama bought into the respectable view that "speaking in sound bites" was a pejorative. But this reflected a misunderstanding of the news, which is the water in which every president must swim. Reporters and headline writers need something catchy and memorable or they will all end up with different interpretations of the news in a newsmaker's remarks. What was the point of Obama's using his valuable time to give a speech when the only people who absorbed it other than the few hundred people in attendance were those watching on C-SPAN or maybe MSNBC? That's thousands of people, to be sure, but out of an electorate of 130 million. The only way the rest of the world would hear about the speech was through news reports, videos, Facebook, Twitter, and so forth. And the best way for them to convey the point of the speech was with a phrase, a line, a couple of sentences that framed the message or crystallized a theme with an image or a metaphor that stuck. That wasn't to say Obama's political speeches should have been a bunch of hackneyed ideas strung together. But there was room between all sound bites and no sound bites, and for months the president didn't find it.

The basic problem with Obama's speeches was that they had many beautiful paragraphs but not enough tight, memorable sentences. In rationalizing the president's loquaciousness, his aides often fell back on analysis of the fragmented media marketplace. This was true enough, but earlier presidents confronted a news climate with plenty of turbulence, including cities with a dozen or more loud daily newspapers. What for generations had cut through the noise were the very catchphrases that Obama disliked. Joel Benenson pointed out that Mario Cuomo, for whom he once worked, was a complicated thinker but knew how to get to a sound bite. Cuomo had famously said that the best politicians campaign in poetry and govern in prose. Even the president agreed that he sometimes overlearned the Cuomo lesson and governed too prosaically. Now he had to find at least a little poetry again—something serviceable but not too grand.

————

ANOTHER COMMUNICATION PROBLEM Obama faced from 2009 through mid-2012: He was often the only major player on the field. When Axelrod engaged in Monday-morning quarterbacking, his mind went to the late Chicago Bears star Walter Payton. For several years it seemed as if the Bears quarterback handed off the ball to Payton on every play. It got boring and predictable. "We did to the president what the Bears used to do to Payton," Axelrod said.

Obama wasn't a camera hog, but he could be a bit of a control freak and he feared that surrogates with their own pet policy agendas might take him off-message. He wasn't comfortable with prominent figures who might not be easily managed by his White House, which routinely denied requests for Cabinet members to appear on television. The president had Hillary Clinton in his Cabinet, but his controlling White House never took to Richard Holbrooke, Elizabeth Warren, or other camera-ready, larger-than-life characters who might have taken some of the pressure off him had they been allowed to represent the administration more often. Time after time, Obama promoted from within instead of reaching out for harder-to-control but better-qualified people to serve in his administration. He never followed (or even showed awareness of) FDR's example of hiring "dollar-a-year men." New York's mayor Michael Bloomberg would have been a perfect choice for a special assignment convincing American businesses to invest in the United States, but he was never asked.

Of course, the largest of the larger-than-life figures was Bill Clinton. The president and the former president had disliked each other intensely in 2008, circled each other warily in 2009 (when Obama waited six months into his presidency to call him), warmed up a little in late 2010, when Clinton helped calm the left in the lame duck session, and settled into what Hillary Clinton described as a "complicated" relationship—yin and yang—in 2011. Part of the contrast between the two men revolved around communications. Obama's rendition of his own record in 2011 and early 2012 unconsciously reflected his frustration at having to repeat it yet again, as if it should be self-evident to anyone paying attention. Clinton understood this. During his 1992 campaign and the first three years of his presidency he had refused to repeat refrains; it bored him to do so. But in 1996, facing reelection, he began repeating, "We're building a bridge to the twenty-first century." Now Obama had to do the same. Senator Dick Durbin, as close to the Obama White House as any senator, argued that Obama's ambitious jobs bill failed in part because "there was a lack of repetition. Lots of good speeches but not enough repetition," he said, repeating himself for emphasis. David Plouffe agreed in theory, pointing out that it was the moment you got exasperated at repeating something that your point began to sink in.

It turned out that Clinton was better at explaining Obama's record than Obama was himself. Because he hadn't expected much from Obama, Clinton's description of his achievements reflected delighted yet understated wonder that the current president had done so much for the country. This tone of pleasant surprise, combined with his immense (and ever improving) gift for explaining complicated policy matters in ways people could understand, left a powerful impression. Countless people told Clinton that they realized how good a record Obama had only after listening to the former president describe it. That Clinton was better than Obama at enumerating Obama's achievements was no small irony. It wasn't as if Clinton had forgotten 2008 and his anger over what he considered to be Obama's use of the race card against him.* But here he was, pulling a man he didn't much care for over the finish line.

WHEN HE SPOKE at Walter Cronkite's funeral at Lincoln Center in 2009, Obama told the audience that the legendary anchorman was great because he understood that "the American people were hungry for the truth, unvarnished and unaccompanied by theater or spectacle." This was the core of his view of communicating: that it could be done without adornment and succeed.

As the 2012 campaign moved into full swing, he admitted that this was wishful thinking. He told the interviewer Charlie Rose that his biggest regret as president was that he hadn't developed a consistent message in his first two years. There were plenty of reasons why, and most of them started with him. "The mistake of my first couple of years was thinking that this job was just about getting the policy right, and that's important," Obama told Rose. "But, you know, the nature of this office is also to tell a story to the American people that gives them a sense of unity and purpose and optimism, especially during tough times." He would focus now on conceiving a new story and selling it in the battleground states that would determine his fate.

---

* After Obama won the 2008 South Carolina primary, beating Hillary Clinton, Bill Clinton implied that it was because he was black. When Obama's team accused Clinton of injecting race into election, Clinton said it was Obama who had made the contest racial by accusing Clinton of having done so.

10

Missing the Schmooze Gene

The president often mentioned his impatience with "the bubble," which referred not just to Secret Service protection but to the air of unreality at the top. The metaphor fit his natural restlessness. It spoke to the artifice and isolation of the presidency that sometimes caused him to feel trapped. He yearned for the simple pleasure of driving a car or browsing in bookstores. His effort to escape the bubble accounted for everything from the ten letters from average people he read and responded to each day (preselected, of course, by the White House Office of Correspondence), to his role as assistant coach on his daughter's soccer team and the pleasure he took from remaining close with Chicagoans and other nonpolitical friends who knew him before he was famous and could make him laugh.

Obama prided himself on his self-awareness, his ability to stand a step removed from his circumstances and apply a sense of perspective. It was one of his best qualities and proved critical to smart decision making on the job. But it didn't always serve him well on the bubble question. The steps he took to keep it real with the outside world did little to address the insularity of his White House and his inability to establish more relationships outside his administration, especially with members of Congress.

Self-assessment should have told Obama that it was his habits that were worsening the problem. If he genuinely wanted to escape the bubble, he would have to make connections outside his circle. Even when he traveled with the explicit purpose of getting outside the tunnel vision of Washington, he often hung out with his staff instead of the local members of Congress and other important regional figures who knew the area best. Making an unscheduled stop at a restaurant (though not so unscheduled that the advance team hadn't made sure the owner wasn't a Joe the Plumber type) wasn't usually much more than a photo-op.* Maybe there was no escape, but Obama's way of operating condemned him to the very fate he claimed he sought to avoid.

By 2011 Obama's failure to reach out was hurting him inside the Democratic Party, where donors, elected officials, and party activists soon made insularity their single most frequent criticism of his presidency. Democratic senators who voted with Obama found that their support was taken for granted. Many would go two or even three years between conversations with the president, which embarrassed them (constituents were always asking about their interactions) and eventually weakened Obama's support on the Hill. The president had good relations with Harry Reid (who despised socializing anyway) and Nancy Pelosi, as well as with three or four others. Most of the other senators, not to mention House members, were rarely invited to the White House for anything except big parties. This included powerful committee chairs who might have helped the president on legislation. By late 2012 many members of Obama's Cabinet had gone six months or a year without speaking personally to the boss. Not once in the first term did the Obamas invite Bill and Hillary Clinton over for dinner in the residence.

Bill Clinton, who even now was rarely reluctant to point to Obama's shortcomings in private, told friends he was puzzled by the president. He thought he was surprisingly good at the hard things, like foreign policy, and surprisingly bad at the easy things, like connecting to more than ten people and making them feel as if he liked them.

It was hard to assess the consequences of this operating style. No one could specify something in the Washington gridlock that would have gone differently if only the president had been more of a schmoozer; no landmark bills would have passed or wars been averted. In his hyperrational way, he applied a balancing test to the social part of the job. Obama figured he had good family reasons to curtail his socializing. He had missed a chunk of his daughters' childhoods. For nearly six years, from early 2003, when he first started running for the U.S. Senate, to late 2008, when he was elected president, he had been on the road almost constantly. In late 2006 Michelle had signed off on a presidential campaign with the condition that he return to Chicago in the evenings after a day of campaigning. This proved to be impossible. He had been raised without a father and was determined, now that he lived over the

---

* Samuel Wurzelbacher, aka "Joe the Plumber," was an employee of a plumbing contractor who got into a discussion with Obama during the 2008 campaign in Ohio in which Obama spoke of "spreading the wealth around." Republicans seized on the comment and Wurzelbacher went on to be a conservative activist.

store, to have dinner with Sasha and Malia at 6:30 almost every night when he wasn't traveling abroad. Afterward he often dropped by receptions in the East Room, but he saw his evenings as mostly time for contemplation and for getting a head start on the next busy day.

His friends said the trade-off was worth it. "Maybe by not schmoozing he won't get that extra $100,000 from that guy he kinda knows," said George Haywood, an old friend. "But if you take care of your core, you're a more content human being. That makes you better off and, if you're president, makes the country better off."

The president was sure the whole "not reaching out" business was another false media narrative. He could play golf with John Boehner every week for all the difference it would make, he said. Boehner agreed. In 2011 the speaker insisted he had no interest in "roasting marshmallows at Camp David." The president was annoyed that after a hugely successful legislative record in his first two years he was being depicted as failing with Congress because he didn't have drinks with congressmen and senators on the Truman Balcony. When reporters in late 2012 questioned the insularity, he had a retort ready: "When I'm over here at the congressional picnic and folks are coming up and taking pictures with their family, I promise you, Michelle and I are very nice to them, and we have a wonderful time—but it doesn't prevent them from going on to the floor of the House and, you know, blasting me for being a big-spending socialist."

Nice to members of Congress at a picnic? The president went on to raise the case of Governor Charlie Crist, who lost the support of Florida Republicans in 2010 because of a photo of him embracing the president. He said that Republicans feared becoming "too cooperative or too chummy" with him lest they face primary challenges. This was true, but it was his job to forge relationships with the few who had the guts to talk to him, not look for ways out of the age-old practice of using perks and personal contact to lubricate the gears of government.

———

Suffering fools had always been part of the presidency. George Washington held weekly dinners with legislators—senators one week, congressmen the next. Franklin Roosevelt filled part of many workdays with fifteen-minute meetings with individual members of Congress, some of whom got to stay for cocktails that FDR mixed himself. Ronald Reagan and House Speaker Tip O'Neill traded barbs in public but made time for plenty of jokes in private.

By contrast, the Obamas, with the help of Valerie Jarrett, adopted an informal code in the White House. Obama would bring members of Congress into the White House for large meetings and maybe even give them a ride on *Air Force One* when he went to their state, but the socializing they craved, the invitations to dinner or a movie, were not often part of the package.

His excuse for not having the GOP leadership over more often was that he had repeatedly invited them and they usually said no. And he had unpleasant memories of intensely courting Republican senators in 2009 to no avail. After passage of the Recovery Act, which won the support of three moderate Republican senators, he received no Republican support at all on his other major legislative victories of 2009 and 2010. He spent many hours with Maine Republican Olympia Snowe, whose objections to Obamacare (including some from the left) he was sure he addressed. But under pressure from her leader, Mitch McConnell, she too voted no.

Obama believed that the days of politicians in Washington settling everything over bourbon and branch water (or, in the case of Reagan and O'Neill, a couple of beers) were over. It used to be that if a president leaned on a member to change his vote, most of his constituents wouldn't find out. But in the age of instant access to voting records and twenty-four-hour cable, the threat of being "primaried" trumped any influence that might come from a ride on *Air Force One* or a trip to Camp David.

Besides, Obama liked to think of himself as nontransactional, above the petty deals, "donor maintenance," and phony friendships of Washington. Here his self-awareness again failed him. In truth, he was all transactional in his work life. He reserved real relationships for family, friends from before he was president, and a few staff. Everything else was business. The senators and billionaires who longed to brag about their private advice to the president were consistently disappointed. Defensive on this point, Obama didn't believe that listening to powerful blowhards was generally worth his time. But that is the thing about relationships: They're investments that don't necessarily pay off right away. His failure to use the trappings of the presidency more often left him with one less tool in his toolbox, one less way to leverage his authority.

It was a sign of his talent that he was quite good at a part of the job that he didn't much enjoy. At fundraisers he was lithe and charming and, most of the time, seemed fully present in the moment. Flashing that thousand-watt smile and exchanging pleasantries were enough for some, but others yearned for at least the impression of friendship, or what passes for it in Washington.

Obama wasn't a loner, just a relatively normal person—warm with his friends—who preferred not to hang out too much with people he barely knew. This was a fine quality in an individual but problematic for a president. Part of the explanation lay in his upbringing. He hadn't spent his early life planning how to become important, as Johnson and Clinton had. Nor was he a legacy, soaked in politics from an early age. No one had to instruct the Roosevelts, Kennedys, Bushes (and Romneys) on how to build lists and get credit for their gratitude. Bargaining was in the background of most of Obama's predecessors. Eisenhower learned to negotiate with balky allies during the Second World War, and Reagan gained bargaining experience as president of the Screen Actors Guild. Unlike Reagan, Clinton, and Bush, Obama had never been a governor herding state legislators, and his experience closing deals with Republicans in the Illinois State Senate and the U.S. Senate was minimal. (It was no coincidence that the last two presidents before Obama who went directly from the Senate to the White House were John F. Kennedy in 1961 and Warren G. Harding in 1921, and neither got much done with Congress.) In Democratic Chicago he rarely had to talk to people who fundamentally disagreed with him. His self-image was that of a bridge-builder, but he came up so fast that he'd never built a big one.

The president didn't have the schmooze gene. Politics self-selects for certain traits, the most common of which is an essential neediness, an emotional hole many politicians are trying to fill that makes them crave attention, thrive on the artificial calories provided by superficial relationships, and make the personal sacrifices necessary for public life. Obama's childhood in Hawaii was marked by a peculiar combination of abandonment and unconditional love. It bred self-reliance and security. By the time he left Chicago for Harvard in 1988, he had the ambition and willingness to sacrifice that is standard equipment in politicians, but he lacked the neediness that is usually part of the package. As he ascended, this made the inherent neediness of other politicians, CEOs, and other high achievers an abstraction for him, not a shared condition. The backslapping, stroking, gripping, and grinning that were second nature to politicians like Clinton and Biden were often chores for Obama. During a scene in *By the People*, a documentary about the 2008 campaign, Obama complains loudly to his staff about having to work rope lines. Where Clinton usually found such contact energizing, Obama frequently found it enervating. There were exceptions; at the end of a campaign, when the competitive juices were flowing, he liked pressing the flesh just fine, but he rarely stuck around to soak up the love longer than the schedule demanded. He didn't *need* to.

———

MOST OF THE president's subordinates didn't care that he wasn't big on small talk. They continued to be impressed with him in their official interactions. Often he would say nothing during long stretches of a briefing; those who didn't know him thought his mind was elsewhere. Then he would interject with something from page 32 or 56 or 63 of the briefing material from the night before, a question or comment that showed that he had both done his homework and developed a sophisticated understanding of the complex issues at hand. This could be intimidating. He prided himself on being conscious of the effect the presidency had on people telling him hard truths, but his briskness and focus didn't leave much room for out-of-the-box thinking.

While Obama was personally gracious, he could be politically stingy in expressions of gratitude, especially in comparison to the norm among politicians. Most elected officials made almost a science of their list of contacts; Obama didn't give it much thought. Of course, not every supporter can go to the parties and receive the nice letters and calls. And not every president can operate in the style of George H. W. Bush, who graciously thank-you-noted his way to the White House (though it didn't keep him there). But the list of those who felt excluded by the Obamas was long. It included everyone from people who hosted fundraisers for him in their homes to loyal sub-Cabinet officials, important senators, and old friends from Chicago. They may have gotten a Christmas card.

Obama was somewhat better with staff on this score. He didn't send off the type of friendly emails that bosses often use to keep morale up among the troops (his email list was too small), but he compensated occasionally with phone calls and letters. When he ran into Assistant Treasury Secretary Michael Barr on the White House Portico, the president thanked him for his efforts on the Dodd-Frank financial reregulation and other matters. Barr was stunned when Obama followed up with an exceptionally warm handwritten note, with its distinctive and orderly lettering. After Solicitor General Donald Verrilli argued for the Affordable Care Act in the Supreme Court, the reviews were scathing. But not from the president, who called to express his appreciation.

Outside of the Obama orbit and those who had suffered some hardship, many of his notes weren't truly personal. Starting in his Senate days, his staff would type up letters to important people that Obama would then carefully write out in longhand, a practice that he continued in the presidency. He didn't understand why the recipients cared so much about a handwritten letter. The historical importance of a letter from the president was something he shrugged off. "He fundamentally doesn't relate to their impact because he wouldn't particularly care if he got one," Pete Rouse said. The same went for telephone calls, a source of pride for those on the receiving end. He phoned members of Congress, key supporters, major CEOs, and other influential players when their names were on a call list prepared by staff, and though he often suggested names for that list, he hardly looked forward to making contact. He handled the calls well enough, but many important ones slipped through the cracks. For instance, he called neither Alan Simpson nor Erskine Bowles to thank them for chairing his deficit-reduction commission. Democrats routinely complained that there were many fewer calls than they were used to under Clinton, and the politicians and supporters who did receive a call sometimes found it a bit forced. Amid the charm and relaxed bonhomie, they could tell the president would rather be doing something else. After word spread that this was not exactly his favorite activity, they knew for sure that the calls were more dutiful than sincere.

Nancy Pelosi thought Obama was plenty sincere but that "he always projects his decency on to other people." When Mitch McConnell said the most important thing was to get rid of him, she expected that the president would be furious in private. But he just waved it off. That was the essence of the problem that Democratic politicians had with him—that he floated above the fray. Pelosi had grown up in the scrum of Baltimore politics. As a child, "Little Nancy" often kept the ledger where her father, the mayor of Baltimore, tracked favors he had granted or owed. Absenting oneself from the grubby requirements of politics was unimaginable for her.

Harry Reid agreed. During the 2011 debt ceiling crisis, Reid made up a list of Democratic senators for the president to call. Obama dutifully worked his way through the list but complained to his staff the entire time. Why do these guys need this? Are they so insecure that they can function only if they get to tell people, "Hey, the president called me!"? When the purpose of a specific call was explained to him, he was fine with it, but if he were asked to call five members of Congress a week just to stay in touch, he wouldn't comply. The plain fact, one of his senior aides said, was that he simply didn't like phone calls and notes: "He fundamentally doesn't understand how important it is. It's not in his DNA. He'd rather go exercise for another half-hour than bullshit with a member on the phone."

Obama didn't intuitively understand the ego gratification that association with a president provided. "They have two pictures with me. Why do they need three?" he complained one day to an aide after some visitors came by. The aide felt the comment summarized Obama's feelings about the ceremonial parts of the job, most of which he could do without. The president, she thought, was a strange combination: a gifted campaigner oddly clueless about the importance of retail politics; a natural president but not a natural politician. This was the opposite of the conventional conservative critique, which was that all he knew how to do was campaign and couldn't govern.

Michelle Obama had her own reluctance about making nice to legislators. On more than one occasion, the president was reminded that when Lyndon Johnson brought small groups of legislators over to the White House for stroking, Lady Bird would take their wives on private tours. Obama said Michelle would never do that. She considered the congressional lunches she was compelled to attend an ordeal.

Of course, nothing the first couple did could ever be enough. When they stood for a total of seventeen hours over two weeks for pictures at 2011 White House Christmas parties, the people invited to other parties without pictures complained. If the president signed fifty posters and books at a campaign event, he would disappoint the five hundred people who didn't get a signature. Throughout the day he was always signing one thing or another, often ten or twenty documents at a sitting. It was understandable that someone who didn't have a passion for rope lines and thank-you notes would think he had done what the job required.

––––––

OBAMA'S PROCESSING OF his failures—some combination of awareness that he was overconfident, missing his old rhythm, feeling he got played—made him a harder, sometimes colder person, at least for a time. As one old friend put it, "It's a little sad to see. Except with his family and closest friends, the sweetness is gone." He had always known abstractly that politics was a tough business, forever telling protégés that if they didn't have a thick skin, they should find some other line of work. But he didn't always take his own advice. He read widely at night on his iPad from various websites, learning exactly what was being said about him. Old friends thought he was hurt by some of it.

Obama wasn't as self-pitying as many politicians, but he often complained about how hard the job was. Early on, one of his first big financial supporters, a Chicagoan, brought him up short in the Oval Office by saying, "You wanted this. We all worked like hell to put you here. Stop complaining." Obama smiled and said he was right and not enough people talked to him that way. This supporter always knew Obama had a huge ego—anyone challenging Hillary Clinton with so little experience had to have one—but he thought Obama had been humbled by the opposition's intransigence. He had never failed to bring anyone around before, and it changed him.

You could see it at public events in 2011, before he put on his friendly game face for the campaign. For those who knew him, and for many who didn't, his vibe was unmistakable in the East Room: I'll flash a smile, then, please, someone get me the hell out of here. It wasn't that he had to be back in the Oval Office for something urgent. He just didn't want to hang out for an instant longer than he had to, even with long-lost Chicago friends. The quality that his girlfriend from the 1980s, Genevieve Cook, described as "a bit of a wall—the veil," was back. The encounters when Obama would stand very close and use his height and star power to leave admirers swooning were rarer, except at fundraisers, when he knew he had to turn it on. He sometimes exuded an unspoken exasperation: I saved Detroit, the Dow is up, we avoided a depression—I have to explain this to all of you *again?*

When the president got away from elites and spent time with those he called "ordinary folks," he relaxed. Even if they disagreed with him on certain things, most Americans still liked and trusted him. The fact that he wasn't a typical politician and stayed above the fray was a huge asset in their minds. The same traits that hurt him in Washington helped keep his poll numbers afloat. As time went on, he began to enjoy his trips out of town—not the fundraisers (as many as six in one day at the height of the campaign) but the other interactions. In his second term, he told friends, he would spend much more time outside Washington.

THE PRESIDENT'S PREFERRED escape from the claustrophobia of the White House was golf. Where Clinton routinely took mulligans, Obama got annoyed if he thought someone was missing shots to keep the president from losing too badly. ("This is bullshit," he muttered to Marvin Nicholson, the White House trip director, after Nicholson blew an easy putt.) He usually golfed with underlings who were strong golfers, like Nicholson, Reggie Love, Ben Finkenbinder of the press office, and David Katz of the Energy Department, or with old friends rather than with other politicians or A-list types. He knew that even some of his friends thought this was a missed opportunity, but he didn't care. Golf was for relaxation, not business, and unlike most golfers he preferred to separate the two. He felt that he didn't recharge when he was with other politicians—it wasn't genuine downtime—and he needed that.

Same with poker. Where Truman played with important lawmakers and the chief justice as well as his cronies, Obama usually opted for the latter only. He hung out, ESPN blaring in the background, with a rotating group of friends and administration officials that included his old law school friend Julius Genachowski (now head of the Federal Communications Commission), Ron Kirk (the U.S. trade representative), Denis McDonough ("McDonough can't even afford cable," Obama joked one night when the soon-to-be chief of staff bid low), Pete Souza, the White House photographer, and George Haywood, a businessman who had once traveled the world winning thousands of dollars counting cards at blackjack.

If Obama had free time, he liked to read novels; Emma Donoghue and Daniel Woodrell were recent favorites. The whole family embarked on a project in 2012 to read classic American novels together, like *Catcher in the Rye* and *Tender Is the Night*. The president set to work on a new book of his own, written in collaboration with Elie Wiesel, the author and Holocaust survivor with whom he forged a strong personal bond. On TV, *Homeland* was a particular favorite. When he was briefed on a possible sleeper terrorist, he replied, "Sounds like *Homeland*!" He liked the show so much that he would sometimes close his office door on weekends, pretend to be working, and put on old *Homeland* episodes.

EVERYONE WHO KNEW him well said essentially the same thing: There were not "two Obamas" as there had famously been "two Clintons," the brilliant policy analyst and clinical political strategist and the volcanic and self-pitying victim of his own appetites. Obama spoke more candidly (and more profanely) when the press wasn't around, especially when it came to political calculation.* But most of the time he was pretty much the same calm and self-contained guy inside the bubble as he was in public, with one big exception.

In public, Obama rarely chose to talk about being the first black president, but in private, after hours, when the conversation flowed freely, it was never far from the surface. He knew that it mattered and that it changed the nature of the opposition to him. He didn't lash out at racist critics; that wasn't his style, even among his closest friends. But the intense racial consciousness that he had nurtured in his own

---

* For instance, in March of 2012, the president's private comments to Russian prime minister Dmitry Medvedev, caught on an open mic at a nuclear summit in South Korea, included a reference to his inability to reduce nuclear stockpiles during the campaign season: "This is my last election. After my election, I have more flexibility."

mind since childhood was more apparent in private. He knew that if he crossed a certain line in reacting to criticism, he would hand his enemies a weapon: "See, he's like all the rest of them." It was better for him to be perceived as "different," with all the challenges that brought.

This stifling of himself, the inability to swing at certain pitches, made him, as one aide who saw him nearly every day put it, 5 percent more aloof than he had been before coming to the presidency. Inside the White House this could take the form of an icy contempt. In March 2011 former Arkansas governor Mike Huckabee, parroting Dinesh D'Souza's outlandish book *The Roots of Obama's Rage*, said twice in a radio interview that Obama's worldview had been shaped by "growing up in Kenya," where he had learned to hate British imperialism. When a White House aide informed the president that Huckabee had just acknowledged that he "misspoke," Obama replied coldly, "He knows what he said. He knows what he meant. He knows what the truth is." Leaving an event at Miami-Dade Community College, where the young Latino students inspired him, he got angry thinking about opponents of the DREAM Act. "They're just bullies. Who could hate these kids?"

THE BUBBLE MAY have hurt the president most by preventing him from getting the real story about what was going on in his own administration. As in any organization, the truth was sanitized or eliminated entirely as reports made their way up the chain of command. Part of Obama's job was fighting that bureaucratic imperative, and he didn't always succeed.

Both Franklin Roosevelt, a former assistant secretary of the navy during the First World War, and Lyndon Johnson, who had run a region for the huge New Deal–era National Youth Administration, knew where the bureaucratic bodies were buried, and it helped them immensely. By contrast, Obama's lack of experience in government hampered him on management questions. He was committed to making his administration run more efficiently, but he didn't have the fingertips for it.

The president tended to hire former Hill aides who didn't know their way around large organizations, and they in turn hired people like themselves. His efforts to incorporate new approaches to management foundered. Despite the president's desire after the 2008 election to bring in stars from Silicon Valley, the White House lured exactly one manager from the huge tech companies that were reshaping the American economy, Andrew McLaughlin of Google. He quit after a couple of years, frustrated by the ignorance of government officials about technology (the federal government spent $78 billion annually on IT, much of it wasted) and the failure to tap the enthusiasm of federal employees. The contrast with the Chicago campaign's digital focus was glaring.

There were bright spots. Obama was the first president to use performance-based budgeting. With little public notice, the "Cuts, Consolidations and Savings" budget from the Office of Management and Budget saved about $20 billion through 2012. The president liked to brag that the Department of Health and Human Services' Head Start program introduced competitive grants for the first time, and the Department of Education reduced its total number of programs from thirty-eight to eleven. He was always leaning on Defense Secretary Leon Panetta to find "commonsense" Pentagon savings.

Of course, old Washington hands knew that "reorgs" inevitably failed, as agency heads and the congressional subcommittee chairmen who oversaw them dug in to defend their turf. Jeffrey Zients, deputy director of OMB, spent a year trying to reorganize the Commerce Department, the office of the U.S. Trade Representative, and other agencies for global competition in the twenty-first century. He got nowhere with Congress. Had Obama enjoyed better relationships on Capitol Hill, he might have convinced lawmakers to give him the reorganization powers that he needed to restructure the government.

The unpleasant fact was that in some areas the White House had become almost dysfunctional. Relations with Cabinet-level departments were so tangled that it was often hard to get decisions made. While centralizing the national security apparatus at the White House worked well enough (unless you happened to work at the State Department), domestic agencies had to deal with several competing power sources inside the White House that each got to say, "It's the White House calling." Staffers in the agencies thought the obnoxious presidential aide Jonah on the HBO spoof *Veep* was only a slight exaggeration. The White House staff had become so big and arrogant that it was tripping over itself and driving the agencies crazy. Often they were sidelined for no good reason. Early on, the Department of Transportation was never asked if $48 billion out of $787 billion in stimulus money was really enough for infrastructure, when it could easily have handled three times that amount. And even now the Department of Housing and Urban Development continued to sit at what HUD Secretary Shaun Donovan called "the children's table" on big housing decisions.

Too often the assumption in the White House was that the agencies were irrelevant backwaters to be ignored or circumvented. This was a common complaint in recent administrations, but the problem seemed especially acute to those committed public servants across the federal government who had looked forward with such excitement to working for Barack Obama.

———

THE COMPARISONS BETWEEN Obama and Clinton and Obama and Johnson weren't fair. Clinton was the most natural politician in memory, yet even his Olympic-caliber schmoozing skills did nothing to protect him from impeachment. Johnson, a former Senate majority leader known for his persuasiveness with former colleagues, had earmarks to hand out and a filibuster-proof supermajority in the Senate on every issue except civil rights.

But Obama didn't do himself any favors by undervaluing the importance of personal relationships in getting anything done in Washington. His not especially creative staff hardly helped. On the domestic side, the policymaking process was simultaneously ad hoc and super-controlled, a combination that led to risk-averse decisions when decisions were made at all. In 2008 Obama accused McCain of not being able to multitask; now his White House staff sometimes seemed to have the same problem, focusing on only one issue at a time. And the reverence for the boss within the White House was a little unhealthy. The close-knit group surrounding Obama had his back but also his front, obstructing his ability to draw close to people outside the inner circle who might help make him a better president.

11

The Keeper of the Essence

Through 2012 Obama had a poor relationship with the business community, which eventually deteriorated to the point where it threatened not just his ability to get things done but his donor base. The fault lay largely with thin-skinned business leaders who were offended by what they viewed as his antibusiness rhetoric (mild by historical standards) and his resistance to their opinions on taxes and regulation. But blame also rested with Obama and with his senior counselor, Valerie Jarrett, who the president described as a big sister, so close to the family that she went on vacation with them to Hawaii and helped them buy gifts for one another. Jarrett, who met Michelle and Barack in 1991, before they were married, quickly became a lightning rod, even a scapegoat for the president in elite circles. Her power over policy was episodic, but she dominated his connections to the outside world.

Jarrett, a former executive at a Chicago housing company, wore two hats: As head of the White House Office of Public Engagement, the White House Office of Intergovernmental Affairs, and the White House Council on Women and Girls, she was the point person for business, women, minorities, state and local officials, and other constituencies. But she also was what some called the "Keeper of the Essence"—the defender, protector, and avenger of the first family. Even many of those not suffering from jealousy thought her roles were in conflict. They felt Jarrett was often uncomfortable with people she didn't know, a handicap in such a political job, and that her closeness to the president and first lady gave her an unfair edge in battles over policy and personnel.

———

In 2009, after Obama chose his economic policy team, the CEOs who had supported his campaign had a legitimate question: When will there be someone inside the White House who truly speaks our language? By that they didn't mean officials who, between stints in government, had worked briefly on Wall Street (a category that included several officials) but people who had run a major business or spent their careers in markets and knew from firsthand experience the challenges that companies faced. These business leaders were sophisticated enough to know that the skills required for effective government service are often different from those in business; they weren't calling for a whole team of former CEOs at Treasury and in the White House. But *none?* To have no one in the room in the middle of an economic crisis who truly had an understanding of business seemed foolhardy, even hostile. It didn't escape their notice that during the BP oil spill in 2010, no one in the White House picked up the phone and called the CEO of Exxon-Mobil or another oil company.

Ronald Reagan had Donald T. Regan, a former chairman of Merrill Lynch. George H. W. Bush had Nicholas Brady of Dillon Reed and Jim Baker, a former Treasury secretary and revered figure in the corporate world. Clinton had Robert Rubin, former head of Goldman Sachs. George W. Bush, himself a Harvard MBA, turned much of his White House over to business (though doing so didn't give him a heads-up on the impending economic disaster). The charge that Obama had no one inside his White House with business experience other than Jarrett was false. One of his closest friends from Harvard Law School, Michael Froman, spent his career mostly as a senior executive at Citigroup. He handled international finance issues from the National Security Council and was consulted on a wide variety of business policy matters. Jeff Zients, chief performance officer and then deputy director of OMB, was a successful entrepreneur. But for the most part, Obama hired people like Tim Geithner, Larry Summers, Gene Sperling, and Cass Sunstein—academics and former government officials, not CEOs. Even his first commerce secretary, former Washington governor Gary Locke, didn't come from business.

When business leaders challenged Obama directly on this point, the president always said the same thing: Valerie Jarrett was a former CEO. "When he'd say that, we just looked at each other in disbelief," one CEO who backed Obama in 2008 recalled. This wasn't the level of business titan these men (the critics were almost all men) had in mind. The Chicago-based real estate business that Jarrett briefly ran, the Habitat Company, had $2 billion in assets, but it was widely known to be Dan Levin's company. He was founder and chairman. In early 2007 Levin promoted Jarrett to CEO, but she held the job for less than two years before coming to Washington, and for at least half of that time she was working hard for the Obama campaign.

New York snobbism toward Chicago played a part in the disregard of Jarrett, and no doubt some sexism too. It turned out that Jarrett had more boardroom experience than patronizing critics knew. She had chaired the Chicago Transit Board, the Chicago Planning Commission, the Chicago Stock Exchange, and the University of Chicago Medical Center, and she had served on the board of the Federal Reserve Bank of Chicago. None of this changed the widespread impression in the business community that she was not the full-fledged former CEO she claimed to be.

Some of the patronizing of Jarrett was a case of shooting the messenger. It wasn't fair to blame her for, say, the National Labor Relations Board decision against Boeing moving a plant to South Carolina (later allowed) or a Commodities Futures Trading Commission ruling that added new regulations. Many business leaders, not to mention voters, didn't seem to get the concept of an independent regulatory agency. They blamed everything they didn't like coming out of Washington on Obama, even if the president was often only indirectly responsible for far-flung decisions in a huge federal bureaucracy. And of course, when they complained about taxes and regulation their demands were simply at odds with administration policy.

Before the 2012 campaign intruded, the president hosted a monthly lunch for a group of one hundred CEOs, arranged by Jarrett. At best, these were exercises in "checking the boxes," as one Obama friend put it; more often, they were a waste of everyone's time. Some of the executives felt lectured to; others believed the president and Jarrett sounded receptive but rarely followed up. The visitors routinely left the White House unimpressed. A CEO in the semiconductor industry, for instance, paid a call on Jarrett and pointed out that he was paying only 9 percent taxes on his Asian operations and had no incentive to move those jobs back. Jarrett offered him no policy ideas in response. "When we go to the White House we talk to people we wouldn't hire," he said.

From the White House's perspective, the CEOs needed to get real; just because some job creation idea might sound appealing didn't mean it could be brought to fruition. When Obama challenged his visitors on substance, such as where they would make up the lost revenue for the Treasury that would come from a tax amnesty on their overseas earnings, the CEOs felt he wasn't listening. In fact he was puzzling through the problem, hoping someone would come up with a formula to make it work. He had no ideological or even political objection to the business agenda, only a practical one, and the visiting business leaders were of little or no help in solving it.

When the president challenged a CEO on a substantive point, it was often an experience the corporate chieftain hadn't had in many years. Like the president of the United States, he, too, was surrounded by people unwilling to go toe-to-toe with him. "You run a company and you're just not used to people disagreeing with you," remarked Robert Wolf, a former UBS banker and a friend of Obama. While the president, with his background in the classroom, got an intellectual charge out of these policy arguments, his visitors usually did not. Obama's best friend, Marty Nesbitt, himself a CEO, had a theory that businesspeople came to the White House with something to get off their chest but were too scared to say it to the president, who had more facts at his disposal. This was their moment to say, "Pay attention to us!," and afterward they felt chagrined that they hadn't given the president a piece of their mind.

Because they were unwilling to attack Obama directly, Jarrett often became the punching bag. By 2011 CEOs were complaining that the White House had a "Hyde Park vibe"—a reference to the Chicago neighborhood that the Obamas called home. One Wall Street CEO said that the president viewed intellectuals as a cut above political operatives and two cuts above businessmen, whom he often brushed right past in social situations. Being worth a billion dollars wasn't going to get the president and his people to believe that your insights were better than anyone else's. CEOs grew resentful that a president only a few years past student loan debt didn't appear to care much what they had to say.

It was true. He didn't have a lot of patience for their complaints. The president was annoyed with people like Jamie Dimon, CEO of JPMorgan Chase, whom he'd known from when they both lived in Chicago, for leading the lobbying charge against the Dodd-Frank bank reregulation, as if nothing should change after the banks brought the country to the brink of economic collapse. And Dimon was one of the better ones. Obama felt bankers as a group were ungrateful or didn't even remember that he pushed the second $350 billion portion of the $700 billion Troubled Asset Relief Program (TARP) bailout through a reluctant Congress in early 2009 (just before he was sworn in as president) and soon stabilized the U.S. financial system with stress tests and other remedies. After all the drama, the bank bailouts ended up costing taxpayers only $24 billion—much less than the savings and loan bailouts of the early 1990s—but they were politically painful for Obama; they helped fuel the Tea Party anger that cost the Democrats the House and hobbled his presidency. And the bankers' reaction? As one of the president's friends put it, likely echoing Obama after hours, he saved their sorry asses and all they could do was whine about him or Jarrett or some tax favor or bonus they thought they deserved.

Handling the egos of CEOs was not something Obama had ever done before. The president had never been a governor, a job that would have given him plenty of experience convincing companies to move to his state. Obama and the country desperately needed businesses to invest in the economy, but he didn't understand intuitively how to do it, didn't have a feel for how to motivate businesspeople, who are more suggestible than he perhaps understood. The complex psychology of business confidence was only partly about their tax rates and the threat of regulation; the real problem was personal: They had an intuitive sense that Obama didn't particularly like them, and they responded in kind.

"We got a lot of Barack Obama's Wall Street money," Spencer Zwick, Mitt Romney's finance director, said after the election. While their wives often stuck with the president, the Masters of the Universe who had supported Obama in 2008 began deserting him en masse. More than 15 percent of all the money Romney raised, nearly $150 million, came from New York, which meant mostly from Wall Street. Tens of millions of that was Obama '08 money that the president and Jarrett had failed to keep.

———————

HARRY TRUMAN SAID that if you want a friend in Washington, get a dog. Obama got a dog but decided early on that he also wanted some real friends around, so he invited his Chicago buddies Nesbitt and Eric Whitaker to visit often, and he gave Jarrett pride of place in his White House. This was understandable; every president deserves having people he can fully trust at his side.

But there were sound reasons why Kennedy didn't give his "Irish mafia," Kenny O'Donnell and Dave Powers, much in the way of line responsibilities and why Clinton decided that Bruce Lindsay, a close adviser he had brought with him from Arkansas, should have no official portfolio. George W. Bush's best friend, Roland Betts, stayed out of government, and his other confidant, Don Evans, went across town to be secretary of commerce. Unlike those aides, Jarrett ran a fiefdom that was supposed to be in fair competition with other sections of the White House. Under normal circumstances, she would be offering ideas in meetings to be embraced, debated, or rebutted by her colleagues running different departments. But in the Obama White House, Jarrett didn't have to bother with much of that. She expressed her views one-on-one with the president. Some colleagues said it was as if a CEO made his irritable and overprotective sister the head of marketing. Others thought Jarrett was more like an adoring mother who thought her son could do no wrong.

Jarrett had had no formal role in any of Obama's campaigns, preferring to exercise her influence as "friend of the candidate." This had caused friction with David Plouffe, the 2008 campaign manager, though he later learned to steer clear of her. Rahm Emanuel, the incoming chief of staff, was so determined to keep Jarrett out of the White House that he tried to convince Governor Rod Blagojevich of Illinois to appoint her to fill Obama's Senate seat. Neither the governor, soon embroiled in scandal, nor Jarrett was interested.

Once in power, Jarrett had great influence on personnel matters and on issues related to women, minorities, the gay community, and who got invited to the White House. She had little to do with foreign policy unless it involved trade. Nonetheless she often accompanied the president overseas, where she would frequently take one of the half-dozen seats alongside the president in bilateral meetings, which meant one less seat for a policy expert.

In staff meetings and conference calls with the president's political advisers, Jarrett rarely said much. Her explanation—"I don't talk just to hear myself talking"—did not satisfy her critics. "If you have a dissenting view, say it in the room," one argued. "If you want to advocate for something, do it in the room, not later with the president." In meetings with Obama, she often lingered afterward, which left other aides to guess what she said to him after they departed. And she could and often did wander up to the family quarters after hours, which led to her nickname "the Night Stalker." "Valerie is so brilliant about power," said one former White House official. "She makes people do what they can to please her because they know that if they want something done with him [the president], they need her as an ally."

Jarrett felt this widespread perception of her role was inaccurate and peddled by disgruntled former White House officials. "If I have something to say, I don't hold back in meetings so I can have a private conversation with the president. I respect the process," she said. "No one can say that Valerie went in to talk with the president and changed his position on X." She said that when she was having dinner with the Obamas in the residence, they were relaxing and talking about their children or what happened on *Downton Abbey*, not policy. She and the president "compartmentalized." She denied that there was any more conflict between her personal relationship and her line responsibilities than there would be for Axelrod or Plouffe or anyone else who both worked for the president and enjoyed a friendship with him, though neither of those two vacationed with the boss.

Jarrett was the gatekeeper not so much to the Oval Office, though she played a role there too, as to the good graces of the Obamas. Sometimes she had a valid reason to protect the president: This friend from Harvard Law School talked too much to reporters; that old buddy from

Chicago had ties to Tony Rezko, a Chicago businessman and felon who had once befriended the Obamas. And sometimes she didn't. Sometimes she was acting on instructions from the president and first lady, and sometimes she only made it seem as if she were. Her power came in the ambiguity between the two.

Within the White House, Jarrett rarely confronted anyone in person when she was unhappy with them, which people didn't appreciate. For second-tier officials, her weapon of choice was the blistering email. If she thought someone got in her "lane" or had wronged the president, she threw what one former senior staffer described as a "brushback pitch" that would churn the stomach and maybe even ruin the week of the person who received one. It wasn't just that she had influence over who got invited to everything from state dinners to the small party for family and inner staff at the White House swimming pool on the Fourth of July. The problem was that in carrying the imprimatur of the president she had a way of making even the most loyal aides who had been with Obama from the beginning feel as if they had exposed him to harm or let him down. Perhaps they had erred on some (usually minor) matter, but it mortified them to think the president they revered might have been told by his closest counselor that they weren't looking out for him. Even though she didn't seem to be a grudge holder, this tendency to jump to conclusions about people hurting the president did not endear her to the White House staff. Pete Rouse and David Plouffe were loved, as was Rahm Emanuel, when he wasn't hated. Valerie Jarrett was feared.

Jarrett's critics didn't fully appreciate that fear can be a useful form of discipline in an institution famous for leaking and in-fighting. One veteran of the chaotic Clinton White House wished Clinton had hired a "Valerie Jarrett type" to scare people. More important, when she went out of her way to help someone, she was usually doing favors for people who deserved them, not for donors looking to buy access. Her role in keeping the White House free of influence-peddling was often overlooked, as was the help she offered to young staffers, especially women.

Besides her line responsibilities, Jarrett helped handle the hundreds of small but important decisions that a president must make every day, from what gift to give a foreign leader to who should get the Presidential Medal of Freedom and which Democratic critic needed to be told to cool it (for example, Donna Brazile during the 2010 Gulf spill). She protected the Obamas in ways both good and bad. It made sense to shield them from hangers-on and build in family time that she knew they craved. But this constant urge to protect could also indulge their resistance to socializing, which meant that the role of compensating for the president's missing schmooze gene fell to no one. "They're not going to stand for all those pictures," she'd say, acutely sensitive to their moods and preferences. But what if those pictures with donors or old friends were important politically? What if he could use someone to tell him "Dammit, Barack, inscribe those twenty-five letters tonight!" Jarrett rejected the idea that he needed her to "teach him good etiquette" or remind him to perform other political chores. Early on, she told a pair of old Washington hands who paid a call, "He doesn't feel he needs to thank his friends." They were supposed to understand that it was all for a greater cause. At the same time, the idea that he didn't use his plane as a perk was a myth, she said. He wandered to the back on *Air Force One* to chat with senators and House members when he was flying to their states. When Republican Senator Lamar Alexander (a gettable vote on some issues) complained of never being on *Air Force One* with Obama, the White House let it be known it had a picture of him aboard, which merely annoyed the senator more while ignoring his larger point: that Obama was missing a chance to build bridges.

By late 2011 the bridges the president wanted to build were outside of Washington. He handwrote letters each evening, Jarrett said, in reply to the average Americans whose letters had been selected for him to read that day. *This* was what he should be doing with his time, she said, not going to dinner parties in Georgetown or massaging the egos of politicians and old acquaintances.

As for others getting closer, Jarrett put out the word early on that "We're not making new friends"—that the president and first lady were busy enough without expanding their personal circle after arriving in the White House. In truth, the Obamas did make some new close friends in Washington, including Attorney General Eric Holder and U.S. Trade Representative Ron Kirk and their wives. But the friend club was small. This was the Obamas' prerogative, of course, and the outer ring of friends understood it, though they didn't appreciate Jarrett's being the one who shut the door. They may not have understood, of course, that if it weren't Jarrett, it would be someone else.

Jarrett's influence on policy was quiet but often effective. Her mother, Barbara Bowman, was a renowned expert in early childhood education, an issue Jarrett pushed inside the White House. (The president eventually made it a centerpiece of his plans for a second term.) But much of the time her thinking was opaque. Reading Jarrett became a nervous pastime in much of the White House. It required interpreting sighs, glances, cleared throats, even terms of endearment. "It's all an elaborate mind game where if you've made a mistake or even if you haven't, Valerie will in effect say, 'I forgive you, sweetie,' and that's supposed to mean you're back in, but it doesn't really mean that," said one former White House official. "If she calls you 'sweetie,' run!"

———

WHEN IT CAME to tensions with the business community, the answer was supposed to be Bill Daley, who had worked in a senior position at JPMorgan Chase and had scores of friends in that world. But within days of his arrival as chief of staff in late 2010, Daley quickly found himself sharing power with the triumvirate of Jarrett, Plouffe, and Rouse. It was reminiscent of Princess Diana saying of her husband and his mistress, "There were three of us in this marriage, so it was a bit crowded." In Daley's relationship with the president, there were five.

He had expected to be heavily involved in the 2012 campaign but was effectively excluded from it, as he had been in 2008. Plouffe's focus was reelection, communication, and messaging, which left room for Daley to work on policy and legislation. But because he had been gone from Washington for a decade, Daley didn't know the players or the subtleties of the protocol anymore. Inside the White House, he ruffled feathers. After he canceled an 8:30 a.m. meeting that was too big to accomplish anything, second-tier aides were upset. "No one would accuse me of being a morale guy," Plouffe said one day in mid-2011, "but morale is terrible." Advised that he needed to keep the troops happy, Daley, normally an affable and popular boss, replied within earshot of staff, "Well, fuck happy. Everybody should just get up in the morning and be thankful they work in the White House."

Daley and his deputy, David Lane, were outnumbered. They came to think that Rouse's nice-guy manner belied his abilities as a knife fighter. Rouse was close to Majority Leader Reid, whose chief of staff, David Krone, lived with Alyssa Mastromonaco, a White House deputy chief of staff whose loyalties, like those of most White House officials, were to Rouse. Daley felt hemmed in by Rouse's loyal Washington network. "It wasn't all on him [Daley]," Rouse admitted after Daley's departure. "We weren't the most welcoming crowd."

On the Hill, Daley got along well with Boehner, another easygoing midwestern Catholic of the same generation, but Reid was a different matter. Throughout 2011 his relationship with Daley deteriorated.

Reid's position as majority leader was rock solid because he worked tirelessly for the Democratic caucus. But it was hard to see what he liked about the job. The world in which he operated gave new meaning to the word *frustrating*. "How would you like to be Harry Reid and need sixty votes just to go to the bathroom?" asked his longtime aide,

Jim Manley. In March 2010, shortly after the Obamacare bill signing, Mitch McConnell told Reid, "That's it, Harry. We're not getting anything done [from now on]." He was as good as his word, delaying or blocking even the most noncontroversial nominations and bills. Only looming budget deadlines could yield minor progress.

If anything, Reid was too loyal to the president, which enabled Obama to stay more detached from the Senate than he should have been. Reid handled so much of the care and feeding of the caucus that Obama spoke even to Democratic senators he genuinely liked no more than two or three times a year. Reid thought the president was too hands-off, too above the fray, but he was willing to undertake most of the herding chores as long as he got the respect from the White House that he surely deserved.

Here Daley fell short. First Reid was embarrassed to be left uninformed on a handful of minor matters. Then came an interview Daley gave in late October 2011 to Roger Simon of Politico. After telling Simon that the first three years of the Obama presidency had been "ungodly" and "brutal," he said, "On the domestic side, both Democrats and Republicans have really made it very difficult for the president to be anything like a chief executive."

Reid was incensed. He had worked tirelessly to advance the president's agenda, most recently on the jobs bill, and resented the chief of staff saying there was an equivalence in the obstruction. He called the president to complain about Daley, and not for the first time. Obama responded by expanding Rouse's duties, a signal to Washington that Daley's days were numbered. When Daley—frozen out of the inner circle, disgusted with Washington, eager to spend more time with his new wife—finally resigned ten weeks later, the president called Reid to give him a heads-up before the news broke. Obama had hired Daley to help him get reelected; now he realized he didn't need the skills of the old Chicago machine when he was building a new one of his own.

Even when he was being edged out, Daley always liked the president personally and felt he was more normal than most of the politicians and CEOs he knew. "He stays cool and doesn't act like he takes this stuff too seriously," Daley said later. "I don't think he'll ever have a stroke."

Jarrett, dismayed at the announcement of Daley's appointment, no doubt played some role in his departure. But as usual, she left no fingerprints.

12

"We Got Him!"

Unlike Richard Nixon and Bill Clinton, Barack Obama generally didn't consider his political adversaries, however despicable, to be his "enemies." He tended to reserve that word for terrorists who sought to kill Americans. Obama's legacy in national security would likely be his efforts to kill them first, through a combination of raids on their compounds and missiles and bombs delivered by drone aircraft. The CIA and the U.S. military's Joint Special Operations Command, known as JSOC, together took out more terrorists—and a few innocent bystanders —than Al Qaeda killed on 9/11.

It took roughly fifteen pages in the President's Daily Briefing to summarize all of the active terrorist plots around the world. While the political world obsessed over the Iowa Straw Poll, the president was deciding whether he had enough evidence to kill someone seven thousand miles away and, if so, how he could at the same time avoid killing innocent people surrounding the target. This was war on a daily basis, out of public view but almost always on his mind. The way he compartmentalized it, 2011 was still about policy; 2012 would be more about politics.

The "targeted killings" of scores of terrorists were always popular with Americans, which was why such a historically significant program for years received so little public scrutiny. The constitutional law professor-turned-president went to pains to have civil libertarians such as Harold Koh, legal counsel to the State Department, explain why the semisecret program was legal under the 2001 Authorization for the Use of Military Force that Congress passed after 9/11. The irony of banning the use of torture but expanding the use of death in a combat setting did not escape Obama, who was well-informed on the Geneva Conventions and the other bulwarks of international law that upheld the distinction.

Obama also understood that targeted killings were not new in American history. Long before drone technology allowed the CIA to kill from the sky, the agency's "wet work" involved occasional assassinations of civilians and foreign political figures standing in the way of U.S. interests (the plots against Cuban leader Fidel Castro failed but others succeeded). During the Vietnam War, the CIA and the U.S. military killed hundreds of Viet Cong leaders through targeted assassinations as part of the Phoenix Program. After congressional hearings, President Gerald Ford in 1975 barred presidentially approved assassinations. This meant that use of the word *assassination*, with its political connotations, gave way to *targeted killings* that could be placed in the context of war. It was a euphemistic distinction. Under Obama, attendees at meetings of the Counter-Terrorism Board of Directors had another reason for avoiding the term *assassination*. Jeh Johnson, then the general counsel to the Pentagon, thought that the assassinations of Martin Luther King and the Kennedys made it unmentionable.

Perhaps the best analogy to the operation performed in Abbottabad, Pakistan, by Navy SEALs on May 1, 2011, came from the Second World War. After the Japanese attack on Pearl Harbor on December 7, 1941, U.S. forces prevailed at the battles of Midway and Guadalcanal, but casualties were heavy. The Japanese military remained largely intact, and the fascist leadership in Tokyo still expected to win. The mastermind of the attack on Pearl Harbor was Isoroku Yamamoto, the Harvard-educated commander of the Japanese fleet. "Get Yamamoto," FDR ordered Navy Secretary Frank Knox. On April 18, 1943, a squadron of P-38s intercepted and shot down the plane carrying Yamamoto. The impact on morale in both the United States and Japan was immediate. Much heavy fighting lay ahead, but the psychological balance shifted with Yamamoto's death.

———

MOST AMERICANS REMEMBER only two or three big things about presidencies of the past. For this president, one will be the killing of Osama bin Laden, who planned the murder of thousands on American soil on September 11, 2001, and declared war on the United States. Obama, who had been advised by Chicago political consultants in 2002 that his name sounded too much like Osama to succeed in politics, vowed for years that if he ever became president he would get bin Laden. His handling of the demise of the Al Qaeda leader spoke volumes about the deliberative risk-taking he brought to the presidency.

On a February day in 2009, less than a month after assuming office, Obama invited the new CIA director, Leon Panetta, to the White House for a one-on-one meeting. In 2008 both Hillary Clinton and John

McCain had criticized Obama as rash for promising to pursue Al Qaeda over the border into Pakistan, a U.S. ally. Panetta already knew that Obama was dead serious about keeping that campaign promise, and now he learned just how focused Obama was on bin Laden. Obama was low-key, as usual, but Panetta could tell he was appalled by how Bush and the entire intelligence establishment had for years all but given up on finding the Al Qaeda leader. It was one thing to ratchet down public expectations; no sense issuing "Wanted: Dead or Alive" statements, as Bush had unwisely done in 2001, especially when the trail was cold. But why was the CIA devoting so little time and energy to tracking leads? This was another reason the president was glad to see Michael Hayden, the holdover CIA director since 2006, go. He told Panetta he wanted to "redouble" efforts to get bin Laden and other leaders of Al Qaeda.

From the start, Obama defined Al Qaeda, not the vague concept (or tactic) of "terrorism," as the enemy. The president could frequently be heard asking John Brennan, his counterterrorism chief, "What's the AQ focus?" If there wasn't a direct connection, or if the collateral damage to civilians would be too great, he would nix the attack. He was leery of too much activity in Yemen, where drone strikes were killing suspected terrorists in a place far removed from the front. "I'm trying to get out of Iraq, Afghanistan, and Libya," he said one day. "I don't want a fourth war." Nonetheless he became president just as the technology for drone aircraft was improving rapidly, and he signed off on a much more extensive CIA drone program than under President Bush. Fears of "blowback"—terrorists retaliating for drone attacks—were pushed aside.

For all the precedents in the twentieth century, this was a new kind of warfare in American history because it centered so many of the operational details in the Oval Office, where the president made specific decisions on who shall live and who shall die. In public, Obama only rarely discussed drones, which were technically classified but had long since become part of the national dialogue. When asked by CNN in 2012 if he struggled with the policy, he replied, "Oh, absolutely. If you don't, then it's very easy to slip into a situation in which you end up bending rules thinking that the ends always justify the means."

The bin Laden raid was not one of those decisions. The end, for virtually everyone, justified lethal force. But first they had to find him. For the first year and a half of the Obama administration, the CIA worked harder on getting bin Laden than at any time since November 2001, when Defense Secretary Donald Rumsfeld failed to provide more U.S. forces to block escape routes at the battle of Tora Bora and bin Laden and his high command slipped away. Now, nearly a decade later, the Agency reviewed old files and tracked down long-neglected intelligence assets in the region. Dick Cheney later claimed that waterboarding Khalid Sheikh Mohammed 180 times was the key to finding bin Laden, but Panetta assured John McCain that this was false and that the break in the case—the identity of bin Laden's courier—came from a suspect who was interrogated but not tortured. Because Obama banned torture by executive order on the third day of his presidency, the CIA had to rely mostly on careful spadework. In mid-2010 reports surfaced that the courier had been tentatively located, and by August the CIA was focused on a million-dollar compound in a residential area of Abbottabad, just five hundred meters from a Pakistani military academy. Suspicion mounted that bin Laden was hiding in plain sight.

In the months that followed, the president became heavily involved in every aspect of the chase, "about as active as any project that I've been involved with since I've been president," he said later. As planning proceeded, four options were presented to him: a commando raid on the compound, a surgical drone strike aimed at bin Laden, an air assault with precision-guided munitions (with greater firepower than could be provided from drones) that would obliterate the compound and everyone in it, or waiting until better intelligence surfaced before going ahead. But the waiting had already gone on for months, and as winter turned to spring the president decided it was time for a decision.

Along with the many meetings on bin Laden, Obama went about his other business, of course, including laying the groundwork for the reelection campaign he announced at the beginning of April. Former New Jersey governor Jon Corzine, soon to face legal problems as a result of the collapse of his investment firm, helped kick off the Obama campaign with an April 27 fundraiser at his Manhattan apartment. Among the donors present was a New Jersey woman named Virginia Bauer, whose husband had died on the 105th floor of the North Tower on September 11. Bauer, a member of the 9/11 Memorial board, had met the president before but didn't really know him. This time, she said, something came over her that she couldn't quite explain. Without thinking about it in advance, she pulled the president aside, touched his arm, and whispered, "When are we going to get Osama bin Laden?" Obama looked startled, and an expression Bauer later described as "strange" crossed his face. "You know when you have an icky feeling that you shouldn't have asked the question?" she said. "I felt uncomfortable immediately." Instead of a long pat answer about all the efforts under way—the answer she had heard for years from politicians trying to placate the 9/11 bereaved—he said simply, "We're working on it," and quickly moved off.

The next day, Friday, April 28, the National Security Council held its final meeting to decide on a course of action. Intelligence reports put the odds at 50–50 that it was bin Laden in the compound, which made a drone attack a bad choice. If the drone missed, bin Laden would escape and the United States would be humiliated. But the risks of a commando raid were high too. How many gunmen were inside the compound? What kinds of weapons did they have? Would they take hostages? Was the place booby-trapped? No one had a clue. The chances of the SEALs sustaining heavy casualties—maybe being wiped out entirely—were significant.

Only Panetta was gungho for a raid by SEALs. "Mr. President, we can do this," he said. "If the American public knew the information that we have now, they would expect us to act." And only Joe Biden was against any military action at all. He thought the intelligence was too weak and the political costs of failure too high. Biden wasn't shy about saying that if the mission failed, there would be no second term.

Everyone else in the Situation Room was tacitly supportive of military action but deeply conflicted. Defense Secretary Bob Gates, the only one present with long experience in the executive branch and possessing the greatest stature of anyone in the Cabinet on national security issues, was against a raid with ground forces, insisting that the CIA had presented only a "circumstantial intelligence case." The defense secretary told the others that he recalled sitting in meetings as a young NSC staffer in 1979 when the Carter administration, eager to free the fifty-two Americans being held hostage by militants in the U.S. embassy in Tehran, first debated what was to become the Iran hostage rescue mission. The military informed President Carter that the mission had a "high probability of success," Gates remembered. But Desert One ended in humiliating failure, aborted after three of the eight helicopters malfunctioned, with one crashing into a C-130 and killing eight American servicemen. The memory of U.S. soldiers dragged by terrorists through the streets of Mogadishu, Somalia, in 1993, depicted in the book and film *Black Hawk Down*, also weighed heavily on the discussion. At one point, the defense secretary explicitly invoked Murphy's Law: If anything can go wrong, it will.

Gates and Admiral Mike Mullen, chairman of the Joint Chiefs of Staff, were worried that even a successful mission would complicate the war in Afghanistan and rupture relations with Pakistan—or worse. If they learned of the raid, angry Pakistanis might seize the SEALs as hostages, creating a major crisis. It went unsaid what the hostage-taking in Tehran did to Carter's presidency. Gates's point, which he expressed to Obama in an Oval Office session separate from most of the rest of the group, was that missing bin Laden or getting the wrong guy was only one kind of failure. He wanted the president fully aware of the strategic risks before he moved forward.

Gates and Mullen backed an option offered by General James "Hoss" Cartwright, vice chairman of the Joint Chiefs, to launch a drone mission involving the use of a top-secret "magic bullet," a thirteen-pound small tactical weapon that would kill just bin Laden. The idea was to nail "the Pacer" (as bin Laden was sometimes called by intelligence services) as he took his daily stroll in the garden inside the compound walls. The technology was new and unproven, but Gates felt a raid by SEALs was an even less attractive option.

The problem with an air strike or drone strike was that it would be hard to identify bin Laden's body in the smoking wreckage, feeding rumors that he was still alive, and innocent women and children would likely be killed, which would help the propaganda efforts of the other side. The military was so dug in to the bombing position that it took the president himself to notice that in the SEALs raid option, the helicopters needed more backup on the Pakistani side of the border. He ordered a contingency plan, which later proved important.

The fourth option, watch and wait, still had a few adherents among lower-ranking officials. Mike Leiter, who headed the National Counterterrorism Center, was against taking any action for now. He suggested waiting longer and "pulling the intelligence thread." "We've been pulling this thread for six months," the president replied, impatience in his voice.

Obama later told the author Mark Bowden that he planned to try bin Laden in civilian U.S. courts were he to be captured alive. But such contingencies were barely a part of Situation Room discussions, which mostly assumed that bin Laden wouldn't survive any American operation.

Besides Panetta, the others who favored a raid were tepid in their support. Hillary Clinton argued all sides and noted several times during the meeting that it was "a very tough call." The secretary of state finally said it was "51–49" to go because it was the best chance to get bin Laden since he fled Tora Bora a decade earlier. Biden asked a lot of questions and worried that the U.S. embassy in Islamabad could be overrun. Out of sight of most of the others, he again counseled against the raid and later marveled that the president made the decision "alone."

The president wanted Bill Daley in the room, a privilege often extended to chiefs of staff under his predecessors. Valerie Jarrett and the rest of the staff were kept in the dark, but they had plenty of company, including Michelle Obama and Bill Clinton, neither of whom was aware of anything until the mission was successfully completed. (The rule that no one outside the Situation Room could know had to be applied uniformly.) Daley was amazed at the president's willingness to take such a risk. He said later that the evidence of bin Laden's presence in the compound was so weak that it wouldn't have been enough to convince even a Cook County judge to issue a search warrant.

The April 28 meeting started at 5 p.m. and lasted until about 7:30, at which point Obama said he was going to the residence to think about it overnight. "The people advocating action knew that if we were wrong there would be severe geopolitical consequences," he said later, referring obliquely to himself. But he felt it necessary to find a little distance from the risks and operational details and think more broadly about what was best for the country. "At that point there's some serenity that you've made the best possible decision you can." In a casual tone he added, "And you do a little prayin'."

Just as he had when proceeding on health care reform over the objections of all of his top advisers, Obama was placing his presidency at least partly in the hands of fate. "Are you still feeling lucky?" Rahm Emanuel had asked him in September 2009 when health care reform was hanging by a thread. "My name is Barack Obama and I'm sitting here, so, yeah, I'm feeling pretty lucky," Obama said then. The feeling persisted. Through diligent preparation, he improved his odds and made his own luck.

In the end, he echoed the 50–50 odds offered by the CIA: "Look guys, this is a coin toss. I can't base this decision on the notion that we have any greater certainty than that." He left for the residence without disclosing his decision to the group.

Early the next morning, he asked that Tom Donilon, John Brennan, and Denis McDonough—his senior national security team at the White House—meet him in the Diplomatic Reception Room on the ground floor of the White House. Obama was preparing to board *Marine One* en route to inspect tornado damage in Alabama, give a commencement speech at Miami-Dade College, and meet with wounded congresswoman Gabby Giffords and her husband at Cape Canaveral. At 8:20 a.m., on the way out the door, he told the trio, "It's a go. We're gonna do the raid."

After Obama made his decision, Admiral William McRaven, who oversaw the operation from a base in Afghanistan, told him that the Navy SEALs could launch the raid on either Saturday, Sunday, or Monday, depending on weather conditions. Saturday was the White House Correspondents Dinner, and someone raised the possibility that a snafu in the operation might prevent the national security team from showing up at the dinner, arousing suspicions from the hundreds of reporters in attendance. After the president returned from Florida, a lively conversation on the subject ensued late Friday. Obama broke in sharply: "Stop! I want everyone to know that we are not delaying because of the White House Correspondents Dinner!" He thought doing so would be "incredibly irresponsible." It turned out that bad weather in the region on Saturday led to postponement until Sunday.

Speechwriters who knew nothing of the activity in the Situation Room gave the president a draft of his humorous speech. It included a joke: "Poor Tim Pawlenty. He had such promise. Except for that unfortunate middle name: bin Laden." When the president deleted the line, a puzzled David Axelrod—also in the dark—protested that it was funny. Obama said it wasn't. Axelrod said it was. The president, betraying nothing, insisted that the joke was "so yesterday." It was dropped.

Saturday night at the Washington Hilton, Obama was in good form, lightly mocking a dour Donald Trump (on firing Gary Busey from *Celebrity Apprentice*: "These are the kinds of decisions that would keep me up at night") and putting on a smiling poker face when comedian Seth Myers joked, "People think bin Laden is hiding in the Hindu Kush, but did you know that every day from 4 to 5 he hosts a show on CSPAN?"

"That was a little bit of acting going on there," the president said later. "My mind was elsewhere." The following week, critics marveled at the performance. His ability to compartmentalize, a skill shared by all effective presidents, let him fool the world.

On Sunday, May 1, the day of the raid, orders were sent closing the White House to any visitors. When Katie Johnson, the president's secretary, asked if an exception could be made for Zach Galifianakis and the cast of the hit movie *The Hangover*, who were scheduled for a private tour, she was told no.

That Sunday Obama played nine holes of golf at Andrews Air Force Base and went to the Situation Room at 2 p.m. Senior officials were milling about as the hours of waiting began. Before long, Obama realized that the main conference room wasn't receiving the instantaneous updates he craved. He wandered into an adjacent room where the Pentagon had set up communications for real-time information. Air Force General Bud Webb offered his chair, but the president waved him off and took a seat on a folding chair in the corner of the small unadorned room, where he sat without speaking as the mission unfolded. Others wandered in, their eyes on a timer that showed how much was left of the forty minutes designated for the members of SEAL Team 6 to be on the ground.

"This was the longest forty minutes of my life," the president said later, "with the possible exception of when Sasha got meningitis when she was three months old and I was waiting for the doctor to say she was all right."

It began badly, as a chopper failed to clear the compound wall and made a crash landing. Clinton held her breath. Biden fiddled with his rosary ring. Gates, who said later that he felt like he was having an aneurysm, stared straight ahead; no one dared look at him, lest they rouse the unspoken memory of Desert One. A soon-to-be-iconic photograph caught some of the tension, though Clinton later said she had her hand over her mouth because of allergies.

Even when McRaven learned that the SEALs in the chopper were safe, everyone knew the hundred other ways the mission could go wrong. With the chopper down, the SEAL team had to break through the wall, giving people in the house plenty of warning. Was the place booby-trapped? Would the bodyguards engage in a prolonged firefight? In the White House basement it was assumed that the answer to both questions was yes.

McRaven, narrating developments by audio, didn't change his intonation in the slightest as the mission was amended. After the SEALs entered bin Laden's house, the video connection to the White House was lost for several minutes, and long stretches of silence descended on the room. The president and his team knew that resistance was lighter than expected, but not much else.

Finally, the commanding officer of SEAL Team 6 said, "For God and country—I pass Geronimo, EKIA." Enemy killed in action.

With bin Laden confirmed dead, those present let out a sigh of relief, cautiously anticipating the best. But when Mullen saw Biden put the rosary ring he'd been touching back in his pocket, he told him, "Not yet." Even quiet celebration would have to wait until the choppers were back across the Afghanistan border and the identity of the body confirmed with DNA evidence. Clinton later said that the room held its collective breath until the choppers cleared Pakistani airspace. By then Obama had inspected photographs of the corpse. He prohibited the release of any photos. "We don't trot this stuff out as trophies," he later explained.

With all the SEALs miraculously safe and uninjured, it was time to spread the word. It turned out that all the White House phone numbers for Bill Clinton were out-of-date, a sign of Obama's distant relationship with the former president. Bush was called first, and then Obama asked the secretary of state where he could find her husband. Mullen felt he needed to reach General Ashfaq Kayani, head of the Pakistani military, as soon as possible to alert him. Biden and Donilon began alerting congressional leaders. From there, of course, it would inevitably leak.

The group wandered upstairs to the Oval Office, where the president allowed himself a moment of triumph: "We got him!"

Arun Chaudhary, the official White House videographer, was invited in with his camera, the first of many efforts to make sure the story was properly recorded for history and, of course, for credit around the world. "I'm proud of you," Obama told Panetta on tape. "You guys did a great job."

Before the fate of the mission was clear, Donilon had asked his deputy, Ben Rhodes, to work on a statement. Rhodes was mortified. He was certain that writing triumphantly when the operation was still under way would jinx it and that the speech draft would look ridiculous. When bin Laden was confirmed dead, Rhodes assumed the president would soon go on television to announce it. But it wasn't certain that Obama would make a statement that night for fear of inflaming the situation. Of the principals, only Panetta thought it was a good idea. He argued that it was preferable for the message to come from the president rather than from some Pakistani colonel. But Obama's first inclination was to keep everything quiet and delay going public until the next day. That was the Obama style: low-key, even in victory.

Then Mullen called General Kayani, who pleaded for an announcement from the White House that night to explain why an American chopper was on Pakistani soil. It wasn't until after 8 p.m. that the decision was made to tell the world. The statement was written in Bill Daley's office in less than an hour, with Obama telling Rhodes that he should connect the mission directly to 9/11. The president rewrote and line-edited the speech until the last minute, which meant that Rhodes had to sprint with the changes to the teleprompter operator in the East Room because Obama was already striding from the Oval Office to the Blue Room, where he would pause only briefly before turning right and making the long televised walk down the carpet to the camera.

At 11:35 p.m., Obama announced, "The United States has conducted an operation that killed Osama bin Laden, the leader of Al Qaeda, and a terrorist who's responsible for the murder of thousands of innocent men, women, and children." From there, he was focused on getting three major ideas across in a short address, whose ratings ended up being double those for the State of the Union and second only to the 2009 Inaugural, despite the late hour. The first was to connect the raid directly to September 11 and its painful aftermath: "The empty seat at the dinner table. Children who were forced to grow up without their mother or their father." Then, after recounting the long hunt for bin

Laden, he noted that this was not a war with all of Islam. Finally, he returned to the theme that had propelled him ever since the 2004 Democratic Convention in Boston: "Tonight, let us think back to the sense of unity that prevailed on 9/11. I know that it has, at times, frayed. Yet today's achievement is a testament to the greatness of our country and the determination of the American people."

These were platitudes, but they also contained the ambition of his presidency in a nutshell: to do big things and do them together. As his team prepared the speech that evening, Obama instructed that finding bin Laden was part of pushing back against the fatalism creeping into the political culture, the idea that we can't solve big problems anymore. They're too hard, too vexing. Here the trail had gone cold for nearly a decade, and now they had gone out to get him and done it cleanly, with no losses.

Afterward, walking down the colonnade bordering the Rose Garden, the staff could hear chants of "USA! USA!" coming from a throng of several hundred people, mostly college students who had stopped studying for exams and gathered on Pennsylvania Avenue in front of the White House. The president had gone directly from the East Room to the residence, but he said later that he could hear them too.

NOT EVERYONE IN the White House even knew anything out of the ordinary had happened. Anita Blanchard, the Chicago ob-gyn who had delivered the Obama children and was one of Michelle's closest friends, was staying as a guest in the residence that night. As usual, Blanchard went to bed early. The next morning at breakfast, she and the president happened to enter the family dining room first. She said, "Good morning, Barack" (Blanchard was part of a tiny circle of intimates who still addressed the president by his first name) and nothing else. Obama gave her a puzzled look. Finally, he said, "We got bin Laden last night." Blanchard looked up from her breakfast and said, "We did?"

Her husband, Marty Nesbitt, emailed congratulations and heard back from the president: "Just doing my job."

Later that morning, John Brennan, the president's counterterrorism chief, went to the press room and began what Denis McDonough later called "a collective barf" of early reports in public. Senior staffers were aware that early fragmentary reports in the immediate aftermath of any major event are almost always wrong. Brennan, trying to make a good story even better, was far out ahead of the facts, telling the world, for example, that bin Laden was armed when the SEALs confronted him. Other developments were taking place even as Brennan spoke. "Fedex delivered the package," Rear Admiral Samuel Perez, commander of the carrier group that included the ship carrying bin Laden's body, emailed the Pentagon that morning. That was code for bin Laden's being buried at sea after photographs and DNA testing, a precaution against any on-land burial site being used to advance his martyrdom.

Pentagon officials were furious that SEAL operations were being discussed publicly and that Gates's opposition to the raid had already leaked. When Gates came by the White House two days later, he stopped in the office of the national security adviser. "I have a new strategic communications approach to recommend," Gates told Tom Donilon drily. What was that? Donilon asked. "Shut the fuck up," the defense secretary said.

The following day Obama went to New York. At the September 11 Memorial on Vesey Street, he met privately with a few family members of those who died. He spotted Virginia Bauer, pointed his finger at her, and smiled broadly: "I remember! I've been thinking of you the whole time. Now you know what I couldn't tell you." She later remembered hugging and kissing the president and telling him to "give those SEALs a big hug and a kiss from all of us." Bill Daley was standing nearby and heard the story of what had happened the week before. "You must have freaked him out," he told Bauer.

———

IT WAS CLEAR from the moment the SEALs killed bin Laden that Obama would exploit the event for his campaign. He had told Panetta that that day was the "most important single day of my presidency" and he wasn't going to pretend otherwise. The campaign knew that this success was central to the depiction of Obama as a strong leader and that strength had always been the number one quality Americans say they are looking for in a president.

Less than a year after bin Laden was killed, the Obama campaign released a tough web ad that quoted Mitt Romney saying, with reference to bin Laden, "It's not worth moving heaven and earth to find one person." Republicans cried foul. How dare the president brag about his performance on fighting terrorism. It was unseemly, they argued across cable TV, a point they had neglected to make about Bush's 2004 campaign. Donald Rumsfeld came forward to say that going after bin Laden was an "easy call." Rumsfeld obviously knew that this was a bum rap; he had failed to make the right call himself when he wouldn't provide the ground forces necessary to seal off bin Laden's escape from Tora Bora in 2001.

Romney claimed that "even Jimmy Carter" would have launched the raid. On December 7, Pearl Harbor Day, he spoke at the Republican Jewish Coalition Forum in Washington and lambasted Obama for adopting a foreign policy of "appeasement" that "betrays a lack of faith in America." At a White House press conference the next day, Ben Feller of the AP asked the president about the appeasement charge. Obama had been stewing about Romney's national security insults going back to the 2008 campaign, when Romney said in his withdrawal speech that he needed to back John McCain because both Barack Obama and Hillary Clinton would "surrender to terror" if elected. Obama paused, then said evenly, "Ask Osama bin Laden and the twenty-two out of thirty top Al Qaeda leaders who have been taken off the field whether I engage in appeasement. Or whoever's left out there—ask them about that." This was the badass Obama, the one his supporters loved to see, and it signaled that he would toughen up once the 2012 campaign began in earnest.

Biden went so far as to compare the "audacious" bin Laden decision to D-Day in 1944, the Inchon landing in North Korea in 1950, and even George Washington crossing the Delaware in 1776. These analogies were figments of Biden's grandiosity, of course, but the historic nature of the event was beyond dispute. And Obama defying Gates and the military was reminiscent of John F. Kennedy overruling the Joint Chiefs and congressional leaders during the 1962 Cuban Missile Crisis. In that case, the uniformed military favored air strikes of Cuba, but Kennedy opted for a naval blockade of Soviet ships carrying nuclear materials. Years later retired Soviet and Cuban leaders revealed that had the United States bombed Cuba, the Soviets would have launched a tactical nuclear strike. Obama didn't face imminent nuclear war, and in that sense the geopolitical stakes were far lower for him than for cold war presidents. But by decapitating and steadily dismantling Al Qaeda, he lessened the chance that weapons of mass destruction would fall into the hands of terrorists.

It wasn't just that some of Obama's enemies sought to deny him credit for shaping history; they lied about him. A group of former CIA officers and SEALs made a video they titled *Dishonorable Disclosures* that attempted to smear the president for betraying secrets, much as Swift Boat Veterans for Truth had ripped John Kerry in 2004. The same wealthy donors who had first underwritten the Kerry attack were behind this effort too. Press reports quickly confirmed that the film was backed by birthers, and it never penetrated the mainstream media. Other attacks did. After the Obama campaign posted Davis Guggenheim's seventeen-minute film valentine, *The Road We Traveled*, Karl

Rove wrote in his *Wall Street Journal* column, "Mr. Obama did what virtually any commander in chief would have done in the same situation. Even President Bill Clinton says in the film 'That's the call I would have made.' For this to be portrayed as the epic achievement of the first term tells you how bare the White House cupboards are." In truth, Rove twisted Clinton's words to suggest the exact opposite of what the former president meant. "He took the harder and the more honorable path," Clinton said of Obama in the Guggenheim film. "When I saw what had happened, I thought to myself, 'I hope that's the call I would have made.'"

After he retired from government, Bob Gates was frequently asked about the bin Laden raid, and his answer was always the same: "My Republican friends don't like to hear it, but that was the gutsiest decision I ever saw a president make." Admiral McRaven agreed: "I'm not a political guy, but they [the president and his national security team] were magnificent in how they handled it start to finish."

THE LARGER ISSUE of how to regulate the power of this or any president to order killings remained unresolved. In September 2011 a drone attack killed Anwar al-Awlaki, a U.S. citizen and Muslim cleric whose incendiary web sermons inspired both the 2009 massacre at Fort Hood, Texas, and the attempted bombing of an American plane.* While no one doubted Awlaki's villainy, a later drone attack also killed his sixteen-year-old son. As other examples of collateral damage piled up, Obama increasingly felt the need to explain himself publicly.

He proposed putting "a legal architecture in place" for himself and future presidents. "There's a remoteness to it that makes it tempting to think that somehow we can, without any mess on our hands, solve vexing security problems," he said of the drone attacks, which by 2011 were used mostly to kill Taliban fighters, not members of Al Qaeda. Obama was worried that a successor wouldn't be as careful as he was in assessing targets, though the expansion to so-called signature strikes (targeted on "likely" enemy combatants, not specific individuals known to be dangerous) had already greatly increased the casualties.

---

* On November 5, 2009, Nidal Malik Hasan, a U.S. Army psychiatrist, opened fire at Fort Hood, killing thirteen and wounding twenty-nine at the army base. On December 22, 2009, Richard Reid, the so-called shoe bomber, tried to detonate explosives on a flight from Paris to Miami with explosives in his shoes.

POLITICALLY THE DRONE attacks and bin Laden's death helped lift the long-standing impression of military weakness from the shoulders of Democrats. Even if the party lost, 2012 wasn't likely to be 1980 all over again. Barack Obama wasn't Jimmy Carter, and not just because he and his military leaders had planned much better this time. Ever since the 2004 Senate campaign, when his opponents in both the primary and the general election self-destructed in separate sex scandals, fortune had smiled on Obama. Luck, he knew, favored the prepared mind, but any president still had to catch a few breaks, and he usually had.

The boost in Obama's approval ratings after the killing of bin Laden was much shorter than Chicago expected. His numbers rose to 52 percent after the dramatic speech, but by the following weekend were back down to 44 percent in several polls. Within five weeks Mitt Romney was leading the president narrowly again in head-to-head matchups. The economy was sagging again. By summer and the debt ceiling crisis, Obama's popularity would sink to the lowest point of his presidency.

Those numbers were misleading. Absent a major crisis, the killing of bin Laden stripped the Republicans of a weapon, that Democrats are weak on national security, which they had used to win seven presidential elections of the postwar period. Foreign policy would not be important in the 2012 campaign, but over time voters would factor Obama's performance on fighting Al Qaeda into their overall assessment of him. "Bin Laden is dead and General Motors is alive," Biden liked to say on the campaign trail. It wasn't so simple; undecided voters, even those who didn't pay close attention, were making a more complicated decision. Looking ahead from mid-2011 the more likely outcome was that they would bury Obama's success overseas in their complaints about his performance at home.

13

Obama's Low Point

The period surrounding Barack Obama's fiftieth birthday on August 4, 2011, was the lowest point of his presidency—in the polls and in the president's own mind. When David Plouffe saw gas prices spike in the spring of 2011, he told senior staff, "The summer is going to suck." But neither he nor the president nor anyone else in the White House knew just how bad it would be.

For nearly four months the Republican opposition held the full faith and credit of the United States hostage. Conservatives, bolstered by the Tea Party, finally had the hammerlock on the process that Grover Norquist and the movement's other leaders had dreamed of for years. The Washington drama of mid-2011 was dreary but instructive, a window on a political party that, flush with victory in the midterms, veered to the right and lost sight of the country's true center.

The man most responsible for walking the fine line between pragmatism and extremism was John Boehner, first elected in 1990 from a district outside Cincinnati. The White House thought Boehner was handicapped by a searing political experience that rarely seemed to turn up in profiles of the speaker. In early 1999, after serving four years as the House Republican Conference chairman, the fourth-ranking position in the leadership, Boehner lost his position to Representative J. C. Watts of Oklahoma. Boehner had been caught up in the Byzantine politics surrounding Newt Gingrich's departure as speaker. Normally there was no way to recover from such humiliation, but he did, maneuvering his way back via his relationship with House Speaker Denny Hastert, a fellow midwesterner.

Obama's team believed this comeback made Boehner a fearful, skittish leader, always worried about being dumped again by conservatives in the caucus. The speaker's aides, not surprisingly, saw him as an exceptionally resilient man underestimated by the White House. They said the White House mistook Boehner as "either a weak leader or a lazy drunk," as one Boehner confidant put it. Senior staff in the speaker's office believed "the Dean Martin schtick" disguised how hard he worked—up at 5:30 reading the papers, Drudge, Real Clear Politics—certainly not the sun lamp he was wrongly accused of using (some of his family shares his dark complexion).

Boehner had run into trouble in his career, most conspicuously by passing out checks from the tobacco lobby on the House floor in 1995, for which he apologized. But he had also cut big deals with Democrats Ted Kennedy (on "No Child Left Behind") and Max Baucus (on taxes) and knew his way around a hard-knuckled negotiation. Obama, on the other hand, had almost never truly negotiated with Republicans, not even in Springfield, where he wasn't in the leadership of the Illinois State Senate. All the glowing profiles of his time as editor of the *Harvard Law Review* negotiating skillfully with conservatives there weren't relevant to operating in Washington, where intellectuals had little influence on the process. He also had what Boehner considered an irritating habit of lecturing him on the merits of various proposals and how the country would react to them, as if his knowledge of substance and political logic would somehow change the speaker's mind.

Obama liked Boehner more than the speaker liked the president, or at least said he did. "Boehner reminds me of all the people I served with in Springfield. He's like the head of the local Kiwanis Club that gets elected to the state legislature," Obama told his aides, drawing a bit too heavily on clichés about country club Republicans. In Illinois, he said, he knew and respected such legislators, played poker and golf with some, and he believed Boehner was serious about getting something done along the median strip of American politics. This all struck Boehner as patronizing.

Republicans snickered, but Obama genuinely saw himself as a centrist. He had long believed that government was too big and inefficient, that regulations could stifle innovation (which was why in 2009 he appointed his old friend Cass Sunstein to head the Office of Information and Regulatory Affairs at OMB, where he eliminated hundreds of them), and that huge deficits were unsustainable—all core conservative positions that he felt pragmatic liberals should embrace. He strongly favored trimming discretionary spending, as long as the cuts didn't bite until after the economy recovered. No one had to talk him into supporting a pay freeze on federal workers or auditing federal agencies to find programs to cut. Long after the passage of Obamacare, he complained privately that he had tried repeatedly to put something in the bill reforming the medical malpractice system—something real that would hurt the trial lawyers who bolstered Democrats. But Republicans, who had championed such reform for years, wouldn't even talk about it. The president figured that it was a cynical play; if they solved the malpractice problem, the GOP would no longer be able to raise money from the doctors who suffered under onerous malpractice premiums.

The same went for public pensions. Months before Scott Walker was elected governor of Wisconsin, Obama told aides that pensions had become "ridiculous—they're bankrupting the states." He knew this from personal experience in the 1990s in Springfield. Like other freshman state senators, he had been assigned to a boring committee, in his case, the one overseeing pensions. Illinois state employees could retire at age fifty with 90 percent pay, "magic money," the president called it. He hoped to reform the federal pension system and reviewed federal sick day rules that gave federal employees twice or three times as many sick days (often taken as vacation) as in the private sector. With Virginia a swing state in 2012 (tens of thousands of federal employees lived in northern Virginia), pension reform struck his political team as a loser. But Obama wanted this big cost-driver on the table along with reforms in TRICARE, the health care system for the uniformed military and their families. He was a pragmatist, dammit, not a paleoliberal preserved in amber.

Spring training for the big negotiations came in March and April over the CR, the continuing resolution, a jerry-rigged parliamentary mechanism by which Congress votes itself enough money to keep the government open. The CR related only to the executive branch's day-to-day operating expenses, not Washington's credit-worthiness or entitlement obligations. By April Congress was working on its seventh continuing resolution in six months, a sign of dysfunction under the House leadership of both Pelosi and Boehner. But Joe Biden wasn't alone in thinking that all of the haggling over the CR—complete with threats of a government shutdown—was a good thing. "Let's have a showdown now and get it out of our system," Biden told his aides. He didn't have to remind them that the last time the government briefly shut its doors, in 1995, President Clinton came out a big winner over Speaker Gingrich.

This thinking would later be filed under "Be careful what you wish for." The 2011 confrontation over the CR ended up being an eerie bit of foreshadowing of an important 2012 campaign theme and a harbinger of trouble between the White House and Capitol Hill.

The climax came over federal support for Planned Parenthood, which provided health services far beyond contraception to millions of women who often could obtain such services nowhere else. In a one-on-one visit in the Oval Office just before the CR deadline on April 8, Boehner told Obama he must cut Planned Parenthood, which had become a punching bag for the right. Obama was adamant that funding for the program must stay in, and Boehner agreed. But after Obama and Boehner shook hands on the CR, Barry Jackson, Boehner's top negotiator, tried to pull a fast one. At 3 a.m., three hours after the deadline for shutting the government, Jackson told Jack Lew, director of OMB and a White House negotiator, that Planned Parenthood funding was gone.

Later that morning Lew went to the president and said he didn't know what to do: The other side was acting as if the negotiations were still going on. Obama promptly called Boehner and said, "I don't get it. The American people are depending on the idea that when we shake hands, it's done." Planned Parenthood funding stayed, and the threat of a government shutdown ended that day, at least for a while.

In announcing the CR deal, Boehner bragged that he had cut $38.5 billion from the 2010 budget in exchange for keeping the government open. This seemed like a genuine shrinkage of government after two years of hundreds of billions in new spending. But a few weeks later, the Congressional Budget Office reported that after savings from winding down the wars in Iraq and Afghanistan were added to other previously scheduled reductions, the true cuts in discretionary spending amounted to less than $1 billion. (In typical Washington fashion, the size of the cuts depended entirely on which budget baseline was used.) This was shocking news inside the House majority caucus. It turned out that Jack Lew, who knew more about the budget than anyone in Washington, had taken Barry Jackson to the cleaners.

When House Republicans found out that their speaker had been outfoxed—that the CR deal cut tens of billions less than they originally thought and preserved a bunch of social programs they despised—they were furious. Many freshmen had arrived in Washington early in the year with a demand that the budget be balanced *right away*, by $1 trillion in immediate cuts. They never acknowledged that this was not only logistically impossible but sure to thrust the economy into a depression. Now Tea Party activists were being forced to settle for less than 0.1 percent of the cuts they had rashly promised constituents. All of it was "a big nothingburger," as one member of the GOP leadership admitted privately.

With the CR deal behind him, the risk-taking president was looking ahead toward a historic Grand Bargain that might bring trouble with liberal Democrats but would secure his legacy for fiscal prudence and all but sew up his reelection. This was hubristic. After barely avoiding a government shutdown, Obama figured he had already had his 1995-style precarious moment. But he neglected a key historical fact: The

Gingrich Republicans in 1995 owed their majority (and in many cases their specific seats) to Gingrich, who could whip them into line, even if it meant conceding to Clinton. This time it was the reverse: The Tea Party was whipping its own leadership. The freshmen and many more senior members not only didn't owe Boehner their seats, but they only reluctantly accepted him as speaker. No one knew it yet, but that was a recipe for paralysis.

IN APRIL 2011, shortly after the near-shutdown, Paul Ryan released his budget, the most radical policy blueprint to come out of official Washington in a generation. It simultaneously shredded the social safety net, swept away the country's seed corn of investments in the future, and adopted discredited supply-side economics. Even Gingrich called it "radical right-wing social engineering." More than any other document or speech, the Ryan budget represented the immense stakes of the 2012 election.

In this first version, Ryan privatized Medicare entirely for those under fifty-five. (Later he offered an option to remain in the existing system.) He block-granted Medicaid to the states, which would effectively mean nearly a trillion dollars less in health care for the poor. And of course, he repealed Obamacare, which, combined with the Medicaid cuts, would have sent the number of uninsured Americans well north of 60 million and left hospital emergency rooms—the least cost-effective form of health care—swamped.

The proposed Ryan cuts in discretionary spending were devastating, with everything from medical and scientific research to college loans and food stamps facing cuts of 30, 40, even 50 percent. In total, nearly two-thirds of the Ryan cuts came from programs directed at the poor. How to find $80 billion by cutting federal pensions, $29 billion by eliminating government supports for home mortgages, $47 billion from transportation projects? If all of the pain was in the service of fiscal responsibility, the reaction of policy experts might have been different. But unlike Simpson-Bowles, this was not a deficit hawk budget. It contained $2 trillion in new high-end tax cuts, which, even with Ryan's own optimistic assumptions of economic growth, meant the budget would not be balanced for several decades.

Ryan had charmed editorial writers into praising his honesty in grappling with entitlements, which had been known for years as the "third rail" of American politics. And it was true that many Democrats were cowardly in failing to acknowledge that the growth in Medicare was unsustainable. Having been burned by his strong support for

George W. Bush's privatization plan, Ryan left the largest entitlement program, Social Security, untouched. Even so, his budget was worthy of the woman Ryan had described in 2005 as his biggest inspiration in public life: Ayn Rand, author of libertarian novels like *Atlas Shrugged.*

Ryan's budget caught the White House by surprise. In his State of the Union in January, Obama had proposed what his aides liked to call "an Ike budget." Responding to the midterms, he had offered to join with Republicans in tackling entitlements. As usual, the president hadn't offered specifics, but he believed it was in his political interest to get some kind of long-term deficit reduction deal. "Then Paul Ryan gave us the finger," recalled Austan Goolsbee, chairman of the Council of Economic Advisers.

So Obama, in his own way, gave it back. In a speech at George Washington University, the president said Ryan's proposed budget wasn't "serious" and "would lead to a fundamentally different America than the one we've known." These were strong words at the time. The White House knew that elites would give Ryan credit for bravery, but average Americans wouldn't approve of what Obama called "changing the basic social compact in America." The White House wasn't aware that Ryan would be in the audience at GW, which gave the news of his presence—and his anger over the president's criticism—extra coverage. Many Democrats feared that Obama had erred in elevating a rival as smart as Ryan, and Obama himself later regretted embarrassing him. But at the time, the president felt that calling Ryan out sharpened the historic choice facing the country.

———

FOR THE PRESIDENT, a Grand Bargain on the deficit was about more than reelection. He felt at the time that it was critical to a successful second term. He told his senior staff that without a debt reduction blueprint he wouldn't have the "credibility" to push infrastructure and other "progressive stuff" in 2013 and 2014. If he could get a long-term deficit deal that "protects our priorities"—that didn't "savage investments" in education and research or shred the social safety net—he could then move forward after the election "from a position of strength."

When Obama and Boehner finally played golf in mid-June, they agreed that a big, historic deal was actually easier than a small deal— that if they settled on $2.5 trillion, critics would say they weren't doing enough. But if they went for $4 trillion or $5 trillion, the size would give the deal historical stature and hush at least some of the skeptics.

Grover Norquist emphatically disagreed. His expectation of complete victory drove his strategy and his instructions to GOP lawmakers.

He was contemptuous of fellow conservatives who wanted to talk to Democrats. When conservative lawmakers called him for his thoughts, as they did almost every day, he asked them all the same question: "Why would you cut a deal between now and the election when you're going to get a Republican president and a Republican Senate in 2013?"

Republicans felt they had reason to be distrustful of deals that contained both tax increases and spending cuts. Invariably, they said, the final deal featured a lot more of the former than the latter. They were right about that. Spending cuts were often dropped altogether in such deals when the Democrats held power, and efforts to reform the tax code in the House Ways and Means Committee or Senate Finance Committee were always doomed. Norquist considered closing loopholes just a backdoor form of tax hikes.

This was why Boehner didn't have a lot of time for Norquist. He had to live in the real world, where a promise of tax reform—lower, flatter rates that raised revenues by cutting deductions—was the only way forward for Republicans. The speaker's problem was that his caucus was living in Groverland.

For years the powerful *Wall Street Journal* editorial page set the tone on taxes for the GOP, and now it trashed the Grand Bargain talks. "A tax increase now for the promise of tax reform later won't fly," the paper thundered, arguing that the Tea Party was right to be suspicious that Obama's promises of spending cuts would ever materialize. "We'll see unicorns first." The editorial gave Eric Cantor ammunition against Boehner's argument that Obama's big concessions on entitlement reform were meaningful. Boehner realized this and immediately called the president at Camp David to say, "I'm going to have to walk away from this right now."

Had Obama been less wishful in his thinking, that would have been the end of it. "When Boehner walked away the first time, we should have called it a day and gone to some sort of Plan B [on avoiding default]," Axelrod said later. "But the president wanted to give it a try." Obama, with backing from Jack Lew, figured Boehner's move was a negotiating ploy. The talks moved forward, and on Sunday, July 17, the parties, assembled at the White House, came closest to a deal, though discussions continued over complex budget baselines and how to structure the $800 billion in revenue increases without raising tax rates.

The week of July 18 was when it all unraveled. For months a bipartisan group of six senators, dubbed "the Gang of Six," had been meeting periodically in Senator Mark Warner's office. In July the Gang, which consisted of the five senators on the Simpson-Bowles Commission plus Warner, still didn't have a plan, only a framework, but they wanted badly to insert themselves into the debate. Now, with exquisitely poor timing, they went public. On Tuesday morning the Gang of Six held a press conference announcing a plan that included $1.2 trillion in revenue increases, which was $400 billion more than was being secretly discussed by Obama and Boehner. Dick Durbin stressed that the Gang's work was not done, but few heard the caveats. Rob Nabors, a key White House negotiator, called Barry Jackson and said, "Have you seen this? Tom Coburn signed off on bigger tax hikes than we did. This changes things for us."

Obama being to the right of the Tom Coburns and Saxby Chamblisses and Alan Simpsons of the world wasn't going over well in the Democratic Party, to put it mildly. When Lew visited the Senate Democratic caucus, liberal senators ripped into him. Barbara Mikulski of Maryland noted that week that if the United States had had a parliamentary system, Barack Obama would have been voted out of office.

The Gang of Six plan may not have killed the Grand Bargain, but it sure didn't help. Obama's inexperience as a negotiator was showing. "He is the most naïve and inexperienced negotiator to ever set foot in the Oval Office," a top aide to the House leadership said later. On Wednesday Obama told Boehner in the Oval Office that, per the Gang, he needed $400 billion more in revenue on top of the $800 billion they had tentatively agreed to. Boehner didn't threaten to blow up the deal at this point, and the White House thought negotiations were continuing. In truth, Boehner, under pressure from Cantor, Ryan, and other Republicans, was getting cold feet. Boehner's office later tried valiantly to deny he had bowed to his caucus, as the president and his team had concluded, but several members admitted privately that this was what happened. Ryan's argument to the speaker was the same as Norquist's: Why negotiate a long-term budget deal before the election? He and the rest of the leadership were so sure they would get "the whole enchilada"—House, Senate, the presidency—in 2012 that they now felt concessions on taxes were pointless.

On Friday, July 22, Obama suffered one of the most severe setbacks of his presidency. For eighteen hours Boehner wouldn't call the president back, a sign of disrespect for the office for which Boehner paid little price in the press. When he finally did, he said the whole thing was off. "You can't put Humpty Dumpty back together again," he told the president. Obama, caught off-guard, offered to return to the $800 billion in revenue increases they had agreed on before the Gang of Six intruded. Boehner said it was too late. Obama was furious. After an uncomfortable twelve-minute call, Boehner hung up and told his staff, "Ooh, he was hot. He's really upset." At 6:30 p.m. the president went to the White House press room with the bark ripped off. He blasted Boehner in strikingly personal terms. "I couldn't get a phone call returned," he said. "I've been left at the altar now a couple of times." Less than an hour later Boehner coolly told the world what he thought happened. "The White House moved the goal posts," he said. "Dealing with the White House is like dealing with a bowl of Jello."

On Friday night Boehner sent a letter to his caucus, saying, "A deal was never reached, and was never really close." The White House was enraged when Boehner claimed that Obama "demanded" the extra $400 billion. In truth, he had introduced it late in their talks, a clumsy gambit that reflected his inexperience as a negotiator. But he had quickly withdrawn the extra $400 billion (only $40 billion a year over ten years, by the way, a relatively small amount in the context of a $4 trillion deal) when Boehner objected. The bottom line was that Obama had in fact moved the goalposts, but then he quickly moved them back. Still, it was highly unusual in any negotiation, business or government, for one side to terminate the talks just because the other side tossed in something from left field. The customary response in such situations was to dismiss the new offer out of hand and resume negotiating. Boehner's failure to do so reinforced the president's interpretation that he couldn't move forward because he didn't have the support of his caucus. When the leader of the House turned around, there was no one following him.

Across the country it was Obama, not Boehner, who was blamed for weakness and poor leadership, for not "working his will" with Congress, as the author Bob Woodward put it. He was president, after all. But this analysis might have expected too much of Obama, given the historical context. Charles Peters, the founder of the *Washington Monthly*, suggested substituting *man* for *president* and *woman* for *Congress* and asking if it was reasonable to expect a man to "work his will" on a resistant woman. In modern relationships, men and women are coequal branches of government, equally able to cooperate or block the will of the other. Obama wasn't any weaker or less competent than an unpersuasive spouse. His sin was overconfidence that everything would work out by the time of the deadline, as it had so often in the past.

Obama and his team would later acknowledge that, as one aide put it, they had "overestimated John Boehner's political courage." They knew the risks of trying and failing to cut a historic deal but thought that if the president could pull it off he would fulfill his promise to bring people together and change the arc of American politics. Only much later, after the election, did they breathe a sigh of relief that the Grand Bargain of 2011 was never struck.

TIM GEITHNER USED various gimmicks to push the moment of truth from spring to summer, but the government simply had to make good on its obligations by August 2. He was angry with the business community, which never believed the politicians wouldn't figure something out and thus brought no pressure to bear on Republican House members. Even after being briefed extensively about the horrific consequences of default by a Republican, Jay Powell, a former Treasury undersecretary in the first Bush administration, the House firebrands of the right continued to brandish the threat. Their argument was simple and easy to understand: To raise the debt ceiling, the budget must be cut by at least the same amount.

The White House felt the rhetoric was getting scary. Austan Goolsbee's heart sank when he heard Senator Pat Toomey of Pennsylvania say that after default, the United States should prioritize the bondholders—in other words, pay China first. Toomey would follow with paying Social Security recipients and the military and leave it at that. *After the default.* This was insane! Goolsbee estimated that default would send GDP down by 15 percent, a much steeper drop than during the Great Depression. Under Toomey's approach, after bondholders, Medicare and Medicaid recipients, the beneficiaries of unemployment insurance, and the military were paid, there was not a dime left over for any other function of government.

Toomey and many Tea Party Republicans viewed default as a cleansing mechanism that would lead to an automatic balanced budget and, most important for them, a dramatic shrinkage in the size of government. "It's reasonable," said Bruce Bartlett, a Reaganite economist chastened by the facts, "if you think sticking a knife in your eye is a good way to deal with glaucoma."

But finding another treatment wasn't easy. Liberals on cable TV were all of a sudden playing the tough guy. It was all about the psychology of power, they argued. Obama should "call the question"—be like Reagan firing the air traffic controllers or Nixon, pursuing what he called his "madman theory" in bombing North Vietnam in 1969. The madman theory dictated that you don't mess with the president because you're never sure what he might be capable of doing.

This was not exactly Obama's style, but Durbin nonetheless thought the president's "ace in the hole" was the Fourteenth Amendment, which said, "The validity of the public debt of the United States, authorized by law . . . shall not be questioned." Some lawyers thought "authorized by law" gave the Treasury the authority it needed to keep the government open. Bill Clinton was among them. Back in May Clinton had ruminated at a conference of the Peterson Foundation that a default of a couple of days "might not be calamitous." Bill Daley called Clinton and told him this was "deeply unhelpful." The White House, sensitive to Clinton's long-standing complaints that Obama was politically inept, saw the gaffe as evidence that the former president had no clue how to operate in the new 24/7 media culture.

The Fourteenth Amendment argument got a full hearing before the former University of Chicago constitutional law professor. Lawyers explained that Section 4 of the Amendment, ratified in 1868, referred to special Civil War obligations and that the Supreme Court would not likely apply them to a modern-day political crisis. That was good enough for the president. When told that he would win the political argument by taking a bold stand, Obama snapped, "We can't purposely tank the economy to make our point." Even a miraculously favorable ruling from the Supreme Court would come weeks after a constitutional crisis had been laid atop a debt ceiling crisis, by which time there wouldn't be much of an economy left to save.

The end of July, Valerie Jarrett remembered, was the nadir. With friends telling him to ignite a constitutional crisis and enemies cavalier about default, he felt trapped.

———

AFTER THE COLLAPSE of the Grand Bargain on July 22, it wasn't clear there was enough time to avoid a catastrophe. Obama figured the best way to move fast in the thirteen days before the default was to have Biden and McConnell, who had stayed in touch throughout, hammer out a deal to save $2.4 trillion. That was more than enough to cover Boehner's consistent bottom line, which was that the cuts must always be equal to or greater than any debt ceiling increase. After much back-and-forth among Boehner, Pelosi, Reid, McConnell, and the White House, the parties agreed on $1.2 trillion in ten-year spending caps (basically slowing the growth of spending) and authorized the creation of a supercommittee to find the other $1.2 trillion. If the twelve-member supercommittee couldn't agree by November 28, automatic cuts would be "triggered." Under a quarter-century-old budget mechanism, a process of "sequestration" would then kick in, the details of which became the subject of haggling for most of the next eighteen months.*

———

* Sequestration, the use of hard spending caps to enforce budget discipline, dates back to the Gramm-Rudman-Hollings Budget Control Act of 1985.

Sequestration was an eye-glazing abstraction in the country, but it quickly became a Washington obsession, the equivalent of arguing over the tailoring of a straitjacket. With $600 billion devoted to automatic cuts to important domestic social programs and other functions, the White House assumed the other $600 billion would be obtained through automatic tax hikes. The whole idea was to make the trigger as uncomfortable as possible to compel more reasonable budget decisions. But continued Republican phobia about tax hikes was such that it couldn't even be included as a bogeyman. The White House was amazed that the GOP preferred to trigger $600 billion in defense cuts. Republicans figured they would shift those cuts to the domestic side if they won the election. Defense Secretary Leon Panetta and others assured the White House that if Obama won, defense contractors would successfully pressure Republican lawmakers for a deal that protected the Pentagon from the knife. This was a major miscalculation, though that wasn't clear until early 2013, when Republicans blithely let the defense cuts go into effect.

For days it looked once more as if Boehner couldn't deliver his caucus. As tension mounted, Obama again crossed swords with Cantor. This time the issue was what was known as the "second vote" on raising the debt ceiling, which would have taken place right in the middle of the 2012 campaign, when Obama could least afford to look weak once more. Republicans loved the way the summer had gone and wanted one more showdown before the election. Obama, who knew the only way out of a second crisis would be deep entitlement cuts, was adamant on this point: He would veto any agreement that included a short-term deal on the debt ceiling. He dug in hard with his bottom line: No second vote, no more hostage taking. Or, as his staff liked to say, *This shit must stop!*

Boehner described the president in a late-night call as "moaning and groaning and whining and demanding" as he delivered his veto threat. Obama denied that account to Bob Woodward but acknowledged, "I was very angry about how he [Boehner] had behaved" and deeply concerned about a default in five days' time.

As he complained glumly to aides, Obama tried to think of analogies for what the Republicans were doing. Imagine that in 2007 Nancy Pelosi had told President Bush, "Pull out of Iraq now or we'll default." Geithner had his own analogy. "They're arsonists," he said one day at the White House. "Incompetent arsonists," Dan Pfeiffer deadpanned.

Fortunately for Obama, McConnell was already on record supporting an end to debt ceiling blackmail, at least in the short term, which forced the House's hand. Obama and Boehner congratulated each other on the phone and on August 1 the Budget Control Act of 2011 passed both houses of Congress. No one in either party was happy with the result. Democratic Congressman Emanuel Cleaver called it a "sugar-coated Satan sandwich."

————

WASHINGTON HAD ESCAPED economic Armageddon thanks only to a balky Rube Goldberg contraption that kicked everything down the road. The feeble effort, reflective of deep political dysfunction, led Standard & Poor's on August 6 to downgrade the U.S. government's credit rating from AAA, where it had been since the ratings began in 1941, even though the ability of the strongest country in the world to pay its bills was never in question. A credit agency disgraced during the 2008 economic crisis now spread the bad feeling a little farther, a move that was both unwarranted and somehow appropriate.

The downgrade was sour news for the U.S. economy, already buffeted by ill winds from the European Union. On August 8 the Dow dropped 634 points, with consumer confidence plunging and the job market freezing in place. For business, confusion and uncertainty are far bigger disincentives to investment than marginally higher taxes and slightly more regulation. But most of the gloomy predictions by conservatives turned out to be wrong. The downgrade "hurts people. You know, car loans, home loans, all these things are gonna go up," Paul Ryan said. This received wisdom—the economic basis for the Ryan Plan and the entire GOP antigovernment agenda—turned out to be false, as the failure to cut spending in the short term had no discernible impact on interest rates, which stayed low.

After it was over, Obama said he was convinced that Boehner sincerely wanted an agreement but just couldn't get anyone else in the Republican leadership to come along. Pete Rouse wasn't so sure. "I personally think we were a little naïve," he said when the wounds were still fresh. "Boehner never made a serious effort to close the deal. Rouse was struck by the president's idealism, even when he had been kicked in the teeth. Obama still believed that, at heart, politics was about people doing what they thought was right for the country. "He believes he can convince anyone with the power of his mind that he's not a purist and is willing to compromise," Rouse said later.

The debt issue was too complicated for most Americans, who cared much more about jobs. But in 2011 it became a surrogate for the deeper and, for Democrats, more dangerous question of whether the government could *do* anything. Heading into 2012, the answer seemed to be no.

ON AUGUST 4, 2011, Obama's fiftieth birthday, the Dow plunged more than 500 points, its steepest decline since before he took office. U.S. and European investors were deeply anxious about the failure of Washington to fix its economic problems.

Amid the bad economic news, a resilient Obama celebrated his birthday at a celebrity-filled party at the White House. Obama showed no sign of being demoralized by recent events. Valerie Jarrett said he had as much fun as at any time since his wedding. As the evening wore on, the music changed and guests started doing the Slide and the Dougie. "I felt like I died and went to black heaven," Chris Rock said later. "Think about this fucking moment: A bunch of black people doing the fucking Dougie in the house that slaves made."

The first family retreated to Camp David for a much smaller celebration. It was, per the president's wishes, an all-sports weekend. He and nine male friends competed in every contest available, from basketball to bowling to air hockey. It was mostly a mix of old friends from Hawaii and Chicago and included only two members of his staff, Jarrett and Reggie Love.

If the president was down, he didn't let on. At one point, Jarrett realized he was comforting *her*, bucking her up. His friends vented for him. While none wanted to spoil the weekend by getting too angry, they were all quietly furious on his behalf. What was the deal with S&P? The ratings agency even managed to mess up the numbers when announcing the downgrade. You would have thought they would cross their t's and dot their i's before announcing something so momentous, and, for the birthday guests, so unpatriotic. John Rogers, a Warren Buffett protégé and prominent fund manager, passed the word that weekend that Buffett thought the whole thing was ridiculous. If you're a rich country with your own printing press, you can't default, Buffett said. Rogers felt that the agency would never have downgraded the United States if Bush were president. It was only the enmity toward the president in the business community that let S&P feel free to do so.

At the end of the summer, the president's friends all used the same word to describe him: *frustrated. Deeply frustrated.* There were no histrionics, only a gnawing disappointment that left him pensive. He had simultaneously exasperated his base, lost to Republicans, and failed to sustain the recovery. His friends were disheartened and his enemies emboldened. Over the August recess he assessed his own performance and concluded he had been "timid." Going forward, he would draw bright lines. "I may win or I may lose this election," he told staff and friends who talked to him around Labor Day. "But I'm going to win or lose fighting for what I believe in."

––––––––

OBAMA TRIED TO be stoic. David Plouffe thought he was "better suited for politics in Scandinavia than here," by which he meant that he was a logical and unemotional person in an illogical and emotional capital. He undertook a rigorous assessment of what went wrong in the debt ceiling fiasco and concluded that he had been playing way too much of an inside game. He realized more clearly that he needed the American people behind him to get anything more accomplished. From now on, he would travel widely outside Washington and make sure the public knew that if taxes went up, it was because of Republican intransigence against his "balanced approach."

The first forays after the fiasco were not auspicious. At town hall meetings in Iowa, the president was peppered with questions—Why are you focused on the deficit instead of jobs? Why wouldn't you compromise?—for which he had no good answers. On September 2 the August jobs report showed unemployment stuck at 9.1 percent and disturbing trend lines, with June and July jobs figures adjusted downward and the number of those "marginally attached to the labor force" up. The numbers weren't nearly as bad as in early 2009, when the economy was losing 750,000 jobs a month. But that was on Bush. This was on Obama.

Obama looked up and down at the report on his desk five times, squinting at it to make sure he was reading it was right. For the first time since World War II, the economy created no new jobs—neither job loss nor gain. Nothing. "How can this be zero?" the president asked. Plouffe thought it was the perfect metaphor for his predicament a year before an election.

His allies in the press were peeling off. At the end of the summer Obama grew perturbed at the *New York Times* editorial page for making him read what he saw as "distracting" attacks "over my orange juice." When he met with the paper, columnist Tom Friedman criticized his communications strategy. Obama admitted as usual to not having a clear message but conceded no other mistakes. He implied that he expected the *Times* to be on his side, which didn't go over well with the group of independent-minded journalists.

Earlier Andy Rosenthal, the editorial page editor, had asked the president if he realized that he was dealing with radical extremists who hated not just his policies but him as a person. When Obama said he knew that, Rosenthal said *Times* readers were wondering why he didn't just hit back at them. "I can't do that every day," the president said.

"I'm not suggesting every day," Rosenthal replied. "Just once in a while."

Senator Carl Levin from Michigan echoed the point. In preparation for Obama's Labor Day speech to the AFL-CIO in Detroit, he sent the president the "Give-'em-hell" speech that Truman delivered to a Detroit crowd on Labor Day in 1948. To Levin's disappointment, Obama used part of the speech but not the strongest part, where Truman hammered "Republican reactionaries" and said of his enemies, "They have come to the point where they will stop at nothing." Levin felt that Obama believed that was true, but wouldn't say it. He recalled that the Detroit crowd winced when, in reference to their hometown bad boy Eminem, the president replaced "hell" with "heck." "I told him bluntly, 'I think you're afraid of being labeled a class warrior,'" Levin said. Obama nodded, lost in his own thoughts.

––––––––

"IS OBAMA TOAST?" That was the headline on the cover of the November 3, 2011, edition of the *New York Times Magazine*. Nate Silver, the author of the paper's FiveThirtyEight blog, wrote the story, which described the president as a "slight but not overwhelming underdog." Mitt Romney struck Silver as "a skilled debater, a cautious candidate and a smart man—exactly what you want when the fundamentals otherwise favor you." In his case study of what would happen to the president if the economy ground to a halt instead of growing at a little more than 1 percent a year, he calculated that "Obama would only have a 17 percent chance—about one in six—of winning a majority of the popular vote."

In Chicago Jim Messina practically choked on his breakfast. Obama was trailing the front-runner, Romney, by 3 or 4 points in national polls but looking better in battleground states. Messina fired off a rebuttal to the *Times Magazine* and vowed that after winning the election, his trophy would be a framed copy of the "17 percent chance" cover with the president's signature. David Axelrod happened to be in St. Louis when he read Silver's story. He noted that in September Silver had predicted that the St. Louis Cardinals had only a 1 percent chance of winning the World Series. In October, one strike away from elimination, they won it in seven.

The wounds from this period stayed fresh. Months later, when a group of staffers were chatting with the president, Ben Rhodes, a veteran of 2008 who enjoyed Obama's trust, began playing an informal parlor game to find the lowest of the low points over the years. Was it losing to Hillary Clinton in New Hampshire? Reverend Jeremiah Wright exploding? The frustration after failing to win the Ohio and Texas primaries? Scott Brown seeming to derail health care by winning a Senate seat in early 2010? The BP oil spill? The midterms? Finally, the president ended the little game: "The debt ceiling."

14

The Clown Car

As bad as things were going for Obama, he had one big advantage: the opposition. Nearly a dozen different Republicans led in party polls at various points during 2011 and 2012, including such implausible candidates as a nasty right-wing congresswoman from Minnesota known for attacking the patriotism of her colleagues; a poorly informed former CEO of a pizza company with no experience in government; a snarling, pornography-fighting former senator from Pennsylvania who lost his seat in 2006 by 18 points; a disgraced speaker of the House whose former colleagues in his own party thought his erratic behavior and serial adultery made him unfit for high office; and a vulgar New York egomaniac with bad hair and a weakness for conspiracy theories. Each won a moment in the media sun that burned the Republican Party.

Several of the candidates and potential candidates were more entertainers than active politicians. Three of them—Sarah Palin, Mike Huckabee, and Newt Gingrich—had contracts with Fox News that paid them handsomely to say outrageous and thus bankable things on a regular basis. (Gingrich had to give up his gig after entering the race.) The combination of the number of primary debates (twenty-two) and the entertainment value of the GOP's new reality show spelled trouble for the party from the start.

The main thing the candidates had in common was their eagerness to outdo each other in trashing Obama. Other than Jon Huntsman, Obama's former ambassador to China, each used a tired insult around the theme of Obama's not being fully American. Mitt Romney said he was "slightly European," Michelle Bachmann claimed that he had "anti-American views," Herman Cain figured he may have been born in Kenya, and Newt Gingrich echoed the far-fetched theme offered by the author Dinesh D'Souza that the president was a "neocolonialist." In truth, Obama's improbable life saga—hard to imagine in any other nation—was a tribute to the sense of "American exceptionalism" the GOP candidates kept claiming he lacked.

For those Tea Party members suffering from "Obama Derangement Syndrome," the president was both a communist (left) and a fascist.

Obama's overreliance on the teleprompter often put up a barrier between him and the public, though there was a racial subtext to some of the criticism.

Roger Ailes, the founder of Fox News Channel, was so paranoid that he once came in over the weekend to work in a supply closet because he feared his office in the News Corp. building was bugged. When Steve Jobs heard that Glenn Beck had called Obama a racist, he ordered all Apple ads off Fox immediately.

Grover Norquist (holding his famous no-tax pledge) borrowed tactics from his Marxist-Leninist enemies. He set the tone for House freshmen with his aim to "make government so small it could be drowned in a bathtub."

Ohio Secretary of State Jon Husted tried to prevent Obama from winning Ohio by throwing up more barriers to voting as part of the GOP's voter-suppression project. There was a concerted effort in nineteen states to restrict Democratic turnout, especially among young people and minorities.

Florida's new law effectively ended all voter registration drives, an activity the League of Women Voters had undertaken in the state for nearly a century. A federal judge struck down the law as "harsh and impractical" as well as unconstitutional. But early voting days were cut, leading to long lines.

Steven Spielberg told campaign manager Jim Messina (left), "You're only the Rolling Stones once." Backed by less public enthusiasm than in 2008, Obama's campaign built a new Chicago Machine that combined technology with old-fashioned shoe leather that resembled "governors' races on steroids."

8

9

The Chicago campaign included a secret annex called "the Cave" (above) where twentysomething analytics geeks sometimes worked until 4 a.m. using Big Data for state-of-the-art microtargeting of voters. Their breaks included Gangnam-style riffs and instruction on the subtleties of *Seinfeld* episodes. There was trouble in digital paradise. Tensions developed with the Tech section run by hipster Harper Reed (right), whose code writers from tech companies had a culture clash with staffers from political backgrounds.

10

Valerie Jarrett's overlapping roles as senior official and personal confidante made her feared in the White House, where she failed to rally American business to the president's cause. Her nicknames included "Keeper of the Essence" and, because of her ability to go into the residence after hours and influence the Obamas, "the Night Stalker."

11

12

Obama seemed to be missing the schmooze gene present in most politicians, who complained that his lack of personal relationships in Washington was hampering his presidency. It wasn't that he didn't like people. He simply preferred people, including children, who satisfied his curiosity and told him things he didn't know.

13

At the White House Correspondents' Dinner the night before the May 1, 2011, raid that killed Osama bin Laden. Obama puzzled aides in the dark about the raid by deleting a bin Laden joke written for his comic speech as "so yesterday."

14

The iconic photo of the president and his national security team when the SEALs' helicopter crashed outside the bin Laden compound. Three days earlier, a 9/11 widow asked a startled Obama at a fundraiser, "When are we going to get bin Laden?"

15

Obama and House Speaker John Boehner quarreled. The president thought Boehner wanted a "Grand Bargain" in July 2011 but was forced out of it by the GOP caucus. The Republican Party's decision to hold the U.S. economy hostage to its agenda convinced Obama that this was the low point of his presidency.

The president believed House Budget Committee Chairman Paul Ryan, a devotee of the libertarian novelist Ayn Rand, was bent on eliminating the social compact that had existed since FDR's New Deal.

The GOP "clown car" primary candidates all raised their hands to say they wouldn't accept even a 10:1 ratio of spending cuts to tax increases, which indicated the party was committed to shrinking the government and lowering taxes, not deficit reduction.

Casino magnate Sheldon Adelson, originally for Newt Gingrich, spent more than $100 million trying to beating Obama and the Democrats even though he was a social liberal. Mark Hanna, William McKinley's campaign manager in 1896, envisioned the 2012 campaign when he said, "There are two things that are important in politics. The first is money and I can't remember what the second one is."

George Romney (with young son Mitt), a CEO and 1968 presidential candidate, spoke out against the GOP moving too far to the right. Mitt Romney revered his father but refused to emulate his challenge to right-wingers and his policy of releasing all of his tax returns. Trying to avoid his father's career-ending gaffe just caused him to make more of them.

19

Stuart Stevens (left), Romney's chief strategist, argued for a relentless focus on jobs and the economy: "Obama thinks this is an eharmony.com election. We think it's monster.com." Others said the campaign should have defended Romney's record at Bain Capital and humanized him.

The machine hums with rigorous testing and annoying emails: Teddy Goff (gesturing) and Marie Ewald cracked the code on Internet fundraising, increasing it tenfold to more than $150 million a month. Some supporters "drunk donated" with smart phones when Obama seemed in trouble.

22

Obama brought up his game on the stump, but his heart was with his campaign staffers, who he said were much better at organizing than he was when he was young. An innovative Facebook app was a big success, and two million volunteers executed flawlessly on the ground.

Obama's relationship with blacks and Latinos was strong but not always easy. Here he is on the verge of reaming out Professor Cornel West, for saying he wasn't progressive. While West, who called him a "black mascot of Wall Street oligarchs," other African American leaders felt his policies were pro-black even if he didn't call them that.

Obama hugs Representative Luis Gutiérrez, who later accused him of "bragging about deporting kids." The president's unilateral decision on the DREAM Act brought Gutiérrez and other Latinos around.

25

Michelle Obama's ad with Cristina Saralegui, "the Latina Oprah," helped sew up the Latino vote. Wondering off-camera if the Obamas planned to have more children, Saralegui pointed to the first lady's midsection and asked, "Is the factory closed?"

Son tantas, tantas cosas...

At a fundraiser in Boca Raton, Romney was caught on tape saying that 47 percent of Americans saw themselves as "victims" who wouldn't "take personal responsibility and care for their lives." The comment crystallized doubts about Romney and weakened any chance for a comeback.

28

The videographer of the "47 percent tape," Scott Prouty, a South Florida bartender with a social conscience and a history as a hero in an Everglades rescue, was more offended by Romney's cavalier comments about inhumane conditions in Chinese sweatshops: "I wanted to shout, 'Would you want your wife working there, Mitt?'"

29 30

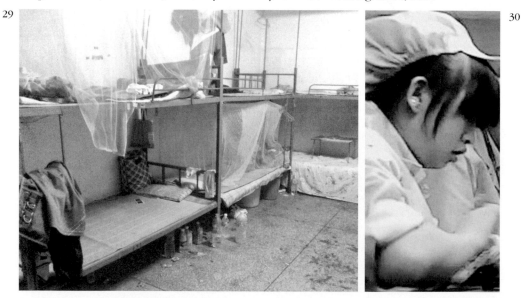

Backstage at the Democratic Convention Obama watches Bill Clinton's nominating speech. The two men had a difficult relationship, but Obama was glad to have what he called his "Secretary of Explaining Stuff."

Obama preps for the first debate with Ron Klain (left) and John Kerry as Romney. The president was 0–6 in rehearsals and not absorbing advice from his worried coaches to be less boring. "I'll be fine. I'm a game-day player," he said. But he wasn't.

33

The voter-suppression forces got the worst of both worlds: court decisions allowing "Souls to the Polls" and an angry backlash that drove black turnout in key states higher than 2008.

34

After Donald Trump offered the president $5 million for his college transcripts, comedian Stephen Colbert made an off-color offer of his own to Trump, which the Obamas watched "over and over."

After Hurricane Sandy, Governor Chris Christie of New Jersey helped Obama look presidential. Christie, who hadn't wanted to run in part so he could keep going to Burger King, planted a question with a reporter, allowing him to reendorse Romney.

Receiving Romney's concession call after a victory he found sweeter than 2008. Earlier in the evening, when told he had won, the president said, "I'll believe it when Fox calls it."

Romney's poll-watching ORCA system failed, only one of the many digital errors by the self-described "numbers guy." He was so confident of winning, he hadn't prepared a concession speech.

Barack Obama ✓
@BarackObama

Follow

Four more years. pic.twitter.com/bAJE6Vom

← Reply ⟲ Retweet ★ Favorite ••• More

811,256
RETWEETS

302,493
FAVORITES

8:16 PM - 6 Nov 12

Flag media

After victory, the most retweeted photo to date.

Obama with family after the official swearing-in on January 20. In a second term, the president would still face an obstructionist House but would make progress on immigration and other issues and prevent the country from moving sharply right.

It wasn't long before Obama Derangement Syndrome infected the primaries. After Governor Rick Perry of Texas said he had just consulted with Donald Trump and still wasn't sure about Obama's birth certificate (six months after the president released it), Joe Scarborough, a conservative GOP congressman turned MSNBC host, predicted, "People will look back at these Republican candidates some day and say, 'What idiots. What total absolute idiots.'" Even "low-information voters" who paid little or no attention to stories about Obama's early life could tell there was something kooky about the claim that he wasn't born in the United States. They sensed that it was odd and nonsensical for Romney to call Obama an "appeaser" when he had all but pulled the trigger and blown Osama bin Laden's brains out.

Romney was a serious man—intelligent, analytical, qualified for high office—but he was running for president in a political party that was no longer serious. Its remedies for the budget, a broken immigration system, war with Iran, and a dozen other issues were badly out of step with American voters. The debates were mostly held before Tea Party crowds that hooted down questions from moderators and cheered only the most right-wing pronouncements. None of the candidates tried to moderate his or her views with an eye to the general election or even the broader goal of seeming presidential. The news media, thrilled to have reality TV characters liven up the primaries, went along with the fiction that most of the candidates onstage had a genuine chance of being nominated.

By late 2011 reasonable Republicans were worried. It was one thing to support candidates who were more antiabortion than the American public; Republicans had won five presidential elections under such circumstances. But now issues like contraception were on the table. Former Pennsylvania senator Rick Santorum said the birth control used by tens of millions of single women was "*not* okay because it's a license to do things in the sexual realm that is counter to how things are supposed to be." Even if the White House sacrificed some conservative Catholics by battling with the U.S. Conference of Bishops on including free contraceptives as part of Obamacare, the issue was a loser for the GOP. The same went for pandering to the base's disdain for the theory of evolution and other matters of science. Just because climate change had lost its saliency as an issue for Democrats didn't mean it was helpful to the party to have several Republican candidates say it was a hoax. Bachmann's rejection of science risked real harm to women; with no evidence behind her claims, she told millions of *Today* show viewers that the HPV vaccine, now routinely administered to young women to prevent cervical cancer, should be avoided because it caused mental retardation.

Under normal circumstances, politicians benefit from sustained public attention. Not this time. Comedians and bloggers enjoyed a daily feast of material with which to make Republicans look ridiculous: Gingrich's $500,000 revolving line of credit at Tiffany's and plea to his second wife for an "open marriage";* Bachmann not knowing that Libya is in Africa and that Lexington and Concord are in Massachusetts (not New Hampshire); Santorum saying that John F. Kennedy's 1960 speech on church-state relations "made [him] want to throw up" and accusing Obama of being "a snob" for saying everyone should have a chance to go to college; Herman Cain confessing, "I don't know the president of Ubeki-beki-beki-stan-stan." Each gaffe faded in a day or two, but they left a cumulative impression. Federal Judge Richard Posner, a barometer of principled conservative thought, complained that the GOP had become "goofy." Columnist Charles Krauthammer referred to the field as "bumbling clowns." Even Pat Robertson, godfather of the religious right, worried about the impact on the general election: "Those people in the Republican primary have got to lay off of this stuff."

———

ABOUT THE ONLY thing that pleased hardheaded Republicans was that Sarah Palin wasn't jumping in. According to a GOP operative who knew her well, Palin's thinking was that if she ran and lost the nomination, it would hurt her lecture fees, as it did Rudy Giuliani's when he went from front-runner to also-ran in 2008. Better to flirt with running as long as she could to keep the money flowing in, then play kingmaker. (She eventually endorsed Rick Perry.) Chicago ardently hoped she would make the race. "If I could pay her filing fee, I would," Jim Messina said in mid-2011.

Few Republicans were happy with the announced candidates. Roger Ailes didn't think Romney was a real conservative, but he didn't trust Gingrich not to blow up and wreck the GOP's chances. "He's like a guy who's sitting calmly on the podium and suddenly he puts scrambled eggs in his hair," Ailes told friends. In the spring of 2011 Romney held his second meeting of the year with Rupert Murdoch, who was no more impressed than when they met in 2008 and 2010. "I didn't care for him at all. He sounded like he was running for president of Bain and Company," Murdoch said afterward. The News Corp.

---

* Rush Limbaugh argued that Gingrich, not his second wife, Maryann, was the "victim" and that the way Gingrich handled the matter "showed character."

founder was eager for Governor Mitch Daniels of Indiana to get into the race.

Daniels and Huntsman were the ones who scared Chicago most. They passed the reasonableness test (even though Axelrod was furious with Huntsman for telling him to his face that he wasn't intending to run at a time when he was busy building a campaign). Boston was confident that his family's reluctance would keep Daniels from the race, and it didn't worry about Huntsman, whom Romney knew through elite Mormon circles and dismissed. Sure enough, when he got in, Huntsman made little impression; instead of filling the television screen, he seemed to shrink within it. Bill Clinton, anxious for a moderate to make headway in the GOP for the good of the two-party system and the country (and hardly likely to lose sleep if Huntsman beat Obama), called Huntsman to offer his advice, but to no avail. It wasn't just the Obama connection that hurt; Huntsman was simply too moderate for the party. "I believe in evolution and trust scientists on global warming. Call me crazy," he tweeted when it was clear he no longer had a chance. The candidate who at first worried both Boston and Chicago was Tim Pawlenty, a former governor of Minnesota who described himself as a "Sam's Club Republican." If he played well in New Hampshire, Romney was in trouble. But Pawlenty hadn't read enough political history to know that if he just hung in for a while, he would have his moment to shine. Instead, strapped for cash and chagrined that he had lost his nerve and failed to confront Romney for sponsoring "Obamaney Care" in Massachusetts, he shocked his own aides by dropping out on August 14 and driving home to Minnesota.

Surprisingly, neither Boston nor Chicago was much worried about Governor Chris Christie of New Jersey. Stuart Stevens, who had advised him on his 2009 campaign before he became Romney's chief strategist, didn't think he would get in; David Axelrod thought his temper would eventually get the better of him. Roger Ailes, whose temperament made Christie look calm, disagreed. In the fall of 2011 Ailes hosted a small luncheon at his New York estate for Christie, who was now his choice. Limbaugh flew in on his private jet for the occasion. Christie gave the group three reasons for not running: It was too early in his tenure as governor; he had four kids and needed to make some money, which might not materialize if he ran and lost; and he admitted, "I still like to go to Burger King and I'm not going to lose it [the weight]." The Burger King line was intended to be funny but wasn't received as such, according to a person at the lunch. Later, when everyone from Nancy Reagan on down in the GOP wanted him to run, Christie was tempted but still felt the timing wasn't right, as it hadn't been in 2005, when the New Jersey Republican Party asked him to run for governor four years before he was ready.

If the Tea Party had a candidate, it might have been easier for more moderate Republicans to rally around an alternative. But all season long Tea Party members found fault with their choices. Romney, Gingrich, and Santorum had all supported bailouts or earmarks, a cardinal sin in the mind of Tea Partiers. Huntsman was seen as too liberal (even though he had a strong conservative record), and Cain flamed out. Many gravitated to Ron Paul but found they couldn't stomach his isolationist views on foreign policy, By the end the Tea Party hadn't helped any candidate and had badly hurt itself.

The prevailing mood in the Republican Party was summed up by Alex Castellanos, a Republican consultant nudged out of the Romney campaign in 2008. "We're waiting for Superman," Castellanos said. "We're waiting for a 'New Republican' the way Democrats in 1992 were waiting for a 'New Democrat' and got one with Clinton."

––––––––

FOR A TIME it seemed that Governor Rick Perry of Texas was the answer to the prayers of conservatives who didn't trust Romney. He entered the race suddenly on August 13 and shot into a double-digit lead in the polls. His hard-right views and Reaganesque bearing were popular, though some prominent Republicans had doubts early on. Norquist kept asking Rove why he didn't like Perry, and Rove finally answered, "The guy's an empty suit. Everyone in Texas knows it."

Perry said some things that confirmed the impression and drove home the point that the new GOP front-runner was on the fringe of American politics. Where Romney in June hedged on the source of climate change but said there was evidence it was taking place (leading Limbaugh to claim, "He can say bye-bye to the nomination"), Perry said climate scientists embraced the theory "just to make money." He called homosexuality "a deeply objectionable" lifestyle and charged darkly that Federal Reserve Chairman Ben Bernanke would be treated "pretty ugly down in Texas" because of the Fed's "treasonous" policies. His associations raised eyebrows. A large Perry prayer rally was organized in part by a Christian sect called the New Apostolic Reformation, whose founder, C. Peter Wagner, claimed that Japan was controlled by demons. The press learned that the Perry family leased a hunting camp that, until recently, had been called "Niggerhead."

By October it was clear that Perry wasn't Superman, and neither were any of the others. "It's hard for a lot of Republicans to get a woodie this year," Castellanos concluded.

One explanation for the GOP ennui was that Republicans were out of new ideas and rapidly rejecting their old ones. Obama was the first president in modern memory to face an opposition party that repudiated many of its own positions to make a political point. The cynicism was startling by any historical standard. Most of the Obama initiatives savaged by the GOP presidential candidates in 2012 had originally been embraced, even originated by Republicans. The most famous example, the individual mandate for health insurance, was hatched in 1994 in the Heritage Foundation and championed by Mitt Romney in 2003 in Massachusetts. A cap-and-trade system for carbon emissions wouldn't have gone anywhere without the efforts of C. Boyden Gray, a senior adviser to Reagan and both Bushes. (Gingrich strongly endorsed it in 2007.) The START arms control proposal was first offered by Reagan in 1982 and negotiated by the first Bush administration. Almost all of the specific provisions of the American Jobs Act that Obama launched in September 2011 were supported before his presidency by large numbers of pro-infrastructure Republicans, none of whom had the courage now to restate their support.

———

FOR MONTHS THE true winner of most of the GOP debates was Barack Obama. The press, obsessed over which Republican candidate won or lost each contest, kept missing the bigger story: the growing damage to the GOP brand. Primary debates were carried only on cable, which meant that the ratings were never higher than a few million. But with so many debates, each hyped by the sponsoring news organization, tens of millions of Americans saw at least snatches the next day on TV and online. The picture wasn't pretty for the GOP. It showed a party of colorful fringe candidates expressing ideas of limited or no appeal to general election voters. The far-right audiences that viewers glimpsed (or heard) were loud and disrespectful, further marginalizing a party already plummeting in the polls.

The Romney campaign despised all the primary debates and the networks' preference for entertainment values. On the weekend before the New Hampshire primary, ABC News had a debate on Saturday night and NBC News the next morning, which required that the candidates do debate prep at 6 a.m. Romney especially loathed the goofy showbiz introductions of CNN and other sponsors that forced the candidates to enter to excitable voice-overs and thumping music as if they were contestants on *American Idol*. His biggest problem was with Fox. When his campaign complained to Fox about having six thousand people in a raucous live audience, the reply was, "Fine, don't show up." Romney's team felt the implicit and sometimes explicit message from the networks was that not showing up or even complaining would affect coverage of their campaign.

———

THE FAULT FOR allowing so many debates lay with Reince Priebus, a Wisconsin lawyer who became chairman of the Republican National Committee in January 2011. He knew the party had lost control of the process, but he didn't have the muscle to get the candidates to reject the invitations of the TV networks. Priebus was a competent chairman, and his informal trade with Rove—the RNC's lists of donors and supporters in exchange for super PAC money—stabilized the party's finances. But the fact that he even had the job reflected the GOP's cluelessness about the changing demographics of the country.

In late 2008, after the election of the first black president, the GOP elected its first black party chairman, Michael Steele, a former lieutenant governor of Maryland. Moments after he won on the sixth ballot, Steele heard members of the RNC muttering "This won't work" and "What's the point?" as they left the room. Steele chalked it up more to poor sportsmanship than racism, but he was struck by how many complaints flowed in from members when he took his outreach program to Harlem. Several RNC board members recommended cutting the budget of his new "Coalitions" initiative, which was aimed at broadening the party's base.

Steele faced a daunting task rebuilding the GOP, which was demoralized after the 2008 wipeout and lacked the control of Congress or the White House that is usually necessary to raise money. In the wake of Obama's win, many big donors gave up on the RNC and moved to super PACs. A more persuasive party chairman might have been able to keep more of that big money in party coffers, but the charge that Steele failed in his job—accepted as a given within the GOP—was unsupported by the record. He erased the party's debt that he inherited, raised a record $198 million, revived moribund state parties by coordinating with Tea Party offshoots, tripled the number of small donors to more than a million, and, not incidentally, helped engineer a smashing victory in 2010, with the biggest gains in the House since 1938. Any other chairman would likely have been reelected based on performance. His reward was to be booted from the job.

Steele's problems began shortly after he took office in early 2009 when Democrats accused Rush Limbaugh of being the "de facto leader of the GOP." This was also an attack on Steele, and he defended himself by telling the truth: "Limbaugh's whole thing is entertainment. Yes, it is incendiary. Yes, it is ugly." As night follows day, any criticism of Limbaugh within the Republican Party must be followed by an apology, and Steele quickly offered one. Within weeks he was branded a gaffe-prone maverick. There was truth to it: He adopted a goofy hip-hop pose for a photograph, wrongly told Sean Hannity that the GOP wouldn't take the House in 2010, and agreed with CNN's Roland Martin that white Republicans were "scared" of him.

But in retrospect, most of what were seen at the time as Steele's embarrassing gaffes—distancing the GOP from the Arizona immigration law, expressing doubts about the war in Afghanistan (which led neoconservatives to call for his resignation), and rejecting the party's forty-year Southern Strategy, which he said "alienated many minority voters by focusing on the white male vote in the South"—were prescient attempts to modernize the party. Too prescient. Just after the big GOP victory in the midterms, the RNC's political director Gentry Collins, ambitious to be party chairman himself, released a fiery letter of resignation accusing Steele of putting the RNC into debt by borrowing at the end of the 2010 campaign and terminating a get-out-the-vote effort called the "72 Hour Program." (This was an effort designed by Rove, in which party operatives from Washington flooded congressional districts on the last weekend before the election; it had worked in 2004 but failed badly in 2006 and 2008.) According to Steele, Collins had earlier sent Steele a memo recommending both such courses of action. In any event, Collins was out of line: The borrowing in the fall of 2010, the main weapon used against Steele, was standard practice at the end of a campaign and fully justified by the spectacular 2010 results.

Steele realized later that he could have survived the gaffes (which were fewer than Romney's) and the borrowing, but not the wrath of the GOP establishment, which was angry at him for giving RNC money to the states for party building instead of to the usual collection of Washington-based consultants and vendors. His critics, whom he identified as Rove, Norquist, and Boehner's and McConnell's political handlers, leaked to the *Washington Times* and the Daily Caller that the African American party chairman was incompetent. "They needed control back," Steele said later. "I just wasn't their boy." His sacking was emblematic of an inflexible, hard-edged party with little use for diversity or outreach.

THE BALLOONING DEFICIT under Obama should have been a potent campaign issue for the GOP, which had once stood squarely for fiscal responsibility. But that party was dead.

The Republicans' lack of seriousness about reducing the deficit was demonstrated at an August 11 debate in Ames, Iowa. Following up on a question from the conservative columnist Byron York about what ratio, if any, between spending cuts and tax increases the candidates might find acceptable, Fox News anchor Bret Baier asked, "Can you raise your hand if you feel so strongly about not raising taxes, you'd walk away on the 10-to-1 deal?" Romney and his rivals all raised their hands, and only Huntsman later regretted it. The moment was a TV gimmick—would-be presidents need not raise their hands like schoolchildren—but it came to symbolize how far Republicans had drifted from reality. The tourniquet the GOP fashioned for itself on taxes was beginning to cut off its circulation. Jack Kemp, the late congressman, HUD secretary, and 1996 vice presidential candidate, had tried to teach Republicans to wrap tax cuts in a gauzy bandage of compassion. The advice hadn't stuck.

The bloodlust of party activists began to seep through. At the Reagan Library on September 9, Brian Williams asked Perry about the 234 executions carried out in Texas during his time in office, "more than any other governor in modern times." After the audience cheered this dubious distinction, Williams wondered what Perry made of the applause. Neither Perry nor any of the other candidates took issue with the cheering or thought to explain, as Reagan often did, the care that should attend each wrenching decision.

Republicans had long been the party of military strength, but the candidates (only one of whom, Perry, was a veteran) proved themselves insensitive to those serving in the armed forces. At the Fox News–Google debate in Orlando on September 23, Stephen Hill, a gay soldier risking his life in Iraq, asked a question via a YouTube video about the Don't Ask Don't Tell policy repealed by Obama. The audience booed Hill, then cheered Santorum when he said coldly that he would reimpose the ban on gays in the military. No one onstage disagreed or thanked Hill for his service. After the debate, Santorum and Gary Johnson, a libertarian candidate allowed to take part that night, were critical of the booing. Romney said nothing.

Perry learned the hard way in Orlando about the consequences of showing compassion in a GOP primary. Already slipping in the polls, he came under attack from Romney for a Texas policy providing tuition for the children of undocumented workers. "If you say that we should not educate children who have come into our state for no other reason than they have been brought there by no fault of their own, I don't think you have a heart," Perry said. He quickly learned that heart doesn't sell within the GOP. Boston and a couple of pro-Romney super PACS went hard at Perry on immigration and his numbers tumbled.

This was a critical juncture of the campaign. Romney could have easily brought Perry to earth with ads targeting his 2010 book, which called Social Security, a hugely popular program even within the GOP, "a Ponzi scheme." Matt Rhoades, Romney's campaign manager, later admitted, "We could have beaten Perry with just Social Security." But at the time Romney was "flipped out" by Perry, as one senior Romney official said. Stuart Stevens figured they should go to Perry's left on Social Security and to his right on immigration: a pincer effect to finish him off. The harsh tone on immigration was shortsighted. With the DREAM Act suddenly on the table, even Gingrich took a more compassionate view than Romney of how such children (soon to be dubbed "Dreamers" by the Democrats) should be treated.

At a CNN debate on October 22, Perry counterattacked by mentioning that Romney employed illegal aliens to do yard work at one of his homes. Stevens and his partner, Russ Schriefer, looked at each other in surprise. They hadn't prepared the candidate for an attack dredged up from the 2008 campaign. When an agitated and transparently political Romney said, "So we went to the company and we said, 'Look, you can't have any illegals working on our property, I'm running for office for Pete's sake, we can't have illegals,'" Obama operatives watching in Chicago erupted in joy.

The net effect of these early exchanges was to place Romney to Perry's and Gingrich's right on immigration—so far right that it was much harder for him to scamper back to the center. For years almost every serious candidate for the nomination in either party weighed each comment he made for how it would play after the conventions; Obama's refusal to propose cutting the Pentagon's budget and Hillary Clinton's opposition to negotiating with Iran were 2008 examples of that calculation. But Romney was apparently under such pressure from xenophobes inside the GOP that he thought he didn't have that luxury. His senior staff knew the campaign had overreacted to dark forces within the party. But at the time it was as if Romney could handle only the obstacle in front of him, with no thought of what lay down the road. He was so intent on clobbering Perry that he knifed himself for November.

———

ONLY A MONTH before entering the race, Perry underwent spinal fusion surgery. It didn't go well. He wore conspicuous soft orthopedic shoes instead of his customary cowboy boots and couldn't sleep. Before the November 9 debate at Oakland University in Auburn Hill, Michigan, the university hosted a reception for the candidates. Two guests in attendance said that Perry, "obviously high" on something, was babbling and staring straight into space. His chief strategist, Dave Carney, later insisted Perry was taking no medication but had not slept at all the night before because of the pain. In any event, the debate was a fiasco for him. Perry said he would eliminate three federal agencies, but couldn't remember the third. "Commerce, Education and the—what's the third one there? Let's see," he stumbled, before Romney suggested the Environmental Protection Agency. "EPA, there you go," Perry said, though it was clear from his puzzled expression that he had another agency in mind. "Seriously?" moderator John Harwood asked. "You can't name the third one?"

"The third agency of government I would do away with—the Education, the Commerce. And let's see. I can't. The third one, I can't," Perry said. "Oops."

Later in the debate, Perry said he meant to call for the elimination of the Energy Department, and in the spin room afterward he told reporters, "Yeah I stepped in it, man." The focus on his gaffe, one of the most embarrassing personal lapses in the history of presidential debates, overshadowed the underlying point sinking in with viewers. Perry, only recently the front-runner for the nomination, wasn't merely too addled to be president. He had a radical view of downsizing the federal government that enjoyed little support with general election voters. But none of his rivals defended any of the departments. In fact all were on record trashing the EPA, an agency whose mission was backed by wide margins in polls.

"Yeah it was embarrassing," Perry said later. "But here's what's more important. People understand that our principles, our conservative principles, are what matter." Those far-right views did indeed matter, though not in the way Perry and his rivals imagined.

———

WITH PERRY SELF-DESTRUCTING and Cain forced out by multiple charges of sexual harassment, it was time for another front-runner to emerge. In late 2011 Newt Gingrich, whose senior staff had quit en masse in June in protest against Callista Gingrich's running the campaign (and running up her husband's $500,000 tab at Tiffany's), surged into the lead in the polls. He was a serial adulterer and "inconsistent, erratic, untrustworthy, and unprincipled," as former New Hampshire governor John Sununu described him, but also a nimble thinker and gifted at using language to pack a punch.

While smash-mouth politics had been around since the dawn of the republic, it had faded in the late twentieth century, before Gingrich's ascent. In the four decades in which the House was in Democratic hands, moderate Republican minority leaders like Gerald Ford and Robert Michel fought hard for their ideas but maintained a civil tone. Gingrich believed their decency had prevented the GOP from winning. In 1990 he wrote a memo to Republicans called "Language: A Key Mechanism of Control." His list of "Optimistic, Positive Governing Words" included *common sense, courage, liberty, strength,* and *vision*. His list of "Contrasting Words," to be used relentlessly against Democrats, included *bosses, greed, lie, pathetic,* and, of course, *taxes*. The GOP internalized Gingrich's message, took control of the House in 1994, and proceeded to run linguistic circles around Democrats, turning inheritance taxes into "death taxes" and efforts to advise seniors on living wills into "death panels."

Now Gingrich turned his vitriol to a new target: Bain Capital, the private equity firm founded by Romney. He took his ammunition from a heavy-handed twenty-eight-minute film called *King of Bain: When Mitt Romney Came to Town*, which described Bain and Romney as "corporate raiders" who "played the system for a quick buck." The film was produced by Barry Bennett, a Republican consultant who had recently worked for a pro-Perry PAC, and directed by Jason Killian Meath, who created ads for Romney's 2008 campaign but later left Stuart Stevens's firm. By late 2011 Perry too had begun referring to Bain and Romney as "vultures" who "pick the carcass clean and then fly away." This was yet more blowback on Stevens. Working in 2010 on behalf of California gubernatorial candidate Steve Poizner, Stevens had produced an ad in the GOP primary attacking Meg Whitman for her ties to Wall Street that included pictures of circling vultures.

Chicago was already planning to slam Romney for his role at Bain; the Obama team knew that the Democratic media consultant Bob Shrum had used Bain to great effect when making anti-Romney ads in 1994 for Ted Kennedy, who pulled away from Romney in a close race that year and won reelection to the Senate. For months researchers in Chicago had dug up everything from old Securities and Exchange Commission filings on Bain to the blueprints for Romney's car elevator in his new $12 million home. Some of the embarrassing stories were leaked; others were held in reserve. Axelrod was delighted to see Republicans laying the groundwork for his coming attacks, though in the amnesiac world of presidential politics, he didn't expect anyone to remember.

As the Iowa caucuses and New Hampshire primary approached, Gingrich began losing altitude. Backed by a super PAC financed by billionaire casino owner Sheldon Adelson, he doubled down on attacking Bain. "You have to ask the question, 'Is capitalism really about the ability of a handful of rich people to manipulate the lives of thousands of people and then walk off with the money?'" he said. Suddenly a counterattack began. "What the hell are you doing, Newt?" former New York mayor Rudy Giuliani cried, echoing the *Wall Street Journal.* "I expect this from Saul Alinsky!" Giuliani said that Gingrich was acting "ignorant" and "dumb." Under a withering assault from pro-Romney super PACs, Gingrich lost both contests.

To repair his message for South Carolina, Gingrich began emphasizing older incendiary themes he had explored over the years, including changing child labor laws so that black kids could learn the work ethic and get paid for janitorial and other work at schools. At the same time, he stepped up the frequency of his demeaning description of Obama as "the food stamp president," without mentioning that the sharp increase in the food stamp program resulted from the recession that preceded Obama's taking office and that most food stamp recipients are white.

Juan Williams, an experienced African American journalist and Fox News analyst (recently fired from NPR for making a politically incorrect comment on "Muslim garb"), decided Gingrich must be called out on it. "The code was, 'We've got a bunch of lazy black kids who need to work,'" Williams said later. "Republicans had created a bubble—another galaxy—on the race issue and no one outside it had asked why they wanted to incite racial passions." Santorum had also made a racially insensitive remark on welfare, telling Iowans, "I don't want to make black people's lives better by giving them somebody else's money; I want to give them the opportunity to earn the money." (Santorum later denied he said the word *black*, arguing that what he actually said was *blah*, though the tape clearly indicated otherwise.) Gingrich had been scoring points off debate moderators all season long, so Fox executives, while approving the line of questioning, warned Williams of the reaction he could expect. Undaunted, Williams used the Fox News South Carolina debate, on January 16, 2012, Martin Luther King Day, to press Gingrich.

When posing his first question, Williams recalled a woman at a black church in South Carolina asking, "Why do you refer to President

Obama as 'the food stamp president'? It sounds as if you are seeking to belittle people." Before Williams even finished the question, the audience began hooting.

Gingrich's "Well, first of all, Juan" was so patronizing that it drew appreciative laughs before he said anything else. He went on to accuse Obama of putting more people on food stamps than "any president in American history," adding acidly, "I know among the politically correct you are not supposed to use facts that are uncomfortable." The exchange was the big news of the night, and Gingrich went on to win South Carolina handily. Williams received thousands of hostile emails, many of them referring to him as a "nigger." Racists called his home number, frightening his wife.

Soon enough, the racial appeals boomeranged. Even black voters most disappointed with Obama were reminded that old racial attitudes die hard. Almost all of them would be there for him in November, thanks in part to a Republican clown car that wasn't so funny anymore.

ON JANUARY 23 the remaining candidates met in Tampa, where Romney once again moved too far right on immigration. He launched the idea of "self-deportation," undocumented workers who couldn't find jobs going back to their country of origin on their own, leaving parents, siblings, and children. Stuart Stevens said later that he had never heard the phrase before the debate; it hadn't been part of the prep. But he and Romney were under the disastrous misimpression that Latinos were divided on the issue. Stevens argued that some immigrant families that had relatives abroad on waiting lists would support the idea of undocumented workers leaving the United States to take their proper place in line.

In fact "self-deportation," a phrase first heard in the California immigration fights of the 1980s, was an offensive concept to almost all Latinos. Somewhere in the lobe of Romney's brain devoted to pandering he figured that self-deportation would work as a "dog whistle"— a coded message—to the anti-immigrant crowd. But it left a much stronger impression on those it was directed against. This would not be the last time in 2012 that a dog whistle ended up being heard by Americans for whom it was not intended.

In Chicago David Axelrod thought that whatever the specifics on immigration, there was "a tonal problem" emerging for Romney, a "mean-spiritedness" that he later said Romney never recovered from. On a mid-February conference call with senior staff, Axelrod said, only half-joking, that maybe it would be better to run against Romney than San-torum, who was much more authentic.

Joel Benenson's polls showed that if there was an enthusiasm gap, it was on the GOP side. The projected wave of Obama-hating Republicans rushing to take part in 2012 never materialized. Turnout was low in Florida, Ohio, Pennsylvania, and other battleground state primaries. Benenson found that Obama supporters were much more enthusiastic voting for him than Romney supporters were voting for their candidate. This should have been a warning to Boston not to depend on depressed turnout within the Democratic base.

In March, Rick Perry turned in a funny performance at the Gridiron Club in Washington that captured some of the damage done by the 2012 Republican primaries. "Y'know, every once in a while, Herman Cain, Michele Bachmann, and myself will get together. We'll kinda act silly, we'll say some stupid things—you know, kinda like old times," Perry joked. Then, referring to an ad featuring a plutocrat rolling down the window of his limousine, he said, "It's weird standing next to [Mitt] on the debate podium. I keep waiting for him to say, 'Pardon me, would you have any Grey Poupon?'"

15

Playground of the Superrich

The idea of billionaire-backed super PACs attacking Mitt Romney for being a capitalist was . . . rich. It was also destructive. The same super PACs that had done so much to help Republicans in 2010 hurt them in early 2012.

Romney began tanking even before Chicago barraged him with negative ads. In a CNN poll, his unfavorable ratings rose an astonishing 19 points between November 2011 and March 2012. He went from leading Obama 51 to 47 percent in head-to-head matchups to trailing 54 to 43. The president won an end-of-the-year agreement to extend the payroll tax holiday, but he did little else of note in this period. So the best explanation for Romney's tumble was the terrible publicity of the clown car debates, combined with the attack ads launched against him by Newt Gingrich via Sheldon Adelson.

Had Adelson not pumped $16.5 million into Gingrich's campaign, Gingrich would likely have run out of money after Romney crushed him in the Florida primary on January 31. The race would have effectively ended then, giving Romney two and a half more months to unify the party. Without super PAC backing from Foster Friess, a Wyoming-based evangelical Christian who made his fortune running mutual funds, Santorum wouldn't have been able to afford any television ads at all. After surprising the political world in the Iowa caucuses, he might have won a couple of primaries on fumes in February, but he would not have had the funds necessary to win eleven primaries and nip at Romney's heels all the way into April. As it was, if Santorum, with Friess's backing, had won Michigan, he likely would have won Ohio and quite possibly the nomination.

Overall, super PACs in the primaries hurt the GOP. While they helped Romney derail Gingrich, they proved to be a net negative for the front-runner. Without them, Romney would not have faced six months of withering criticism from fellow Republicans that softened him up for Obama's attacks. Instead of spending more than $85 million in the primaries, he would have had that money to defend himself against Obama's early ad buys over the summer.*

Gingrich had no regrets. He told a friend in May, after Romney clinched the nomination, that none of the negative ads Adelson ran against Romney would matter because Adelson was now prepared to spend unfathomable amounts on behalf of the nominee. Gingrich added that he heard that sixteen other billionaires secretly pledged $10 million or more apiece to help Romney and Republicans win in the fall. The amount of money spent in 2012 by super PACs and other independent groups would end up increasing tenfold compared to 2008. "It's not going to even be close," Gingrich said with his usual self-assurance. Given the history of money in politics, this seemed like a reasonable bet at the time.

———

THROUGHOUT MOST OF the twentieth century, wealthy individuals had often thrown their weight around in state and local elections, but they have had a harder time buying the presidency. Reforms first launched by President Theodore Roosevelt banned unlimited corporate donations. National party committees paid for the travel of presidential nominees but not often for advertisements or get-out-the-vote efforts. Individual contributions from the rich rarely matched the efforts of unions and state and local party organizations (urban machines for the Democrats; county courthouse politics for Republicans) that handled most of the electioneering, even for president. The cash doled out by "bag men" more often came from these local sources than from multimillionaires.

Occasional heavy hitters—General Motors executive John J. Raskob for Franklin Roosevelt and the Democrats in 1932, insurance magnate W. Clement Stone for Richard Nixon in 1972, and currency trader George Soros for John Kerry and the Democrats in 2004—made news with their largesse, but none could fairly be called a kingmaker. Between the post-Watergate reforms of 1974 and the election of 2008, campaigns operated under a new wave of regulation, including public financing of general election presidential campaigns. Loopholes allowed for unlimited donations to the DNC and RNC, but this mostly empowered donors contributing or bundling tens of thousands of

---

* Santorum could also have won the nomination had his talks with Gingrich about forming a unity ticket borne fruit. But after several conversations, the two men couldn't agree on who would be on the top of the ticket.

dollars, not tens of millions. Until *Citizens United* in 2010, billionaires didn't have a big appetite for politics.

So finding the best analogy to the renewed class-based politics of 2012 requires going all the way back to the election of 1896, when Republican William McKinley outspent populist Democrat William Jennings Bryan by more than 10 to 1. McKinley's legendary campaign manager, the Ohio industrialist Mark Hanna, liked to say, "There are two things that are important in politics. The first is money and I can't remember what the second one is."

Hanna went to New York in early 1896 to highlight "the reality of the danger" of Bryan, whom the pro-Republican *New York Times* depicted as a "mongoloid." Several large banks kicked in 0.25 percent of their capital holdings to Hanna and the McKinley campaign. Cyrus McCormick sent 7,500 field agents for his reaper to spread the word that if Bryan won, he "would run the company at only half capacity," a widespread effort among the wealthy to scare voters about what would happen to "job creators" if the Democrat prevailed.

The heirs to Hanna and McCormick and other industrialists of the Gilded Age were Karl Rove (who described Hanna as his role model) and Charles and David Koch.

The Koch brothers sat just behind Bill Gates and Warren Buffett on the list of wealthiest Americans. Their father, Fred Koch, built oil refineries for Stalin in the Soviet Union before he turned sharp right in the early 1960s and became a major backer of the John Birch Society. After the founder's death, his four sons fought bitterly over his estate, with Bill and Fred, echoing the government's position, filing lawsuits that charged Charles and David with multiple violations of environmental laws. Charles and David eventually took full control of Koch Industries, which owns pipelines, refineries, paper mills, synthetic fiber manufacturers, and chemical plants, among other businesses. With sixty thousand employees and $115 billion in annual revenues, it is the second largest (after Cargill) privately held company in the country. The extreme secrecy surrounding the conglomerate extends to the dozens of bland-sounding libertarian organizations backed by the family.

The Kochs claimed devotion to free market principles while shunning the transparency that has always been essential for properly functioning markets. "The secrecy seems hypocritical," *Forbes* reported in an otherwise respectful profile. Not coincidentally, their huge political investments were always tied to advancing the company's economic interests. Because tighter controls on carbon emissions would cost Koch Industries tens or even hundreds of millions of dollars, spending a few million to fund groups devoted to climate change skepticism was a bargain for the brothers. Their good deeds too were often at odds with the company's record. David, a survivor of prostate cancer, generously underwrote cancer research even as the company lobbied relentlessly against the regulation of carcinogenic chemicals like formaldehyde.

Perhaps the best example of the family's muscle-flexing was a subsidiary called Koch Supply and Trading LP, one of the world's largest energy traders. Koch Industries hired lobbyists to pressure the Securities and Exchange Commission (SEC) and the Commodities Futures Trading Commission to weaken new regulations on derivatives. The term of the progressive CFTC chairman, Gary Gensler, was set to expire at the end of 2013. A Romney victory would likely mean that the Kochs could essentially handpick Gensler's successor, much as Ken Lay, CEO of the soon-to-be-disgraced Enron Corporation, chose the chairman of the Federal Energy Regulatory Commission, Curtis Hebert, when George W. Bush became president in 2001.

In 1980 the Kochs supported Ed Clark, the third party libertarian alternative to Ronald Reagan, but in the years since they steadily gravitated toward the Republican Party. Starting in 2003, Charles Koch hosted twice-a-year secret retreats at fancy resorts aimed at convincing other superrich conservatives to make multimillion-dollar political donations to the GOP. At the June 2011 conference, held at a Ritz-Carlton near Vail, Colorado, Koch in his welcoming remarks named thirty-two people who had already given at least $1 million to Republican candidates and asked the other three hundred attendees to do the same.

According to a surreptitious taping of his speech, Koch described the election as an investment opportunity, a chance for donors to win "the best possible payoff" for their efforts. But he was also apocalyptic about the stakes. The 2012 election will be "the mother of all wars," he told the gathering, a battle "for the life and death of this country," aimed at removing from the presidency the man he described as "Saddam Hussein."

It was hard to tell why the Koch brothers were so convinced that Obama was ruining America. Their net worth had increased 58 percent since the recession began in 2008, while for the rest of the country median family net worth dropped 40 percent. Their family fortune grew from $50 billion to $62 billion in 2012 alone, giving the Kochs plenty more to invest in like-minded candidates.

Cyrus McCormick in 1896 had nothing on the Koch brothers in 2012. When a group of midwestern Democratic senators blamed the Kochs for helping defeat the DISCLOSE Act, which required transparency in campaign donations, the Kochs, in a rare moment, fired back publicly, telling workers at Koch-owned companies (like Georgia Pacific) in New Jersey, Illinois, and Michigan to go public with the message that their home state senators were jeopardizing their jobs. Then the Kochs, who for years had specialized in targeting Democrats for political ruin, made their own contribution to the annals of political chutzpah: They accused the senators of composing a Nixonian "enemies list."

FOSTER FRIESS WASN'T a super PAC billionaire, just a "billionaire wanna-be," as he liked to say, since his fortune was only several hundred million dollars. But the seventy-one-year-old also differed from the other superrich players in his rejection of negative advertising. His mother had dropped out of school in eighth grade to pick cotton in order to save the Texas family farm, and she took seriously the Baptist admonition "Hate the sin but love the sinner." Or as his friend Lou Holtz, the former football coach at Notre Dame, told him, "Criticize the performance but not the performer." So he didn't pay for Santorum, who had run cutthroat campaigns in the past, to get personal. The closest the Santorum campaign came was "Rombo," a thirty-second spot featuring a Romney impersonator running through an empty warehouse, using a machine gun to shoot mud at a cardboard cutout of Santorum.

Friess also steered clear of directly funding attacks on Obama. He just thought Obama's "worldview was 180 degrees opposed to everything [Friess] was trying to accomplish" in the private sector. "He probably never met a payroll or knew people who gained success through our free enterprise system," Friess said. "Seems like most of his contacts are academicians and political figures." Friess later gave money to the Kochs, Crossroads, and other super PACs attacking Obama, but, remembering his mother, he could never work up feelings of malice toward the president. "I have to confess that watching his acceptance speech in Chicago in 2008 brought tears to both Lynn [his wife] and my eyes as we saw the joy that exuded from the people gathered there," he said.

UNLIKE THE KOCHS and Friess, Sheldon Adelson had no background in right-wing politics. "Look, I'm basically a social liberal," he said after the election. He noted that he was pro-choice, backed stem cell research, supported the DREAM Act, and—after experiencing Israel's medical system through his wife, an Israeli doctor—declared himself "in favor of a socialized-like health care." He opposed Obamacare because it let "medical decision be based upon money" instead of offering "cradle to grave" coverage, as Israel did. Adelson, whose $20 billion net worth had been amassed mostly during the Obama administration, said he was a Democrat until attending the 1992 Republican Convention in Houston, where he realized Republicans were "less selfish" and more focused on the good of the country.

After propping up Gingrich, Adelson pledged $10 million to Restore Our Future (Carl Forti's pro-Romney super PAC), $10 million to Karl Rove's Crossroads GPS, $10 million to the Koch brothers' various organizations, and $10 million to super PACs dedicated to winning Congress for the Republicans. He would eventually pump a staggering $100 million into GOP campaigns—about five times as much as the previous record holder. The 2012 election would be a real-world test of whether one superrich man could affect the outcome.

Adelson made no secret of what he wanted from Romney and the Republicans in exchange for his lucre: an end to all support of a two-state solution to the Israeli-Palestinian conflict, a position to the right of the American Israel Public Affairs Committee and the vast majority of the Israeli public. When Romney went overseas in July, the trip was most noted for his gaffes. But he also made news by attending a fundraiser in Jerusalem with Adelson, who owned a pro-Likud newspaper in Israel and was close to Prime Minister Benjamin Netanyahu. Afterward Romney took time out of the campaign to stop off in Las Vegas for an audience with Adelson. The first trip Paul Ryan made after his selection as Romney's running mate was to see Adelson.

Adelson liked to say he wasn't seeking an ambassadorship, just better treatment at the White House Hanukkah party: "If I'm fortunate enough to be invited to another, I want two potato pancakes because the last time I was there [under Bush], they ran out of latkes." This was charming but incomplete. Like the Koch brothers, Adelson sought to buy the election to protect his business interests. His company, the Las Vegas Sands Corporation, did 90 percent of its business overseas, in Singapore and Macao. He paid a mere 9.8 percent in foreign taxes on those billions. Under its repatriation plan, the Obama administration was committed to making him pay his fair share of U.S. taxes, preferably at 39.6 percent; Romney's policy was to let him continue to avoid them.

After a former Adelson partner, Steven Jacobs, charged that Adelson's

Macao operation was corrupt, the Obama Justice Department began investigating whether Sands violated the Foreign Corrupt Practices Act, a law from the 1970s that barred U.S.-based companies from engaging in bribery abroad. The SEC launched a separate probe into the casino company's operations. Adelson, denying any wrongdoing (and threatening to sue Democrats who recklessly repeated the charges), said he was bankrolling Republicans because of the president's campaign of "vilification" against him. Friends reported that the seventy-nine-year-old magnate was under the impression that Romney as president would drop the investigations because they had no merit. Given the tsunami of bad publicity this would cause, a Romney White House would be unlikely to do so, at least at first.

Whatever specific policies were affected, the impression of a president in the pocket of a billionaire was disturbing even to some major figures in the GOP. Norquist, who was married to a Palestinian Muslim and supported changes in U.S. policy in the Middle East, said that Romney wanted Adelson's $100 million so badly that he "would do anything to please him." Norquist attributed every word Romney uttered on foreign policy to his efforts to kiss up to Adelson.

Not that Norquist objected to separating billionaires from their money. In 2005 he had shocked conservatives by inviting one of their main bogeymen, the billionaire liberal George Soros, to his Wednesday Group meeting, mostly so he could ask him how much he spent trying to elect John Kerry the year before. When Soros said $27 million, Norquist was amazed that a man of his wealth had tried to buy the presidency on the cheap. Seven years later Norquist recounted how little Soros spent and said the Republicans would never make that mistake.

SOROS WAS SORE at the White House for much of the 2012 cycle. The Hungarian American investor and philanthropist, who became famous when he made more than $1 billion on a Wednesday in 1992 betting against the British pound, had given $8 billion away, much of it to build democracy in Eastern Europe. He became a right-wing target after backing the legalization of drugs and vowing to beat Bush, whom he detested. The organization he helped fund in 2004, Americans Coming Together, built grassroots infrastructure that proved essential to Democrats in later campaigns. That year he hosted the first New York fundraiser for Illinois state senator Barack Obama.

Soros helped Democrats some in 2006, but he wasn't active in 2008, when the Obama campaign made a big point of discouraging independent expenditures. But the billionaire didn't see why that should make him radioactive. He was a brilliant man who knew as much about international finance as anyone, and he was incredulous that the president wouldn't seek his advice beyond a short conversation or two on the phone. Obama knew Soros was erudite and even heroic, but he didn't think it was prudent to be seen spending time with the world's most famous speculator, who, not incidentally, had once been convicted by a French court of insider trading. Michael Vachon, a Soros adviser, met with Valerie Jarrett at the White House in 2009 and said, "George would like to have a conversation with the president. He feels like he's on the team but can't talk to the coach." Jarrett replied, "The coach is very busy."

In September 2010 Soros wanted to discuss climate change with the president, and with the Democrats strapped for cash and the midterms only six weeks away a meeting was finally arranged at a hotel in New York. But by then it was too late for donor maintenance; the two men seemed to be talking past each other. When Soros made some political observations, the president said, in a way that struck Soros as arrogant, that everyone has an opinion about politics, but "this is something I know a little about." The message was: Leave the politics to me. Afterward Soros felt he hadn't been heard and that it was pointless to try to stand in front of an avalanche from the other side—that $5 million, $10 million, even $20 million from George Soros wouldn't change the outcome in 2012.

In 2011 Soros was especially upset not to have been consulted by the administration about the Arab Spring. He had done more than anyone in the world to spread democracy; it was something he "knew a little about." He had intended to sit out 2012 until he saw the rise of the conservative super PACs. Then he quietly contributed to a few grassroots organizations and congressional campaigns and five weeks before the election gave $1 million to Priorities USA, the pro-Obama super PAC, because he was "appalled by the Romney campaign, which is openly soliciting the money of the rich to starve the state of the money it needs to provide social services." Soros and his team rejected any comparison to the Koch brothers, Adelson, or the Chamber of Commerce. He pointed out that they were promoting policies in their own self-interest. Soros, who opposed the Bush tax cuts and the rest of the Republican agenda and had no business before the Obama administration, argued that he was motivated by the public interest.

———

THROUGH MUCH OF the twentieth century, class rhetoric was an important part of progressive presidential campaigns. Theodore Roosevelt lambasted the "malefactors of great wealth." Franklin Roosevelt excoriated "economic royalists" and said, "I welcome their hatred." Harry Truman argued that Republicans favored "a return to the Wall Street dictatorship" and wanted big business to "take over the country lock, stock and barrel." John F. Kennedy, hardly a populist, said after steel executives raised their prices, "My father said all businessmen are S.O.B.s but I didn't believe it until now."

Then, after defeats in the 1980s, Democrats concluded that their party had moved too far left, and they began to downplay anticorporate arguments and to harvest campaign donations from the wealthy. To raise unlimited "soft money" in the 1990s, Bill Clinton courted Wall Street. In 2008 so did Barack Obama, who ended up raising more money there than did John McCain.

The idea that Obama was somehow antibusiness wasn't borne out by his record in the presidency. Obama hired an economic team with close ties to Robert Rubin and other fixtures of Wall Street, and he attached few strings to the bank bailouts. His mention of "fat cat bankers" on *60 Minutes* in September 2010 was viewed by oversensitive millionaires as evidence of malice toward the wealthy. In fact it was a sign of his inexperience. He was substituting rhetoric for action and would have been better off walking softly in public while wielding a bigger stick. Worried about alienating business, he backed off from an executive order that would have forced corporations doing business with the federal government to disclose their contributions to the Chamber of Commerce. While part of him wanted to exploit the public anger toward bankers, his heart wasn't in it. Like Clinton, he refused to take class-based politics much beyond championing the middle class.

But if Obama didn't resent the wealthy, he didn't believe their material success entitled them to any more authority over public life than anyone else. In his youth, he had actively challenged corporate power abroad, first in the movement to force Occidental College to divest from businesses selling to the South African apartheid regime, and then privately, when he worked for a short time in business. His first job after graduating from Columbia in 1983 was with an outfit called Business International, which compiled reports about economic conditions in foreign countries. His mother, Ann, wrote to a friend that he "call[ed] it working for the enemy" because it was helping businesses prop up foreign dictators. In his book *Dreams from My Father*, Obama described himself in that period as "like a spy beyond enemy lines."

Conservative critics crudely superimposed these youthful attitudes on the president, where they didn't fit. His best friend, Marty Nesbitt, was the CEO of a Chicago-based airport parking business, and Obama felt friendly toward plenty of other business executives, and not just because they gave him money. But he didn't feel he needed to spend his time stroking their egos and pretending that he thought they were the smartest people in the world just because they were rich.

————

As OBAMA TOOK office, the country was paying the price for the excesses of a second Gilded Age. For three decades Wall Street had steadily transformed the American economy into a wealth-creation machine for the few. In 1950 finance, insurance, and real estate accounted for 11.5 percent of GDP. By the beginning of the new century, these asset-shuffling industries had nearly doubled, to 22 percent of all economic activity in the United States. In 2010 the six largest banks owned or serviced more than half of all American mortgages and more than two-thirds of all mortgages in foreclosure. The big banks, revered by elites but often operating outside the law, had been sanctioned more than two hundred times and coughed up more than $50 billion in fines since 2002. The average compensation for the men who ran them was more than $17 million a year, which was about 250 times that of the average worker. (In the 1950s CEOs made twenty times as much.) They spent more than $30 million a year on lobbying and employed 234 registered lobbyists. It was no wonder that Obama's friend, Senator Dick Durbin, said of the U.S. Senate, "The banks own this place."

In Springfield in the 1990s, Obama was appalled at how the financial services industry misled consumers on credit card debt. He read articles on predatory lending by a Harvard Law School professor named Elizabeth Warren, who argued that many people in finance just didn't want to admit that they made their money by creating "tricks and traps" to squeeze more out of Americans who couldn't afford extra credit card fees, home equity loans, and all the other debt they were amassing. Warren was a bankruptcy expert but also a cultural critic focused on how certain occupations could corrupt the soul. In private life, before she had to watch her words so carefully, she spoke often about the need of elites to create psychological separation between what they did specifically (working, say, on arts programs for a tobacco company or in the legal department of a bank) from the bad things that others in their companies might be doing. They rationalized their careers by thinking that they weren't responsible for anything damaging that they hadn't done themselves. Those in finance felt genuinely that they were engaged in work that was mildly socially constructive as well as lucrative. To discover that they had been part of breaking the backs of millions of American families was hard to admit. These people were not the mafia, Warren said; they gave to charity and thought they led good lives. But after luring unsuspecting Americans into financial trouble before the Great Recession, they suddenly found themselves lowering the boom, spending their days generating profits for their banks by taking away the homes of people earning $42,000 a year, showing no mercy for people working three jobs and struggling to make all of their payments on time.

Warren championed class-based arguments that would eventually work their way into the marrow of the 2012 campaign. As head of a congressional inquiry into the TARP bailouts, she grilled Treasury Secretary Tim Geithner on the no-strings-attached deals offered during the last days of the Bush administration, when Geithner was president of the New York Federal Reserve. She was critical of Obama for not doing more to prevent foreclosures, but she felt the president had stuck his neck out in getting new regulations on credit cards and in insisting that Warren's baby, the new Consumer Financial Protection Bureau, be included in the Dodd-Frank reform of the financial system.

Senior White House officials in 2010 and 2011 came to dislike Warren; they thought she was a self-promoter who never seemed to get around to praising the president in her speeches and TV appearances. They pointed out that when Obama, believing she was too controversial to be confirmed to run the CFPB, asked her to make up a list of alternatives, she named only candidates whom she knew weren't interested, in the hope of getting the appointment for herself after all. All the sniping was irrelevant. Warren was on her way to being the new populist star of the Democratic Party.

―――――

THE 2012 ELECTION was shaping up as the most explicit contest over class since the Nixon era. Republicans sought to return to Nixon's class-based mobilization of white middle-class voters against liberal elites who coddled the poor. There were still votes in that strategy, but the new class struggle took on a different pattern. It was, as even Warren Buffett put it, a war of the wealthy against the middle class. The prize was control of the federal government and all the levers that offered to rig the rules even more on behalf of the privileged. If a small group of billionaires succeeded in firing a president they despised, they would naturally feel some ownership, if not of the government itself at least of his successor, a man who, as much as any other presidential candidate in memory, came from their world.

Eight of Mitt Romney's ten biggest donors were Wall Street firms. In early 2012 Crossroads GPS disclosed that 90 percent of its $70 million in donations was raised from just twenty-four people. (At the time, Obama would turn on the charm for a couple dozen people at a fundraiser and raise maybe a million.) As the campaign heated up, *Citizens United* was allowing one side to raise nearly seventy times as much as the other per wealthy backer.

In retrospect, Pete Rouse thought, maybe David Plouffe should have resigned from the White House in 2011 and gone to run the pro-Obama super PAC. Bill Burton, a former deputy press secretary in the White House, had cofounded one called Priorities USA Action, but at first it was raising a pittance compared to Rove and company. Burton, who had been the point man in the 2008 Obama campaign arguing against independent expenditures, found that many of the large New York Democratic donors asked the same question: Why aren't super-rich Chicagoans like Penny Pritzker and Jim Crown, two major fundraisers going back to Obama's 2004 campaign for U.S. Senate, kicking in to the super PAC? The answer was that they opposed super PACs on principle, as did the president. And their wealthy friends were having trouble working up enthusiasm for Obama. Given that, Burton's goal of raising $100 million seemed impossible. In January of 2012, Priorities USA spent almost as much on salaries to its three employees ($43,779) as it raised altogether ($58,816).

As late as the fall of 2011, the president and Axelrod agreed that the contrast with Republicans would be better if there were no pro-Obama super PACs. This talk of campaign finance reform led to profane outbursts from Rahm Emanuel. "No actual voter gives a fuck about any of this!" he said repeatedly, both before and after leaving to run for mayor of Chicago. It became a source of tension with his old friend Axelrod.

But one day in early 2012, Jim Messina peered at a white board in his office that totaled GOP super PAC fundraising and called in Axelrod, who said, "We've got to tell the president." They informed Obama that he would be badly outspent if he didn't authorize Democrats to give to the Burton super PAC. The president, who had no problem sacrificing his campaign reform principles on the altar of reelection, agreed. He signed off on campaign officials appearing at Priorities USA events. But he refused to appear at big super PAC events himself, as

Romney did. Clinton had attended many similar "soft money" events when he was president and let donors sleep in the Lincoln Bedroom. Obama wouldn't go that far. He preferred to be a little bit pregnant.

Over time wealthy Democrats (though not Pritzker and Crown) began kicking in, but Burton would have to be smarter and more nimble than Republican super PACs just to keep his old boss in the big money game.

———

FOR ALL THE hurt feelings in the business community, most of the gripes boiled down to taxes. Obama's plan would raise marginal income tax rates on the wealthy from 35 percent (which few paid in full) to the Clinton-era level of 39.6 percent. Then there was the president's effort in 2010 to end an obvious unfairness in the tax code that benefited only extremely wealthy investors. Under Obama's proposal, "carried interest," the compensation structure of fund managers, would be taxed as ordinary income instead of at the capital gains rate, which was less than half as high. The idea was crystallized by Buffett, who thought it was simply wrong for him to pay at a lower tax rate than his secretary. Even before Obama unveiled the Buffett Rule, Democrats believed it made no sense for hedge fund managers to pay at the lower rate. After all, the commissions and fees that they reap (customarily 20 percent of their clients' profits) are not, strictly speaking, capital gains because the managers themselves rarely owned the stocks. This was the kind of niggling fact that lobbyists for Wall Street had no trouble burying.

As a former lobbyist for the industry put it, if you were selling companies for two or three times what you paid for them, it was hard to argue that it would change your business model if carried interest was eliminated and you paid taxes like anyone else. On the margins, higher taxes might make some deals too risky, but it was hard to imagine many. As one dealmaker put it, if CALPERS, a huge pension investor, were paying KKR a $40 million management fee on a private equity deal, CALPERS would be plenty unhappy if KKR scotched the whole thing because its executives would pocket less under a reform of carried interest. "The tax piece for the private equity guys is a very small part of what you look for in a deal," the dealmaker said.

But the practical effects were considerable. "You can't create jobs at the same time you're at war with the private sector," said Brian Mathis, a hedge fund manager who was with Obama early. That war was "because of their hurt feeling. Period. Full stop." After being spoiled by Clinton and Bush, who treated them as opinion leaders, business leaders couldn't understand why Obama wasn't ingratiating himself. It offended these captains of industry and finance that everyone else in the world except the president of the United States gave them what they considered their due.

If Democrats had gone after carried interest alone, they might have won. But Max Baucus, chairman of the Senate Finance Committee, insisted on also targeting another, much more commonly used tax break that allowed the sale of private partnerships to be taxed as capital gains, not ordinary income. This break was more defensible than carried interest, and the idea of a new "enterprise tax" aroused the opposition of thousands of real-estate ventures and other businesses far afield from the hedge fund world. The Democrats' aim was to prevent tax lawyers for these partnerships from using more than a dozen loopholes to keep taxes low, but it had the effect of slowing and eventually ending efforts to confront the carried interest discrepancy.

In the meantime, the anger and self-pity on Wall Street was off the charts. In mid-2010 Stephen Schwarzman, the leading McCain supporter in the Blackstone Group, which in 2008 gave more money to Obama, was addressing board members of a nonprofit organization in New York when he let loose. "It's a war," Schwarzman, whose net worth exceeded $8 billion, said of the struggle over carried interest. "It's like when Hitler invaded Poland in 1939."

When Obama heard about this, he was furious. He couldn't believe a pillar of the financial establishment was comparing him to a Nazi. Schwarzman's office issued an apology, and his relationship with the president would eventually take a different course.

———

IF THEY HAD their druthers, Obama haters would have run a vicious and personal campaign. A planning document sent by political consultants to the super PAC of Joe Ricketts, the billionaire founder of Ameritrade, whose family owned the Chicago Cubs, said this: "Our plan is to do exactly what John McCain would not let us do [in 2008]: Show the world how Barack Obama's opinions of America and the world were formed and why the influence of that misguided mentor [the Reverend Jeremiah Wright] and our president's formative years among leftwing intellectuals has brought our country to its knees." The document, which Ricketts apparently never saw, lamented that Obama had successfully sold himself in 2008 as something he wasn't: "The metrosexual black Abe Lincoln had emerged as a hyper-partisan, hyper-liberal elitist politician."

No super PACs in 2012 ran ads with those harsh anti-Obama themes. Voters were disappointed in him and ready to hear that someone else could do better at creating jobs, but they liked him personally. And the order of battle had changed. Axelrod thought it would be harder to get away with swiftboating this time because both sides enjoyed technological advances that allowed them to fight back more success-fully. And the cable culture had changed. In 2004 Kerry had no MSNBC (then a politically neutral channel) and no social media—essentially no liberal infrastructure—to help him repel the attacks. The same was true for Bill Clinton during impeachment. Now a Democratic president had more allies.

This would prove to be a problem for the forces dedicated to de-feating Obama. Instead of launching surprise attacks in various media markets, noticed by few except the target audience, their every move was suddenly subject to blowback from the fact-checkers and bloggers relied on by the still-influential mainstream media. Then there were the legal impediments. Perversely, super PACs had a hard time mak-ing positive ads, in part because the law allowed them to include only stock still pictures obtained from agencies, hardly the stuff of riveting ads, not footage of the candidate they were supporting speaking di-rectly into the camera, which was the most effective kind of upbeat appeal. The lawyers warned this was a form of coordination with the campaign, and therefore not allowed.

So-called dark money groups that didn't disclose donors were al-ready making assertions in their applications to the IRS that would have caused serious problems for ordinary taxpayers. Crossroads GPS, which would end up spending $70 million in untraceable money in 2012, told the IRS in a confidential 2010 filing that it would focus on public education and legislative policy and that trying to influence elections would "not constitute the organization's primary purpose." Rove's orga-nization had to claim this benign purpose in order to win recognition as a "social welfare" nonprofit. Skirting the law this way made it harder for the dark money groups to take the gloves off in their ads.

Super PACs that disclosed donors had more leeway. But unfortu-nately for Republicans, the highly negative ads that these super PACs had long specialized in were no longer working as well. Their focus groups told them that Obama was already a known commodity and that voters reacted harshly to ads that made him look evil. So the super PACs settled for a dull knife and a series of dull issue ads that played thousands of times on TV but were remembered by almost no one. It also turned out that door-knockers saying they were from Americans for Prosperity or mass emails from the Club for Growth were a waste of everyone's time and money. Super Pacs—like the Republican Party as a whole—were wedded to media that was very twentieth century. A tiny handful of billionaires and their hired political guns were about to offer a master class on how to blow $600 million.

16

The Book of Mitt

One of the striking things about the 2012 election was how little Mitt Romney's Mormon faith mattered. Evangelical Christians, who believed Mormonism was a cult, who had told pollsters for years that they could vote for a black, a Catholic, or a Jew for president but never for a Mormon, voted overwhelmingly for Romney.

Romney's reluctance to talk in any detail about his Mormonism may have helped ease the concerns of voters. But the repression of his true self could make him seem pinched and robotic to those who didn't know him personally. Romney was highly regarded, even revered, by most of those who met him in school, church, and the business world, where he was considered a talented innovator in finance and a friendly and supportive colleague. These were his natural habitats, and he was comfortable within them. That could not be said of him in politics.

Romney didn't engage in the normal banter of politicians. When he went into the makeup room before a TV appearance, for instance, he generally didn't speak to the makeup artists and often didn't shake hands or even thank them afterward. Examples of his oblivious awkwardness were legion, from asking African American kids during the 2008 campaign, "Who let the dogs out? Who? Who?," to telling a local baker in 2012 that his cookies looked like they came from the 7-Eleven store. He informed NASCAR fans that some of his best friends were owners and made fun of the cheap raincoats they wore at the race. He placed a $10,000 wager with Rick Perry during a debate, insulted the British preparations for the Summer Olympics, mentioned that his wife had "a couple of Cadillacs," and lectured a heckler at the Iowa State Fair, "Corporations are people, my friend." Eventually the expectation of a gaffe meant that odd comments that might pass unnoticed from another politician—"I'm unemployed too" and "binders full of women"—stuck to him.

The most common indictment of Romney was that he stood for nothing. An incomplete list of issues on which he flip-flopped included abortion, immigration, the Iraq War, gays in the military, the minimum wage, the virtues of blind trusts, TARP, the Obama stimulus, the assault weapons ban, the no-new-taxes pledge, waivers for welfare reform, climate change, and whether an individual mandate for health insurance was good for the whole country. Thanks to YouTube he was held more accountable for changing his position than were politicians of the past.

But it was wrong to suggest that Romney was a fake. He was a genuine throwback to the 1950s, when men wore white shirts to work and women had dinner waiting at home. Ronald Reagan rode restorationist themes into the White House in 1980, and Republicans figured that maybe there was one more election in which nostalgia for a lost America could carry the day. Like Ward Cleaver, Romney was a paragon of old-fashioned values, if not in business than at least in his personal life. His expletives consisted of words like "Gosh-darn," "Shoot," and even "H-E-double hockey sticks." But if the candidate sought to conjure memories of *Leave It to Beaver*, *Ozzie and Harriet*, and *My Three Sons*, he apparently wasn't a believer in *Father Knows Best*, at least as it applied to his own dad.

Like Al Gore and George W. Bush, who ran for president partly to meet or exceed their fathers' expectations, Romney had daddy issues. His eldest son, Tagg, told the *Boston Globe* after the election, "[My father] wanted to be president less than anyone I've met in my life," a denial of lifelong interest in the office that was also said of Gore and the younger Bush. That wasn't quite true; Romney was plenty hungry for high office. But his ambition was alloyed with filial obligation.

While Romney worshipped his late father and followed in his footsteps, he often turned his father's legacy on its head. As governor of Michigan, George Romney enjoyed a reputation as a principled man—the journalist Theodore White found him almost embarrassingly sincere—while Mitt Romney was often viewed as a smart but slippery politician with few convictions. Romney senior, an ardent believer in civil rights, thought the GOP's 1964 presidential nominee, Barry Goldwater, was taking the party too far to the right and he refused to campaign for him; his son did not speak out against even the most extreme right-wingers. As chairman of American Motors in the early 1960s, George denied himself a $100,000 bonus and declared that no executive should be paid more than twenty-five times the factory wage; Mitt's private equity deals often showered huge profits on executives and investors while average workers received little or nothing. George, a strong supporter of expanding the franchise, was the darling of the Michigan chapter of the League of Women Voters, which drafted him to chair a constitutional convention to rewrite the state constitution. His son said nothing when Michigan and Florida passed legislation in 2011 that drove the League of Women Voters out of those states.

As a presidential candidate, George released twelve years of his income tax returns; Mitt reluctantly released two years, though he insisted that Paul Ryan and his other vice presidential possibilities give the campaign lawyers who were vetting them a full ten years of returns. George Romney, HUD secretary under Nixon, pushed for integration of housing and the end of "urban renewal" projects that had destroyed neighborhoods all over the country; Mitt told a closed-door fundraiser in April 2012, "Things like Housing and Urban Development, which my dad was head of, might not be around" when he became president.

In 1968 George Romney was the front-runner for the Republican nomination until he told a local Detroit TV interviewer, "When I came back from Vietnam I'd just had the greatest brainwashing that anyone can get," a reference to U.S. military commanders painting a rosy picture of the failing war. In the wake of the novel and movie *The Manchurian Candidate*, which depicted brainwashing of an American by North Koreans, this was a crippling error, though it came in the context of an appealing admission by Romney that he had changed his mind and now opposed the Vietnam War. The elder Romney insisted to his dying day that it was the entrance of a much wealthier moderate Republican, Nelson Rockefeller, into the race, not the reaction to his interview about Vietnam, that caused him to withdraw three weeks before the 1968 New Hampshire primary. Either way, his humiliation left a lasting impact on his twenty-year-old son. Mitt learned that rich men hold the power in politics and that a single gaffe can end a political career. In 2012, with his father's "brainwashing" experience seared in his mind, he developed a "Don't think about a pink elephant" problem. The more he tried to be cautious and avoid gaffes, the more he made them, like a son who repeats his father's mistakes despite every effort to avoid them.

The saga of the Romneys and the auto bailouts might have been ripped from Sophocles or Aeschylus. Because his father had run American Motors and he grew up in Michigan around carmakers, Romney thought he knew the issue better than anyone, and he grew touchy when challenged on it. So it was no small irony that his November 18, 2008, *New York Times* op-ed piece, "Let Detroit Go Bankrupt," eventually helped doom him both in his native state and in Ohio, where tens of thousands were also employed by the auto industry.

Romney claimed that he always favored the "managed bankruptcy" that Obama implemented and that the *Times* headline should have been "How to Save Detroit." Stuart Stevens went so far as to say that

the "anti-Romney" headline writer at the *Times* (never publicly identified) might have single-handedly swung a presidential election. The
headline hurt, but it would have faded had the facts been on Romney's
side. They were not.

For two years Romney kept trying to say that of course he wouldn't
have let Chrysler and GM go under, and it made him furious that Michigan and Ohio voters didn't believe him. But he had no way to prove
he was willing to break from his market principles at the time. Later
he claimed that the government guarantees he endorsed at the end of
his *Times* op-ed amounted to a willingness to have the government
support the auto companies. This was disingenuous. He knew perfectly well that government guarantees are meaningless unless there
is private capital to guarantee in the first place, and there was none
available in the grim economy of early 2009. Obama's auto task force,
headed by Steven Rattner, approached every possible private lender,
including Bain Capital. No one was interested, even on favorable terms
that slashed the automakers' labor costs. Without government help, GM
and Chrysler might not have faced full liquidation, but more than a million people would have been thrown out of work at a time when the
economy could least afford it.

In 2009 Romney called Obama's bailout "crony capitalism" but offered no plausible alternative. His later explanations of what he would
have done differently became increasingly convoluted and confusing,
even to his campaign staff. Michigan's Republican governor and the
Republican-owned *Detroit News* didn't buy it. No one inside his campaign dared give him advice on the subject. It cut too close to home.

———

MOST VOTERS IN 2012 knew nothing of George Romney's centrist record, but they suspected that his son might govern as a moderate, as
he had in Massachusetts. Romney played on this sentiment. His pitch
was subtle and highly unusual. As the columnist Michael Kinsley first
pointed out in October 2011, he might win "because his supporters
are convinced that he's a liar"; they were betting that he didn't actually
believe the right-wing things he said during the primaries and would
govern from the middle. In other words, they would support him
not in spite of his flip-flops but because of them. It was a comforting
assumption—that the "adult" Romney would show up eventually—but
it was flawed. If Romney truly intended to push back against the right
wing and show his moderate colors, the time to do it would have been
before the election, when suburban women and other swing voters
were in play.

There were two interrelated reasons why it should have been in Romney's interest to push back against wackos: To prove to swing voters that he wasn't the captive of the right wing and to show that he had the guts and toughness to be president. Faced with a similar situation on his left after he wrapped up the Democratic nomination in June 1992, Bill Clinton held a press conference to attack a female rap star, Sister Souljah, for making antiwhite comments. The message to moderates and independents was unmistakable: I will attack left-wing Democrats occasionally to prove I'm not their prisoner. It worked well, setting Clinton up for a successful nominating convention that unified and broadened his party. To Chicago's relief, Romney never had his Sister Souljah moment. Perhaps it was impossible. "He couldn't have done a Sister Souljah," Grover Norquist said later. "People would have gone, 'He's not a real conservative.'" In fact Romney had to keep moving right. After Fox's Bret Baier questioned him aggressively about his flip-flops, Romney told CPAC in February that he was a "severely conservative Republican governor," which was both infelicitous and factually untrue.

Candidate Romney was trapped in a right-wing universe that civilian Romney, the one from the business world whom people admired, would have found ridiculous. Instead of denouncing Donald Trump for suggesting that the president wasn't born in the United States, Romney welcomed Trump at a Las Vegas fundraiser just a day after the man conservative columnist George Will called a "bloviating ignoramus" went on CNBC and doubled down on his "birther" fiction.

Unlike John McCain, Romney did nothing to restrain the trash-talkers whose paths he crossed. Rather that rebuking a woman supporter in Euclid, Ohio, who said at a May event that Obama "should be tried for treason," Romney ignored the comment and launched into a long answer to the woman's question. He looked the part of president but was having trouble showing the fortitude that Americans expected in the Oval Office.

ROMNEY TRUSTED FEW people and viewed campaign consultants with skepticism. As a former management consultant, he believed that their advice was peripheral to the decisions at hand. But the political decisions he made on his own were often perplexing.

In early 2011 aides gingerly suggested he get the issue of his income tax returns behind him at a time when few voters were paying attention. He rejected the advice. This gave rise to informed speculation that, like many wealthy taxpayers, his investment losses in 2008 and 2009 were so heavy that he paid little or nothing in taxes, which would have dogged him throughout the campaign if it became public. In preparing for another presidential run, he could have adjusted his returns to pay a respectable amount, as he finally did in September 2012 on his 2011 returns. But doing so would have cost him millions and violated a leadership principle he established for himself. "If I had paid more [taxes] than are legally due I don't think I'd be qualified to become president," he told ABC News in July.

For months Romney promised to release his returns at tax time in April 2012, at which point the primaries would presumably be conveniently over. Even conservative commentators said that the governor's position suggested he had something to hide. For months Stevens had advised him to get some returns out, and finally, on January 23, he agreed to release his 2010 taxes only. The big news was not his income—$21.7 million in 2010—but the rate at which he paid taxes, 14 percent, which was expected by those who understood carried interest but came as a surprise to much of the public. (This was almost certainly a higher effective rate than he paid in the years when he was not running for president.)

Romney had told reporters only days earlier that he had made "not very much" money from outside speaking fees, but his two-year haul from the chicken-and-peas circuit totaled more than $600,000. While this wasn't outrageous by the standards of big-time politicians, Romney looked as if he thought hundreds of thousands of dollars was scarcely worthy of notice. Worse, he and his wife had money in Swiss bank accounts (until 2010) and in the Cayman Islands, a notorious haven for tax avoiders. This didn't make Romney a tax cheat; the Caymans are a place where many private equity funds park money collected from international investors (often investing in American companies) who frequently prefer to pay at the rates of their respective countries rather than U.S. rates. But complicated descriptions of the structure of funds hardly lessened the impact of the story, which was sure to resurface in attack ads.

The candidate's tax embarrassments were just one sign of his cluelessness about public perceptions. In preparing for the 2012 campaign, neither Romney nor his aides focused on his image as a Richie Rich character. Romney decided to stand by MassCare (his health care plan in Massachusetts) and to project comfort with who he was, a wealthy businessman. But his personal fortune was a largely unmentionable subject in Boston. Despite the car elevator at his new La Jolla home, Romney thought of himself as a cheapskate who made sure his sons were not raised as entitled rich kids. Even Bob White, the former Bain partner who was thought of at campaign headquarters as Romney's alter ego, apparently did not warn him that his wealth was a political problem, though he later briefed campaign officials about the complex details of Romney's holdings.

This was a classic example of a candidate heedlessly avoiding an important personal issue, in this case, his image as a plutocrat. Romney credited his parents for raising him right but seemed clueless about the advantages in life afforded by what Warren Buffett called "the lucky sperm club." He said later he believed that class in America should be discussed only in "quiet rooms." That was a pipe dream in 2012, when voters retained their anger at rich people who seemed to play by their own rules. "If Romney's going to be Michael Douglas, that guy's not going to win," Stevens said in April 2012, referring to Douglas's infamous character Gordon Gekko in the movie *Wall Street*. "He doesn't have to be Michael Douglas."

But he was Gordon Gekko. Somehow the candidate had not thought about the political ramifications of offshore accounts, overstuffed IRAs (with tens of millions, clearly out of step with the intention of the retirement accounts, which was to encourage middle-class savings), and a new $12 million California vacation home whose construction could have easily been delayed a year or two. In their 2010 returns, the Romneys wrote off $77,000 for Ann's dressage horse, Rafalca, whose prancing preparations for the Olympics became a running joke on late-night TV. Romney, who by 2012 had been actively running for president for five years (and had thought about it for ten), should have anticipated how this would look. As one senior campaign aide put it, "He should have said to his accountants and money managers, 'I'm running for president, get me out of all of this.'"

———

THE 2012 ELECTION was expected to be defined by billionaire-backed super PACs and a wealthy GOP challenger. Imagine the surprise in Boston when, starting in April, Romney, the candidate with financial expertise, faced what Stuart Stevens called "a perpetual financial crisis." The comedian Andy Borowitz joked that "Romney spent $76 million to beat a serial adulterer and a mental patient in a sweater vest," but it wasn't so funny for Republicans.

Like almost all conservatives, Romney opposed campaign finance laws in principle; now he was handcuffed by them. Under the law, an individual can give up to $2,500 to a candidate for the primaries and another $2,500 for the general election. The latter amount cannot be used for television until after the convention, which in 2012 was at the end of August. Having spent so much during the primaries, Romney was strapped. He had to get through four months (May through August) before he could begin to use his general election money. Obama, with no primary challenge, didn't have this problem. Meanwhile the highly touted pro-Romney super PAC reinforcements could not, by law, coordinate with the campaign, and their ineffective ads quickly made them almost a nonfactor. To stay competitive with Obama, Boston figured that Romney had to raise about $100 million a month, all of it from donors who had not already "maxed out" (given $5,000). Starting in May, Romney achieved this, but not without consuming huge amounts of time and energy.

There was a way out, of course. Romney could have reached into his own pocket, as he had in 2008, when he gave his primary campaign $45 million, about a fifth of his fortune. But he vowed not to do so again. A Romney family friend said that the candidate's reasoning involved personal considerations and a concern that he would once again look like a rich guy trying to buy the presidency. Some Republicans wondered why they were being asked to dig deeper while the candidate himself didn't do so. The campaign quietly borrowed $20 million in July, but by that time thousands of airings of anti-Bain ads had gone largely unrebutted. By not wanting to reinforce his image as a wealthy man, Romney gave Obama an opening to do just that.

———

ROMNEY'S TACTICAL APPROACH could be summarized by the old playground taunt: "I'm rubber. You're glue. Whatever you say bounces off me and sticks to you." It was a tried-and-true approach in past elections but didn't work so well in 2012.

The idea was a refinement of Karl Rove's old rule that candidates do best when they go after their opponents' strengths, not their weaknesses. Thus Republicans went after Al Gore on the environment in 2000 and after John Kerry on his heroic Vietnam War record in 2004. Under this theory, if you strip the other candidate of his assets, he has nothing left to run on. Taken further, if you strip your adversary of his weapons, he has nothing left to fight with. Romney had first adopted the rubber/glue tactic back in 2002, when he ran against Democrat Shannon O'Brien for governor of Massachusetts. O'Brien, picking up where Ted Kennedy's successful 1994 Senate reelection campaign left off, pounded Romney over Bain. Instead of changing the subject, as he had against Kennedy, Romney counterattacked. He charged that O'Brien's running mate, Chris Gabrieli, who ran a venture capital firm, was the one who invested heavily in Bain-run companies like Ampad and GST Steel, the same companies that Kennedy (and later Obama) charged with causing painful layoffs. Romney claimed in 2002 that he had been off running the Salt Lake City Olympics and had no involvement in those deals. The jujitsu against O'Brien and Gabrieli worked. Bain was neutralized as an issue in the gubernatorial campaign and Romney won.

Fast-forward to 2012, when Obama and pro-Obama super PACs went after Romney's connections to Bain and charged that he was still CEO and full owner, even if off in Salt Lake City running the Olympics. Once again Boston responded with a ferocious barrage. Every time the president or first lady visited a company, college, or nonprofit that had benefited from a Bain connection—and hundreds of institutions had portfolios with such investments—the Romney campaign screamed hypocrisy. But this time the tactic didn't work. The press understandably thought that owning a mutual fund that contained companies that, unbeknown to most investors, contained Bain financing hardly disqualified someone from criticizing Romney over Bain.

Even so, Romney aides spent most of 2011 with a false sense of security about the Bain connection, in part because a former Bain executive who ran for Ted Kennedy's Senate seat in 2010, Steve Pagliuca, had endured only one nasty *Boston Globe* editorial on his connection to the firm. (They didn't seem to notice that Pagliuca lost in the Democratic primary.) And Romney's rivals in the 2008 presidential campaign had largely left the subject alone. By the 2012 cycle, it seemed like awfully old news. But Perry and Gingrich went hard at Bain, and Chicago made it a theme of Obama's campaign. Axelrod figured that if Bain was Romney's "calling card," Obama would take a leaf from the Rove playbook and go after his opponent's strength.

Obama paid no price for it. The fact-check features in the *Washington Post*, the Annenberg Center, and elsewhere found that Chicago was wrong in claiming that Romney still had responsibility for Bain Capital's investments after he left to take over the Olympics. But the Democratic base loved that the president was finally throwing punches, even if they were misdirected.

Throughout the year both parties left misleading impressions about the company that Romney had founded. Republicans pointed to Bain as evidence that Romney had a record as a job creator. But the point of Bain's investments was profit for itself and its shareholders, not job creation. At many Bain-owned companies, payroll was reduced and workers left in the lurch after the takeover. Democrats meanwhile often made it seem as if private equity was a disreputable business. In truth, Bain helped underwrite several fledgling companies and resuscitated others. All told, private equity proved to be more productive than most brands of modern-day capitalism; at least it focused on real companies in the real economy, not the casino of derivatives, credit default swaps, and other exotic products that, as former Fed Chairman Paul Volcker put it, contribute nothing to wealth creation.

In May Newark's Democratic mayor Cory Booker defended Bain Capital as having "done a lot to support businesses, to grow businesses." He called an Obama attack ad linking Romney to layoffs at a Bain company "nauseating." Chicago panicked and made Booker, a longtime Obama supporter, recant. His statement, which he taped himself, looked almost like a hostage video. Stephanie Cutter, Obama's deputy campaign manager, later said Booker's defense of Bain was one of the most frightening moments of the entire campaign because it undermined Chicago's depiction of Romney as an overdog. She needn't have worried. Romney's Bain connection was just one brick in a wall that was going up between him and the middle class.

———

RATHER THAN REACHING out, Romney just kept attacking Obama's strengths. First, Boston tried it on women's issues. After Democrats began alleging a "war on women," Romney and his surrogates could have ignored the attacks and tried to move to friendlier terrain. Instead they accused the president of being hostile to stay-at-home moms. This didn't work either. The gender gap didn't budge. Nor did the gap among minorities. Romney almost never ventured into the inner city or even to minority areas of the suburbs, although any sensible look at the country's demographics would have told him that simply turning out the Bush base from 2004 wasn't going to cut it. He needed to find new voters and streak toward the center "as fast as you can," as Nixon always advised GOP candidates to do after their primaries were over.

The issue on which he most urgently needed to reposition himself was Wall Street. His private equity background was worsened by the perception that he sided with the big banks, which were the subject of scorn in every focus group conducted since 2008. After he went on the ticket, Paul Ryan urged Romney to attack Dodd-Frank from the populist left. He argued that the new law, signed by Obama in 2010, had enshrined too-big-to-fail, favored large Wall Street banks over smaller regional financial institutions, and made the government too cozy with the banks. Advisers prepared a PowerPoint that showed Romney how going after Obama on Dodd-Frank could work on several levels at once. Romney wouldn't bite. It would have meant challenging his peer group. His Wall Street friends had spent millions lobbying against

Dodd-Frank as too restrictive, and he couldn't very well go all the way to the other side of the issue. But he absorbed everything he heard, and later, at the first debate, the populist line would pop out.

More often Romney got the timing of his pandering backward. If he was going to visit Liberty University, founded by the Reverend Jerry Falwell, it should have been in 2011 or early 2012 at the latest. But there he was on May 12, 2012, delivering a commencement address on family and marriage (which he said should be between "one man and one woman") at Liberty when he should have been at a nonsectarian university, moving toward the center. The same poor timing afflicted his media relations. In 2011 Romney kept conservatives at arm's length, refusing interview requests from Fox and telling people privately that he didn't want to be owned by the base. But then, after the primaries, when he should have been signaling his independence, he complied with most interview requests from Fox (especially the softball *Fox & Friends*) as well as from other conservative media outlets, drawing the line only at requests to show viewers the Michael Jackson moonwalk he performed privately for family and friends.

THE THEME OF the 1992 campaign was trust versus change. Voters trusted George H. W. Bush much more than Bill Clinton, who had been revealed as a serial philanderer and a "Slick Willie" on political matters. But Clinton won easily because the appetite for change trumped any personal concerns. Axelrod thought 2012 was a "trust" election, which he defined more broadly than personal trust. The questions for the voters would be: "Does this guy empathize with me? Does he identify with me and fight for me and my interests?" He was confident of victory because the research showed that voters answered those questions yes about Obama and no about Romney. "That is who Obama is and that's what he cares about," Axelrod said. "It's hard to make that case if you're Mitt Romney, who has spent basically his whole life fighting for Mitt Romney."

Boston thought 2012 was a "change" election, like 1992 or 1980, when a much-maligned former governor (Ronald Reagan) beat a hapless liberal incumbent (Jimmy Carter). In this climate, all of the charges and countercharges were just chaff. Stevens developed a "Day One" TV ad campaign to convey the impression of the action Romney would take upon assuming office, though it contained no job-creation plan beyond lower taxes, repealing Obamacare, and less environmental regulation of the kind that slowed approval of the Keystone XL pipeline from Canada.

In January Romney was campaigning in Florida, flush from a big win in New Hampshire. At a Courtyard Marriott in Palm Beach, he met with Chris Ruddy, the founder of Newsmax and a reliable barometer of conservative sentiment. Ruddy told him that to win the whole thing he needed specific plans for helping the middle class that he could use to "triangulate" (a favorite expression from the Clinton years), to find a new position above and between Obama and the other Republicans.

"What do you mean?" Romney asked. Ruddy brought up student loans, which Obama had greatly expanded. They were essential to helping young people get the training they needed to make it into the middle class. Romney asked Ruddy if student loans are so important, what is *your* plan? Ruddy said he didn't have a plan but figured Romney's campaign could come up with one. It never did. Beyond claiming implausibly that private markets could lower tuition and attacking Obama for taking the middlemen banks out of the process (which in 2010 had freed up tens of billions for new loans), Romney never offered anything on the issue.

And Ruddy didn't agree with the Romney camp that it was too late to cook up something new on immigration. Sure, conservatives would be upset, but not as many as Romney thought. "If he had embraced some version of the DREAM Act, he would have gotten away with it with the base," Ruddy said later. Instead he let Obama outflank him and even left the concept of "self-deportation"—anathema to Latino voters—in the GOP platform.

———

FOR ALL THE flip-flops and botched management of the conservative base, Romney's basic approach remained consistent. At Bain he was the "closer," the CEO who would work through the major deal points, saying whatever was necessary to get to an agreement. In politics this meant saying what was necessary to get past Rick Perry, Newt Gingrich, Rick Santorum, the GOP Convention, the debates, and anything else that stood immediately in his path. "The way the campaign was run was 'Whatever it takes to get us through the day,'" one senior aide said, arguing that the circumstances of a long primary season and a candidate badly matched to his party ruled out any other course.

In an earlier era, Romney might have gotten away with it; politicians who shifted their positions always seemed to stay one step ahead of the media sheriff. But as Chicago soon realized, technology had changed the old equations. Mitt Romney wasn't truly running against Barack Obama. He was running against other versions of Mitt Romney, preserved forever on easily accessible videotape.

17

Boston Mad Men

In his late fifties, Stuart Stevens was still into adventure sports. He cycled 450 miles, mostly uphill, in the Pyrenees, and skied a hundred kilometers to the North Pole. He celebrated the latter achievement by getting naked with Eskimos and Russians of both sexes in an overheated igloo. Every hour, one of the revelers, fortified by vodka, was required to exit and run naked once around the igloo in temperatures of around 40 degrees below zero—good preparation for the insanity of a presidential campaign.

Stevens, a Mississippi native, had a couple of pairs of cross-country skis propped up in the corner of his campaign office, but the Romney campaign's chief strategist rarely had time to use them. For two years he was either on the road with Romney or working at the Commercial Street headquarters almost around the clock, leaving only to exercise or sleep for a few hours. Whatever the campaign's chief strategist lacked in long-standing ties to the governor, he made up for in influence over almost every part of the operation. By force of intelligence and personality, he dominated the inner circle of advisers and enjoyed Romney's confidence even when plenty of people inside and outside the campaign were gunning for him. Like James Carville in Bill Clinton's 1992 campaign, Stevens, a Hollywood scriptwriter and author of charming travel books when he wasn't running campaigns, offered bits of humor and history with his relentless spin.

Until 2012 Stevens's favorite experience in politics had been working for George W. Bush in 2000. Brought in by his friends Mark McKinnon and Karl Rove, he had bonded with Bush, who always made sure Stevens was there for debate prep. In 2008 he and his media consulting partner, Russ Schriefer, at first worked for John McCain, whom Stevens had despised in 2000. They made a spot about Romney's serial flip-flops ("Americans want a leader, not a follower") that never ran but was leaked when they jumped ship to the Romney campaign.

Stevens believed that the 2012 GOP nominating process was different from almost every nomination since Eisenhower's. With the exception of 1964, when Barry Goldwater was nominated instead of Nelson Rockefeller, the GOP's tradition of primogeniture demanded that the inheritance go to the first son, the one whose "turn" it was. Nixon, Ford, Reagan, Dole, both Bushes, and McCain all won in part because it was their turn. Stevens argued that though Romney was runner-up in 2008, it wasn't necessarily his turn or his party. He was a northeastern governor in a southern party, a Mormon in an evangelical party, a supporter of health care reform in a party hostile to it. "Romney has to *steal* this nomination," Stevens said in the spring of 2011. "Left to its own devices, the party won't move to him." He was right about that, though he didn't mention that his candidate would have to knife his rivals with tens of millions in attack ads before he could steal the prize.

Stevens had what he termed his "unified theory" of the Romney campaign. He called 2004 the first "post-9/11 election" and said the only way President Bush had won reelection was to make it a referendum on the war on terror. Similarly 2012 was the first "post-crash" election. Romney, as the only candidate other than Herman Cain who had been a CEO, would need to talk constantly about the economy. That was the strategy all season long, even after Romney, at his friend Bob White's suggestion, hired veteran GOP operatives Ed Gillespie and Ron Kaufman for additional political heft and sought outside advice from media consultant Mike Murphy and other Stevens haters.

Stevens was sure that all the abuse Romney was taking in the press would prove to be meaningless. He compared 2012 to 1992, when the George H. W. Bush White House underestimated Bill Clinton: "I can't tell you how many meetings I sat in where they'd say, 'Who is this fat fuck from Arkansas? *He's* going to beat George Bush? Are you kidding me?'"

Stevens believed that when the White House changed parties it went to the person most unlike the incumbent: vigorous Kennedy after dowdy Ike; Reagan's sunshine after Carter's malaise; Bush's "honor and dignity" after Clinton's scandals. Romney represented the sharpest break from Obama because he knew about business and how to create jobs. He was the only candidate who could talk credibly about the private sector launching companies. "If the question is about health care, we lose," he said.

In mid-2011 Stevens's theory of the case was simple: Beating Obama would be "either easy or impossible" depending on the state of the economy. If unemployment fell significantly, Obama would win; if it stayed above 8 percent, he would lose. Voters consistently put the economy and jobs at the top of their list of concerns. Their take was,

"It's the economy and we're not stupid," Stevens liked to say. "More Americans lost their jobs under Obama than under any president in American history. End of story." But was it? That the bulk of those job losses were in early 2009—the result of Bush policies—seemed to Stevens to be a quibble. He didn't think voters were likely to spare the president any blame. If Chicago was betting on the maturity of voters to place Obama in historical context with Bush, Boston was betting on their ADD.

Stevens thought Obama had only one way to survive in such a climate: Check into the Betty Ford Clinic of public opinion and issue a mea culpa. By acknowledging failure and asking for a chance to start over, the president might be able to appeal to the voters' spirit of forgiveness. It had famously worked for Clinton after he was defeated for reelection as governor of Arkansas. McCain had played the remorse card so often that he sometimes seemed to be looking for some issue to prey upon the mercy of the public. The gratuitous advice to Chicago to apologize was ironic coming from Stevens, whose candidate wrote a book called *No Apology*. But he was adamant. Chicago "will do it. I can't tell you when, but they will," he said in mid-2012.

Of course, for Chicago, Apollo 13 rules applied: Confession of failure was not an option. The president could acknowledge mistakes, especially in communications, and repeat "long way to go" platitudes, but to prostrate himself before the public would hasten exactly the Jimmy Carterization of his presidency that Boston sought. Stevens knew this, of course, but he kept trying to get a drumbeat for apology going in the press.

Stevens argued that when the president went on the road and touted economic success stories at this battery plant or that biotech lab, he was doing victory laps. "It's Mission Accomplished!" he shouted, conjuring Bush's premature declaration of victory in Iraq on board an aircraft carrier. He charged that Obama was "uniquely blocked" in acknowledging disaster: "It's like a hospital kills a lot of patients and they say, 'Not everyone died.' Or the 1988 Dukakis campaign after Willie Horton saying, 'Most prisoners on parole don't kill.'"

Stevens believed that Obama was presumed guilty and had to prove to the voters that he was innocent. Chicago's belief that the president's likability would prove decisive was a fantasy. "They think this is an eHarmony.com election," Stevens said. "We think it's a monster.com election." Everything would turn on who could find you a job.

The message discipline was impressive. Every press release on the economy had not just "Believe in America" but "Obama Isn't Working," a slogan borrowed from a Tory campaign in Great Britain that included a Photoshopped picture of a long line in front of what was described as an "unemployment office." If Boston was responding to something Obama had said, the Romney home page would feature a picture of Hillary Clinton with her line from 2008: "Shame on you, Barack Obama!"

Stevens's goal was to impose a Depression-era context on the race. When Obama called the anemic May 2011 jobs numbers "bumps in the road," Stevens, the off-season writer, retorted, "If John Steinbeck were alive, he'd be writing about those 'bumps' as human beings." He compared the "bumps in the road" comment to McCain's "the fundamentals of the economy are strong" gaffe of September 2008. But he was overreaching. His first ad for Romney, in November 2011, showed a clip of Obama saying, "If we keep talking about the economy, we'll lose," the point supposedly being that Obama didn't want to dwell on the economy. But the clip, wrenched out of context, was Obama quoting McCain in 2008. The press called Romney on it, and a ticked-off candidate demanded to review every future statement from his campaign, which slowed down the volume of video releases and ads. It was an early sign that playing loose with the truth would get you busted by fact-checkers in 2012.

The problem for Romney and Stevens was that they had no Plan B. The great corporate planner and his wily strategist had no strategy for winning if the economy got marginally better or Obama attacked, which they knew he would eventually. Worse, Boston felt no need to paint a positive, humanizing picture of their candidate.

IF THE CHICAGO subculture was the Cave, with its twentysomething analytics experts, the equivalent in Boston was the editing suite that Stevens built in-house for the fiftysomething (or sixtysomething) team he called "Mad Men." Axelrod leaped on the moniker, accusing Romney of being in a "time warp." But Stevens said he was out to find the best ad men in the country, to "get the speed onto the field." Rather than hogging most of the work for himself and Schriefer, he assembled a group modeled on Reagan's famous 1984 "Tuesday Team," which produced a memorable convention film and legendary spots ("There's a Bear in the Woods") that were brilliantly narrated—often while drunk—by the late Hal Riney.

Nearly three decades later, Tom Messner, a Tuesday Team member who originated the idea for Reagan's iconic "Morning in America" ad, was one of Stevens's Mad Men. So was James Dalthorp, who coined "The Ultimate Driving Machine" for BMW, and Jim Ferguson, the campaign's creative director, who thought up "Beef—it's what's for dinner." With his long white hair, ever-present Parliaments, and 1970s tattoos, "Fergy" looked like an aging member of Hell's Angels. When he signed on to Bush's 2004 reelect campaign he traveled to Kennebunkport, where he told Bush, "Look, if I do this, will I have to worry about pictures of a corkscrew up my ass appearing in some magazine?" Bush laughed and said, "If you got 'em, I'd like to see 'em." In 2011 Fergy had noticed a news story about an Iowan laid off from his job at a grain elevator who could find only part-time work as a grave digger. The story made him cry, and Boston thought it would do the same for voters when turned into an ad.

It didn't. The Mad Men weren't breaking through the clutter with their spots. Neither were Chicago's TV ads, but Boston's real contempt was reserved for the spots made by the pro-Romney super PACs. The Mad Men liked to point out that Rove was a direct-mail guy in a world where direct mail was nearly dead and that he had no business making decisions about which TV ads should run. One pro-Romney super PAC ad, in heavy rotation in May, offended their sense of craft, especially the decision to have the woman in the spot describing her problems in the Obama economy played by an actress. "With all the unemployed women, they use an actress!" one complained. "It's like a Vietnam ad in 1966 using an actor instead of a real soldier."

The Mad Men laughed at the billionaires who paid second-raters top dollar to produce subpar ads. "Those who can, do [congressional, gubernatorial, or presidential] races. Those who can't, do IE," one said, referring to the independent expenditure ads produced by super PACs. "They're not doing races because they can't win races. Fucking great idea: Get people who can't win races and give them $200 million to spend. Wonderful."

Even as the pro-Romney super PACs helped destroy Gingrich's campaign, Boston felt handicapped by them. Dan Senor, a senior aide and foreign policy adviser who had served as the Bush team's spokesman in Iraq, compared super PACs to uncontrollable drunks in a saloon. Stevens's analogy was to a newspaper being told what story it had to put on the front page. He rejected the notion that super PACs could do the campaign's dirty work without blowback to the candidate for going negative. The campaign, he said, had survey data showing that viewers assumed that all super PAC ads were Romney ads, even though Romney didn't appear in the spot to say, "I approve this message."

The Romney campaign and the pro-Romney super PACs weren't allowed by law to coordinate, and they didn't; no one wanted to have to hire lawyers after the election. In fact a schism developed between them. Boston was furious to learn that the Koch brothers scheduled their billionaires conclave in San Diego on the same June weekend the Romney campaign was bringing campaign officials, policy experts, Karl Rove, Condoleezza Rice, and even a few journalists (Fred Barnes of the *Weekly Standard*) to rub shoulders with rich donors and the candidate in Park City, Utah. When the Kochs refused to change the date, it was a sign that they weren't going to take their lead from Romney, whom they didn't much like in the first place.

———

BOSTON'S DIGITAL DIRECTOR, Zac Moffatt, believed that it wasn't necessary to match Chicago point for point, just to pick five or six things in digital and do them well. The main goal was "to separate motion from movement." Motion was about fads—say, live-tweeting every event. Was this really necessary? He noted that when Obama's kickoff rally in Columbus, Ohio, didn't fill the arena, Twitter ate the president's team alive with no need for Boston to weigh in. "You can build a lot of stuff and get marginal return," he said.

This was rationalizing a severe competitive disadvantage. Chicago had been building digital capacity for six years, while Boston decided it couldn't afford it. In April 2011 Alex Gage, the founder of Target-Point Consulting, a Republican opinion research firm that pioneered the use of consumer data in politics, approached the Romney campaign. Gage's firm had begun using the term *microtargeting* in 2000. (He later learned it was originated by the medical profession for laser surgery.) He had compiled opinion research for Republican candidates from Gerald Ford in 1976 to Romney in 2008, and after noticing Obama job postings for data scientists, he saw what he called a "data arms race" coming. So he went to Boston and pitched "Romney Abacus," which he described as a centralized voter contact database not unlike what Chicago was building. The project would need to be located in Salt Lake City, he said, because the data scientists in Boston and Silicon Valley were almost all Democrats, an indication of the "geek gap" (Democrats had many more of them) that harmed GOP recruitment of brilliant techies.

But that wasn't the immediate problem. Gage, whose wife, Katie Packer Gage, was Romney's deputy campaign manager, knew the fate of Romney Abacus when he saw the distracted Boston high command diddling their smart phones during the meeting. They were like most people, suspicious that the Big Data talk was mumbo jumbo. Stevens, who monitored Twitter obsessively but didn't tweet himself, liked to remind people that the quants on Wall Street never saw the subprime mortgage crisis coming. He and his colleagues were in no mood to spend a couple of million dollars experimenting with analytics. Romney himself never even heard the presentation.

The campaign had reason to be skeptical of the GOP consultants. It was already paying an eye-popping $33 million to what was known as the "FLS Mafia," a reference to a company called FLS Connect (whose partner, Rich Beeson, was Romney's political director), and a sister firm called TargetedVictory, cofounded by Zac Moffatt. The latter was among nine Republican organizations on a single floor in a single office building located at 66 Canal Center Plaza in Alexandria, Virginia, which the conservative blogger Erick Erickson called the "locus of evil" in the Republican Party. Erickson thought they were rip-off artists whose only competence lay in fleecing candidates. Rove's Crossroads Media and Restore Our Future, the pro-Romney super PAC run by former Romney aide Carl Forti, were on the floor, as well as outfits with names like Digital Franking and Americans for Job Security. It wasn't clear what any of these consultants and super PACs did to actually help Romney get elected. They spent a lot of time consulting lawyers to make sure they violated no campaign finance laws when they ate lunch together. Only much later did they realize that not only were they allowed to coordinate, they should coordinate. But by then it was late in the game and their clashing messages had already squandered millions. None of these firms delivered anything resembling the media work in Chicago of Jim Margolis and Larry Grisolano or the analytical work of the geeks in the Cave.

The closest to the latter was Alex Lundry, a data scientist on leave from Alex Gage's firm to help out in Boston. But the Romney campaign was never data-driven. Lundry was like the lonely commander of the Alamo watching Santa Anna's vast army coming over the horizon. Where Chicago had fifty-four geeks building and analyzing models, Boston had only ten data scientists. The campaign did some good Twitter analysis, and Lundry borrowed TargetPoint's National Dialogue Monitor, which built fever charts that incorporated every mention of a candidate by hundreds of media outlets. But that tool just confirmed what Stevens and the others didn't want to hear: that Romney's reputation was taking a beating in mid-2012.

Boston produced no original data products and was always playing defense against Chicago's Optimizer, which it tried and failed to reverse-engineer. Without its own Cave-like modeling, Boston was flying blind, unable to make full use of the RNC's voter file and vulnerable to the faulty definition of "likely" voters that afflicted Gallup and other pollsters. Neil Newhouse, Romney's pollster, fell into a similar trap. His projections relied on 2004 and 2010 turnout models but lightly weighted 2008, when Republicans lost. That meant that Boston would have a skewed view of the race all the way to Election Day.

Moffatt argued that the other side could have the best database in the world but it wouldn't make any difference if it had the wrong message. He conceded in June that the Dashboard database reportedly being worked up by the Obama team would be cool. But the advantage of, say, having canvassers with special handheld devices (later largely abandoned by Chicago) seemed overblown to him. A canvasser could only hit around forty-five doors a day and talk to about twelve people, handhelds or not. What Moffatt didn't realize was that the efficient Obama field team was talking to the twelve they needed and ignoring the rest.

JUNE 1 WAS a bad day for the economy but a good day for Boston. The May jobs report showed only sixty-nine thousand new jobs, and the March and April figures were revised downward. Axelrod traveled that day to Boston to give a fiery speech at the state capitol castigating Romney's record as governor. The idea was to juice the line of attack focused on how Massachusetts was forty-seventh out of fifty states in job creation under Romney. But the event was a fiasco. He was met by festive pro-Romney hecklers sent from Romney's Commercial Street headquarters who drowned out his awkwardly delivered message. One GOP protester blew bubbles; another, a former Rhodes scholar, dressed in a space suit left over from when the Romney campaign was ridiculing Gingrich for his space colony reveries, denounced Obama's "astronomical" deficits.

Stevens respected Axelrod's work in 2008, but now he went out of his way to trash him. He emailed that Axelrod had "an obsession with Romney that is verging on the DeNiro character in Taxi Driver." He chose to believe a bogus story about Axelrod being present in national security briefings and pointed to focus groups showing that he was less popular than Donald Trump, who Stevens said had standing not just with the conservative base but with blue-collar voters and fans of his TV show. That night, Stevens emailed the author:*

When is Obama going to acknowledge the incredible human tragedy

---

* All of Stuart Stevens's emails included here were to the author in 2011 and 2012.

that has unfolded under his administration? More poverty, more unemployed, more homes lost. . . .

This race won't be close . . . but forget that, what about his legacy?
Axe has become a cross between Haldeman and Baghdad Bob.*

Stevens said that Chicago staffers, blinded by their hatred of Romney, failed to see that people didn't care about his dog Seamus being
strapped to the roof of his car (reprised by *New York Times* columnist
Gail Collins in every column that referred to Romney and noted in almost every Chicago focus group). "They think it's a *Travels with Charley*
election," he said, referring to the John Steinbeck travelogue about his
crosscountry trip with his dog. "We think it's a *Grapes of Wrath* election."

The one-liners in the middle of the night just kept on coming: "For
the president of the United States to ask 'What's my narrative?' is right
up there with Dustin Hoffman asking, 'What's my motivation?' when
he's a tomato at the top of *Tootsie*," Stevens said later that night by
phone. He argued that for Obama to ignore the unemployed while he
sought his place in history by pushing health care reform was "arguably criminal. It's like condemning all those people to misery."

As the summer began, Stevens was feeling especially good. He said
publicly that now Romney could run the campaign he had been planning to run all along, focused on Obama's failures to fix the economy.
Privately he all but pitied the Obama campaign. He was sure it had
wasted $25 million in May on spots that didn't move the needle up in
a single media market. After the election, Chicago's decision to front-
load its ads over the summer became a shorthand explanation of why
he won. In fact Stevens was right that all of the early Obama ads barely
affected the polls in an exceptionally stable race. But there was something ominous for Romney going on beneath the surface of the electorate in battleground states that wouldn't be clear until after the election.

Stevens placed his faith in right track/wrong track numbers. Only
26 percent of the public thought the country was on the right track, he
said, which was why Romney would eventually win easily. The strang-
est thing of all, Stevens said, was that a president who had begun his
career working with the unemployed on the South Side of Chicago
wouldn't even meet with them now. "Those people have become 'the
disappeared,'" Stevens claimed, as if they were Central or South Ameri-

---

* Bob Haldeman, who came out of the PR business, was Nixon's chief of staff before being
convicted in the Watergate scandal. "Baghdad Bob," whose real name was Muhammad Saeed
al-Sahhaf, was Saddam Hussein's information minister and became known during the 2003
Iraq War for his absurdly optimistic briefings.

can dissidents who simply vanished. He didn't mention that Romney wasn't venturing into the inner city either.

Obama could talk about subjects other than the economy, but it wouldn't matter, a confident Stevens said. The ammunition Chicago was saving was for naught. An ad reminding voters that Romney had money in the Cayman Islands? "It's like showing up at the Tet offensive and saying, 'Your shirttail is out.' No one cares," Stevens said. On this point, he would prove to be mistaken.

Stevens's theory was that this was not "a Seinfeld election," a reference to Jerry Seinfeld pitching his pilot as "a show about nothing." The 2012 contest was most definitely about something, and because it was so obviously about one issue, Romney had the luxury to lay off the ad hominems against Obama in favor of an advertising campaign featuring the patronizing "he's a nice guy who isn't up to the job" line of attack. This didn't sit well with conservatives, who booed Romney at the Orlando Tea Party debate in 2011 for denying that Obama was a socialist. And it surprised Axelrod, who expected a vicious frontal attack.

"When you buy a new car you don't have to hate the car you're trading in, you don't have to admit that you made a terrible mistake buying that car four years ago," Stevens said. "We don't want to make you think you were a dumb motherfucker four years ago for supporting Obama." In this spirit, the RNC made an ad with the tagline "He tried, you tried—it's OK to make a change."

————

AFTER THE ELECTION, Boston was criticized for not humanizing Romney more. But that may have been a futile exercise. In 2008 Romney ran an ad featuring Robert Gay, a former Bain partner who credited Romney with mobilizing the entire firm in a successful search for his missing fourteen-year-old daughter. In 2012 Restore Our Future, in a move that raised eyebrows among campaign finance watchers, bought time for the same heartwarming ad in Arizona and a couple other primary states. But it didn't move any numbers. "It didn't work because he didn't need to be humanized," Stevens said. He compared it to trying to make a wide receiver in football play center instead. Voters didn't want to see Romney in another position, especially one that didn't play to his strengths on the economy.

The same logic led Stevens to explain away all the gaffes Romney made during the primary season: "News flash!—people already knew he was rich and didn't care because they wanted to be rich, too." It had ever been thus. Jackie Kennedy's equestrian habits hadn't hurt JFK— had in fact made the couple more glamorous—and Ann's dressage horse being in the Olympics would be just fine. Romney's awkward attempts to relate to the unemployed—"There were a couple of times I wondered whether I was going to get a pink slip"—were cringe-worthy but easy enough to avoid repeating. And these stories, even with YouTube, evaporated in a day or two for everyone but the Democratic base.

Or so Stevens—and, by extension, Romney—believed. They aired no ads on the Olympics or good deeds in the Mormon Church or testimonials from Staples employees who had good jobs because of Romney. All of this would eventually come at the Republican Convention, but by then impressions had been allowed to harden. The Mad Men failed to understand that whatever the state of the economy, the character and humanity of the person who might assume high office is always of great significance.

———

ERIC FEHRNSTROM, a senior Romney adviser, told CNN that after the primaries "everything changes" and it's no longer necessary to worry about conservatives so much. "It's almost like an Etch A Sketch. You can try to shake it up and start all over again." A media frenzy ensued, but once again Stevens dismissed the importance of the mistake. This election was all about Obama, who had said in 2009, "If three years from now, the economy is no better I'll be a one-term president." Boston was confident that any price Romney paid for Etch-A-Sketching would be small compared to Obama's broken promise on the biggest issue of the day.

Much of the GOP establishment thought little of Stevens's strategy and began speaking out in early July. Rupert Murdoch, new to Twitter but loving it, weighed in first, tweeting that Obama's Chicago team "will be hard to beat unless he [Romney] drops old friends from team and hires some real pros. Doubtful." The *Wall Street Journal* editorialized that a "coasting" Romney campaign was "slowly squandering an historic opportunity." The laser-like focus on economic conditions wasn't cutting it, the newspaper said. "We're on its email list and the main daily message from the campaign is that 'Obama isn't working.' Thanks, guys, but Americans already know that." Bill Kristol wrote in the conservative *Weekly Standard* that "the campaign's monomaniacal belief that it's about the economy and only the economy and that they need to keep telling us stupid voters that it's only about the economy, has gone from being an annoying tick to a dangerous self-delusion." But the *Journal* and Kristol were delusional too. They and other conservative critics wanted Romney to lay out a clear agenda on taxes, spending, health care, and other issues—a suicide mission considering the strong support Democrats received on all those issues.

Even as Romney got hammered all summer on Swiss bank accounts, his tax returns, and Bain, Stevens remained confident. Some campaign finance rules—like the one stipulating that, until the nominating conventions, campaigns could only spend money on TV ads that had been raised explicitly for the primaries—were hurting them over the summer but would soon be in the past. While Romney lacked the power of incumbency to rake in contributions (a huge asset for Obama), he made up for it with prodigious fundraising, spearheaded by the indefatigable Spencer Zwick, whose firms made more than $20 million off the campaign. Stevens got a chuckle over reporters complaining about Romney's light schedule. He was spending most of his day raising money, nearly three-quarters of which would go for ads on CBS, NBC, Yahoo, and the other parent media companies of the campaign press corps.

Boston liked the way the race was shaping up. By mid-July Obama had spent $100 million in advertising in swing states, and, while some polls showed marginal upticks, he had not gone over 50 percent in any state or built the lead Chicago had hoped for. But Stevens was unaware at the time of how much money Obama was putting into its field operation—and how effectively that money was being spent. Chicago had bet on the summer and Boston on the fall, when it expected to dominate the airwaves.

Stevens knew that between the 8:1 spending advantage that Romney enjoyed among super PACs and the greater amounts of campaign cash that he raised in the spring and summer, Boston would have a financial advantage. Both sides agreed in July that the president would be outspent after Labor Day. The only question was how badly.

———

FRIDAY, JULY 13 was an unlucky day for Romney. A story in the *Boston Globe* that made him look dodgy on the timing of his departure from Bain was taking him off message. His claim that he left Bain for the Salt Lake City Olympics in 1999 was critical to his avoidance of responsibility for the bankruptcies, layoffs, and outsourcing that Obama was emphasizing. Obama went on TV to reinforce the message that Romney was principal owner and CEO of Bain Capital for three years after that date. Stephanie Cutter suggested that by signing SEC documents saying he was CEO but telling investors he had no role, Romney exposed himself to a possible felony charge. This was overreach, and Chicago backed off.

Knowing the story would continue another few days no matter what he did, Romney went on five TV networks to declare the whole thing "the height of silliness" and to lay down his marker on his tax returns: He would release returns from 2010 and 2011 and no more.

After midnight Stevens was in an especially combative mood, but he began his email calmly: "One of the things I learned the hard way coming up in politics is to let the data tell you what is happening not what you think might be happening." Whatever the noise from the trail, it wasn't working for the other side. "If I was Obama, I'd be asking for a $100 million refund," he wrote, arguing that Chicago's ads had done almost nothing to move the numbers, and the president couldn't win with 46 or 47 percent of the vote. But then the toll taken by the week's events began to show through in his missives: "I've found that when Dems try to get into this chest pounding stuff about how tough they are, well, it rarely ends well for them."

Stevens left the North End headquarters for the all-night gym in his apartment building. After 1 a.m. he was on the phone with the author, a touch of menace in his voice. "They're doing a birther campaign," he said. "Obama was saying, 'You want my birth certificate? Fine, I want your SEC document.'" Obama had wrecked his brand, he said. He was good at a certain kind of campaign—noble-sounding, unifying, above the fray—but now was running a different campaign. Chicago would regret unleashing these furies, he predicted. "We're not bad at this," Stevens said quietly of the dark arts of politics. "We know how to do this. Now we have permission to make it a character campaign."

When asked what that meant, Stevens began talking about the president's background. "We've never had a president we knew as little about as Barack Obama," he said, sounding like a radio talk show host. Stevens had been reading Ed Klein's *The Amateur* and David Maraniss's *Barack Obama* and didn't seem to find enough ammo there, so the subject turned back to Bain and how the Obamas' church, colleges, retirement funds, and favorite charities all had their investments tied up in Bain-financed companies. "He's such a hypocrite on this," he said. Stevens insisted that focus groups had liked this tortured argument, but soon he was on to the next Obama outrage. The week before, he said, the president devoted a mere forty-two seconds in a forty-four-minute speech to the plight of the unemployed. "That's a psychotic break."

Harry Reid's reckless suggestion, unsupported by facts, that Romney hadn't paid taxes for ten years sent Stevens into a late-night emailing frenzy. He accused Chicago of scraping the bottom of the barrel: "Romney will win this thing—would probably win if the election were held tomorrow—and it will serve the purpose of really exposing a moral bankruptcy of so much of the Obama legacy. They became Birthers and worse."

The next night, August 7, he tried to spark more media outrage over Reid's charge, which Stevens knew Romney could disprove only by releasing his tax returns:

> Did you compare it to McCarthyism? Why is Obama allowing this to continue? Talk about a man with no core. . . .
>
> This is a man who won't even release his college transcripts? What he is doing is proving everyone on the right who we thought was crazy to be accurate. Just a guy who gamed the system and really doesn't believe in anything. Goes to college on Bain money and then attacks Bain. Turns Reid loose as a mad McCarthyism birther. You do know that the "source" for Reid is Axelrod, don't you?

Not surprisingly, Axelrod insisted that neither he nor anyone else connected to Obama gave the story to Reid. The idea that Reid's unsubstantiated charge "proved" that the right-wing crazies were "accurate" was itself a little unhinged.

It was hard to tell if Stevens genuinely believed that the president was "psychotic" and should turn over his college transcripts because they were tainted by Bain or was just whipping himself into a frenzy like a football coach at halftime. Either way, for a talented, rational, hardheaded political operative with the right relentless message on the economy to fall prey to Obama Derangement Syndrome was a sign of how far that affliction had spread in the political culture.

18

A Message Built to Last?

It sometimes seemed as if the president saw everything about political campaigns through basketball and poker. When faced with a setback, he liked to recall the 1991 NBA season, when Michael Jordan and the Chicago Bulls lost the first game of the finals to the Los Angeles Lakers on a three-pointer by Sam Perkins. Even the Chicago press wrote off the Bulls, who went on to win four in a row and launch a storied sports dynasty. Obama's confidence could also take the form of a hoops metaphor. In February Governor Brian Schweitzer of Montana asked him if he had what it took to beat Romney. At first the president seemed annoyed by the question, then he said his campaign would "block" Romney at every turn: "We're the Miami Heat and he's Jeremy Lin."

For most of 2011, "blocking" Republicans meant playing defense on taxes and budget deficits. Polls showed that independents wanted the president to focus on the deficit, which many of them viewed almost as a character issue. Plouffe and the president had tried to adjust accordingly. The result was even more delay in returning to a jobs agenda. But after the debt ceiling fiasco, Obama decided to move left and double down on the Democratic base. The phrase, which originally meant to double a bet in blackjack, was overworked now, applied to everything from doubling Haitian relief efforts to a Kentucky Fried Chicken sandwich with meat for buns. Obama used it twice in his 2012 State of the Union speech, proposing that the United States "double down on a clean energy industry" and praising other countries for "doubling down on education" as many states at home fired teachers. The president, a poker player, liked the idea of prudent bets that could pay off big in the future.

In his reelection campaign, this meant betting on the rapidly growing coalition of women, minorities, young people, and gays that was sticking with him, and worrying less about being a transformational leader who floated above politics. Given that composition of his base, it was natural that he would highlight issues like women's health, immigration, student loans, and eventually gay marriage instead of chasing after a Grand Bargain and trying to woo independents with claims of fiscal rectitude. His economic message would stress fairness, not austerity.

Romney too doubled down on his base, but he was forced to do so by the realities of the GOP. He had to bet on conservative cards to have any chance of being the Republican nominee. Politicians with fewer options win fewer hands. And the cards he played were consistently worse than the president's, the bets riskier and less connected to the center of the action. Polls showed that the policy ideas that Romney advocated were much further outside the American mainstream.

Of course, Obama was taking chances too. This was the first presidential campaign since Walter Mondale's disastrous effort in 1984 in which a candidate boldly endorsed tax increases. It helped that Warren Buffett agreed. The billionaire's *New York Times* op-ed piece, entitled "Stop Coddling the Super-Rich," made it harder to depict the president as an antibusiness populist, and it gave the president a line he would use throughout the campaign: "Warren Buffett's secretary should not be paying a higher tax rate than Warren Buffett." But Obama still had to convince low-information voters—people with better things to do than pay attention to politics—of his careful distinction between taxing the wealthy and taxing them. His victory depended on poor and middle-class Americans suspending their natural aspirations to be rich for long enough to notice that the game was rigged against them. The main conclusion of the series of Saturday political meetings the president began hosting in the Roosevelt Room was to "raise the stakes" in 2012. His legislative program, speeches, and messaging would all be directed at reminding voters that they faced a historic choice.

The message about the stakes had begun not with Obama or his consultants but with the voters themselves. It was in the endless focus groups that Binder, Grisolano, and David Simas, an emerging talent who ran opinion research, began to hear the musings that eventually became the line "This crisis wasn't created overnight, and it won't be solved overnight." This view reflected a maturity on the part of voters whose expectations had been lowered. But their anxiety also created a sense of urgency. The line "make-or-break moment for the middle class" that Obama used on the stump came straight from a white middle-aged woman in a focus group.

It helped that he genuinely believed it. The president told friends that he might not be reelected, but he was going to go down fighting for what had brought him into politics in the first place. Harry Reid liked hearing Obama talk that way. He thought the president would lose his remaining credibility with Senate Democrats if he didn't pivot to jobs, and thus was relieved when Obama called him the day after Labor Day 2011 to say he would be addressing a joint session of Congress on the need for a major jobs package. Everything in the $447 billion American Jobs Act that he championed around the country that fall—extending unemployment benefits, the payroll tax holiday, tax credits for hiring, road and bridge construction, modernizing schools— had been supported in the past by the Republican leadership.

When Republicans predictably rejected the jobs bill, they looked like Lucy pulling away the football every time Charlie Brown tried to kick it. But the president didn't care about seeming ineffectual. Throughout late 2011 and 2012 the point was to make the GOP look mean, out of touch, and not to be trusted with the power of the presidency. "Every election is the most important election in our history," Obama liked to say at fundraisers. "But let me tell you, this one matters. This one matters. This one matters."

IT WOULD TAKE time to bring back the base. Many liberals were still sore that Obama had let Wall Street–friendly officials dominate economic policymaking and failed to prosecute bankers for fraud. They wanted Guantánamo closed (though there was no place to put the prisoners) and Bush-era torturers brought to justice. Despite the achievement of universal health care coverage after a century of trying, many progressives remained disappointed that Obamacare didn't include a public option. Most of all, they insisted that he stop being passive and move on the offensive.

With major legislation dead until the next election, Obama decided to double down and raise the stakes on classic progressive ideas. He traveled to Osawatomie, Kansas, where on December 6, 2011, he delivered what his staff considered one of the most important speeches of his presidency. Osawatomie was the site of a famous Theodore Roosevelt address in 1912 outlining a progressive political philosophy Roosevelt called "the New Nationalism." Obama had long admired Roosevelt's pragmatic progressivism. A quote from TR, chosen by the president, was woven into his Oval Office rug: "The welfare of each of us is dependent fundamentally upon the welfare of all of us." Kansas was bright red, but it was also the home state of Obama's white grandparents and it had helped connect him to the heartland in 2008.

The historian Doris Kearns Goodwin talked to Axelrod about Roosevelt, the subject of her next book. They agreed the analogy fit. Roosevelt was sensitive to the gap between Gilded Age fortunes and the rest of society. While his attacks on moneyed interests were sharper than anything Obama could get away with a century later, TR's message resonated. "This country succeeds when everyone gets a fair shot, when everyone does their fair share, and when everyone plays by the same rules," Obama said in Osawatomie, echoing not just Roosevelt but Bill Clinton in 1992 and many of his own themes in 2008. Then he leaned into a line that came close to the kind of sound bite he normally disliked: "This is a make-or-break moment for the middle class, and all those who are fighting to get into the middle class."

In December, Obama got a chance to show he was fighting. House Republicans overreached by insisting they would agree to extend the payroll tax holiday for a year only if the rest of their right-wing agenda (repealing Obamacare, voucherizing Medicare, slashing programs for the poor) were enacted. For a week before Christmas, everyone from Republican senators up for reelection to the *Wall Street Journal* editorial page said the House GOP caucus was shooting itself in the foot. Obama surrounded himself with average Americans who explained what $40 less a week or $1,000 less a year in their paycheck, if the holiday wasn't extended, would mean for them. The optics, in the Washington vernacular, were outstanding for the White House, and Senator Chuck Schumer advised Obama to "make them sue for peace." Finally, on December 23, Boehner caved and admitted he hadn't handled the issue right. His staff conceded that it was the worst week of his speakership.

IT WOULD TAKE years, even decades to know whether the Obama presidency was truly make-or-break for the middle class. Campaigns, by contrast, are made or broken on a shorter time horizon. To fend off the forces arrayed against Obama, his team would have to drive a consistent message.

Here the mathematical tools of the Cave were less useful. The quants pushed "experiment-informed programs," a methodology popularized by liberal statisticians that analyzed how messages were received by different audiences (comparing delivery by ads, phone, mail, door knocks). But Analytics wasn't yet able to design the messages in the first place. That took the political experience and judgment of people like Axelrod, Grisolano, Benenson, and Simas. "If you don't have the right message and the right strategy, you can have the greatest analytics in the world and you're still the *Titanic*," Benenson said. Just as the medical profession couldn't use "comparative effectiveness" statistics to address all patient needs and the educational establishment had to avoid standardized testing as a panacea, the Obama campaign knew it needed to keep a little humility about the numbers.

So Chicago decided to match its quantitative modeling with some qualitative noodling. In 2011 Benenson designed an "ethno-journal" program in which one hundred swing state residents wrote in on-line diaries six times in sixteen days, detailing their economic lives, then answered eight to ten nonpolitical questions on such subjects as their feelings about their job, their aspirations for their children, and their views of their community. The 1,400 pages of transcripts showed an American working class that was less focused on getting ahead (the phrase *American Dream* didn't seem to be in their vocabularies) than concerned about not falling behind. It seemed as though every week in the ethno-journals someone wrote about putting food that was too expensive back on the grocery shelf or skipping a night at the movies. Their optimism was fragile, if it existed at all.

Chicago's takeaway, which informed the tone of campaign ads and the president's speeches, was to show sensitivity to their anxieties and avoid the word *progress* in describing economic conditions. Plouffe occasionally forwarded a collection of "verbatims"—excerpts from ethno-journals, focus groups, and polls—to the president so that he could hear more voters describe their lives in their own words.

Benenson was a numbers guy, but he liked to remind people of the sign that hung in Albert Einstein's office in Princeton: "Not everything that counts can be counted, and not everything that can be counted counts."*

AS THEY PREPARED for the 2012 State of the Union, the message mavens knew that Osawatomie wouldn't be enough. Alarmed by polling that showed voter confusion about what Obama stood for, Benenson told Axelrod that the campaign needed a simple line, an organizing principle. "Our problem is not that we don't have the right message," Benenson said. "We're just not saying it simply. It's so easy to draw the contrast and we're not doing it!" Benenson's idea for a memorable message was "An economy built to last." He thought it conveyed the president's long-range vision and focus on fundamentals. It didn't hurt that the line, originated by management guru Jim Collins, had worked for years for Chevy trucks. The president decided to try it in the State of the Union.

---

* The quote comes from William Bruce Cameron's 1963 book, *Informal Sociology: An Introduction to Sociological Thinking.*

Obama's poll numbers on the deficit weren't as bad as some imagined. Voters thought the two biggest causes of the deficit were the wars and the bailouts. The stimulus and health care reform were far behind as culprits. Benenson and Binder were impressed by how well respondents could contextualize recent history. Almost all of them understood that it was Bush who landed the country in this mess. The centerpiece of the Republican agenda on Capitol Hill—more tax cuts for the rich— was extremely unpopular. "This was the campaign where Democrats finally took the theory of Reaganomics straight on and turned it on its head," Benenson said later.

Even so, Democrats were having a hard time getting people to absorb how extreme the Republicans had become. Bill Burton and Sean Sweeney convened focus groups in the spring for their pro-Obama super PAC and found that the Republican position was, literally, incredible to respondents. When informed that Romney supported something called "the Ryan Plan" that voucherized Medicare, slashed education, and included more tax cuts for the wealthy, the people in the focus groups didn't believe any politician would propose it.

The top two reasons focus group members gave for sticking with Obama were that no president could solve the problems he faced in just four years and that Romney would have to learn on the job; they didn't buy that his business background would make him competent on Day One. Many thought he had the wrong kind of business experience. This played into the Obama campaign's Bain narrative, which was focused less on attacking the company itself than on showing that Romney hadn't created jobs when running it.

But message remained a challenge for Obama, who knew that "Republicans want to cut more and Democrats less" wasn't going to be a winning theme. Larry Grisolano was sure what else wouldn't work: bragging about economic recovery. "The problem with 'We're getting back to normal,'" he said, "is that normal sucked for most people too." The toughest group for Obama was forty- to forty-nine-year-olds, the "Anxiety Generation," with stagnant incomes, kids going to college, and parents retiring. The challenge was to convey that the president was committed to putting the middle class on a more stable course. Over the months, whenever the seas got rough, Stephanie Cutter always reminded herself that the auto rescue, outsourcing, manufacturing—all of the specifics they raised had to be connected to the struggles of ordinary people. "The middle class is our North Star," she said.

———

FOR SEVERAL WEEKS in mid-2012, Axelrod and Cutter barely spoke to one another. Axelrod believed at the time that Cutter had accepted an invitation to appear on one of the networks that was meant for him. (He later concluded that the fault lay with a Cutter underling.) Cutter, who had worked as an Axelrod deputy in the White House, was a skilled communicator and strong on execution, a talented Democratic operative with experience handling Ted Kennedy and John Kerry. She rightly thought that she was better on TV than Axelrod and should represent the campaign not just online (where her jabs at Bain and other subjects were developing a cult following) but on the networks. She was right that the boys' club around the president didn't always pay her the proper respect. But she was relentlessly territorial—her nickname inside the campaign, "the Ninja," referred to more than her kickass anti-Romney videos—and that she was no match for Axelrod in either strategic vision or understanding of the president. Pete Rouse began to fly regularly to Chicago to smooth out that rivalry (among others) and to coordinate campaign rhetoric with official administration policy. Before long, Cutter and Axelrod repaired their friendship and stoutly defended one another.

Inside the White House, Plouffe kept the political ship on an even keel. Setbacks—disappointing jobs reports, say, or disturbing economic news from Europe—were taken more in stride than in the past. Plouffe had always been calmer than the easily agitated Democratic fundraisers he called "the bed-wetters." Now he convinced other battle-tested staffers to be philosophical about the ups and downs of Washington. When something went wrong, they liked to say to one another, "It's New Hampshire," which was code for an event that, like the loss to Hillary Clinton there in 2008, was merely a bump in the road.

One of those bumps was Obama's formal campaign kickoff at Ohio State University on May 5. The crowd at the indoor arena, estimated by the Columbus Fire Department at fourteen thousand, would have been huge for a Romney event, but it was underwhelming by Obama's 2008 standards. Despite roughly four thousand empty seats, Obama staffers urged attendees to move onto the floor of the arena. The idea was to make the event seem more crowded on television, but the cameras predictably panned to the vast empty spaces above. While the president gave a rousing speech, conservative websites normally confronted with rapt Obama audiences had no trouble finding video of people in the crowd yawning and checking their iPhones. The *New York Times* described the rally and another that day in Virginia as at times conveying "the feeling of a concert by an aging rock star."

———

THERE WAS ONE issue in 2012 that gave Obama the chance to stop the yawning and make history: gay marriage. The country was in transition on the subject. In 1996 Bill Clinton felt compelled to sign the Defense of Marriage Act, which defined marriage as between a man and a woman, but he did so at 1:00 a.m. because he wanted minimal press coverage for a bill he didn't really believe in. At that time, a mere 27 percent of Americans favored same-sex unions. In 2004 Karl Rove arranged for referenda banning gay marriage to be on the ballot in eleven states, and the resulting turnout among evangelicals was considered decisive in Ohio, where President Bush beat John Kerry by fewer than 120,000 votes. Without the backlash against gay marriage, Bush would have been a one-term president.

By 2012 forty states had approved statutes or ballot measures banning same-sex marriage. Even as Republicans like Dick Cheney, Ken Mehlman, and John Bolton endorsed same-sex marriage, the political risks of joining them were considerable. Nearly half of the country now supported the idea, but the opposition was not restricted to red states. While attitudes among many Democrats and independents had shifted in the eight years since Kerry's campaign, Chicago wasn't sure by how much.

For months Obama stuck to his awkward position that his views on same-sex marriage were "evolving." This was doubtful. Sixteen years earlier, during his first campaign for the Illinois State Senate, he had told a local gay newspaper, "I favor legalized same-sex marriages," which meant that he was either pandering then or holding back now. He took comfort that his dawdling paralleled Lincoln's careful evolution on the issue of slavery, which displeased impatient abolitionists in 1860. The president's position reflected where Americans were in 2012, still in transition. Housing Secretary Shaun Donovan's support in 2011 was seen as a handy wink to the LGBT community that the president would move on the issue after being reelected. Gay fundraisers, who accounted for one-sixth of Obama bundlers, seemed fine with the straddle, especially since the end of Don't Ask Don't Tell in late 2010 and Obama's decision to stop defending the Defense of Marriage Act in court. The president was under little pressure to "evolve" right away to full support of marriage equality.

Then Joe Biden appeared on *Meet the Press* and dropped a "Joe bomb." He noted that he was "absolutely comfortable" with gays and lesbians having the same legal rights as anyone else. Biden, who until recently had what one aide described as a "Village People" conception of gays, had just been to a fundraiser at the home of HBO executive Michael Lombardo and his husband in Los Angeles, where he was genuinely moved by his conversation with the adorable children of gay parents. On the air he engaged in a little sociological analysis of the impact of popular culture. "I think *Will and Grace* probably did more to educate the American public than almost anything anybody's ever done so far," he said in reference to the first TV hit with major gay characters.

Biden's appearance ignited a round of news stories that the vice president was off-message and implicitly endorsing same-sex marriage. Contrary to published reports, Biden never apologized to the president, though they both later used the same formulation to describe Biden's gaffe: that he had "gotten out over his skis." Obama was unhappy because of the way it was handled, not the policy change.

The president insisted that Biden had simply beaten him to the punch, that he intended to support gay marriage before the convention. He told aides that he was surprised no one had asked him how he would have voted on Governor Andrew Cuomo's marriage equality bill had he been a New York state senator; he would have answered that he supported it. But there were no definite plans on the schedule and no political incentive to fully endorse gay marriage. Chicago was nervous about the issue because it didn't play well among many swing state independents.

Looking forward, the impact of gay marriage on the campaign was tricky to calculate. Two days after Biden's appearance, North Carolina voters overwhelmingly approved a ban on same-sex marriage. According to exit polls, large numbers of African American voters there supported the ban, and many black ministers in North Carolina and other states continued to thunder from the pulpit against gay marriage. Obama nonetheless moved forward with plans to make his own statement on the issue the day after the North Carolina vote. He was never going to give a bold speech à la Lyndon Johnson's "We Shall Overcome" address to the nation in 1965 on civil rights. Such a speech would be "too much in-your-face," as Dan Pfeiffer put it, for voters who were still in transition.

Instead the White House called Robin Roberts, an African American coanchor of ABC News' *Good Morning America* to ask if she wanted to interview Obama the next day, May 9. In contrast to his tortured answers to the question in the past, the president appeared comfortable on the air as he said, "At a certain point, I've just concluded that for me personally, it is important for me to go ahead and affirm that I think same-sex couples should be able to get married." He stressed that it was still a matter for the states to decide but that working with staff in same-sex relationships and listening to Malia and Sasha talk naturally about their friends with same-sex parents made it difficult "to explain to your child that some people should be treated differently."

A chorus of conservatives immediately charged that Obama was playing politics. In truth, the specific timing was politically motivated, but the underlying decision was not. It wasn't that Romney and the Republicans intended to bludgeon him over it; independent voters and pro–gay marriage donors like former RNC finance chairman Lewis Eisenberg and hedge fund managers Paul Singer and Daniel S. Loeb wouldn't allow them to do so. But the decision on balance was still more likely to hurt Obama, especially among black and Latino voters, where even a marginal drop-off in support could prove devastating. And evangelicals who supported Obama in 2008 might vote for Romney over it.

The objections to gay marriage turned out to be more muted than expected, in part because the ranks of the leadership of the religious right had thinned. Jerry Falwell was dead, Pat Robertson and James Dobson passé, and Franklin Graham, the son of Billy Graham, had dipped into birther politics and challenged Obama's Christianity, thereby discrediting himself as a credible spokesman in mainstream media. Even as Ralph Reed's Faith and Freedom Coalition prepared literature attacking the president on the issue, Chicago stepped up its outreach to religious voters in North Carolina, Virginia, and Ohio, confident it could cut into Romney's lead among them.

After all the political calculations, the fact remained that Obama had done something historic. Staffers in Chicago certainly thought so. Many found themselves watching the interview with tears in their eyes. In a *Newsweek* cover story entitled "The First Gay President," Andrew Sullivan confessed to the same: "I was utterly unprepared for how psychologically transformative the moment would be. To have the president of the United States affirm my humanity—and the humanity of all gay Americans—was, unexpectedly, a watershed. He shifted the mainstream in one interview."

But it was not a shift that either campaign wanted to dwell on. Chicago realized that any undecided gay or straight independents knew about the decision and didn't have to be reminded of it, while those Democrats who objected shouldn't be reminded either. And Boston understood that, as Steve Schmidt, McCain's 2008 campaign manager, put it, the GOP was "on the wrong side of history" on this one. Almost everyone in the country had a friend or family member who was gay, which meant that the movement for marriage equality proceeded at a pace much faster than the struggle for civil rights.

Amid all the commentary about the decision, few noticed the concrete political benefits for the president in solidifying his base and energizing his fundraising. Good values—of dignity, respect, humanity—would prove to be good politics too.

———

WITH GAY-BASHING OUT of bounds, Republicans settled for attacking Obama as excessively political. "Team Obama has turned the candidate of hope and change into a ferociously political animal," Alex Castellanos wrote in May, confident that Romney would win. Castellanos cited Obama's being caught on an open microphone telling outgoing Russian Prime Minister Dmitry Medvedev, "After my election I [will] have more flexibility." He quoted a poll showing that 67 percent thought Obama's decision on gay marriage was made "for political reasons," while only 24 percent said he did it because "he thinks it's right." Castellanos argued that these were ominous findings for Chicago and called into question the president's entire strategy. The numbers suggested that Obama had been brought to earth as just another politician and was on track to squander his greatest asset, the transcending of red state–blue state distinctions that had launched him as a national figure at the 2004 Democratic National Convention.

Even if the advice hadn't come from Republican strategists with suspect motives, Chicago had no intention of letting up on its barrage of anti-Romney ads and videos or otherwise changing its approach. Obama believed that one of the secrets of his success in 2008 was sticking with the strategy even when the campaign ran into choppy waters. Retooling was for other campaigns. Theirs was about consistency and execution of the master plan. Besides, throwing punches was popular with the Democratic base and made him look tough. Obama was the rare candidate unhurt by going negative.

The single most important strategic decision of the campaign was to spend heavily in the middle of 2012 instead of in the fall. Here Chicago took a leaf from the Bush family playbook. In 1988 Vice President George H. W. Bush defined Democratic nominee Michael Dukakis over the summer. In 2004 his son, the incumbent, did the same to John Kerry. Labor Day, the traditional kickoff of the fall campaign, was now too late for much persuasion. Axelrod believed that by September and October voters had made up their minds and tuned out the barrage of ads. This turned out to be right. Exit polls would later indicate that

70 percent of 2012 voters had decided by Labor Day, and Obama won that group 53–46. That meant that to win, Romney would have had to carry the other 30 percent by 58–41, a nearly impossible feat.

Jim Messina and the Chicago contingent came to the Roosevelt Room in May for a final sign-off on spending more than $100 million defining Romney in the summer rather than hoarding the money for the fall. The meeting, later depicted as high drama, was in fact anticlimactic. Obama wanted to know all the risks, how strapped the campaign would be in October if fundraising didn't pick up. But for all the expressions of concern about "uncharted waters," neither he nor anyone else questioned the basic strategy. The poker-playing president wasn't pushing new chips to the center of the table, just leaving his stack where it was.

———

A MYTH DEVELOPED later in the season that Chicago was bent on depicting Romney as a flip-flopper until talked out of it by Bill Clinton, who favored making Romney out to be a "severe conservative." In truth, Clinton talked them out of nothing. The original flip-flopper line—"Governor Romney has no core," as Plouffe said on *Meet the Press* on October 30—was meant to sow dissension in the GOP primaries. It was never intended by Chicago to be the brickbat that clocked Romney in the fall.

The personal relationship between the two presidents had improved, but it still wasn't good. When they played golf the previous September at Andrews Air Force Base, they didn't talk much. Clinton, a more experienced golfer, was having what he later called a "really horrible" round. He had expected to win and was annoyed that Obama was beating him by a few strokes. As president, Obama decided on the rules and they didn't include mulligans, a Clinton specialty. Afterward the Andrews clubhouse was booked for a wedding, which spared the two presidents from having to chat more.

Even Clinton aides thought the media narrative that Obama must consult the Clinton oracle to win was false. Hillary Clinton had been up in the polls by more than 30 points against Obama in 2008 and lost. Why should the president defer to her husband about politics? Bill Clinton was rusty politically, his instincts dulled not just by age but by his continued unwillingness to learn how to use a computer. (George H. W. Bush, by contrast, took to it in the 1990s.) Clinton liked to say that the big innovation of his 1992 campaign was the blast fax. Social networking was an abstraction to him, though he was a gifted synthesizer of the digital trends changing the world. His aides feared what would happen should he ever open an email account; God knows what trouble he could get himself into, they thought. But operating politically in 2012 entirely offline was like flying blind.

The result was that sometimes Clinton was out of step with the Obama message, like saying that Romney's business career was "sterling" and that perhaps the tax cuts for the wealthy should be extended. He was upset with himself for these slips from the Democratic script, and when he came to Chicago in June for a conference sponsored by the Clinton Global Initiative, he met with Axelrod and Messina and was contrite.

Clinton liked to point out that in the fifty-one years since President Kennedy took the oath of office, Republicans have had twenty-eight years in the White House; Democrats have had twenty-three. In the same half-century, the economy has produced 66 million private sector jobs—42 million of them under the Democrats, 24 million under the Republicans. "No one states these facts," he told audiences.

By this time the Obama campaign had long since decided that, for all his shortcomings, Clinton was not merely an asset but a central player and must be given his own night at the Democratic National Convention. Although his frequent advice was only rarely taken, his stature as President Prosperity in the 1990s was essential. In July Obama called Clinton to ask him to give the nominating speech for him in Charlotte and Clinton accepted.

CHICAGO'S STRATEGY HAD three stages: First, lay down a positive message in the battleground states in early 2012. Second, hit Romney hard on Bain in the spring and summer so that he could no longer run as an economic oracle. Third, lay out a vision for the future at the Convention in September that would take them into the fall on an uplifting note.

The rationale for the Bain bashing was obvious. His experience running Bain was what Axelrod described as Romney's "calling card" for being a jobs-creating president, and the card didn't look good on inspection. Poll respondents were presented with a straightforward description of the way Bain took over companies and asked if these were the normal things businesses have to do to keep afloat or simply wrong. The research came back strongly negative on the company. David Simas said the whole point of the anti-Bain campaign was to say, "Just because Romney's successful doesn't mean it's going to help you." Week after week he waited for three messages from the other side: positive spots on Bain, the Massachusetts record, and Romney as a human being. They never came.

Axelrod thought Stuart Stevens's key strategic mistake was centering the whole campaign on Romney "not being Barack Obama." They "spent not one dime fleshing out Mitt Romney—a huge mistake." Candidates can't win if they are no more than "cardboard cut-outs," Axelrod thought. Voters are looking for three-dimensional characters, and it was naïve to think otherwise.

———

IN JUNE OBAMA laid out his argument for reelection in a speech at a community college in Cleveland. The White House had placed a lot of importance on the speech and was upset when even political analysts who usually supported the president found it too long and unmemorable. Benenson fretted that they needed to land a few more blows before the Convention.

At least the people inside the White House were beginning to reach out more. Jon Carson was getting high marks for coordinating well with Democratic constituency groups at the Tuesday "Big Table" meetings. The day after the Cleveland speech, David Plouffe, Jon Favreau, and Dan Pfeiffer and his deputy, Jen Palmieri, hosted a group of a dozen Democratic Party insiders who had a lot of contacts in the press and often appeared as surrogates on TV. Most of the insiders entered the meeting skeptical. "I know these White House guys. They don't listen well. They never have," said one. But he and the other surrogates felt a change at the meeting, a sense that these insular White House aides were genuinely extending themselves. Plouffe told the group that they should read the Cleveland speech carefully because it was the campaign narrative going forward.

This sounded fine, but Obama's whole approach to winning the election still felt fuzzy. Jim Manley, a former top aide to Harry Reid, attended the meeting. He was asked immediately afterward if he knew yet what the president's message was. Manley paused to think for several seconds before saying, "Nope."

———

SOME OF CHICAGO'S logic came from corporate marketing. Benenson argued that when you're a leader in a category, like Apple or Walmart, you must establish a cost for switching to another brand. It could be higher prices, less convenience, worse service. Obama needed to do the same with Romney. That's where negative campaigning came in: to make the voters feel they would pay a price for abandoning the president in favor of someone they didn't know much about. This wasn't all negative. BMW, for instance, might imply that a Mercedes was also comfortable but that you just didn't feel the road the way you did in a BMW. It was all about tapping into the emotional "switching costs."

Chicago couldn't understand why Boston hadn't done its "permission ads" (giving voters permission to switch) at the beginning of the year. By the time they launched spots with disappointed Obama supporters reluctantly moving to Romney in late summer, Benenson's response was "You're too late, dude." Only 2 or 3 percent were truly undecided and less than 10 percent even leaners.

Larry Grisolano explained that the core economic question was how Americans can maintain a middle-class standard of living. The election was about protecting what had been gained over many decades. The decline had begun not three years earlier, but twenty. Wages had been stagnant for years. Every issue fell under this rubric: training, health care, education, R&D, technology, and energy independence. The goal for the campaign and for a second term was to stress durable growth. Hence the slogan, "An economy built to last."

The message lasted much longer than the slogan used to encapsulate it. Obama had used "Built to Last" occasionally in the weeks following the State of the Union, but he didn't like it any more than any of the other slogans cooked up over the years, and it disappeared. Other sloganeering failures would follow. One week, the president began repeating a talking point concocted in the White House about Congress's "to-do list." The list contained several rejected jobs proposals and other proposed legislation that no one, even inside the campaign, could remember off the top of their head. One senior adviser who knew nothing about the message before it was announced was appalled: "It sounds like something my wife would ask me to do on Saturday morning."

The bumper-sticker slogan (as distinct from message) that Chicago finally settled on had originated from an unlikely source, Mark Penn, the Hillary Clinton strategist who had said in 2008 that Obama was not "fundamentally American." Penn and Axelrod despised each other, and Penn's relationship with his old partner Benenson wasn't much better. So it was no small irony that the Obama campaign's eventual slogan, "Forward," was almost identical to the "Forward, Not Back" message that Penn fashioned in 2005 to help British Prime Minister Tony Blair win a third term. There are only so many slogans available to an incumbent, none of them particularly inspiring.

The message mavens did better on framing the debate. Obama

began to repeat the line that Romney believes you build an economy "from the top down," while we believe you create prosperity "from the middle out." The keys to victory, Chicago felt, lay in the answers to three questions: Who do you trust? Who's on your side? Who will do better on the economy? They figured the candidate who won two out of three would win the presidency.

Traditional focus groups and an online resource launched by David Simas called "The Community" (in which small groups of voters would offer feedback about breaking events or new ads) yielded consistent results. Undecided voters said of the president, "I like Obama, but I'm disappointed things haven't turned around yet." They said of Romney, "He knows a lot about the economy, but I'm not sure I trust him."

Chicago saw no evidence that a single jobs report moved the numbers even slightly. Voters' views on the economy were conditioned more by personal things: whether their favorite restaurants were crowded, the foreclosed house down the street sold, their spouse got a job. Even when the jobs report was encouraging, focus group participants were downcast if anyone they knew was hurting.

The May polls were all over the lot but showed a tightening race, and some of the internals (the specific breakdowns) were troubling for Obama. Independents, assumed to be fiscally conservative but socially more liberal, didn't react well to the gay marriage announcement. Another bad omen came in the sleepy North Carolina Democratic presidential primary, where 20 percent expressed "no preference" for president. Worse, May was the month when it became clear that the administration's housing policy simply wouldn't be able to work in time for the election. A report by the inspector general for TARP revealed that the Hardest Hit Fund, a Treasury Department program created in 2010 to help homeowners in communities with high unemployment and a steep decline in house prices, had failed spectacularly. A program meant to reach three to four million had helped only about thirty thousand homeowners.

Obama's record, for better and worse, was beginning to catch up to him. Now the Supreme Court was poised to determine the fate of the president's signature achievement. If Obamacare went down, the message would be clear: This presidency wasn't built to last.

19

Obamacare's Close Shave

In late 1934 Franklin Roosevelt decided to move forward on what would become his greatest domestic achievement: Social Security. He assigned his secretary of labor, Frances Perkins, the first woman ever to serve in the Cabinet, to lead the way on designing the program. But Perkins was worried. The Supreme Court was moving toward a narrow interpretation of the Commerce Clause of the U.S. Constitution that would invalidate many of the great achievements of the New Deal. Soon that would include the National Recovery Act, the capstone of FDR's famous First Hundred Days in 1933.

Perkins went to a party and bumped into Justice Harlan Fiske Stone. When she expressed concern about whether an old-age and survivors insurance program (later called Social Security) would pass constitutional muster, Stone, a Republican appointee to the Court and future chief justice, replied, "The taxing power of the federal government, my dear; the taxing power is sufficient for everything you want and need."

―――――

FROM THE EARLY DAYS of 2009, Obama's enemies fastened on his health care reform as the symbol of everything they detested about his presidency. After Republicans, still in the minority, failed to block passage of the Affordable Care Act, they continued their assault on the new law by other means.

At first, the attacks seemed to come from the fringe. When Obama signed the bill in March 2010, almost no one took the legal challenges to the new law seriously. The notion that penalties for not buying health insurance wouldn't pass constitutional muster seemed to be the concoctions of a Georgetown law professor, Randy Barnett, and the attorney general of Virginia, Ken Cuccinelli, without much legal firepower behind them. The consensus in the legal profession was that health insurance was obviously an interstate business and thus its regulation was constitutional under the Commerce Clause.

But a few conservative appellate judges disagreed, and they began ruling against the individual mandate in Obamacare, even as other courts upheld it. The idea that requiring Americans to buy a product was unprecedented and thus unconstitutional began to gather strength in the court of public opinion and was accepted for review by the Supreme Court. By the time oral arguments before the justices began on March 25, 2012. supporters of the law were nervous.

Obama's legal team had long known that it could have trouble convincing the Supreme Court of its Commerce Clause argument. The congressional drafters of the bill, working with the White House, had anticipated that the mandate might need backing as a tax and quietly put language into the statute defining it as such. But because every politician and talking head in Washington was too busy posturing on the bill to actually read it (and who can read 2,700 pages, anyway?), almost no one noticed.

In April 2010, as the new law faced its first legal challenges, Donald Verrilli Jr., then in the White House Counsel's Office, wrote a memo to the president warning him that he might be criticized for telling George Stephanopoulos on ABC News days earlier that the Affordable Care Act included no taxes. The legal team needed his approval for what it called "a powerful hedge"—a backup plan arguing that the individual mandate was in fact a tax and therefore constitutional. Despite concerns expressed by political advisers, Obama agreed to take the heat for flip-flopping on the tax question if it came to that. In the meantime, he was deeply involved in the risky legal strategy on the case, which called for not appealing to the Eleventh Circuit Court of Appeals in favor of going more directly to the Supreme Court. The president wanted the issue resolved before the 2012 election in order to give the Department of Health and Human Services the clarity it needed to move forward with implementing the new law.

By March of 2012, Verrilli was solicitor general, arguing the case of a lifetime before the Supreme Court. The early reviews were harsh. When Verrilli choked briefly after a drink of water, many Democrats took it as a metaphor for his performance. It wasn't entirely his fault, of course. He was cut off 180 times by the justices and allowed to speak for ten seconds or less nearly half of the time. But Verrilli was especially weak in responding to Justice Antonin Scalia's frivolous argument (later endorsed by Chief Justice John Roberts in his opinion) that there was no difference between forcing people to buy health insurance and forcing them to buy broccoli. Why couldn't Verrilli have simply said that, unlike the uninsured free riders in health care who get expensive treatment in emergency rooms paid for by taxpayers, those who refuse to buy broccoli hurt no one else? When Justice Samuel Alito, hardly sympathetic to the government's position, asked him for a statement of his principle on the Commerce Clause, Verrilli should have been ready with a cogent answer he had honed for months. Instead he offered up opaque and almost incomprehensible legalistic mush, the product of overlawyering by the bureaucracy.

The president called White House Counsel Kathryn Ruemmler from *Air Force One* after the first day to ask for transcripts of the oral arguments. While Ruemmler told him that Verrilli was making a persuasive case, most Court observers didn't agree. Larry Tribe, the influential Harvard law professor who had had both Roberts and Obama in his classroom, noticed that during the first of two days of oral argument, Roberts briefly signaled that he was open to the idea of tinkering with federal taxing power. It was obvious from the start that the Commerce Clause argument was unconvincing to Justice Anthony Kennedy (the swing vote) and thus to the Court, but Tribe believed Verrilli hadn't taken the cue to adjust his case and start talking taxes. Verrilli thought the professor and others who made that point weren't paying close enough attention; he had spent the whole first day laying the groundwork for his backup plan, which relied on a complex legal argument that for the purposes of the statute the individual mandate was not a tax, but for the purposes of the Constitution it was.* (The first day's arguments on the Anti-Injunction Act, mostly involved implementation of the law by the states.) While Verrilli didn't get to the constitutional tax argument until forty-five minutes into his hour-long presentation on day two, he did eventually make it, when he could get a word in edgewise.

Obama called Verrilli to buck him up both before and after oral arguments, and to congratulate him after the decision was announced. The onetime constitutional law professor was knowledgeable about the case but by this point mostly kept his hands off it, even though his signature achievement in office was riding on the results. The collapse of the Commerce Clause argument left him in just the political pickle Verrilli had predicted in 2010. Obama had repeatedly said that his health care reform included no new taxes. When the bill was being debated in Congress, supporters defined the consequences of not buying health insurance as "penalties," not "taxes," for the obvious reason that the lat-

---

* The first day's arguments on the Anti-Injunction Act, mostly involved implementation of the law by the states.

ter were more unpopular. Now he was exposed as talking out of both sides of his mouth. It was no wonder the solicitor general downplayed the tax argument before the justices.

Verrilli would be Obama's human shield. Later, it looked to the world as if the law—and arguably the Obama presidency—were saved because Chief Justice Roberts made an argument that should have been offered more forthrightly by the government's lawyers. But Larry Tribe was mistaken. Don Verrilli wasn't missing anything; he was simply being strategic in his approach, though hardly eloquent. And as all lawyers with Supreme Court experience know, the briefs are far more influential with the justices than the oral arguments anyway.

————

IN THE THREE months between oral arguments and the issuance of the opinion, no one covering the Supreme Court had any good intelligence on what would happen. Most suspected the individual mandate would be invalidated, which would be like pulling a thread on the whole fabric of the law. The result would be the ruin of Obama's legacy even if pieces of it survived.

Two days before the decision was announced, the president was serenely confident. "Kathy [Ruemmler] and I are the only ones around here who think we're gonna win this thing," he said. Obama, certain the law was constitutional, thought it would be too activist, provocative, and divisive for the chief justice to write a majority opinion striking down eighty years of traditional deference to Congress on major social legislation. The institutional strength and reputation of the Supreme Court, he said, would carry the day.

The president was watching TV near the Oval Office on June 28 when CNN reported erroneously that the individual mandate had been ruled unconstitutional. He was staring with a furrowed brow at the screen, trying to absorb the early reports, when Ruemmler rushed in with thumbs up and a big smile on her face. Obama and Biden quietly celebrated the survival of what Biden, on the day the bill was signed in early 2010, famously called "a big fucking deal" over an open microphone.

Like CNN, Fox News blew the story, airing a banner reading, "Supreme Court Find Health Care Mandate Unconstitutional." Within minutes, the network caught up to the Court's upholding the law and assumed a more sober tone. Karl Rove's on-air affect was funereal, while anchor Megyn Kelly turned steely, vowing, "The Supreme Court just woke up a sleeping giant."

It took only moments for Obama Derangement Syndrome to become

Roberts Derangement Syndrome, as conservative bloggers who had revered the chief justice turned on him with a vengeance, some even suggesting that he suffered from epilepsy and brain damage. (Roberts did suffer a nonepileptic seizure in 2007, which might have sensitized him to the plight of those with preexisting conditions.) On July 1, Jan Crawford, a CBS News reporter with good contacts among conservatives, reported that two sources "with specific knowledge of the deliberations" said that Roberts had changed his mind in May on the constitutionality of the statute under the taxing power. If true, such a switch was not uncommon inside the Court, even on important cases. The difference this time was that the deliberations leaked, which was unprecedented in modern memory. It was a sign of the times when even the most venerable traditions were discarded for ideological purposes.

Some politicians lost control. In a closed-door meeting of Republicans in the House, Representative Mike Pence, soon to be governor of Indiana, compared the Court's decision to the September 11 terrorist attacks. (He later apologized.) Senator Rand Paul issued a statement saying, "Just because a couple people on the Supreme Court declare something to be 'constitutional' does not make it so," and Glenn Beck starting hawking T-shirts depicting Roberts as a coward.

"I am literally sick over what happened," Rush Limbaugh said. "A giant total fraud was perpetrated on this country. The Supreme Court as an institution is forever tarnished." With his gift for inapt analogy, Limbaugh then said of the individual mandate: "It really is akin to going into a 7-Eleven, and saying to the clerk, 'No, I really don't want to buy any gum.' And the clerk says, 'Well, okay, tax on that is $2.35.'" Neal Boortz, one of the top right-wing radio talk show hosts, summarized the conservative case: "I am so sick to death of calling the play-by-play of the destruction of this great country by power-hungry Democrats and the moocher class."

The jabs at Democrats wouldn't impress independents, who thought all politicians were "power-hungry." But the concept of a "moocher class," however cruel to working people just trying to get some health care coverage, had already struck home with many voters, even if they hadn't heard the term. They didn't pay much attention to politics and didn't know many details of Obamacare, but a majority opposed it because they had a vague sense that something would be taken from them and given to people who weren't as deserving. It would not be the last time the "makers versus takers" argument surfaced in the politics of 2012.

———

FOR ALL THE criticism, the landmark decision was a huge relief to the president. His signature achievement would not be invalidated and thus deemed somehow un-American. The political win was significant. He had come to office promising to "change the trajectory of politics" after nearly three decades of stagnation for the middle class. Part of that change was doing something about the 15 percent of the country—nearly 50 million people—who lacked health insurance and thereby increased the burden on everyone else when they needed treatment. In 2009 Obama was forced by the opposition to choose between health care and his vision of a postpartisan and more cooperative political culture. He chose health care, and the backlash against it soon powered the Tea Party and other elements on the right enraged by what they saw as a power grab by the federal government. Now he had won some measure of vindication.

Romney's response to the decision was to charge that Obama had violated his pledge not to raise taxes on the middle class. With the combination of the tax cuts in the stimulus and the payroll tax holiday, Obama had actually cut taxes on the average American family by about $3,600. The Affordable Care Act was a tax hike on the middle class only if one considered an increase in the cigarette tax to be the same. The charge that Obamacare would separate you from your doctor was untrue (at least for the present), and the notion that costs were going up and the law would add trillions to the deficit were matters of fierce debate. (The nonpartisan Congressional Budget Office didn't think it would.) Romney's charge that 20 million Americans would "lose the insurance they currently have" was grossly exaggerated, though Obama was disingenuous in replying that this would happen to no one. Some businesses planned to pay the fines instead of insuring their employees.

As Romney spoke out against Obamacare, Obama got to work polishing the "happy" speech that had been prepared that week in anticipation of a possible victory. The speech was short, clear on the advantages of the Affordable Care Act, and captured the moral importance of the bill in one sentence. Right off the top he said the Court had "reaffirmed a fundamental principle that here in America—in the wealthiest nation on earth—no illness or accident should lead to any family's financial ruin."

The president wrapped the individual mandate in a cloak of "taking responsibility" and deployed it as a sign of his strength and leadership. The mandate (though he didn't call it that) was essential to make the law work: "That's why, even though I knew it wouldn't be politically popular, and resisted the idea when I ran for this office, we ultimately included a provision [for it in the bill]."

Conservatives immediately began depicting Obama as a liar for say-ing throughout his presidency exactly what Scalia, Kennedy, Thomas, and Alito said in their dissent: that the mandate was not a tax and had not been intended as one. Even though they hated Roberts's decision, Republicans would immediately embrace the reasoning they despised to fashion a political attack.

The *Wall Street Journal* editorial page began the drumbeat that Rom-ney needed to make Obamacare a big issue in the campaign. The edi-torial page editor, Paul Gigot, went on TV to say that repeal should be a "centerpiece" of Romney's campaign because the idea was unpopular with the public and would become more so once it was conceived of as a tax. In fact this didn't happen. The issue lost its salience for Repub-licans almost immediately. It was Democrats who made use of health care reform, especially in ads to Latinos. Later, trying to explain why he lost, Romney would point to Obamacare and its "gifts" to help people stressed by the costs of health insurance. When it counted, Obama had been able to sell his health care plan after all.

In the meantime, the stakes in the 2012 election had just gone up. An Obama win would mean the bill was securely in place; a Romney win would mean repeal. When asked the conventional media ques-tion about whom this would help or hurt in November, Nancy Pelosi looked to history and to the larger purpose of devoting oneself to elec-tive office. "All of us have to take a step back and say: Why are we here?" Pelosi said. "The politics be damned. This is what we came here to do."

But the politics would not be damned in an election year. By dodg-ing a bullet on Obamacare, Obama avoided looking like a loser. The Supreme Court decision was an important psychological threshold for the Obama campaign. The road ahead would be smoother.

20

The Machine Hums

On the day after the Supreme Court ruling on Obamacare, the president flew to Colorado to inspect wildfire damage there. On the way back, he was tired but agreed to a conference call with big donors who had maxed out in 2008 but hadn't this time. He warned them that if "a couple billionaires wrote $20 million checks [for Romney] and have bought all the TV time, we will find ourselves flat-footed in September and October."

May had been a bad month. The economy created only sixty-nine thousand jobs and unemployment ticked up to 8.2 percent. A week after the jobs report came out, Obama, explaining the weak numbers as a reflection of curtailed stimulus spending on government jobs, said the private sector was "doing fine." Even as he walked back the gaffe, Chicago went wobbly under other news. The monthly fundraising totals shocked the campaign high command. Romney outraised Obama $76 million to $60 million, and that didn't include super PACs. Even accounting for the history of these things—that the front-runner consolidates lots of party money when he wraps up the nomination—the news was alarming. Going back to the first-quarter reporting period of 2007, when a rookie only two years out of the Illinois State Senate rocked the political world by outraising Hillary Clinton, Obama had never been bested in fundraising.

For a time it seemed as if Organizing for America was going bankrupt. By mid-2012 the Obama campaign had burned through about $400 million, more than McCain spent altogether in 2008. Chicago employed 786 paid campaign workers, nearly three times as many as Boston. Television advertising represented less than one-fourth of its total expenditures; the usual percentage is closer to two-thirds. Much of the rest was going toward building a huge digital machine that might not work. The campaign was spending so much more than it was taking in that Messina informed department heads they would have to cut $90 million from their planning budgets. If implemented, this would require layoffs and other painful choices over the summer. Only one department saw its budget grow in this period: Analytics. The Cave dwellers would have what they needed.

One night in June, Messina wandered all the way across the Floor to Teddy Goff's office in Digital. It was late and almost everyone else had gone home. "You do understand that if online money doesn't come in, we don't have a path to win," Messina told him. Goff found the conversation frightening. He had been having some trouble managing his staff of two hundred and, distracted by the growing demand for campaign videos and social media content, had been able to raise only a disappointing $15 million a month online. Messina was expecting Digital to hit at least $70 million a month by fall. He had already informed the president that there was no Plan B. The whole campaign strategy depended on moving $65 million from September and October and putting it into June and July to "fill in some blanks" on Romney. They must start harvesting more cash online or they wouldn't have enough money to run much of a campaign after Labor Day.

Around the same time, Dan Wagner made a presentation to senior campaign officials about the Cave's "state prioritization algorithm," which placed a monetary value on each electoral vote so that the campaign could allocate resources with unprecedented precision. Hundreds of millions of dollars in media buys, staff deployments, candidate travel, and other expenses depended on the modeling being accurate. "If you're wrong about this, we're gonna lose," Axelrod told Wagner, with his usual mixture of wry humor and seriousness. "And a lot of this will be on you."

A pair of nerds in their twenties were on the hook for reelecting the president.

THE LIBERAL BASE of the Democratic Party remained wary, if not of the president himself then of the people around him. While the Washington-based progressive groups had a voice at the secret weekly "Big Table" meetings, local activists did not. In June the White House, through Common Cause, began inviting progressive groups to Washington for issues briefings aimed at getting them energized for the campaign. The sessions didn't always go well. At a meeting in a town house across the street from the White House, aides laid out the specifics of the Affordable Care Act to a group of 130 party activists from New Jersey, many of whom had worked their hearts out for Obama in neighboring Pennsylvania in 2008. All morning tension grew. The progressive organizations felt they had been waiting forever for marching orders and fresh instructions on how to engage voters. When Jon Carson pointed the group toward a few inadequate websites for more information, an Essex County party organizer named Cary Chevat blew up. "Websites? Are you kidding me?" Since the last campaign, he and his organization had received almost nothing on the president's accomplishments, only tiresome email solicitations for money. Why had it taken until now, more than two years after passage, to even tell them what was in the health care bill? The head of a local NAACP chapter echoed the complaint—Where's the material to pass out to our people?—and then the South Jersey Democratic organizers weighed in. For a moment Obama's progressive allies were in full mutiny. Instead of being flattered to get briefings and a special White House tour, the group, like several from other states, left freshly disappointed over having been ignored for three and a half years by what they viewed as an arrogant Obama White House.

———

IN 2011 THOSE annoying fundraising emails became a big topic of discussion in Chicago. Teddy Goff and his Digital team thought the videos and fundraising appeals they sent out online had to be creative or they wouldn't stand a chance. They thought it was lame to ask supporters to retweet links. In 2012 they would learn otherwise. It turned out that predicting from your gut which messages or graphics might connect with voters was a fool's errand. Intuition gave way to test results. In direct mail, tests are slow and expensive; online, they're fast and nearly free.

So Goff and his deputy for online fundraising, Marie Ewald, conducted 240 A/B tests on their donation page. They tested everything they sent as many as eighteen times, from the salutation ("Hey" worked especially well) to the wording of fundraising appeals, the size of the donate buttons on the site, and whether an invitation to dinner at Sarah Jessica Parker's house with the president (if the entrant won a lottery for supporters who couldn't afford the $40,000 price tag) should include a reference to Parker as a mother or, in a separate test, *Vogue* editor Anna Wintour as a cohost. Some on the Email List, mostly women, got a Wintour mention in their invitation; others did not. Wintour's video invitation ended with her saying archly, "Don't be late."

For a while, yellow backgrounds generated 10 to 20 percent more email responses than white backgrounds. Who knew? The fundraising emails—more than four hundred in all—appeared hour after hour, day after day because they worked. An elaborate "More Emails Test" showed conclusively that the more fundraising emails that went out, the more money came back—simple as that. Even the $3 ask—just enough to cover the credit card processing—helped build lists and increase a sense of ownership on the part of supporters. The growth in the number of people unsubscribing because they couldn't stand the alarmist emails was much slower than the growth of cash flowing in, and Chicago knew that peeved unsubscribers would end up voting for Obama even if they thought the emails sounded like sketchy pleas from Internet con artists.

Goff concluded that ignoring the human desire not to be annoying may have been the single greatest conceptual breakthrough of the campaign. It turned out to be worth more than $100 million.

A critical moment came when Digital tested thirteen varieties of a special message from the president to the Email List, scheduled for June 26, just two days before the Supreme Court ruled on Obamacare. Among the subject lines tested were "Thankful every day," "Do this for Michelle," "Would love to meet you," and "Some scary numbers." The winner, which netted a projected $1.5 million more than several of the runners-up, was "I will be outspent." "I will be the first president in modern history to be outspent in his re-election campaign, if things continue as they have so far," the president wrote. Obama asked for $3 (more if the recipient had donated before) to fight back against more than $1 billion in ads "trashing me, you and everything we believe in."

"We can be outspent and still win. But we can't be outspent 10 to 1 and still win," Obama emailed, in a classic bit of hype. That level of Republican spending would require super PACs to spend $7 billion or $8 billion, which wasn't going to happen. Chicago feared that it would fall short of its goal of being the first billion-dollar campaign, but not as far short as it was hinting now. By once again opting out of public financing for the fall campaign, Obama was delivering the coup de grâce to a thirty-five-year tradition of campaign finance reform he claimed to champion. After Labor Day, he, like Romney, who also opted out, would have to depend on private donations, not $91.2 million in taxpayer funds. So poor-mouthing would become a campaign tactic. Messina wanted to get the president's email out before the Supreme Court decision on Obamacare because he calculated that a positive decision from the Court might return the Democratic base to the sense of complacency that had hampered fundraising all along.

Messina's worries proved unfounded. The landmark "I will be outspent" email raised $2.6 million in a single day. Two days later the Supreme Court upheld the Affordable Care Act and instead of the base assuming Obama needed no help, it was energized to dig deeper. The last seven days of the month brought in $20 million, far surpassing expectations. Goff could breathe easier now. When Sarah Palin spoke at the Republican National Convention in 2008, Chicago raised $9 million in twenty-four hours, a record at the time. That figure was topped five times in 2012, with the biggest haul exceeding $19 million in a single day after the second debate. The Obama campaign went from raising $15 million a month online in the spring to more than $150 million a month online in the fall. Messina said later that starting in late June the graph on online fundraising looked like a hockey stick.

Digital's biggest tech innovation was "Quick Donate," a mobile app that raised an extra $75 million by letting supporters give money with one click instead of filling out a form. Donors who used Quick Donate gave four times as often and three times as much as those who didn't. The mobile app led to what the campaign called "drunk donating," where Obama supporters agitated by polls showing Romney gains impulsively kicked in before they thought better of it.

Quick Donate was supposed to be a Tech project, but it was engineered by the less experienced code writers inside Digital. This was another example of why tensions between Tech and the other departments hadn't eased much. Tech had some terrific people but was so focused on trying—and often failing—to build cool new apps that it didn't give Digital, Field, Finance, and Comm the workaday tools they wanted.

In June Tech finally came through with Dashboard, which was praised by many field organizers for helping put all of their local efforts at their fingertips. For many Obama volunteers, Dashboard became almost a new social network. It helped tens of thousands tap into the long-delayed Call Tool, which allowed volunteers to join Nurses for Obama, Veterans for Obama, Seniors for Obama, and other subgroups. Jeremy Bird and Mitch Stewart put Dashboard in the category of Better Late Than Never. By the end of the campaign, the gears of the Chicago machine seemed to mesh. "Even in our most fierce head-butting, we'd all finally get up and say, 'We're here for the same reason, right? To re-elect the president,'" Harper Reed said later. "Then we'd all go out and get a drink."

When Dashboard went live, Messina, determined to stay in touch with supporters, sent out a questionnaire to the now 16 million names on the Obama Email List. For the Obama field and fundraising operations, the survey was important in making the machine hum for the rest of the campaign. Every answer was a potential mine of data to make the campaign more efficient. Supporters were asked to rate their level of enthusiasm (to prioritize recruitment of volunteers); disclose whether they planned to donate (to determine who should get the hard sell); guess how close the election would be (those saying it wouldn't be close would get a special message arguing against complacency); and explain "what worries you most about the possibility of Mitt Romney being the next president" (the answers could help tailor attack ads).

Of course, all the fancy technology meant nothing without enthusiasm on the ground. The basic volunteer work of knocking on doors, calling, texting, and emailing involved a certain irreducible level of drudgery that could only endure if fueled by some passion.

———

IN EARLY SUMMER Adam Fetcher, a former spokesman at the Interior Department, was offered a job in Communications in Chicago. He almost didn't take it. The word in Washington was that Chicago was dysfunctional, with messaging being run from the White House, and that his new boss, Stephanie Cutter, was impossibly overbearing. Upon arriving on the Floor, Fetcher found none of this to be true. He watched in awe as Cutter sliced up Romney every day and concluded that the Ninja was one of the party's best assets. Chicago stayed on the offensive through the spring and summer and stomped Boston in the 24/7 media wars. Comm had a TV camera and chair installed in the headquarters in April, the better for Cutter, Messina, Axelrod, and others to beam message. It took Boston until September to do the same.

Chicago had a lot to communicate, most of it negative. In late June the *Washington Post* published a story by Tom Hamburger outlining how Bain had invested heavily in companies shipping jobs overseas, becoming "pioneers of outsourcing." It was something the Obama campaign had been holding in reserve, worried that the story would ripen too far in advance of the election. For months Axelrod had known from "oppo" (opposition) research that not only had Bain engaged in outsourcing, but the company sponsored workshops to help companies learn how to outsource. Chicago learned that when Romney was governor, Massachusetts even outsourced the phone bank for the state's unemployment office. The question now was how well Chicago could exploit all the oppo.

Early July brought signs that the Obama Communications team was clicking. After *Vanity Fair* and the AP ran stories raising questions about Romney's holdings in Swiss bank accounts and funds in the Cayman Islands, all the campaign surrogates seemed to finally get the memo. Democrats of all stripes (including some not terribly fond of Obama) argued on MSNBC, CNN, and even occasionally on Fox that the only reason for a Swiss bank account was to avoid taxes or show preference for a foreign currency, and that George Romney had released twelve years of tax returns, not one. This reflected message discipline usually seen exclusively among Republicans.

With so much juicy material to work with, Chicago's media consultants got creative. When Obama sang Al Green's "Let's Stay Together" to Michelle at the Apollo Theater in Harlem, it had looked and sounded cool; when Romney sang "America the Beautiful" to audiences in the primaries, it had looked and sounded uncool. Could the coolness contrast be linked to Romney's vulnerability on Bain and outsourcing? That thinking led to "Firms," the toughest and best Obama commercial of the campaign. John Del Cecato, an ad maker with Axelrod's old firm, cut a spot with Romney's off-key rendition of the patriotic song illustrated by text about his offshore accounts and outsourcing of jobs and pictures of Mexico, Switzerland, and the Caymans.

At first the president said "Firms" was too harsh. It went back to focus groups, which again loved it. Obama was still worried about the ad, but when Plouffe and Axelrod pushed hard, he relented. The spot had no sound except Romney singing, the Swiss flag flapping in the wind, and the soft Caribbean waves. It broke through.

———

BY JUNE, PEGGY NOONAN, a conservative pundit who normally respected good rhetoric from any source, had given up on Obama as an orator. "Do you remember any phrase or sentence the president has said in a speech or statement the past 3½ years? One? Anything, in all that talking, that entered your head and stayed there? You do not. He is interesting, his words are not." Then she offered a brutal summary of Obama's themes over the previous six months:

> It's not so bad—this indicator is up, and that one.
> OK, it's bad, but it could have been worse—my actions kept us from tanking.
> It's bad, but it's Bush's fault.
> It's bad, but it's the congressional Republicans' fault.
> I have made it less bad, and I need more time to make it even less badder.
> Rich people have fancy cars and car elevators, I stand for jalopies and street parking.

She concluded, "None of it has worked. What does it say of a crisis presidency at a dramatic moment that a president can't make the case for his own re-election, can't find his own meaning?"

But maybe the words the president used on the stump weren't so important in 2012. At the time Noonan wrote the column, Obama was all but sewing up the election.

———

FOR A DECADE, one of the silly frames put on the election was a simple question: Which candidate would you rather have a beer with? The answer was Bush over Gore in 2000, Bush over Kerry in 2004, and Obama and McCain both beer-worthy in 2008. This time Chicago was determined to win the beerfest, so Alyssa Mastromonaco, a deputy White House chief of staff who had determined Obama's schedule since 2007, made sure that the president visited a bar at least once a week on the campaign trail to hoist one. The White House even arranged for a recipe for homemade brew to be released. Romney, a Mormon, didn't drink and thus couldn't compete in this arena, a detail that did not escape Chicago's attention. In the end, Romney would win the white male beer-drinker vote anyway, but Chicago was determined to hold down his totals.

This was especially critical in Ohio, which had more blue-collar workers and fewer Latinos than other battleground states. But a combination of the auto issue and a fired-up African American community kept the polls there remarkably stable. The same was true in Nevada, where the registration efforts of OFA and the unions had dramatically widened the Democrats' advantage in party identification (and where Romney's line that housing prices should be allowed to hit "rock bottom" hurt him badly). Field's third anchor was Iowa. A core of Obama organizers who started there in 2007 had never left. Organization of early voting was well in hand by the end of July.

OFA considered early voting especially important because it gave the campaign the chance to win what were called "low-propensity" or "sporadic" voters, registered voters who didn't make a habit of showing up at the polls. These were the 50 million, more than one-third of the electorate, who mostly went for Obama in 2008 and stayed home in 2010. The Republicans' base of older, white voters went to the polls more reliably. Bringing sporadic voters into the fold well before Election Day was essential.

Finding them was the challenge. Analytics and Field concluded that it wasn't the amount of information on each voter that mattered, but the total number of voters in battleground states about which *something* important could be noted. Vertica and Votebuilder ended up providing that and working just fine. By summer canvassers had sheets with a little notation next to the names of millions of battleground state voters that read something like this: "Voted in '08, not '10. Says she's concerned about environment." This indicated the woman was a "sporadic"—she hadn't voted in 2010—which meant that the Romney campaign and a pollster like Gallup might not score her as a likely voter. But because a door-knocker noted her interest in the environment, she became a prime target for persuasion. If she decided for Obama and needed a babysitter or lift to the polls to vote early, she got one. Banking sporadic voters early—nailing down the 2008 Obama voters who stayed home in 2010—was central to the game plan.

One of the best new tools for Field was dubbed "Airwolf," in homage to the 1980s TV series about daring missions. After volunteers entered voter information into the system and the Cave updated support scores, Airwolf would send voters a personalized email or letter under the name of a local Obama organizer, reminding these supporters to turn in their ballot application, sign up to volunteer, make sure everyone in the household voted, or whatever other message applied. The result allowed Chicago to assist field organizers from hundreds of miles away. Airwolf created the illusion of political intimacy. "I know you from your emails!" a voter would exclaim to an Obama field organizer who had never written to or even heard of the voter before. The Obama staffer would then nod sagely and pretend they knew each other, a small taste of the life of a politician.

By the middle of the summer, Field was firing on all cylinders. Mitch Stewart felt that in 2008, OFA's young organizers had come in and pushed the locals around. Then in 2010 the Obama people on the ground got punched in the face. It matured them. Now the twenty-four-year-old organizers of 2008 were twenty-eight and less arrogant. They were more respectful and more willing to empower the people on the ground. Jeremy Bird's original organizing mentor, Marshall Ganz of Harvard, said that organizers who lacked the passion they felt in 2008 had to replace with their heads what was missing from their hearts. Ganz didn't account for all the volunteers whose hearts still belonged to Obama.

Everyone had their nervous moments. For Stewart it was in June, when Wisconsin, a central section of the Obama firewall, started to look shaky. OFA's normal advantage on the ground was challenged there by Governor Scott Walker, who had built a strong field organization to fight off a recall effort. But it turned out that a large number of Wisconsin voters who opposed recalling Walker supported Obama.

Field had a small target for persuasion. About 30 percent of the electorate could be deemed independent swing voters, but this was misleading because about three-quarters of these voters leaned strongly to one party, usually the Republicans. The GOP's brand had been so tarnished that millions of longtime Republicans were now calling themselves independents or Tea Party members, a fact that would confuse pollsters and reporters for the rest of the season. Only about 7 percent of voters nationally were up for grabs, with many fewer undecideds in the battleground states that were getting all the attention. The upshot was that around a million voters in a handful of states—much less than 1 percent of the electorate—were truly persuadable. That's why the country seemed heading toward what the political scientists called a mobilization election rather than a persuasion election.

Field worried most about young voters. Many had drifted into other pursuits since 2008. So the campaign made a special effort to find the younger brothers and sisters of the old core. The last time, the campaign had one or two full-time organizers at Ohio State University; now they had nine or ten, plus scores of volunteers, scavenging around the clock for votes at the huge Columbus campus.

———

NARWHAL FAILED—"a huge disaster," as one senior staffer put it. A unified data platform, instant access to highly detailed information (beyond support scores) on millions of American voters, would have to wait. It was not yet possible to, say, link a veteran supporting Obama in Ohio to a persuadable veteran from his same army unit in Virginia. Harper Reed's insistence that Narwhal was a success depended on defining it more narrowly as a "data store" for all of the campaign's applications. In truth, Narwhal was always more of a concept than a product. By 2016, maybe even by the 2014 midterms, Democratic geeks might be closer to catching the great toothed whale.

Facebook-targeted sharing, by contrast, was a monster success, especially with the youth vote. OFA started from strength: One way or another, Obama connected to 98 percent of Facebook users in the United States, which exceeded the total number of American voters. In an era in which half of eighteen- to twenty-five-year-olds were unreachable by phone, Facebook was essential for a candidate like Obama. Here the Cave, working with Digital, came through in a big way. They matched Facebook friends against their modeling to determine who was a registration target, persuasion target, or turnout target. By the end of the campaign 600,000 Obama supporters had each used Facebook to contact around half a dozen specific friends identified by Chicago: 3.5 million potential Obama voters in battleground states. Nearly one-third of them, one million people, took some action in response, such as registering. This was a staggering response rate and the debut of a digital persuasion and get-out-the-vote tool that would inevitably be adopted by every campaign at every level. As Messina had predicted, friend-to-friend was the highest form of voter contact, though it was hardly perfect. A Romney staffer, Matt Lira, was encouraged through targeted sharing to contact his Facebook friend, House Minority Leader Eric Cantor, and urge him to vote for Obama.

All year executives at Facebook bent over backward to show no favoritism to Obama. Even so, Boston conceded that the social media explosion helped the president. On Election Day 2008 Obama had 118,000 followers on Twitter (which was then only six months old) and 2.4 million likes on his Facebook page. By Election Day 2012 he had 24 million Twitter followers—more than ten times Romney's following—and 34 million Facebook likes, which was more than three times Romney's. Ann Romney also came late to social media and ended up with only about a tenth as many Twitter followers as Michelle Obama.

Social networking was helpful, but the key to victory was on the ground. On the last weekend of July, Chicago took its new machine out for a test drive. In what was billed as the "It Takes One" weekend (where volunteers were urged to take at least one other person along with them), volunteers from 3,518 different communities participated in more than 4,700 events. This was a show of force that Boston couldn't possibly match. Beyond the intense activity in places like Ohio, Florida, and Virginia, neighborhood teams in California, New York, Illinois, and other noncontested states were given millions of names to call in important battleground areas.

This was just the first of what Chicago called "Dry Runs," elaborate team-building and training sessions involving ten thousand neighborhood team leaders in ten states. These were exactly the marching orders the New Jersey volunteers despaired of ever receiving when they had met with Jon Carson at the White House in June. The training involved get-out-the-vote instructions, message materials, detailed advice from lawyers on voter protection in case of Election Day problems, and even role-playing to enhance voter contact. In meeting rooms and outdoor amphitheaters across battleground states, a paid staffer would jump up onstage and play a disappointed Obama supporter from 2008. Another would show the crowd how to talk to that voter convincingly about health care, the economy, and other issues. The state directors would train the county directors, who would train the field organizers, who would train the neighborhood team leaders. The NTLs, destined to become the building blocks of all Democratic field efforts in the future, would then go home and train their volunteers. By Election Day

Obama would have 900,000 committed volunteers and more than two million who had completed at least one three-hour shift helping to re-elect the president. The overall effect would be the largest political mobilization in American history.

ONE OF THE biggest differences in the competing strategies was that Obama, as Clinton had in 1996, front-loaded his ads five and six months before the election, while Romney unloaded most of his after Labor Day. Eventually even Republicans agreed that the Obama strategy was smarter, and not just because voters get sick of so many ads and tune them out in October. After the election, Alex Gage's "Dialogue Monitor" found that the period from early July until the selection of Paul Ryan for the ticket was especially harmful to Romney. Gage described what he called "the kindling effect": He concluded that Obama's negative ads on Bain, the Cayman Islands, and outsourcing "laid the anti-Romney kindling that the 47 percent video ignited on September 17."

Romney provided plenty of his own kindling over the summer, especially during his much-publicized trip abroad in late July. First, in an interview with Brian Williams on NBC News, Romney offended his British hosts by questioning whether London was capable of running a successful Olympics. Prime Minister David Cameron drily noted, "Of course, it's easier if you hold an Olympic Games in the middle of nowhere," which simultaneously put down Romney and diminished his claim that managing the 2002 Winter Games in Salt Lake City was a significant qualification for the presidency. When London's mayor Boris Johnson shouted contemptuously to a rally of sixty thousand, "There's a guy named Mitt Romney who wants to know if we are ready," he might as well have been Joe Biden revving up the base back in the United States. The trip to Jerusalem was viewed by the press as almost as bad, though Romney's depiction of a Palestinian culture of violence as harming their economy was consistent with U.S. policy. Romney managed to pick up the tacit endorsement of Prime Minister Benjamin Netanyahu, which ended up bringing him little among American Jewish voters who had long since made up their minds.

In Chicago Romney's trip brought laughter and high fives. By August it was clear that the negative ads and the drumbeat of "free media" on Bain and Romney's gaffes were working. When Joel Benenson started polling on Romney in 2010 and 2011, his ratings were about 33 percent favorable to 14 percent unfavorable. He was known by about 50 percent of the public. By mid-2012 Romney was known by 80 percent and his favorables were "underwater," campaign lingo for more people disliking him than liking him, never a problem for the president. Before long Obama's ratings for honesty would be twice those of Romney.

———

THE OBAMA CAMPAIGN had a formal hierarchy and a more informal pecking order of commitment. The latter were ranked on how far back they went with Obama. Among those who held special claim to the spirit of the Obama crusade was Alex Okrent, who took a semester off from Wesleyan University to work on Obama's 2004 Senate campaign. In 2007 he was one of the first to join the presidential campaign, where he struck a charming balance between commitment and fun.

On the morning of July 13 Okrent collapsed at his desk. A colleague tried CPR, but he was unresponsive. The last his friends saw of him, the EMT crew was rolling him off the Floor on a gurney, still pounding on his chest. When word came that he had died, most likely of a heart arrhythmia, everyone on the Floor sobbed. "Our brother Alex has passed away," Messina announced. The shock and grief were like that over the loss of a loved one. Everyone went home for the rest of the day.

A small shrine to Okrent was set up in a corner of the headquarters, where staff and visitors could sit on a cushion, talk about Alex, and sip a little of the bourbon he liked to share. Hundreds of people, including the president and vice president, wrote messages to him on Post-it Notes that were hung in his corner. Friends made buttons depicting his Jew-fro and other quirks. An epitaph emerged: Do it for Alex. It wasn't long before the cut and thrust of the campaign resumed, but Chicago was different now, closer and more committed to the crusade that had brought them together.

21

Demography as Destiny

The numbers told the story of a changing America. In his losing 2008 campaign, John McCain won the same proportion of the white vote as Ronald Reagan did in his 1980 landslide. In 1992 the electorate was 88 percent white. Twenty years later, it was expected by Chicago (although not by Boston) to be 71 percent white.

But that was still nearly three-quarters of the country. Obama's problem was that polls showed his support among white working-class men plummeting, from 39 percent in 2008 into the 20s. If that didn't change, the president would have to improve his 2008 performance among youth, minorities, and women to win. This was the job of Operation Vote, Obama's outreach and base mobilization program, which was run by Katherine Archuleta and Buffy Wicks in Chicago. They couldn't use what Archuleta called a "cookie cutter" approach to constituency groups because the variations were endless. Young people had particular tastes in popular culture that had to be part of volunteer recruitment. Blacks were five times more likely to be on Twitter than any other group. Latinos were heavy users of smartphones because it allowed their children to go online without expensive computers. Women responded especially well to messages defending Planned Parenthood.

Obama's biggest demographic advantage was that old Republicans were dying and young Democrats were turning eighteen and eligible to vote. Chicago planned to make as many as five million kids who had been between fourteen and seventeen in 2008 now welcome the chance to do what their older siblings had done, even if it wasn't as cool this time. Beyond the hip new videos to stream and gear to buy at the Obama store, Chicago used social media to spread the idea of just doing something for Obama, if not skipping class to spend the day knocking on doors then at least sharing an enticing recruitment video with a great sound track on Facebook or Tumblr. Obama's record helped, as word filtered out that he was responsible for expanded college loans and being able to stay on your parents' health insurance until age twenty-six. And it didn't hurt that young people thought Romney was culturally clueless and in the grip of right-wingers. But none of that would be enough to get them to register and vote (preferably early) in the numbers Obama needed. That required relentless organization down to the "dorm captains" assigned to almost every dormitory at every college in every battleground state.

Beyond youth, OFA would have to register African Americans, Latinos, and women detached from the system and lure back to the polls those who voted for Obama in 2008 but stayed home in 2010. The only thing these potential Obama voters had in common was that on balance they suffered more in the recession than Republicans did. Now they would be asked to vote their class interests and their future but not their present-day pocketbooks. The unemployed tended to support Obama; the ones who had seen their portfolios zoom back up in the past four years more often went for Romney. The irony didn't escape Obama World.

———

IN 2008 OBAMA received 96 percent of the black vote. By early 2012 he was polling in the high 80s, with black registration down 7 percent in four years. It seemed that nothing could revive the fervor of 2008. Many black clergymen despised the idea of same-sex marriage and felt reluctant to urge their congregants to work hard for a president who had endorsed it. Stubbornly high black unemployment made it difficult to argue that a black man in the Oval Office had fundamentally changed the lives of black people. Even so, almost all African American commentators still backed Obama, and he had no patience for those who didn't.

Among the dissenters was Professor Cornel West, who had campaigned for Obama in 2008 but grew upset when Obama stopped returning his phone calls. After the election, West learned that Obama's top economic adviser would be Larry Summers, who as president of Harvard had pushed West out of the university in 2002 in a dispute over whether a professor should record hip-hop songs.* West gave speeches around the country saying that Obama wasn't a true progressive and that he couldn't "in good conscience" tell people to vote for him, though he admitted that his failure to secure special inauguration tickets for his mother and brother contributed to his hard feelings.

---

* West left Harvard for Princeton, where he stayed until assuming a position in 2011 at the Union Theological Seminary.

In July 2010 the president spotted West in the front row of the audience for his speech to the National Urban League. Afterward he came down to West's seat and grew angry. "I'm not progressive? What kind of shit is this?" the president hissed, his face contorted. West said later that a brassy African American woman standing behind him told the president to his face, "How dare you speak to Dr. West like that!" and argued after Obama left that the obscenity would have justified removal by the Secret Service had it come from anyone else. In the months following the confrontation West stepped up his attacks, calling Obama a "black mascot of Wall Street oligarchs and a black puppet of corporate plutocrats." He added, "I think my dear brother Barack Obama has a certain fear of free black men. It's understandable. As a young brother who grows up in a white context, brilliant African father, he's always had to fear being a white man with black skin."

As he was recoiling from West, the president drew closer to Reverend Al Sharpton, who had simultaneously shed one hundred pounds and his incendiary approach to public life. (Even former New York mayor Ed Koch had become a friend of Sharpton's.) He had never apologized for his conduct in the Tawana Brawley case, but seemed to be trying to make amends.* In 2008 Obama appreciated that Sharpton defended him from blacks who criticized him for distancing himself from his former pastor, Reverend Jeremiah Wright. Sharpton understood that pushing his way into pictures beside Obama wouldn't be helpful with white voters. He didn't care that Obama was using him for street cred with disappointed blacks.

When Obama learned in 2009 that Sharpton had become a strong supporter of education reform, he invited him and Newt Gingrich to the White House for a private bipartisan discussion on the subject. While Gingrich later swung right to run for president, Obama and Sharpton set to work building a new pro-reform coalition in the Democratic Party. They and Arne Duncan, the secretary of education, were fed up with teachers union traditionalists telling parents that more accountability was somehow harmful. The reformers pulled together around the simple but powerful idea of viewing every education initiative through the lens of what was good for children, not adult constituency groups.

Over time the president made Sharpton feel included, and Sharpton

---

* Tawana Brawley was a fifteen-year-old African American girl from Wappingers Falls, New York, who claimed in 1987 that she had been sexually assaulted by a group of white men and smeared with feces. Sharpton was among those who recklessly suggested that a white assistant district attorney, Steven Pagones, was one of the attackers. It turned out that Brawley made the story up.

returned the favor by becoming one of Obama's biggest defenders. His refusal to criticize the president in any way before the 2012 election signaled to many African Americans that they should follow suit.

But tensions within the black community continued. Sharpton and West got into a shouting match on Ed Shultz's show on MSNBC, when West accused Sharpton of being a stooge for the White House. When defending himself in private, Sharpton liked to point out how black civil rights leaders of the past such as Frederick Douglass, A. Philip Randolph, and Martin Luther King Jr. had handled their relationships with progressive American presidents: Each was respectful. Sharpton noted that King's famous 1963 March on Washington was not directed against Kennedy personally; in fact he met with JFK both before and after the march, as he did on several occasions with Lyndon Johnson. Sharpton's point was that black leaders of the past didn't insult the president, Cornel West–style. "And those presidents weren't black!" he shouted.

After the blowup with West, the president welcomed Sharpton and a half-dozen other black hosts and commentators to the Roosevelt Room of the White House. The subject turned to Tavis Smiley, a PBS host (and cohost of a radio show with West) who was also severely critical of Obama.* Tom Joyner, a strong Obama supporter and host of the top-rated black talk radio show, thought that West and Smiley (neither of whom was invited) were causing other blacks to denigrate the president. He began to mix it up with the author Michael Eric Dyson, who wanted the administration to target its efforts more on particular black needs. Obama jumped in to say he had no problem with Dyson or anyone else disagreeing with him about how to help the needy. What upset him was critics who "question my blackness and my commitment to blacks." He felt the community needed to be a little more sophisticated politically. "If I go out there saying 'black, black,' do you think that will help black people?" he asked, arguing that Congress would never support legislation explicitly intended for African Americans. His legislative program was aimed at helping all Americans but would disproportionately help blacks: "Pell grants? Black people. Health care? Black people."

The president's record showed that he had delivered for African Americans far beyond college loans and Obamacare. The stimulus saved hundreds of thousands of jobs of state and local workers, a large

---

* Some of Obama's African American supporters believed Smiley first turned against Obama in 2007, when Obama decided to announce his candidacy for president on the same day Smiley was holding his "State of the Black Union" convention.

percentage of them black, and provided $850 million for historically black colleges as part of its aid to higher education. The Fair Sentencing Act of 2010 ended the discrepancy in punishment for crimes that involve the same amounts of crack and powdered cocaine. The extension of the Earned Income Tax Credit kept millions of the working poor, disproportionately black, from slipping back into poverty, and the extension of unemployment insurance and food stamps helped millions of African Americans. But with black unemployment at 14 percent and four out of ten young black males still caught up in the criminal justice system, Obama had hardly transformed the community he had sought to join when he was a young man.

By mid-2012 Obama's hold on the black vote was almost complete. His credibility was such that support for gay marriage within the black community went up almost 20 points overnight after the president endorsed it, no matter what the attitude of black clergy. And that was before the political system felt the full force of a backlash against voter suppression that would spur memories of the civil rights movement.

IN THE LATE 1980s, after Reagan signed the bipartisan Simpson-Mazzoli Act reforming immigration policy, the Latino vote seemed up for grabs. Democrats considered Latino voters part of their base, but Republicans thought they could make headway with a rapidly growing Catholic constituency that responded well to pro-family, pro-entrepreneurship messages. Then, in 1994, Republican Governor Pete Wilson of California backed Proposition 187, a punitive law later overturned by the courts that deprived illegal aliens of all public services. Prop 187, still seared in the minds of Latinos nearly two decades later, turned California into a solid blue state and forced the GOP to play catch-up with Latinos nationwide.

George W. Bush, who had been a pro-immigration governor of Texas, emphasized bringing Latinos back into the GOP fold.* He received more than 40 percent of the Latino vote in both 2000 and 2004. But in 2006 nativism, a fever that goes back to the Know-Nothing Party of the 1850s, surged within the GOP base, which split with Bush and

---

* Bush was also enlightened on race. Both of his secretaries of state were African American, and he focused intently on treatment of AIDS in Africa. In late 2009, when a former aide, Ron Christie, an African American conservative, told Bush that his next book, *Acting White*, recounted how some blacks thought Obama acted white, Bush got red in the face and began yelling, "Take it out! Take all of that stuff out! It looks terrible for a black member of my staff to criticize a black president." Christie complied.

turned illegal immigration into a top-tier campaign issue. Bush dropped comprehensive immigration reform, and his administration tripled the fees charged to process citizenship applications, a seemingly small change that alienated Latinos and other immigrants. By 2008 the presence of Representative Tom Tancredo, a vitriolic anti-immigrant activist, in the GOP primaries pushed the other candidates to the right, which sent even more Latinos into the Democratic Party. Soon the nominee, John McCain, distanced himself from his own immigration bill. (He would renounce it entirely in order to get reelected to the Senate in 2010.) Obama hadn't been particularly popular with Latinos in 2008— he lost them to Hillary Clinton by a wide margin in every primary—but in the general election he won the Latino vote by 34 points.

That bought Latinos nothing. About 1.5 million illegal aliens were deported under Obama, far more than under Bush. And the president reneged on his promise to make comprehensive immigration reform a priority. Even a lesser goal, enactment of the DREAM Act, failed at the end of 2010 thanks to Republican obstruction. Many Latinos charged that the president didn't put the same muscle behind the DREAM Act that he applied to repeal of Don't Ask Don't Tell.

In an April 2011 meeting in the Roosevelt Room with Latino journalists and activists, Obama said Republicans should "pay a price" for their obstructionist positions on immigration. Maria Teresa Kumar of Voto Latino replied that both parties should pay a price. When José Díaz-Balart, a Telemundo anchorman from a Republican political family, told the president that "people say" he wasn't sympathetic to Latinos, Obama shot back, "No, *you* say." He vehemently rejected that charge and said the failure of the DREAM Act was the biggest disappointment of his presidency so far.

The story of Obama's contacts with Representative Luis Gutiérrez of Chicago resembled what happened with Cornel West, except with a happier ending. Gutiérrez had been, according to one White House official, "weirdly obsessed with the president." He called often in 2009, claiming an old Chicago friendship, and eventually Obama stopped taking his calls. In May 2010 the congressman got himself arrested during a demonstration in front of the White House protesting the deportations. At Christmas, just after the DREAM Act failed, Obama invited Gutiérrez, Representative Nydia Velázquez, and Senator Bob Menendez of New Jersey to the White House and told them that he expected no legislation on immigration for another two years. "Let's put our thinking caps on," he suggested, and figure out a solution from the executive branch. The president hugged Gutiérrez and the two Chicagoans shared a laugh.

But in 2011 their relationship deteriorated again. Chief of Staff Bill Daley invited Latino leaders in for a meeting and Gutiérrez asked what the "thinking caps" had produced. When Daley said, in effect, nothing, Gutiérrez went ballistic. He even accused the president of sending him a letter that sounded sarcastic, which Cecelia Muñoz of the White House said was ridiculous. "They've been silent for two years and now they're bragging about deporting a million people, many of them kids? I can't shut up about this," Gutiérrez said. He predicted that Obama would still get two-thirds of the Latino vote, but turnout would be so depressed that he might lose the election. The White House was furious with Gutiérrez. After the congressman had promised to keep his complaints private, he went on a national speaking tour blasting the president.

The problem Gutiérrez complained about continued to eat away at the president's Latino support. Muñoz, the White House official responsible for Latino issues, admitted to colleagues that the administration did a "crappy job" of explaining the Secure Communities program, whose aim was stepped-up deportations of hardened criminals, which is what led to the record number of deportations. But she kept telling Latino critics that the climate in 2010 was brutal. Representative Gabby Giffords of Arizona would call up Rahm Emanuel when he was chief of staff and implore him on the phone, "You *gotta* send me more National Guard [to secure the border]." Giffords was worried about losing her reelection fight.*

In June 2011 U.S. Immigration and Customs Enforcement agreed to start using prosecutorial discretion in deciding deportations, but the new policy didn't work on the ground, where ICE agents complained that they couldn't easily make judgments about which immigrants deserved prosecution and which didn't. In the year that followed, the government halted the deportation of only 593 students.

All year the problem festered, and even Latinos sympathetic to Obama grew frustrated. Bill Richardson, the former governor of New Mexico, had become persona non grata in the Clinton wing of the Democratic Party by jumping to Obama in 2008 after explicitly promising Clinton at a Super Bowl party that he wouldn't. He was slated to be secretary of commerce in 2009 (until derailed by a New Mexico scandal) and was as friendly with the president as any politician could expect to be. But in August 2011 Richardson, normally an easygoing sort, broke the festive mood of Obama's fiftieth birthday barbecue in

---

* Giffords won, but in 2011 she was shot in the head by a gunman in Tucson. Still recovering, she declined to run for reelection in 2012.

the Rose Garden. With Jay-Z and Tom Hanks nearby, he bent the president's ear about how the deportations were hurting innocent immigrants, including a disturbingly large number of children. Obama told him he was working on it, but Richardson didn't see any evidence of movement for many months.

Janet Napolitano, secretary of the Department of Homeland Security, claimed to want a more nuanced deportation policy, but her hard-line subordinates, who came mostly from law enforcement backgrounds, dragged their feet on changing the policy. Their people were trained to arrest, not act as admission officers trying to figure out whether a kid did well in school. And the department's general counsel threw up legal objections to easing deportations without a change in the law. But as usual in the government, there was wiggle room in "enforcement standards" and "prosecutorial discretion." Kathy Ruemmler, the White House counsel, recognized that while ad hoc discretion was unworkable, the government could set new rules that made arresting young, law-abiding high school graduates the lowest priority of the department and allowed young people in that category to apply for such status.

On the Hill, Democratic Senator Dick Durbin wouldn't let the issue go. In early 2012 his office received calls nearly every week from young people being deported. Muñoz, a former immigration reformer who was now director of the Domestic Policy Council in the White House, began pushing in meetings for a new policy. Muñoz liked to say internally that "Democrats can no longer rely on Republicans being bigger assholes" on the issue. Now they had to do something.

On June 17, 2012, the president decreed that 800,000 young people who had arrived when they were younger than sixteen, finished high school, and met other requirements could be given temporary status and avoid deportation. "We're happy he's our leader and champion," Gutiérrez exulted. "This is the president we elected." Almost immediately, thousands of young people stepped out of the shadows and formed long lines to apply for new status.

Not everyone was so sure the decision would yield huge political benefits for Obama. It was hard to say whether more Latinos would vote just because others in their community avoided deportation. Many had been directly hurt by the foreclosure crisis, which hit Latinos harder than any other group. Some experts in Latino voting patterns said it would still take the reemergence of someone like Lou Dobbs or Glenn Beck spewing venom to motivate enough voters to match the Latino turnout numbers of 2008.

Just as in gay marriage, the delay in exercising presidential authority inadvertently worked to Obama's advantage. By waiting so long to make his decision, the president gave the media an opening to interpret it as a political act aimed at reelection. But at least they were covering it. Had the decision been announced a year earlier, the story would have been "policy," not "politics," and thus largely ignored by a press corps obsessed by the latter. Instead many more people saw the president showing leadership on immigration—and showing up Romney in the process. Five times Bob Schieffer of CBS News asked Romney if he would reverse Obama's initiative, and five times Romney declined to answer. It was all upside that weekend for the Obama campaign.

Even so, Plouffe and Pfeiffer were nervous about the DREAM Act, which they thought Republicans could depict as amnesty. This turned out not to be a problem. Romney knew that he had to cut into Obama's margins. "We have to get Hispanics to vote for our party," he told a Florida fundraising dinner when he didn't realize the press outside could hear. Anything short of that, he said, "spells doom for us."

OBAMA'S "LATINO TRACK" was almost like running a presidential campaign in a different country, or a country that the United States was about to become. It included messages, voter contact strategies, and celebrities that were off the radar of the Washington press corps.

Everyone knew the Latino giant was stirring, but only the Democrats were doing anything about it.* About 40 percent of eligible Latinos weren't even registered. And of those who were, fewer than half usually voted, compared to about 65 percent participation among all registered voters. To change that, Operation Vote launched an aggressive marketing campaign at soccer matches, boxing tournaments, and Latino beauty parlors and barbershops. (Similar efforts in the black barbershops had been critical in the 2008 primaries.) OFA field organizers attended citizenship ceremonies in battleground states and discreetly asked new citizens if they wanted to register. Messina worried for months that word of the effort would leak and make it seem as if the Obama campaign was politicizing a solemn event.

The campaign hired Bendixen & Amandi, a Miami-based communications consulting firm that specialized in Latino voters. In the past, ads aimed at Latinos ran only at the end of a campaign. Obama's started in March. And instead of merely translating issue ads into Spanish, the usual practice, Chicago created separate and carefully tailored mes-

---

* In 1970 Latinos made up 4.7 percent of the U.S. population. In 2010 the figure was 16.3 percent. By 2030 they are estimated to be almost 25 percent of all Americans.

sages. Roughly a third of all TV viewers now routinely time-shifted the shows they watched, which meant that they saw many fewer ads. Only a tenth of Latino viewers did so. That made advertising on *tele-novelas* and other Spanish-language entertainment programs especially efficient.

The firm's early focus groups were discouraging for Obama. Latinos liked the president personally but didn't think he was effective. Over and over, focus group respondents said, "He hasn't really done anything." They were largely unfamiliar with achievements like the auto rescue and the health care bill, but they knew the president had failed on immigration reform. "He promised a bill and then he deported my next-door neighbor's kid," one said.

The best way out of that hole was to educate Latino voters about Obamacare, which was immensely popular when Latinos learned the details. The pitch was much more direct than in Obama's English-language media. Certain families, the Spanish-language ads said, "will receive economic help from the government to pay for quality [health] insurance." If the election was partly about the role of government in American life, Chicago was betting that Latinos favored a big role. Romney went the other way, targeting his ads at Latino small business owners. They were an important subgroup but made up less than 10 percent of Latino voters.

For the Latino market, the messenger is often more important than the message. The surrogate Chicago chose was Cristina Saralegui, known as "the Latina Oprah." Saralegui had just finished a twenty-year run hosting one of the top-rated shows on Univision, the Spanish-language commercial network that beats all cable networks in the ratings and in some time slots bests NBC, ABC, and CBS too. A Cuban American, she had enormous crossover appeal with Mexican Americans (who made up more than half of Latinos in the United States) and other Latinos. Fernand Amandi, also Cuban American, begged Saralegui to appear in Obama TV spots, and though she had never done anything political before, she finally agreed. By coincidence, her signature sign-off line on her show, "Pa'lante!," translates roughly as "Forward!" Saralegui conducted an "interview" with Michelle Obama in which she pointed to the first lady's midsection and asked, "Is the factory closed?" Michelle said she and the president were done having kids. That exchange didn't air, but Saralegui's ads on Univision and Telemundo were known by almost all Latino voters, and by almost no one in the separate universe of white America.

Sheldon Adelson had a lot of experience hiring Latinos for his Las Vegas casinos, and he urged the Romney campaign to do more to win their votes. Romney's son Craig appeared in an ad speaking Spanish, but it contained only platitudes about his family and didn't penetrate. Neither did a negative spot Republicans ran in Florida entitled "Chávez por Obama," pegged to Venezuelan president Hugo Chávez's comment that he preferred the president over Romney. Negative ads rarely had much traction with Latinos, though an Obama spot attacking Romney for opposing Sonia Sotomayor's nomination for the Supreme Court seemed to resonate in the Puerto Rican community, where turnout would help determine the outcome in Florida. The big difference was volume. Romney ads were far less visible on Spanish-language television; Obama ran 13,232 spots compared to 3,435 for Romney.

In August Obama's numbers with Latinos sagged a bit, and Bendixen & Amandi pushed hard for a big ad buy connected to the DREAM Act. After some resistance, Chicago agreed. The president appeared in a direct-to-camera spot in which he spoke in Spanish of the "buen ejemplo" (good example) offered by the young "dreamers" who were brought to this country illegally as children and stayed to make something of their lives. Native speakers were impressed by Obama's accent, especially in contrast to Romney, who spoke only in English.

Between June and Election Day, many dreamers and their extended families and friends became passionate Obama supporters for a simple reason: fear of what would happen if Romney was elected and reversed the policy. Because these young people had stepped out of the shadows, the government would have their names and be able to quickly deport them.

———

To win, Obama needed the gender gap to stay wide, but he couldn't lose too many Catholic votes. These conflicting goals played out on the issue of contraception.

When George Stephanopoulos of ABC News pressed Romney about his views on contraception during a January primary debate, Boston was livid. The liberal media, it seemed, was trying to make Romney out to be against birth control. But the bigger flap was a confrontation between the White House and Catholic bishops over state-funded contraception. When the administration moved to limit religious exemptions to the Obamacare requirement that employers provide birth control as part of their standard package of health care benefits, Romney pounced.

The issue crystalized tensions within the Democratic Party over implementation of Obamacare. In late January, after a spirited internal White House debate that essentially featured Catholics (Joe Biden and

Bill Daley) against women (Valerie Jarrett and Nancy-Ann DeParle), the president decided on a narrow rule that exempted only churches, mosques, and temples. DeParle, the deputy chief of staff assigned to the issue, later insisted that the policymaking was incomplete and nothing had been set in stone.

But conservative clergy were on fire over the exemption, and two days later they began denouncing the regulation from the pulpit as an assault on religious liberty. A letter from the U.S. Conference of Bishops saying the same thing spread quickly. Regional media and then cable news ignited the story. In Chicago, campaign officials shook their heads at the White House's failure to lay the political groundwork better on an issue of such sensitivity. "It was like getting caught with your pants down," one said.

After the liberal columnists E. J. Dionne and Mark Shields, both Catholics, weighed in on the side of the bishops, the president looked stung. In February he offered a compromise—make the insurance companies, not the government, pay for any contraceptives—and won over Sister Carol Keehan, president of the Catholic Health Association and an Obama ally. Liberals rallied. Obama was like a quarterback on a broken play who scrambled across the line of scrimmage for a first down.

Of course, the conservative base was hardly appeased. Senator Roy Blunt of Missouri introduced an amendment that would allow any employer (not just religiously affiliated institutions) to refuse on religious grounds to include contraception in their health care coverage. This was a pivotal mistake. It allowed women's groups to argue that your boss shouldn't be in your bedroom. The amendment was defeated, and Romney and Senator Scott Brown of Massachusetts, a cosponsor of the Blunt Amendment, found themselves on the defensive with women.

Rush Limbaugh helped the Democrats keep the issue out front. In late February, Sandra Fluke, a Georgetown University Law student, testified before a congressional committee in support of mandatory employer health coverage of contraception. It was an unremarkable appearance that drew little public attention until Limbaugh seized on it and accused Fluke of being a "prostitute" and a "slut." He went on: "If we are going to have to pay for this [the contraception] then we want something in return, Ms. Fluke. And that would be the videos of all this sex posted online so we can see what we're getting for our money."

When asked about Limbaugh's comments on a rope line, Romney said, "I'll just say this, which is it's not the language I would have used." Romney was under no obligation to denounce Limbaugh, but it represented a missed opportunity and another sign that he would do little to reach out to anyone outside the base.

A series of other news stories kept women's health in the news: The Susan B. Komen Foundation for breast cancer research stopped its funding of Planned Parenthood, then reversed itself; Governor Bob McDonnell of Virginia signed a bill requiring some women to undergo a transvaginal ultrasound before receiving an abortion, then reversed himself; and Todd Akin, the GOP candidate for Senate in Missouri, wrecked his campaign by telling an interviewer that there was such a thing as "legitimate rape." The combination of these stories widened the gender gap, which helped the president.

As the campaign heated up, Democrats tried to press the advantage with a series of distortions, starting with the alliterative but unfair notion that the Republican Party was engaged in a "war on women." Chicago did nothing to tamp down the idea, spread widely in radio ads funded by liberal groups, that Romney was against the distribution of birth control and opposed abortion in all cases. In truth, he was against federal funding of birth control and requiring institutions to offer it, and he adhered to a common view of abortion, embraced by all recent Republican presidents, that included exceptions for rape and incest. But he never used his influence to change the Republican Party platform, which continued to have no such exceptions.

Unfortunately for the Romney campaign, that would not be the last the American public would hear about rape before the election.

22

In the Scrum

Republicans in 2012 had differing theories of combat. Boston abided by the old adage "If you're explaining, you're losing." Under this theory, the challenge of a campaign is to stick to message—in this case the weak economy under Obama—and not get pulled off your game by responding to attacks. The other view was summarized by Mississippi's governor Haley Barbour, a former chair of the RNC: "An attack unanswered is an attack admitted." Republicans in the Barbour camp felt Romney got clobbered in so-called free media, the cut-and-thrust of the twenty-four-hour news cycle.

Fox understood that cut-and-thrust better than anyone, but the fantasyland it built to sustain ratings blinded the network to political realities. Roger Ailes couldn't fathom that the assault on Bain Capital might be convincing, so he made no effort to defend the company or Romney, for whom he had no great love anyway. Neither did the Romney campaign, which was cash-strapped until after the Tampa convention. So week after week, the attacks of Chicago and the pro-Obama super PAC went answered.

It used to be that general elections didn't start until Labor Day. Now they were all but over by then. Worse for Romney, the 2012 election had been much more stable than other recent elections. Millions of people made a decision in the winter or spring and never revisited it. Obama's failure to return the economy to full prosperity hurt him, especially with older voters who considered themselves underemployed. But huge numbers of voters who viewed the economy as the number one issue favored him nonetheless.

Republicans were losing the economic argument. Austerity was failing badly in Europe, and it made no intuitive sense that cutting spending would put people back to work. Contrary to the Republicans' claim, the deficit had led to neither inflation nor higher interest rates. Blaming unemployment insurance for encouraging people to be lazy didn't correspond to the suffering of the jobless that voters saw in their own communities. Cutting taxes for the "job creators" may have sounded good to the wealthy and even to small business owners, but tax cuts weren't popular with strapped voters who didn't think their bosses needed fatter incomes.

The Romney strategy was to make the election a referendum on Obama and the economy; the Obama strategy was to make it a choice. Both were wrong. It turned out to be a referendum on Romney and the Republicans.

———

IN THE SUMMER Jim Messina confessed that he had completely misread the Romney strategy. He thought that Romney would pivot away from the base and toward the center in order to woo swing voters. "Instead, they're running the Bush '04 race again—an incumbent's strategy instead of a challenger's." In Boston Stuart Stevens thought that pivoting to the center on immigration and other issues would make his candidate look like a phony. Obama would simply "outbid" them on anything they tried, and it would cost them in the character department.

Paul Begala, an aggressive operative under Clinton, liked to quote Zell Miller, a former governor of Georgia, who taught him that "a hit dog barks." But Romney remained silent on his record at Bain, which stunned Begala. He was helping out Bill Burton's super PAC and was amazed that Romney let Chicago and one tiny underfunded super PAC "define him as Gordon Gekko." Without his business record, Begala said, "Romney was left with nothing but his charm."

The pro-Romney super PACs couldn't compensate for him. While they weren't allowed to coordinate with the campaign, nothing prevented them from working with each other. They held plenty of meetings but advertised on different themes. One week in August, Restore Our Future was on jobs, Crossroads GPS on the deficit, and Americans for Prosperity on the Solyndra "scandal," while the Romney campaign was focused on welfare. These pro-Romney super PACs spent $400 million—more than five times as much as Burton's pro-Obama super PAC, Priorities USA Action. But they had four or five messages and Burton had one: Mitt Romney is bad for the middle class.

The summer ad wars reached a fever pitch when Burton's super PAC posted (but never aired on television) an ad featuring Joe Soptic, a former employee of a Bain-owned steel company. Soptic recounted how, after the plant closed and he lost his insurance, his wife got cancer and died.* The ad implied that Romney was responsible for her death.

———

* Another pro-Obama super PAC ad also cut through. Called "Coffin," it featured a man describing how he was asked to construct a platform at his Bain-owned factory. When he

The press referees immediately jumped on the factual time line, which showed Soptic's wife had insurance from another employer for a time and that Romney was no longer running Bain when the events transpired. After Chicago tried to claim no connection to the ad, reporters dug up the fact that, months earlier, Stephanie Cutter had introduced Soptic and his story to the media on a conference call. This allowed Boston to charge that Obama and his backers were taking the campaign to a new low.

In truth, while the Joe Soptic ad was the most inflammatory spot of the campaign to date, an ad Romney aired on welfare reform was the most inaccurate. It accused Obama of gutting the work requirements of Clinton's 1996 welfare reform bill and "sending a check" directly to welfare recipients without requiring them to work. While the waivers offered to states by HHS Secretary Kathleen Sebelius (and signed off on by the White House) were at first too loose, the White House quickly backpedaled and HHS included explicit requirements that states expand the number of welfare recipients at work. A few liberals at HHS may have wanted to gut the 1996 bill, but they failed. No checks were ever sent without discernible signs of work, and no one in a powerful position ever intended to do so. The ad didn't feature blacks and thus couldn't be scored as racial, but the subtext—Obama is giving your hard-earned money to his people—was hard to miss.*

Romney was going for the anti-moocher vote—the whites whom Ronald Reagan had won with his denunciations of "welfare queens." When Romney in midsummer put nearly 50 percent of his money behind this one spot capitalizing on a bureaucratic snafu, the White House went into a paralyzed crouch. It had thought Obama had political cover because the requests for flexibility came from the Republican governors of Nevada and Utah. (Romney had made his own such requests when governor of Massachusetts.) Now everyone recognized the whole idea of "cover" was dead. Anything was fair game.

While the Romney ad didn't hurt Obama much in the polls, it did effectively shut down the federal government until Election Day. In the first half of 2012, the White House pushed its "We Can't Wait" agenda of small policy initiatives that required no congressional approval and

---

learned the platform would be used to anounce the closing of the plant, he said he felt as if he was "building my own coffin."

* Similarly, Republicans circulated video, posted at the top of the Drudge Report, of a poor African American woman in Cleveland shouting, "Obama has my vote. He gave me a free phone." In truth, a program to subsidize telephone service for low-income Americans was begun by Ronald Reagan and expanded under George H. W. Bush.

let the agencies continue rule-making and other policy formulation. But after the July welfare imbroglio, David Plouffe and Deputy Chief of Staff Nancy-Ann DeParle blocked almost everything for fear of a damaging story on the Daily Caller, Drudge, or Fox that could be turned into a thirty-second ad. Many regulations and nominations were put on hold, strictly for defensive political reasons. For instance, the FDA had a proposed rule barring food handlers from chewing gum or wearing jewelry at work because these items were accidentally falling into the food supply. It was delayed until 2013.

The White House wasn't taking any chances. Obama would have likely opposed military intervention in Syria even if it were not an election year; when the issue came to a head in a July meeting, only the CIA (with the lukewarm backing of Hillary Clinton) wanted a more aggressive policy there. But the prospect of being drawn into another unpopular war was especially unappealing now. With the Democratic base nailed down, the goal was to lure independents, not launch new initiatives or brag about the Obama record. In southeastern Ohio, for instance, Obama was running to Romney's right on coal, airing ads that showed Romney as governor saying, "This plant kills," about a coal plant in Massachusetts he wanted to shut down. When Interior Secretary Ken Salazar, who had won tough races in battleground Colorado, offered new conservation plans that might have helped there, he was ignored. Instead a policy of No Distractions descended over the administration. The idea, said one White House official, was "We've got a strategy. Now don't go fuck it up."

The all-politics focus came straight from the top. "If I lose, my presidency is a footnote," Obama told his senior counselor, Pete Rouse, in the middle of 2012. "All of the progress we made in the first four years would be reversed." By winning, he said, his first-term achievements would be cemented for a generation and he could move forward on promises sidetracked by the Great Recession.

IN JUNE AND JULY Romney undertook his vice presidential selection process with the same analytical rigor he applied to his business career but that had been missing from his approach to data management. From the start, he never believed in geographical picks, and the campaign had no polling that showed selecting Senator Rob Portman of Ohio would help carry that state for Romney. Portman made the final list nonetheless, as did Marco Rubio, Tim Pawlenty, Chris Christie, and Paul Ryan.

Romney's first requirement was what he described as "no surprises."

He hadn't been running for five years just to see his VP choice blow up his chances over something he and his team hadn't anticipated. He wanted someone young, someone who could energize the base, and a "governing partner" who could help his administration and be president immediately if it came to that. The person who best met those four requirements would get picked.

While young and engaging, Rubio had some question marks in his past, especially a flap over his using a credit card from the Florida Republican Party for $160,000 in personal expenses. But the bigger concern was that Romney didn't think that after just a year and a half in the Senate he was ready to be president. Pawlenty (Axelrod's prediction) had proved during his brief presidential campaign that he wasn't exciting to the base, while Portman (Stuart Stevens's choice) met only the requirement of being fully ready to assume the top job if necessary, and even that qualification was marred by his time as budget director in the Bush administration.

Chris Christie came much closer than reporters recognized at the time. He was young (fifty), capable of governing, and appealing to moderates. The base of the party might not agree with every position he took, but he was strongly pro-life and thrilling to party activists. Christie's problem, Romney concluded, was lack of "discipline." Romney never said that this meant his inability to control his weight, but he didn't have to. He had other examples. At a fundraiser one night at the Grand Hyatt in New York, Christie, who was scheduled to introduce Romney, was so late that Romney started speaking without him. When Christie entered the room during Romney's speech, Romney had to stop and introduce him. If this happened only once, no one would have cared, but Christie was consistently late and it annoyed Romney.

Ryan was young, exciting for the base, and his selection would reflect Romney's belief that 2012 wasn't just a referendum on the Obama economy but a big-time "contrast election." The question about him was whether, as a forty-three-year-old congressman, he was ready to be president. But his deep knowledge of the budget and fluency on other issues dazzled Romney, who thought Ryan could help him hit the ground running in the White House. Unlike Christie, he was highly organized—"tight," as Romney said. After listening to Ryan talk, Bob White leaned over to Dan Senor and said, "At Bain, we would have called him 'client-ready,'" meaning that he could be sent out to represent the firm on multimillion-dollar deals. Matt Rhoades, the campaign manager, said Romney was smitten: "It was like talking to your buddy who has just met a girl and he's giddy."

By choosing Ryan, Romney was doubling down on the idea of slashing programs for the middle class in order to pay for more tax cuts. Surprisingly Boston seemed unprepared to answer the question of whether Romney backed the Ryan Plan, which he had called "marvelous" in 2011 but was now less enthusiastic about. Axelrod figured he wanted to be the "ideas candidate" without actually embracing the idea he had just imported.

Teddy Goff reported that Twitter exploded after the Ryan pick and that money was pouring in online. Jeremy Bird said that the troops in Wisconsin were galvanized and newly confident of victory in Ryan's home state. At the White House, Obama told his team that selecting Ryan cemented the analogy in his mind between 2012 and 1964, when GOP nominee Goldwater promised to reverse Johnson's Great Society agenda of Medicare, education, and civil rights. It was, the president said, a clarifying choice.

ON JULY 13 Obama joined Senator Mark Warner of Virginia in front of a fire station in Roanoke. What happened next wasn't noticed by the Romney campaign's oppo staff for five days, but it symbolized the conflict over founding principles and became one of Boston's lifelines after a rocky month of being battered over Bain. About three-quarters into his stump speech, Obama arrived at the place where he ordinarily included himself among the well-off. It was a rhetorical trick first used by Bill Clinton: Get points for saying people like me don't deserve a tax cut. First he calmly said, "A lot of wealthy, successful Americans agree with me—because they want to give something back."

Just as he had borrowed from Massachusetts governor Deval Patrick for part of a 2010 stump speech, he now took a leaf from Elizabeth Warren, running for the Senate from Massachusetts. A video of her delivering off-the-cuff remarks at a house party had gone viral among liberals. "There's nobody in this country who got rich on his own. Nobody. You moved your goods to markets on roads the rest of us paid for," she said, then explained how the workforce was educated by public school teachers, how factories were protected from harm by public police and firefighters, and how society had moved away from appreciation of the New Deal, the GI Bill, and other great achievements of activist government. Warren also championed individual initiative and getting rich ("God bless!"), but said successful citizens should "pay it forward."

Unlike Warren, the president, speaking in a folksy way, crossed the line from preaching commonality to taking a shot at successful people: "I'm always struck by people who think, well, it [success] must be because I was just so smart. There are a lot of smart people out there. It must be because I worked harder than everybody else. Let me tell you something—there are a whole bunch of hardworking people out there."

At this point, the crowd applauded. The firefighters and their families and other middle-class people in attendance liked being told they were just as smart and hardworking as the people who make ten times or a hundred times (or, in the case of some of those who drove the economy into the ditch, a thousand times) as much money.

Then came a section that reflected innocuous intentions on the president's part but went out to the world with a grammatical ambiguity that hurt his campaign, at least temporarily: "If you were successful, somebody along the line gave you some help. There was a great teacher somewhere in your life. Somebody helped to create this unbelievable American system that we have that allowed you to thrive. Somebody invested in roads and bridges. If you've got a business—you didn't build that. Somebody else made that happen. The Internet didn't get invented on its own. Government research created the Internet so that all the companies could make money off the Internet."

The president was trying to make his familiar Abraham Lincoln point about the importance of infrastructure and collective action. Fact-check.org, the *Washington Post*, and other media referees agreed that Obama's awkward "that" in "you didn't build that" referred to "roads and bridges," not businesses. No matter. The president was off his game that day, not just grammatically but in tone. He had spoken often in the past about the importance of championing success. In his inaugural address in 2009, he saluted "the risk takers, the doers, the makers of things," and many of his trips around the country in the years since had been to visit factories and private labs and small restaurants, where he praised all of the qualities of small business owners he was accused of ignoring. But he didn't do that in Roanoke, which gave conservatives an opening. Crossroads GPS cut a spot of small business owners watching the "you didn't built that" clip and saying this confirmed what they always suspected about the president. If the speech hadn't become controversial, Obama's straw men would have remained billionaires. But once the video went viral, many Republican small business owners thought the president was talking about them—telling them that intelligence and hard work had nothing to do with their success.

The episode also played into the "other" theme. "It's as if a Dutch politician—an intelligent, well-meaning Dutch politician—were somehow running for the presidency," the conservative social critic Charles Murray wrote on his blog. "We would listen to him and say to ourselves, 'He doesn't get this country.'" Then Murray went on to repeat the tired talking point that Obama was acting "un-American." The slur seemed contagious. "I wish the president would learn how to be an American," said John Sununu, the former governor of New Hampshire and White House chief of staff. These were not Internet trolls attacking the president's patriotism but prominent conservatives.

Obama and Chicago knew the latest barbs couldn't be as easily dismissed as similar attacks in the past. Axelrod ordered up two ads of a soft-spoken president speaking directly into the camera and explaining how much he respected entrepreneurs. After that, Chicago was unperturbed. Polls showed little slippage, and Romney's ads on the charge never went into heavy rotation, suggesting they didn't get much traction. Ben LaBolt, the Chicago campaign press secretary, had an explanation: "They're not going to win the election based on a lie."

***

AS THEY GATHERED for their convention in steaming Tampa, Republicans weren't enthusiastic about Mitt Romney; their passion came from despising Barack Obama. No fewer than seven politicians who had expressed doubt over whether Obama was born in the United States, including Florida governor Rick Scott and former Arkansas governor Mike Huckabee, were given speaking roles, though not in prime time.* Boston knew that Obama-bashing would only hurt them with the 2008 Obama supporters they needed to win over. So the convention was designed to humanize the nominee.

Just as in Minneapolis in 2008, a hurricane caused the cancellation of the first night of the convention—the first of two hurricanes in 2012 that marred Romney's plans. Limbaugh alleged that the Obama "regime" intentionally forecast hurricane warnings for Florida with the intention of causing the cancellation. "What could be better for the Democrats than the Republicans to cancel a day of this?" he asked. Donald Trump was especially disappointed. Romney had publicly embraced him in Las Vegas in May and signed off on a video of him behind his desk giving a dismal performance review to an Obama impersonator, who is predictably dispatched with Trump's signature line from his NBC show: "President Obama, you're fired." The video, scheduled for the first night, never aired, and Trump plotted his next publicity stunt.

The humanizing of Romney, which should have been launched months earlier in paid media, began with Ann Romney's warm and well-delivered speech. But her meditation on love (including the awk-

---

* After the columnist and presidential candidate Pat Buchanan gave a divisive speech on the "culture wars" during prime time at the 1992 GOP Convention, prime time has been reserved for burnishing the image of the nominee.

ward "I love women!") was free of any stories about her husband that might be remembered even a day later. She was followed by the key-noter, Chris Christie, who rejected the drafts offered by speechwriters, penned his own at the Jersey Shore, then bristled when told by aides during rehearsal that it wasn't good enough. Romney staffers weren't happy when they vetted Christie's speech, but they didn't stand up to him or even notice that he contradicted Ann Romney by saying that his mother taught him that love is less important than respect, a quality he failed to show by not mentioning the nominee until the sixteenth min-ute of his speech. This soon became a theme of the GOP convention: self-promotion over promotion of the presidential candidate.

Worse, the convention looked like a country club or, as conservative media baron Chris Ruddy put it, an Afrikaner Party convention in the old South Africa. Black delegates numbered twenty-eight out of 2,286, down from 167 in 2004, which was partly attributable to the difficulty of recruiting blacks in the age of Obama. Latino delegates were more in evidence, but Latino viewers didn't seem to care; the latter over-whelmingly watched *telenovelas* on Univision instead of the conven-tion. Because the hall was filled with well-heeled Romney delegates, not boisterous Tea Party enthusiasts, the convention seemed to lack the energy of previous GOP conclaves. Some of this was also by design. The Tea Party, unpopular with independents, wasn't mentioned once from the podium during prime time.

In fact three years after they noisily took over town meetings on health care, Tea Party activists were surprisingly absent in Tampa. The movement had been weakened by feuds. In 2011 Amy Kremer of Tea Party Express found herself embroiled in a lawsuit with Mark Meckler and Jenny Beth Martin for pushing her out of Tea Party Patriots in 2009 and stealing the name, which Meckler and Martin denied. Then Martin slowly froze Meckler out of decision making at Tea Party Patriots until, in 2012, Meckler quit. Kate Zernike, who chronicled the Tea Party for the *New York Times*, felt the movement benefited early on from people not knowing what it really was. Now, even as at least a hundred GOP House members embraced radical Tea Party ideas, the name itself was in bad odor and threatening the whole Republican brand.

———

THE LAST TWO nights of the convention featured several fine addresses by former secretary of state Condoleezza Rice, Senator Marco Rubio, and Governor Susan Martinez, among others, but the acceptance speeches were underwhelming. Paul Ryan came into the convention with a repu-tation as a truth teller and left with one, at least among the news media, as a prevaricator. His Boy-Scout-with-a-knife evisceration of Obama thrilled the conservative base but contained a half-dozen misstatements of fact, from implying that a General Motors plant in his congressional district closed when Obama was president (it was shuttered under Bush), to falsely charging that Medicare was raided for Obamacare and attacking the president for not embracing Simpson-Bowles when it was Ryan himself who helped torpedo the commission's recommendations. He also incorrectly charged that the president had begun his administration by focusing on health care, not jobs. (The stimulus came first.)

While these policy distortions might not have resonated beyond the world of fact-checkers and Democratic partisans, a fib Ryan told earlier in the year about running a marathon continued to circulate. Ryan twice claimed he ran a twenty-six-mile marathon in under three hours when in fact his fastest time, according to *Runner's World* magazine, was just over four hours—a nontrivial difference that did not help his reputation for truthfulness.

In Tampa, Republicans were putting all of their money on money. The real convention, the one where someone might be persuaded to act, wasn't in the arena but at the tony Tampa Club, where Karl Rove hosted an Americans Crossroads event for seventy superrich donors. A reporter for *Bloomberg Businessweek*, Sheelah Kolhatkar, accompanied a guest and recorded the session, where Rove said Crossroads would raise $300 million, or an average of more than $4 million from each person in the room.

Rove explained that the undecided voters that Republicans needed were not hostile to Obama, so a soft sell was required. "If you say he's a socialist, they'll go to defend him. If you call him a 'far out left-winger,' they'll say, 'no, no, he's not.'" The key, Rove said, was simply to contrast the president's promises with his record: "If you keep it focused on the facts and adopt a respectful tone, then they're gonna agree with you." No one bothered to ask why, if the soft sell worked, the tens of millions in low-key super PAC ads that had already run were failing to leave an impression.

Haley Barbour provided comic relief with a parody of the Democrats' more effective message: "You know, 'Romney is a vulture capitalist who doesn't care about the likes of you. He doesn't even know people like you—he'll lay you off, cancel your insurance, shit jobs. He's a plutocrat. Married to a known equestrian!'" The room erupted in laughter, though few knew the origins of the joke, an apocryphal story in which a gay-baiting Senator George Smathers was quoted as saying during a 1950 Florida Senate primary that his opponent's sister in Greenwich Village was a "known thespian."

Turning serious, Barbour compared the pro-Romney super PACs to "the charity hospital" or a "big not-for-profit cancer research program that you give to." He concluded by saying, "I know everybody in here wants their children and grandchildren to inherit the same country we did. I honestly believe those are the stakes." The millionaires and billionaires on hand no doubt believed that, but their "charitable" (read "political") impulses conveniently dovetailed with their commercial interests. Unlike most wealthy Democratic donors (who are generally in the game for ego or ambassadorships), most of these donors sought explicit business favors from the government in a Romney administration. For instance, Harold Simmons, who would give nearly $27 million to Republicans in the 2012 cycle, owned a company called Waste Control Specialists that could not return to profitability unless the Nuclear Regulatory Commission changed a rule and allowed the firm to bury depleted uranium left over from the cold war at a private dump in West Texas instead of a federal waste disposal site. Even though the federal government had never allowed the privatization of such dangerous work, Romney said early in the campaign that he would favor such a rule change.

Besides being forums for extracting cash, conventions in recent decades have been judged by the television takeaway. The original plan had called for using precious prime time on the last night of the convention to further humanize Romney. Ted and Pat Oparowski told the moving story of their fourteen-year-old son who was dying from lymphoma in the 1970s. Romney visited the boy often and helped him make a will dividing up his possessions. Boston produced a beautiful ten-minute film that tough critics in both parties called one of the best convention movies ever made. It depicted a man of character, depth, and unusual leadership abilities. But neither the Oparowskis nor the film were seen by a wide TV audience. Both ran early, before network coverage. Romney advisers said the networks would have cut away from the campaign film, as they had in the past. Instead Boston opted for stunt casting that caused it to lose control of the convention just when the big audience was tuning in.

———

ROMNEY HAD FIRST met Clint Eastwood at a fundraiser in California, where he asked him if he would speak at his convention. Eastwood was originally scheduled for the second night, but after the hurricane, he was moved to the third. The trouble began after the film icon arrived in Tampa and awestruck Romney staffers failed to vet his remarks and insert them in the teleprompter like every other speaker's.

"Are you going to talk like you did at the fundraisers?" Russ Schriefer, who was managing the convention, asked him. "Yup," Eastwood replied. "He's Clint Eastwood—*you* argue with him," Schriefer explained later. When, shortly before taking the stage, Eastwood asked for a chair, puzzled Romney staffers complied without asking why he needed one.

Within moments the indelible image of the Tampa Convention was not of a warm and fuzzy Mitt Romney but of an eighty-two-year-old ad-libbing actor holding a peculiar conversation with an empty chair that he said contained an invisible "Mr. Obama." "What do you want me to tell Romney?" Eastwood asked the chair, as if he were Jimmy Stewart's Elwood and the chair held a foulmouthed version of Harvey, the invisible rabbit. "I can't tell him to do that to himself."

Ignoring a flashing red light, Eastwood rambled on for twelve minutes about everything from Guantánamo to the problem with lawyers. Film critic Roger Ebert summed up the verdict on Twitter: "*Clint*, my hero, is coming across as sad and pathetic." Teddy Goff ran into Jim Messina's office to tell him the story was exploding online. It didn't take long for @BarackObama to tweet a picture of Obama and a chair in the Cabinet Room with a caption that read, "This seat's taken."

Afterward Beth Myers and others close to Romney were furious with Stevens and Schriefer for not keeping Eastwood to a script. Conventions, unlike interviews, debates, and candidate town halls, are entirely controllable events, which made this a major unforced error. An annoyed Ann Romney didn't even pretend to defend Eastwood's performance when she appeared on the *Today* show the next morning.

Romney's acceptance speech was widely described as "solid," which wasn't enough to keep it from being overshadowed by Eastwood's act. He told charming stories about his parents and early married life before explaining his business career (though uttering hardly a word about his governorship) and pivoting to a critique of Obama and a recitation of his own five-point jobs plan (energy independence, tax cuts, less regulation, deficit reduction, favors for small business) that contained nothing new. "You need to actually convince voters by making a positive case for the Romney-Ryan ticket," said Bill Kristol, the editor of the *Weekly Standard*. He and many other conservative analysts didn't hear that case. Romney pilloried Obama on foreign policy (he "threw Israel under the bus") but forgot to give a shout-out to American troops serving in Iraq and Afghanistan.* The sarcastic jab at the president for

---

* A tribute to the troops had been planned for Monday night. When that evening's convention was canceled because of the hurricane, Romney aides forgot to reinsert the tribute later in the week.

promising to "heal the planet" won applause in the hall but hardly helped him win the pro-environment independents he needed.

While Romney lumbered through his convention, Obama was on reddit, a crowdsourced social news site known by few of the Tampa delegates, though popular with many of their children. The president answered questions about Internet freedom and other issues for forty-five minutes, typing his answers himself. He mentioned, as he did in most speeches, gottaregister.org, the OFA site yielding impressive new registration numbers, and ended, at Goff's suggestion, with an inside joke for the three million reddit users: "NOT BAD." This was a natural locution for a president whose favorite superlative around the White House was "pretty good." The reddit appearance was another sign that Obama's dominance of the digital campaign was not only not bad, it was a pretty good indicator that he was on a winning track.

THE DEMOCRATS ASSEMBLED at their convention in Charlotte ready to rip Romney's face off. "Ask Osama bin Laden if he's better off now than he was four years ago!" John Kerry thundered. Former Michigan governor Jennifer Granholm twisted the knife with glee: "In Mitt Romney's view, the cars get the elevator and the workers get the shaft." Congressman John Lewis of Georgia cast resistance to voter suppression as the latest chapter in the civil rights movement: "I've seen this before. I lived this before. Too many people struggled, suffered, and died to make it possible for every American to exercise their right to vote. We must stand up, speak up, and speak out. We must march to the polls like never, ever before." But with 23 million Americans still out of work, Democrats needed to offer a more compelling explanation of why they hadn't done better on the issue that mattered most to voters.

For more than two years, Bill Clinton had religiously devoted at least an hour a day to studying the economy and how to fix it. The effort produced great clarity in his thinking and an underrated book. Now he had spent weeks outlining his nominating speech, intent on making it logical rather than rhetorical. To align Clinton's speech with the campaign and avoid surprises, Axelrod asked that he work with Gene Sperling, Obama's director of the National Economic Council, and Bruce Reed, Biden's chief of staff. Both were veterans of the Clinton White House, with their loyalties now divided. As Sperling and Reed spent seven straight hours whittling down their old boss's remarks, they felt a sense of elation. Not once did the former president make a snide comment at Obama's expense, as he had so often in the past. Sperling took the draft to Plouffe, Axelrod, and Obama, who had only a few minor clarifications. Because Clinton took a nap before incorporating Obama's changes, the final draft didn't go out publicly until it was in the teleprompter and being delivered—a habit of Clinton's that left younger, less plugged-in White House aides fretting.

They needn't have worried. Clinton gave one of the best speeches in recent convention history. It worked in part by being less an oration (for which there is little patience anymore) than a talk—a sophisticated and fact-rich argument delivered in an accessible conversational tone that explained the reasoning behind giving Obama a second term. Even the Fox commentators who had brayed for his removal from office in 1998 now conceded that Clinton had scored heavily. Where he seemed to be ad-libbing, the former president was actually inserting from memory sections from his original draft that had been cut for time, then using his huge expressive hands and twinkly half-smile to drive home the point.

Beyond reminding delegates that Obama was inclusive on the big things ("Heck, he even appointed Hillary!"), selling his accomplishments and savaging the "arithmetic" of Republicans, Clinton lambasted GOP obstructionists, something that Obama had been loath to do for fear of looking weak and ineffectual. "They think government is always the enemy, they're always right, and compromise is always weakness," he said. By blaming economic woes on Congress in a way that sounded perfectly rational, Clinton offered more than the imprimatur of a former president; he shredded the Republicans' claim that the Obama presidency was a left-wing departure from his own and lampooned the heart of their argument: "We left him a total mess, he hasn't cleaned it up fast enough, so fire him and put us back in." When Clinton said, "No president, not me, not any of my predecessors, could have fixed in four years the economy that Obama inherited," it was hard to imagine a fair-minded American voter disagreeing. The alternative to Romney, he implied, was to embrace the investment in the middle class that gave the country the prosperity of the Clinton years. Even if this ignored the tech boom and other factors, his buoyant logic suggested the promise of a return to better times.

When the two presidents embraced onstage, Sperling felt as if he were a child of divorce thrilled to learn that his parents were not only talking again but actually getting along. A friend emailed Obama that he should appoint Clinton "Secretary of Explaining Shit," which Obama changed to "stuff" on the stump. It raised the question of whether health care reform might have been more popular had the two men reconciled earlier and Clinton been designated to explain it. Even before the convention, Clinton had agreed to a vigorous schedule of speaking on behalf of Obama. He was a smash with Democratic audiences in battleground states. After the third debate, he had breakfast with Messina in Chicago and agreed to campaign full-time for the last three weeks, which was like having another vice presidential candidate, only better. Clinton relished his new stature in a party that had once been ashamed of him, and he knew that he was helping his wife to be nominated practically by acclamation in 2016, if she chose to run. Obama was just happy to have all the help he could get.

————

OBAMA'S ACCEPTANCE SPEECH was written a week ahead of time, an eternity in Obama World. The most important line in it may have been the simple "I am the president." This was a rebuke to everyone from Joe Wilson (the congressman who shouted "You lie!" during a joint session of Congress in 2009) to Rush Limbaugh and Clint Eastwood. It was directed at all those who had disrespected him or questioned his legitimacy in office. Afterward it resonated especially well with ardent supporters who were waiting for him to stand up for himself.

The speech deftly laid out that the election wasn't merely a choice between candidates and parties but "between two fundamentally different visions for the future." This was the essence of the 2012 contest. Obama's "basic bargain," was a fresh way of framing the New Deal, the Fair Deal, and the Great Society. "My grandparents were given the chance to go to college and buy their home and fulfill the basic bargain at the heart of America's story, the promise that hard work will pay off, that responsibility will be rewarded, that everyone gets a fair shot and everyone does their fair share and everyone plays by the same rules."

The "dial groups" of swing voters responded especially well to the parts of the speech where the president sounded positive and hopeful, a note that the high command took for debate prep. Chicago didn't think voters needed to be reminded that the economic problems Romney blamed on Obama had in fact started under Bush. "Do you think they don't know what Bush did to them?" Benenson asked in his charmingly acidic style.

The speech was not well-reviewed. "Where Clinton entertains and explains, Obama tends to sermonize and exhort," wrote Joseph Lelyveld, former executive editor of the *New York Times*. But Obama covered the points necessary to advance his campaign, which would not have been well-served by high-flown rhetoric. He laid out a pallid, poll-tested second-term agenda that included such crowd-pleasers as a million manufacturing jobs, 100,000 new teachers, and getting rid of subsidies for oil companies. Other items on the agenda—comprehensive immigration reform, action on climate change, raising the minimum wage—would have to wait until after the election. With the Democratic base nailed down, the goal was to lure independents, not please liberals.

To address disappointed voters, the president tried to shift the onus for hope and change from himself onto "you." "The election four years ago wasn't about me. It was about you," he said. "My fellow citizens, you were the change." If depersonalizing the movement diminished Obama, the White House could live with that. With his subdued tone and plain language, Obama sought to convey that he was a humble, farsighted leader on the side of the middle class. While Jon Favreau, as usual, penned the first draft after conversations with the president, Obama wrote the pivotal humility section himself, with an assist from his favorite president. "While I'm proud of what we've achieved together," Obama said, "I'm far more mindful of my own failings, knowing exactly what Lincoln meant when he said, 'I have been driven to my knees many times by the overwhelming conviction that I had no place else to go.'"

If this wasn't quite the frank confession of failure that Stuart Stevens hoped to goad him into, the passage nimbly addressed his reputation for cockiness, as did a self-effacing line about how sick everyone was of hearing "I'm Barack Obama and I approved this message." The absence of other compelling metaphors remained a problem. The stirring paean to citizenship, for instance, was missing an allusion that might linger in the mind. But the ending struck the same notes of destiny and commonality that had carried him so far: "America, I never said this journey would be easy, and I won't promise that now. Yes, our path is harder, but it leads to a better place. Yes, our road is longer, but we travel it together."

Afterward the president was in good spirits. His convention was a success. It showed a unified and relatively centrist party whose members actually looked like America. Michelle Obama's speech had reminded everyone of why they liked her husband personally, and he did nothing to mar the impression.

Public polls showed an Obama bump of 5 points nationally after the convention, but national polls were irrelevant in Chicago, where internal numbers showed only a 1-point gain in battleground states. That was fine. Charlotte had motivated the troops, which was the important thing.

The weak jobs numbers released the day after the convention,

96,000, did nothing to dampen the mood, though they worried Obama economists. With 150,000 new jobs required each month just to keep up with population increases, the Obama job growth record continued to be anemic. Austan Goolsbee, former chairman of the Council of Economic Advisers and still close to the campaign, liked to throw a scare into Obama supporters by telling them that the Bureau of Labor Statistics margin of error was plus or minus 100,000 jobs (until the official revisions, which could be months away). So the whole thing was appallingly random. The presidency might depend on a statistic of dubious validity except as the roughest indication of direction. Plouffe believed that beyond a few data heads, the larger public would care only if the number dipped into negative territory, snapping a streak of more than thirty months of job creation. But with the margin of error, that could seem to be happening even if it wasn't.

Such a report would constitute the "new information" that Plouffe dreaded. He told a dozen top fundraisers in Charlotte that he expected Obama to win unless voters were exposed to news from home or abroad that changed their calculation. Otherwise the game seemed under control.

As the fall campaign began, the president, joined for the first time at a fundraiser by his hero, Michael Jordan, said he couldn't resist a basketball analogy: "We are in the fourth quarter. We're up by a few points, but the other side is coming strong and they play a little dirty. If you've got a little bit of a lead and there's about seven minutes [to go], that's when you put them away."

———

WITH A DAMAGED candidate and the country's demographics lined up against them, Republicans needed more than a limp economy to win the election. But their two biggest assets—a bottomless war chest and concerted voter-suppression efforts—were failing them. The super PAC aerial bombardment was not weakening the will of the people, who had mostly made up their minds oblivious to TV ads. Not a single pro-Romney ad cut through the clutter enough to become part of the conversation. And efforts in state capitals to supress turnout were backfiring.

By now, voter suppression was emerging from the shadows of the campaign as a major civil rights issue. Bill Clinton recalled seeing racial discrimination at the polls in pre–Voting Rights Act Arkansas in the mid-1960s. But he said it didn't compare to 2012: "In my lifetime, nobody's ever done anything quite this blatant."

By late summer it was clear that the GOP's efforts to discourage voting weren't turning out as planned. First, the American Legislative Exchange Council was forced from the battlefield in the wake of the highly publicized Trayvon Martin case. After George Zimmerman killed Martin, an unarmed seventeen-year-old African American carrying nothing but a pack of Skittles, Florida authorities at first said they couldn't arrest Zimmerman because of the state's Stand Your Ground law, which allowed the use of lethal force on the slightest pretext. When word spread that ALEC had won passage of similar bills in more than a dozen states, several corporations, fearful of bad publicity, left the Council. To prevent a stampede of corporate backers, ALEC announced that it would, for now, drop its efforts on behalf of both Stand Your Ground bills and its "vote fraud" legislation, which had already helped lead to new laws in nineteen states.

Meanwhile voter-suppression efforts were not faring well in the courts. In Florida, where the Brennan Center for Justice filed suit with the Obama Justice Department under the Voting Rights Act, a federal judge called the provision of the election law requiring that registration forms be turned in within forty-eight hours "harsh and impractical," and ruled that the bill had "no purpose other than to discourage" constitutionally protected activity. The Obama campaign, the League of Women Voters, the NAACP, and others engaged in voter registration got back to work in time to make a difference.

Unfortunately for OFA, the part of the statute that cut early voting time was allowed to stand—a serious blow to Obama's chances in Florida. The intentionally confusing law let people vote early for eight days in late October, but closed the early voting sites on the last six days before Election Day. So the Obama campaign would have to try to get word out to black churches that they needed the buses on the previous Sunday, nine days before Election Day. It might not work. The "Souls to the Polls" Democratic tradition was central to the ground game in Florida, where 33 percent of those who voted on the last Sunday before the 2008 election were African American and 23 percent were Latino. With polling places expected to be jammed, Bauer's team of lawyers, dubbed the "Legal Brain Trust," would be filing suit to restore early voting in three Florida counties right up to Election Day.

Wisconsin had attached a series of requirements for student IDs, including expiration dates on the cards. Requiring tens of thousands of students to get new IDs would have held down the youth vote. A state judge invalidated the law and allowed continuation of same-day registration, a ruling that Chicago felt tipped Paul Ryan's home state to

Obama. After the election, Wisconsin state senator Alberta Darling, a cochair of Romney's campaign there, said Romney "absolutely" would have won Wisconsin had the voter ID law been allowed to take effect. Because Obama carried the state by 200,000 votes, Darling was suggesting that at least 200,001 legally registered Wisconsinites should have been legitimately discouraged from voting. It was a perfect encapsulation of the hyperpartisan motive behind the laws.

Republican voter-suppression efforts in other key states fared no better. Republican Governor Rick Snyder of Michigan, recognizing that many of the GOP-controlled state legislatures had gone too far, vetoed an election reform bill, explaining that it was poorly drafted. Under pressure, New Hampshire pushed back the effective date of its photo ID bills to 2013. At first, a Pennsylvania state court upheld the photo ID law, though the judge was forced to delay implementation of the statute when the state supreme court ruled that Pennsylvanians would be disenfranchised by it. The Keystone State would, for now, operate under the old rules.

The pendulum began to swing back toward democracy in Ohio too. OFA not only got the GOP's voter-suppression law on the November ballot for repeal, but it changed public opinion. Fearful of losing the referendum, Ohio Republicans in May did something highly unusual if not unprecedented: They repealed their own law, wiping out several voter-suppression techniques. At first glance, that seemed to settle the issue in Ohio. But crafty GOP legislators in Columbus had a trick up their sleeves. When fashioning the bill in early 2011, they had placed the details of early voting procedures in a separate technical measure that they now refused to repeal. This provision barred early voting on the weekend before the election, the period when more than 100,000 African Americans took part in Ohio's "Souls to the Polls." In a close election in the most pivotal battleground state, that could mean defeat for the president.

Like Pennsylvania Majority Leader Mike Turzai, who admitted his motive for restricting voting was to carry Pennsylvania for Romney, the GOP chair in the Columbus area, Doug Preisse, a close adviser to Governor John Kasich, gave the game away to the *Columbus Dispatch*: "I guess I really actually feel we shouldn't contort the voting process to accommodate the urban—read African-American—voter-turnout machine." All the talk of vote fraud as the reason for limiting voting hours gave way to this frank acknowledgment that Republicans didn't want black Democrats to have the option to cast their ballots over the weekend, when they were likely off work and had more time, even if the result was a repeat of the four-hour Election Day lines of 2004. The Obama campaign, seeing Ohio hanging in the balance, sued.

The Republicans had one last Ohio card to play. The RNC hired Washington lawyers Michael Morley and Will Consovoy, products of the conservative Federal Society (which was created in the wake of Lewis Powell's landmark 1971 memo), to represent military service organizations in the case. Their argument was that letting everyone, not just the military, vote in the three days before the election would undermine the military's special status. The VFW, American Legion, and other supposedly nonpartisan service organizations were now officially on Romney's side of a novel legal argument. Boston unleashed a blistering attack on Obama for trying to "restrict military voting." The Obama suit was an "outrage" against "our brave men and women in uniform," the Romney statement said. Like Romney's other distortions, this one traveled far on Fox, even as independent fact-checkers pointed out that the Obama campaign was simply seeking to equalize voting rights for all Ohioans.

OFA won. On August 31 U.S. District Court Judge Peter Economus issued an injunction ordering the polls open in Ohio the last three days before the election. In a last-ditch effort to win partisan points, Ohio secretary of state Jon Husted told the state's eighty-eight county Boards of Election that it would be "too confusing" to comply with the federal court order because a higher court might reverse it. He later gave a speech in Toledo attacking the decision as "un-American" for intruding on the prerogatives of the states, an unwise move during pending litigation.

Bob Bauer was in Charlotte for the Democratic Convention when he took part in a conference call with the clerk of the court, who said Judge Economus would hear OFA's motion to enforce the court order on early voting. With an edge in her voice, the clerk said the judge expected Ohio's secretary of state to appear personally at the hearing, a highly unusual development. This was the clerk's way of hinting that Husted might face a contempt citation if he didn't clean up his act. The clerk told Husted's lawyer that the only way around this outcome was for Husted to immediately rescind his directive to the counties and apologize personally to Judge Economus. Husted complied and apologized for "the misimpression," but he wasn't done yet. After he lost the case on appeal, he issued another thunderbolt through his director of elections, arguing that the Obama suit was partially responsible for making it impossible to extend registration deadlines for the military. This made no sense; the Obama suit had been about extending early

voting, not military registration. Bauer demanded Husted's lawyers rescind the directive and asked them if they really wanted Husted to go
back before Judge Economus after he called the judge's opinion "un-
American." With that, the Ohio secretary of state finally stood down.

But the fight over voter suppression in Ohio and Florida would go
all the way to Election Day.

23

Makers versus Takers

In 1972, as the Watergate scandal was unfolding, Richard Nixon's re-election campaign attacked the Democratic nominee, Senator George McGovern, for his position on welfare. In one ad, sponsored by Democrats for Nixon, the Republicans went after McGovern's 1972 proposal for a negative income tax aimed at ending poverty with tax refunds of up to $1,000 per person. The idea of a negative income tax had originated with Milton Friedman, the godfather of conservative economics, and was proposed by Nixon himself (with the help of his aide Daniel Patrick Moynihan), as recently as 1970. Two years later Nixon, mobilizing resentments, saw political opportunity. The ad showed a construction worker (so-called hard hats were the core of Nixon's base) eating his lunch on a steel beam. "McGovern's bill would make 47 percent of people in the United States eligible for welfare," the narrator intoned. Then he repeated the number: "47 percent."

IT's IMPOSSIBLE TO know exactly why an unassuming blue-collar worker, a man not unlike that hard hat eating his lunch on the construction beam, decided to expose Mitt Romney's private comments at a Florida fundraiser and change the course of the 2012 campaign. Some clues may be found on an inky black September night seven years earlier in the Everglades.

The visibility on the highway that evening was poor, and a car plunged into a ten-foot-deep canal. A six-foot-three man in his early thirties who worked selling motorcycles at a dealership nearby, heard the crash and sprinted hundreds of yards to the canal, where a passerby had already broken his hand punching out the passenger-side window of the quickly submerging car, trying to free the woman, trapped inside by her seat belt. When he arrived at the scene the man plunged into the murky water several times and was finally able to unlock the door from the driver's side, but he couldn't pull the unconscious woman free. The passerby with the broken hand and other bystanders yelled, "Dude, she's gone. She's gone." The man would later say that he had slept well ever since because he kept trying. He knew from having done volunteer EMT work that the woman could live minutes longer. With the help of a bowie knife he was finally able to cut through the seat belt and free the driver, who floated to the surface. He remembered smiling to himself when he was underwater, knowing that he had saved her. As a coworker administered CPR, onlookers peering into the water yelled "Baby seat!" The man dived down several more times, feeling in the pitch black for a baby, but fortunately found no child in the car. The driver, a single mother, survived. Later the mayor and town council of nearby Davie, Florida, gave the man a watch, and Liberty Mutual Insurance Company awarded him its "Life Savers Award" for "outstanding courage and humanity."

The man's name was Scott Prouty and he later said the experience convinced him, "If you *can* jump in, you *should* jump in." Growing up in a white working-class neighborhood in Quincy, Massachusetts, Prouty had known families without enough money for heat. He had seen suffering and suffered himself, breaking his neck playing high school football and later surviving a liver ailment. For as long as he could remember, he had to change the channel if he saw a nature program showing one animal killing another. He had wanted to be a cop, and, later, a lawyer, but he dropped out of Northeastern University and moved to South Florida, where for a time he managed a collection of nightclubs, a business arrangement that ended badly (with Prouty owing a few thousand dollars in back taxes he eventually paid). Now thirty-nine, Prouty was working as a bartender for a high-end catering company. He and his girlfriend devoted long hours on weekends to helping the South Florida Society for the Prevention of Cruelty to Animals. He had traveled to the Galápagos Islands, where he contemplated both Darwinism and Social Darwinism, the heartless nineteenth-century application of Darwin's theory of survival of the fittest to modern capitalism.

Prouty was well-informed about politics, though not the type to get involved in campaigns. His political involvement had extended no further than once attending an anti–Iraq War rally. As a white working-class male, he fit into a demographic group that ended up voting heavily for Mitt Romney. He had no intention of doing so himself; he was a liberal. Besides, he hadn't developed a good first impression of the Republican candidate. At a September 2011 Romney fundraiser at the home of Marc Leder, a private equity fund manager, Prouty had been told that the governor would like a Diet Coke with a slice of lemon. He served it to him with a napkin and said later that he received not even a simple "Thank you," the same you-are-invisible treatment that makeup artists in TV studios had complained about. This was later depicted as a grievance Prouty was nursing against Romney, which he denied. But after the next event, when the whole thing blew up, Prouty realized that he in some ways represented all of the "invisible" service workers who tend to the powerful while keeping their eyes and ears open.

When the catering company was booked to work another Romney event for seventy guests at Leder's house on May 17, 2012, Prouty was intrigued. He wanted to see if Romney said the same thing behind closed doors as he did on television. Before leaving home for the $50,000-per-person fundraiser, he inserted a large memory card into his Canon digital camera, just in case Romney said something interesting. Many of the others who worked the event also brought cameras. Several had catered a dinner where Bill Clinton came back to the work areas to pose for pictures, and they hoped to get one with Romney. No one told any of them that they couldn't bring cameras or even tape the event if they wanted to, as campaign videographers seemed to be doing.

According to Prouty, the governor arrived and departed without shaking hands with the waiters, busboys, cooks, carhops, and others working the event—his attention was on the donors—but that was the least of it. The waitstaff wasn't happy when a Romney aide called shortly before the entourage arrived and insisted that dinner be served twenty minutes early because of the candidate's schedule. That wreaked havoc with the caterers' carefully synchronized operation. And the faster pace wasn't enough for Romney, who, during his remarks, arrogantly told the waitstaff, "Don't slow down. Come in, clear the places," as if, the waiters thought, he was their boss.

By the time Romney was giving instructions to the caterers, it had been several minutes since the bartender placed his camera on the bar with a view of the dining area and pressed "Record."

———

ON ONE LEVEL, the 2012 campaign was simpler and less elevated than 2008. The Republican candidate portrayed the president as a failure on the economy and said a man of his business background could do better. The Democratic president said he'd done as well as could be expected in hard times and that the challenger's business experience— buying companies to extract a profit for investors—was the wrong background for protecting the American middle class.

But this frame didn't do justice to the intensity and complexity of class politics in 2012. Obama could talk about the social contract (or "basic bargain," as he called it in his acceptance speech), but he had to be careful not to focus on the poor, lest middle-class voters turn their resentments on them as they did in 1972. Conversely, Romney had to be careful not to seem too focused on the rich, lest middle-class voters turn their resentments on them as they did during the 1930s. A voter in David Simas's OFA online community summarized the views of many independents: "I'm sick and tired of bailouts to guys at the top and handouts to guys at the bottom."

The class tension was reminiscent of the 1936 election, when the *New Yorker* ran Peter Arno's famous cartoon of plutocrats saying to one another, "Let's go down to the Trans-Lux and hiss Roosevelt." David Axelrod was at a Chicago Bulls game one night when an agitated man came up from his $112,500-a-year courtside seat, tugged at his pants, and said, "Why doesn't Barack just take my whole wallet?" Axelrod replied, "Brother, if you're sitting in those seats, I don't think you have a problem."

Elizabeth Warren's Senate campaign crystallized the class issues that animated 2012. It wasn't that the populist professor ran such a brilliant campaign in Massachusetts against Scott Brown, whom she trailed in a deep blue state until Labor Day. But Warren helped Democratic candidates and even the president craft a story about what had happened in the United States in recent decades. In her stump speech, she walked the audience through the great achievements of late twentieth-century progressivism up until the 1980s, when the United States decided "government works for people who can hire a lot of lawyers and lobbyists." Now "General Electric pays nothing in taxes while young people take on more in debt and seniors have to get by on less." Meanwhile many of these same corporations began exporting good jobs overseas, where the cost of labor was cheap. The decline of unions and a deregulatory mood in Washington let them operate with impunity. Warren thought that after the Great Recession, the United States would return to investing in the real economy instead of finance. "I was wrong—the people who brought us this doubled down."

Warren liked to bring up a movement that had faded even faster than the Tea Party but also left its mark. She recalled that in the summer of 2011, the only number in the public debate was $14 trillion. "That was the only conversation—the debt and how to cut it," she said. "Then Occupy Wall Street fundamentally changed the conversation." Now "the 99 percent" and "the 1 percent" were also part of the public dialogue. If the Democrats could hold the White House, maybe a broader debate might be possible about how to restore fairness and opportunity.

Romney had said in the winter that he wanted that argument held only in "quiet rooms," by which he meant places where like-minded people who understood business might gather. But now even the hushed sanctuaries of the superrich, where donors spent the average yearly salary of an American worker on dinner with a politician, could be breached by some guy with a camera and a YouTube account.

———

MARC LEDER, the host of the Boca Raton event, was an investor with a net worth of more than $400 million.* Inspired to enter the world of private equity after a meeting with Romney at Bain Capital in 1995, Leder specialized in buying ailing companies and stripping them of their assets. At the time of his Romney fundraiser, about 20 percent of the companies recently owned by the firm he cofounded, Sun Capital Partners, had filed for bankruptcy. In late 2011 the federal Pension Benefit Guaranty Corporation accused Sun of pushing Friendly's, a legendary chain of ice-cream parlors, into bankruptcy in order to dodge $100 million in pension liabilities, which were then shifted to the government. Even as Leder denied any wrongdoing, the net effect was the U.S. government saving Sun Capital tens of millions of dollars.

Private equity had its place in the American economy. Barack and Michelle Obama were among the millions whose college educations had been paid for by scholarship funds that benefited from investment in Bain-backed companies. But Romney and protégés like Leder were only "makers" if the profits of shareholders were the sole standard for assessing one's contribution to the economy. Otherwise they might also be regarded, depending on the deal, as "takers" whose pension and tax favors constituted a subsidy from the government far larger than any received by a retiree, a veteran, or a student.

———

A FEW MINUTES INTO his remarks at Leder's home, Romney recalled:

> Back in my private equity days, we went to China to buy a factory there. It employed about twenty thousand people and they were almost all young women between the ages of about eighteen to twenty-two or twenty-three. They were saving for potentially becoming married, and they work in these huge factories that make very small appliances. And we were walking through these facilities, see-

---

* Leder was probably best known to the public for hosting a wild party in Bridgehampton, New York, in 2011 featuring Russian fire dancers and guests having sex in the pool.

ing them work, the numbers of hours they work per day, the pittance they earn, living in dormitories with little bathrooms at the end. The rooms, they had ten or twelve girls per room—three bunk beds on top of each other. . . . And around this factory was a huge fence with barbed wires and guard towers. And we said, "Gosh! I can't believe you, you know, keep these girls in!" They said, "No, no, no. This is to keep other people from coming in."

Prouty had not come to the event expecting Romney to go much beyond his stump speech, but this sweatshop business struck him as both unusual and offensive. The barbed wire and guard towers were to keep people *out*? Who was he kidding? The bartender decided on the spot that the candidate was a menace: "I heard zero empathy in his voice—for anybody. I looked around the room to see if anyone else was disgusted, and no one seemed to be. Romney's tone was, 'Isn't that wonderful that we can share this with the world?' Share *this*? I said to myself, 'If this guy is running the show, he's a danger—almost a socio-path.' It was clear he thought that China factory he visited was a good business model to invest in—it was almost as if he was saying that it would be fine in Ohio too."

Just as Romney was praising the business opportunities of sweat-shop labor, a Secret Service agent wandered near the bar. Prouty placed a bar cloth over the camera, which is visible for a moment on the tape. He figured he had something good, even explosive, and he didn't want to be asked to turn off the camera. When the agent left, he removed the cloth. He was determined to capture as much as he could and make his escape.

After the fundraiser, Prouty didn't watch the sixty-eight-minute tape for two weeks. He worried about what would happen to him and to the catering company (whose owners he admired) if he went public: "I just sat there and said, 'Do it or don't do it. Do it or don't do it.' I asked myself, 'If he gets elected, will I be able to look at myself again?' I went into the bathroom in the middle of the night, looked in the mirror and said, 'You fucking coward.'"

As he weighed what to do, Prouty couldn't get the image of Romney in China out of his mind: "I couldn't believe he could go on a factory tour like that and get such a warm and fuzzy feeling. I was waiting for him to say, 'And I knocked down those fences and improved the work-ing conditions and it became more profitable because of it!' Romney didn't say that, though." Prouty began to do a bit of math on the con-ditions he found inhumane. "Romney said there were twelve girls per room, so eight or ten rooms per "little bathroom" equals more than a

hundred girls using a bucket or squat toilet. They have hoses for show-
ers. They get to leave once a year. All for what Romney called a 'pittance.' I wish I'd been able to shout at the event, 'Would you want your
wife working there, Mitt?'"

Just as he did with the submerged car in the Everglades, Prouty decided to jump in, first by creating a YouTube channel on May 31 that
he called "RomneyExposed." He used editing software to cut the video
into several short clips that included the China comments, muffle the
sound, and darken the pictures to make them harder to trace back to
the Boca Raton event. This also made it more difficult for news organizations to authenticate. Was this current video or years old? Was it doc-
tored? No one watching the clips could tell, though Prouty left a video
ID number on the clips so that bloggers could slice it up and further
disseminate it online. He began learning all he could about slave labor
conditions around the world. By midsummer his Twitter, email, and
other accounts used the photograph of a girl on the cover of Leslie T.
Chang's book *Factory Girls: From Village to City in a Changing China*.
He thought he would need a disguise, and a small Asian girl was the
opposite of who he was. His Twitter handle, @AnneOnymous670, also
suggested that he was a woman, the better to throw people off his trail
when he escalated his video assaults on Romney.

For weeks before the world learned of the full "47 percent" video,
Prouty conducted a guerrilla campaign against Romney on the subject
of Chinese sweatshop labor. He was especially interested when David
Corn of *Mother Jones* magazine reported on July 11 that Romney, contrary to his claims that he wasn't an outsourcer, had in 1998 used a
Bain-connected company he owned, Brookside Capital Partners Fund,
to buy nearly a 10 percent stake in a Chinese factory called Global-
Tech Appliances. It sounded just like the factory Romney described in
Boca, which Boston never denied. The Global-Tech investment, made
when Romney was in full control of Bain, connected Romney to some
of the worst corporate layoffs of the last fifteen years. Global-Tech was
the sole supplier for Sunbeam, whose CEO, Albert J. Dunlap, earned
the nickname "Chainsaw Al" for announcing 6,400 Sunbeam layoffs in
1998, the same year Romney made his investment in the Chinese appli-
ance factory that likely took many of those American jobs.*

The Pittsburgh-based Institute for Global Labour and Human Rights,
a labor-backed nonprofit best known for busting Kathie Lee Gifford
in 1996 for manufacturing her clothing line in overseas sweatshops,

---

* Brookside shared its piece of Global-Tech with Sankaty High Yield Asset Investors, a mys-
terious Romney-owned Bermuda corporation. Both sold their stakes in 2000.

saw the RomneyExposed clips and decided immediately that Romney was talking about Global-Tech. IGLHR's director, Charles Kernaghan, later said that Prouty, whose identity he didn't yet know, spurred him in July to hire Chinese researchers (skilled workers who could obtain short-term employment inside Global-Tech) to document abuses at the plant.* Kernaghan then issued a damning report on the abuses in the Chinese plant once partially owned by Romney. It received little attention. In the middle of a presidential campaign, the media had scant interest in stories about overseas labor conditions, even if they spoke volumes about the Republican nominee. To get more attention, Prouty posted one of the Chinese labor clips on YouTube under the name "Rachel Maddow." Maddow's staff asked YouTube to take the clip down, though she mentioned it on her MSNBC show and posted it for a few days on her site. The clip was retweeted thousands of times, which made Prouty feel as if he was starting to break through.†

Because Maddow hadn't inquired further, Prouty moved to what he called "Plan B." He tweeted David Corn and got no response, so he settled for reaching out to James Carter, who was credited at the bottom of the *Mother Jones* article with helping provide research for Corn. (At the time, Corn didn't know that Carter was the thirty-five-year-old grandson of former president Jimmy Carter.) When Carter saw that he had a Twitter follower named @AnneOnymous670 with some compelling Romney video, he and Corn began investigating whether there was a connection between the clips and Global-Tech. They made contact on August 28, though Prouty disputed the idea that he was "discovered" by anyone. As far as he was concerned, he was already midway through his plan to administer a form of Chinese water torture to a presidential candidate he had come to despise.

Prouty still wasn't ready to part with the entire tape, the release of which he feared would bring down the wrath of the Republican Party on every person working the Boca event. His aim was to time his releases of ten video clips for maximum damage to Romney during and after the Republican National Convention in late August. He made a list for Corn of the most noteworthy moments on the long tape, including Romney disparaging a two-state solution in the Middle East and his remarks about 47 percent of Americans receiving entitlements, but he remained focused on Romney's involvement with Chinese sweatshops. "I

---

* If the researchers were caught documenting working conditions without authorization, they could be tried by China as spies.

† Prouty also posted Chinese labor clips on dailykos.com, but they were removed when they couldn't be verified.

think bragging about buying a sweatshop filled with twenty thousand young girls is more morally objectionable than name-calling on who doesn't pay income taxes," he said later in explaining why he didn't leap first on the "47 percent" comments.

In late August laid-off workers at a Bain-owned company in Freeport, Illinois, Sensata Technologies, made an anti-Romney video of themselves watching Romney talking about doing business in China on the "AnneOnymous670" tape. It was evidence, they thought, that the Republican nominee had no respect for American workers. Prouty warmed to the idea of destroying Romney's campaign. "If I'm going to get in a fight," he said later, "I'm gonna punch the other guy in the face as hard as I can." As he weighed whether to give Corn the whole tape, he consulted a lawyer in Palm Beach who told him that the risks to him far outweighed any personal satisfaction he might get. "Don't do it," the lawyer said, warning that Florida law banned surreptitious taping, not of Romney (a public figure) but of anyone else at the event. Prouty ignored the advice. After talking at length to the *Huffington Post* and the *New York Times*, he chose Corn because of the *Mother Jones* Global-Tech story. But it took Corn many hours to convince Prouty to turn over anything more than untraceable audio. Corn said he could protect Prouty's identity but he needed the full video and to specify where and when the fundraiser took place. Finally, Prouty decided to release the whole tape, but he still took precautions. He donned gloves to prevent leaving fingerprints and sent the full video by regular mail so it couldn't be traced. Corn received the memory card on September 11 and, after checking with lawyers and probing Prouty's past, posted it on the *Mother Jones* website on September 17. The story rocked the presidential campaign as hard as any external event in modern memory.

———

IN BOCA RATON, Marc Leder apologized to the Romney campaign and tried for a time to find the source of the video. He failed. While the camera angle clearly suggested it had been shot from the bar, anyone who knew or suspected the bartender wasn't talking. Prouty quit his job, changed his home telephone number, and for a couple of weeks cut off all contact with the outside world. He felt better than he had in May, when the video was secret. Now, at least, a few friends were aware he had made the tape, so if he disappeared they would know why. But he still had to suppress fears about being up against some of the most powerful people in the country. "At that point, I thought there was a distinct possibility I could end up in the Everglades," he recalled.

Unlike many Americans, Prouty was at best ambivalent about the brief celebrity status that would come with going public. He believed that the focus should be on Romney, not him. He lay low for six months, and watched with satisfaction as the story played out.

As the world learned, beyond his support for Chinese sweatshops, Romney said many things on the tape that didn't sound good. But it was these comments that crystallized the public's worst suspicions about him:

> There are 47 percent of the people who will vote for the president no matter what. All right, there are 47 percent who are with him, who are dependent upon government, who believe that they are victims, who believe the government has a responsibility to care for them, who believe that they are entitled to health care, to food, to housing, to you-name-it. That—that's an *entitlement*. And the government should give it to them. And they will vote for this president no matter what. . . . These are people who pay no income tax. . . . My job is not to worry about those people. I'll never convince them they should take personal responsibility and care for their lives.

Any controversial statement always looks worse if said behind closed doors, especially at a fundraiser, as Obama learned when his comments about rural Americans who "cling to guns and religion" hurt him in 2008. Poor audio and grainy video offer the impression that this is the "real" candidate that the handlers don't want you to see, which imparts more credibility. But "controversial" didn't begin to cover this one. Romney made one of the most serious political mistakes imaginable: He showed disdain for half of the American people he sought to lead.

The key line, the phrase that in retrospect may have sealed Romney's fate, was "My job is not to worry about those people." That is precisely the president's job: to worry about people who can't always look out for themselves. Romney's poor polling on the question of "cares about people like you" was the boulder that blocked his path to the presidency.

Inside the White House, David Plouffe watched the whole sixty-eight minutes on September 17 and emailed top staffers that this would be a big story that they should jump on right away. The president was busy dealing with an exploding Middle East, but he eventually watched a few clips on his iPad. The Chicago reaction was captured by Joel Benenson's simple "Holy shit!" Jim Margolis and company waited a few days to let the story sink in before cutting man-on-the-street ads of outraged voters. Romney, refusing to blame staff, first tried to cast doubt on the veracity of the tape before shifting to damage control and admitting that his comments were "not elegantly stated." Stuart Stevens insisted internally that staffers in Boston keep their heads down and focus on the next big event, which was Romney's upcoming interview with Univision, a mere three days after the full video was posted.

Aside from offending voters, Romney was factually wrong to suggest that all Obama supporters were tax-avoiding takers. Around 60 percent of those who paid no federal income tax were working and paying payroll taxes and sales tax, which meant that many sent a larger percentage of their income to the government than Romney did. The rest were elderly on Social Security and Medicare (20 percent), college students using Pell grants, active-duty military, and the poor. Those earning below around $30,000 a year paid no income taxes because, to reward work, the government, beginning with Ronald Reagan, offered an Earned Income Tax Credit that took millions off the rolls. The Child Tax Credit gave tax relief to families. All of this was now anathema to much of the right, which considered these struggling Americans to be the true "lucky duckies," as the *Wall Street Journal* editorial page called poor people who pay no federal income tax.

Ironically it was often Romney's supporters, clustered in red states, who received more from Washington than they paid in. Academic research showed that if the calculations included "submerged" government benefits like the home mortgage deduction and tax-free health benefits, more than 95 percent of Americans were beneficiaries of government programs at some point in their lives. And if one looked further for subsidies, everything from the sugar on your cereal to the cotton in your shirt was subsidized by the government.

Beyond the numbers, it was the insensitivity, even cruelty of Romney's remarks that immortalized them. Was a mother of a handicapped child not "taking responsibility" when she received help from the government to pay for the child's physical therapy? Was a senior citizen without many assets acting like a "victim" when she applied for Medicaid to pay for a mediocre nursing home? Did college students not "care about their lives" when they got student loans? Obama, appearing on *The Late Show with David Letterman* the day after the fracas erupted, raised variations on these questions, and soon his campaign was out with ads saying that presidents must worry about all Americans.

Romney's standard response was to say that of course he wanted to help 100 percent of Americans. He tried to push an old TV interview with his mother in which she discussed how her husband, George, and his family were on "welfare relief" in the years after they returned to the United States from Mexico. None of it worked. The sense of "entitlement" he excoriated on the tape had been projected onto him. Prouty's 47 percent video stuck because it reinforced an existing narrative of Romney as clueless and out of touch. Now some voters, remembering the Bain layoffs and even his bullying of a gay student in prep school, were ready to add "heartless" to the list. His friends said this perception was horribly unfair to the Romney they knew, a decent man of good deeds in his church, well-liked by those who worked for him. The real Romney, whoever he was, had only seven weeks to make himself known.

———

IN JANUARY 2011 Paul Ryan anticipated Romney's words in Boca Raton. When he delivered the Republican response to the State of the Union Address, he said of Obama's modest agenda, "This is a future in which we will transform our social safety net into a hammock, which lulls able-bodied people into lives of complacency and dependency."

Where was the point at which the safety net became a "hammock"? Ryan seemed to be saying that it was when programs reached a certain overall size. But in entitlement programs, the level of spending reflected the level of need. Spending went up in tandem with suffering, not sloth. Entitlements, however costly and unsustainable for the country, did not by definition encourage dependency.* By global standards, Americans remained extremely hardworking. No studies showed that Social Security or veterans benefits or college loans encouraged laziness. The old welfare system that was abolished in 1996 might have been a "hammock," and the same could arguably be said for limitless unemployment benefits or unmerited workman's comp. But food stamps, children's health programs, and child care tax credits were genuine helping hands for people with little money. To believe otherwise went at the heart of the American social contract that was established during the 1930s and remained unquestioned by prominent Democrats and Republicans in the seven decades since.

Born in 1970, Paul Ryan was a party to that contract. His family owned a construction company in Janesville, Wisconsin, that prospered from the same types of public roads and infrastructure projects (for example, O'Hare Airport) that he later voted against when Obama proposed them. When Ryan was sixteen, he arrived home one day to dis-

---

* The late Daniel Patrick Moynihan argued that tax breaks were also entitlements because they expanded or reduced the cost to the Treasury without changes in federal law. He predicted that the decision in the Carter administration to call Social Security and Medicare "entitlements" instead of "social insurance" would prove disastrous.

cover his fifty-five-year-old father sprawled on his bed, dead of a heart attack. With his older siblings off at college, his mother retraining for a new profession, and a grandmother with Alzheimer's living at home, he grew up fast, developing self-reliance and an easy confidence. He began reading the novels of Ayn Rand, the libertarian political theorist whose objectivist philosophy championed radical individualism and unapologetic selfishness. At Miami University in Ohio, where he paid tuition with the help of the Social Security survivors' benefits he received upon his father's death, Ryan fell under the sway of Professor Richard Hart, a libertarian economist.

After college, Ryan moved to Washington for six years, part of a close-knit assortment of antigovernment conservatives who made their living mostly by working for the government. Through connections, he got a job as a speechwriter for Empower America, the think tank run by Jack Kemp and Bill Bennett. Ryan saw Kemp, who died in 2009, as a mentor, though they held different views of the role of government. Kemp, a former secretary of housing and urban development, believed in lower taxes, but he wasn't a small-government conservative. He favored programs for the poor that Ryan later opposed. Instead of putting their ideology into practice by seeking their fortunes in the private sector, Ryan and his friends plotted to blow up the Washington Leviathan from within.

For Ryan, that meant returning to Janesville and running for office. After a year at Ryan Inc., his only experience in the business world, he got himself elected to Congress in a Democratic district. He won in part by posing in TV ads in a borrowed hard hat and with his sister and infant niece, who looked on television like his wife and child. (He was single at the time.) Ryan turned out to be a natural politician, with a smooth, accessible personality that seemed to bear none of the malice that afflicted so many other shock troops of the right. After becoming chairman of the House Budget Committee in 2011, he raised more campaign money than any other member of the House. Wealthy donors loved his command of arcane budget details and the gentle midwestern earnestness he superimposed on Wall Street values.

By his midthirties Ryan had long since figured out exactly how the world works; in fact he had known since high school. While most young conservatives outgrew their Ayn Rand obsession, Ryan did not. For Rand, a refugee from Stalin's Soviet Union, government and the collectivist impulse were the source of all evil. Poverty, she believed, was entirely one's own fault and could not be remedied. Greed was the only motivator in human nature. In dense, cartoonish novels like *Atlas Shrugged* and *The Fountainhead*, Rand championed lonely and misunderstood capitalists. Legions of modern-day conservatives, including former Federal Reserve chairman Alan Greenspan, her friend and disciple, drew inspiration from Rand, whose 1982 funeral included a six-foot floral arrangement in the shape of a dollar sign.

In 2005, when he was a thirty-five-year-old congressman, Ryan addressed a dinner at the Atlas Society on the hundredth anniversary of Rand's birth. He told the group how *Atlas Shrugged* "inspired me so much that it's required reading in my office for all my interns and my staff." The only debate was over which Rand novel to assign first and which to send out as Christmas presents. "The reason I got involved in public service, by and large, if I had to credit one thinker, one person, it would be Ayn Rand," he said. "And the fight we are in here, make no mistake about it, is a fight of individualism versus collectivism." To show that Rand was consistently "undergirding" his principles, Ryan bragged about his intimate familiarity with her work. "I always go back to, you know, Francisco d'Anconia's speech on money when I think about monetary policy. And then I go to the sixty-four-page John Galt speech, you know, on the radio at the end."

Sure enough, in Congress Ryan took an unorthodox, Randian view of monetary policy. He argued that even after the 2008 recession, interest rates should be raised, not lowered, because fighting inflation was the only legitimate function of the Federal Reserve. Concern about unemployment, per Rand, should not even enter into the Fed's deliberations. However, Ryan departed from his source of inspiration on social issues. After having children, he began regular attendance at church, which Rand had considered a worthless medieval institution. Where Rand supported abortion as a basic freedom, Ryan voted against it even in cases of rape and incest. But there was no sign he repudiated her political theories. He continued to embrace her binary thinking, which divided the world into "producers" and "moochers." In 2011 he said, ""Between 60 and 70 percent of Americans get more benefits from the government than they pay back in taxes. So, we're getting towards a society where we have a net majority of takers versus makers."

Getting to 47 percent takers was tough enough. Reaching 60 percent required counting all Social Security recipients. Ryan had been the floor leader in the House for George W. Bush's 2005 plan to privatize Social Security. This was a bit like being the Maytag repairman. The bill was so unpopular that it never came to the floor, which taught Ryan that he should keep his views on Social Security to himself for now.

In the meantime he needed some help from above. Recounting his years as an altar boy, in early 2012 Ryan sought justification for his small-government views in the Catholic Church. He referred to the doctrine of "subsidiarity," which was enunciated in 1891 by Pope Leo XIII in his famous and astonishingly liberal papal encyclical, *Rerum Novarum*. Ryan interpreted the concept to mean that "government closest to the people governs best." This was, at best, an incomplete definition of subsidiarity, and it became an erroneous one when he added that churches and charities "advance the common good—not having big government crowd out civic society." The theologian Meghan Clark pointed out that in fact the concept means that assistance to the poor should be provided at "the lowest level possible, but also at the highest level necessary." Subsidiarity, she and others in the Church have noted, must be paired with solidarity. The Church must stand with the poor and forsaken in every realm. Pope Leo wrote in *Rerum Novarum* that such solidarity would entail support for a "living wage," collective bargaining, and the concept of "natural justice."

The impact of *Rerum Novarum* was immense. In 1932, as the Great Depression deepened, a New York political operative named Ed Flynn, boss of the Bronx, began a series of discussions with his friend, Governor Franklin D. Roosevelt. Flynn was a Catholic with an intellectual bent and he spoke at length with FDR about Pope Leo and the progressive concepts he espoused in his encyclical. Roosevelt was moving rapidly toward belief in a social safety net provided by government, and, though he was a Protestant, he looked to *Rerum Novarum* for philosophical justification. Two years later his "new deal" incorporated many of these ideas.

Nearly eighty years after that, Paul Ryan tried to turn Catholic teachings on their head. After the House passed his budget, which decimated programs for the poor, the forty-two-year-old Ryan, likely to be a major force in national politics for decades, exulted, "It is so rare in American politics to arrive at a moment in which the debate revolves around the fundamental nature of American democracy and the social contract, but that is exactly where we are today."

———

EVEN CONSERVATIVES WERE gobsmacked by Romney's folly in attacking the American people instead of the other candidate. David Brooks wrote that Romney resembled Thurston Howell, the shipwrecked millionaire on the 1960s sitcom *Gilligan's Island*. Bill Kristol called the remarks "arrogant and stupid." Four Republican Senate candidates running in blue states tried to claim that Romney's comments didn't reflect their values.

But they did. As Ryan's worldview suggested, Romney simply articulated the core philosophy of the Republican Party, circa 2012. It was no surprise that his campaign quickly reemphasized another 47: the nearly 47 million Americans who received food stamps. The point of bringing up food stamps was both to tar Obama with the bad economy and to imply that a black president was providing new benefits to a portion of the population that many whites perceived—wrongly—to be over-whelmingly black.* The problem was the original 47 percent number. If Romney had said 10 percent or 20 percent, his lazy moochers argu-ment might have worked. But 47 percent meant he was attacking *you*, or at least someone you knew well.

In desperation, conservatives went back to McCain's 2008 argument that Obama had told a voter dubbed "Joe the Plumber" that he wanted to "spread the wealth around." The Drudge Report dredged up a video from 1998 in which State Senator Barack Obama said, "I actually be-lieve in redistribution, at least at a certain level to make sure every-body's got a shot." The fact that Romney and every other supporter of any federal income tax believed in redistribution "at a certain level" largely escaped notice.

Boston knew that no counterattacks or damage control would work. While snap polls showed only a modest drop in support for Romney, it would take a few days for the story to circulate among voters on-line and around the watercooler. A week later a *Washington Post* poll showed strong disapproval of the remarks, with 57 percent of indepen-dents reacting negatively. Many in Chicago now believed the race was all but over.

In South Florida, the man who for a time was known as @Anne Onymous670 saw poetic justice in Mitt Romney's fate. Scott Prouty compared Romney to a bird in the Galápagos who inherited a huge pile of fish, more than he could ever eat, while other birds starved. Eventually a stronger bird with nothing to lose knocks the greedy Rom-ney bird out of the way, restoring the balance of nature and allowing everyone to eat at least a little. Romney had made his fortune in part by outsourcing jobs, then had the nerve to complain about U.S. unem-ployment under Obama. He had called those who didn't make enough money to pay income taxes—the people whose jobs he had helped ship overseas—entitled moochers. He had invested heavily in cheap Chinese labor, then bashed China. In the end, trying to be the fittest, he ended up as dinner for the masses.

---

* According to the Census Bureau, 28 percent of those receiving food stamps are African American and 59 percent are white. The big increase in the number of food stamp recipients was due partly to dozens of states that loosened eligibility requirements.

24

The First Debate

After Romney's "47 percent" fiasco, Obama World thought the election was over. Yes, the president could lose, but he would not. His approval ratings were over 50 percent for the first time since 2009. He led Romney by 7 points nationally and 9 in Ohio, a nearly insurmountable lead in an election just around the corner. As Romney suffered through two terrible weeks at the end of September, money and volunteers for OFA began drying up. There was no urgency anymore.

But the fallout from the 47 percent story coincided with exactly the kind of external news that David Plouffe worried could affect the election. On the anniversary of 9/11, armed men launched attacks on a consulate building and nearby CIA annex in Benghazi, Libya. U.S. Ambassador J. Christopher Stevens and three others were killed.

The Benghazi story was quickly politicized. Republicans charged that the Obama White House, invested in its campaign boast that Al Qaeda was on the wane, tried to make it seem as if the attacks grew out of spontaneous demonstrations against a crude anti-Islamic video originating in the United States, not terrorism. Charges of a cover-up began almost immediately. Democrats countered that the initial erroneous reports about the nature of the incident (repeated by UN Ambassador Susan Rice on *Meet the Press*) came from the intelligence community, which is nonpartisan. While the CIA station chief in Tripoli said the intensity of the raid made him believe it was planned, James Clapper, director of national intelligence and hardly an Obama stooge, concluded initially (based on intelligence from around the world) that it was in response to the anti-Islamic video that had already sparked riots in Egypt and the Sudan. (The attacks were later attributed to local terrorist groups retaliating against U.S.-backed counterterrorism efforts in the area.)* Lost in the cross fire were legitimate questions about why

---

* Republicans and some reporters said Obama had declared Al Qaeda "defeated." In truth, he had said on May 1, the first anniversary of the killing of bin Laden, "The goal that I set—to

the U.S. government didn't do a better job protecting its personnel abroad. Hillary Clinton had made repeated attempts to beef up security at U.S. embassies, but the House of Representatives never provided the money.

Romney was so eager to score political points that at first he barged in on the wrong Middle Eastern story. On the morning of September 12, as the world was first learning of Ambassador Stevens's death, Romney went on television to blast U.S. policy in Egypt, where protests against the inflammatory video had taken place. He spoke before the president appeared in the Rose Garden to mourn with the nation and before the bodies from Libya had been returned to the United States. From a campaign stop in Jacksonville, he charged that the career U.S. ambassador in Cairo had "sympathized" with the Egyptian attackers by issuing a mild statement calling for religious tolerance. McConnell, Boehner, and even Fox News distanced themselves from Romney's remarks. The smell of defeat around the Romney campaign had now grown so strong that major GOP donors seriously considered shifting their money from the presidential to congressional contests. The press had begun to write Romney off.

Then, on October 3 in Denver, the president almost threw his presidency away. His disdain for the requirements of politics, his ill-disguised contempt for Romney, and his complacent cockiness caught up to him in a listless and bewildering debate performance in front of 67 million people. The strategy, style, execution, spin—everything went wrong. "We had this inflated lead and we wanted to see if we could erase it in one night," David Simas joked after the election, still wincing.

———

RON KLAIN, the veteran Democratic Party operative who headed Obama's debate prep, had reminded the president over the summer that he would probably lose the first debate. Almost all incumbents do, from Jimmy Carter and Ronald Reagan to both Bushes.* The challenger wins just by being on equal footing with the president for the first time. He gets to seem like a plausible commander in chief without having to defend a record. If he has been through primaries, he's in fighting trim, while the incumbent is rusty. The press, looking for an underdog story, sets the expectations bar higher for the sitting president.

---

defeat al Qaeda and deny it a chance to rebuild—is now within our reach. Still, there will be difficult days ahead."

* Bill Clinton besting Bob Dole in their first 1996 debate is the only contrary example in three decades.

Of course, that didn't explain the dimensions of Obama's defeat. Maybe nothing could. Klain said he would go to his grave not knowing exactly what happened.

From the start, Obama's unexpected lead in the polls had made it tricky to formulate debate strategy. The debate prep team counseled the president to stick with the calm and agreeable tone that had helped give him his lead in the polls. The worst thing that could happen, his coaches figured, was a moment like Obama's patronizing "You're likable enough, Hillary" line in the 2008 New Hampshire debate, which opened the door to her comeback there. It was a real danger. In prep, said one coach, "if you armed him with a scalpel, he took out a hacksaw." When a mock question was posed about Romney's business career, the correct setup answer was to be gracious about his opponent's success before pivoting to the message about the economy. But the president could never deliver the setup with anything but venom. He'd describe how both he and Romney went to the same law school and he became a community organizer while Romney went to make money. It was exactly the sharp-edged and boastful approach his coaches wanted him to avoid.

Worried about a gaffe, Obama's advisers disregarded the risks of a cautious strategy. They sat on a lead, playing not to lose, which of course leads to losing. Obama told his friend Robert Wolf in September that it was "the beginning of the fourth quarter and we're up a few baskets." But it wasn't the fourth quarter. It was the third quarter, too early to run down the clock. A prevent defense in football or a four-corner offense in basketball was premature.

Part of the problem was that the president was uncomfortable with the advice he was getting and dubious that it would work. Early on in prep, Klain suggested they adopt NBA coach Paul Westhead's run-and-gun offense, which emphasized fast breaks for easy points and only a light defense against Romney's shots. "You'll win 162 to 160," he said. Obama wasn't a Westhead fan; he had once coached the Chicago Bulls to a dismal 28–54 record. And he thought the advice was wrong. He accepted it intellectually and internalized it, but it went against his instincts. He never believed he could win the debate with a "wide-open but soft" strategy. He thought he needed to hit Romney, to "get physical" on the court. "He was right, and we were wrong," Klain said later.

The strategy called for Obama to be the explainer, like Bill Clinton at the convention, but this misread the new expectations of the viewers. While Obama's slow, almost ponderous, nonconfrontational style had worked well in his first debate with John McCain in Mississippi in 2008, the context was different this time. In the past, incumbents didn't take shots at their challengers; it was considered unpresidential. The pugilistic 2012 GOP primary debates had changed that, with the most combative candidate usually declared the winner. So now partisans on both sides were looking for their man to land blows. Later Axelrod tried to blame himself: "We were a little phobic about engagement [with Romney] and took it to an illogical extreme. We prepared him for a discussion instead of a debate."

Obama hated debates. He felt they were a circus sideshow. Not coincidentally, he knew he wasn't very good at them. He had despised them since 2004, when perennial candidate Alan Keyes scored points off him in their Senate campaign debates even though Keyes was a hotheaded and erratic candidate at best. In 2008 he lost almost every primary debate to Hillary Clinton. Even besting McCain never brought him much better than passing grades. Debates represented what he couldn't stand about politics: superficial, canned answers with thumbs up/thumbs down reviews by prattling pundits. What did they have to do with the actual work of being president? He thought the format was artificial and relied on stagecraft and debate rules that were irrelevant.

When he was told during prep for Denver that his answer on infrastructure needed to be less than sixty seconds long, he said, "It really deserves sixty minutes." Obama hadn't gone into politics to be a public affairs entertainer, and his writerly detachment from the idiocies of the process had helped him keep perspective. But he failed to absorb that since the days when George Washington made sure he looked good on a horse, politicians have always been required to perform in the theater of the presidency. While the president could be a gifted performer in other venues, he never fully inhabited the role of debater. Now he was like a novelist cast as a politician in a movie. His aloofness set in, as if he were too good for the part.

Lack of practice wasn't the problem. After several warm-up sessions, the president had three full-dress mock debates in the basement of the Democratic National Committee and three more at the Westin near Henderson, Nevada, where the stage was an almost perfect replica of the one at the University of Denver. He went 0–6 in debate prep. Prep was like eating mayonnaise or asparagus or some other food he disliked. The president, who spent his days steeped in policy, was forever in the weeds, offering long, boring answers, talking too slowly, not responding crisply to John Kerry, who was playing Romney well, though he wasn't such a cogent speaker himself.

When one of the eight or nine advisers present offered a critique, Obama didn't disagree, as he had during his cranky 2008 debate prep. He would say, "You're right, that's in the [briefing] book"—then fix nothing in his performance. This failure to bring up his game rattled his coaches.

The prep was going so poorly that the team recommended Obama not discuss the 47 percent video unless asked directly. In rehearsal, Obama kept blowing the topic. First, he would turn it into a defense of the social safety net that was too wonky. Then, when Kerry-as-Romney responded, saying that 47 million Americans were now on food stamps, Obama took the bait and went into a full-throated defense of food stamps, a sure loser in a message aimed at the middle class. "We assumed it would lead to a vituperative exchange that wouldn't be helpful," Axelrod said. One debate coach had a theory about what was in Obama's head: I'm up by seven and can talk about liberal stuff that's good for the country.

Debate prep brought out the truant in Obama. He escaped debate camp at Lake Las Vegas once to visit Hoover Dam and again to deliver pizzas to campaign volunteers in Henderson, where he was overheard telling a supporter on the phone that debate prep "is a drag. They're making me do my homework."

For twenty-five years, Democratic presidential candidates had employed Michael Sheehan, a communications expert and debate coach. After the Denver debate a couple of senior staffers bad-mouthed him for having told Obama it was okay to scribble notes and look at them. In fact Sheehan had worried all along that the president was writing too much. "We kept telling him not to write a novel," he said later. "He wished the whole thing could be an essay exam and he could use two blue books if he needed to."

It's wasn't that anyone was afraid of telling him the truth. "You had no energy again today and weren't driving message," they told him. Obama shrugged and said, "I'll do better." On the eve of the debate, the president told Axelrod, "I'll be fine. I'm a game-day player." On the flight to Denver the staff engaged in gallows humor: "Maybe our guy will bring it when the red light goes on."

At the Westin Hotel, a reporter asked spokeswoman Jen Psaki what was the worst that could happen. "Well, he could fall off the stage," Psaki said. A day later, he almost did.

———

ROMNEY ENDEARED HIMSELF to his top staff with his good humor and refusal to point fingers. "You didn't say '47 percent,'" he told his campaign manager, Matt Rhoades. "Stuart didn't say '47 percent.' I did."

At fundraisers in mid-2012 Romney had informed donors that he had three big chances to turn around his standing in the polls: the choice of his running mate, his convention, and the debates. Ryan didn't give him much of a lift, and the Tampa convention brought no bounce at all, so that left the debates. He had debated thirty-two times in the primaries, but he started his fall debate prep in June, the earliest on record. Beth Myers called debate prep the campaign's "Manhattan Project." It was the reason Romney kept such a light schedule on the campaign trail. The elaborate preparations included policy sessions led by issues director Lanhee Chen, strategy meetings run by Stuart Stevens, and a record sixteen mock debates, with five in three days at a house in Vermont. With Senator Rob Portman playing the president, they practiced Romney's long-awaited pivot to the middle. Stevens and company had timed it well: too late for Tea Party conservatives, hungry for victory, to complain, but just in time for the tens of millions of moderate general election voters only now tuning in. Arriving in Denver, Romney was confident his moment was at hand.

Onstage the tone was set from the beginning. Obama spoke first, but Romney got the jump by mentioning that it was the Obamas' twentieth wedding anniversary. His self-effacing little joke—"I'm sure this was the most romantic place you could imagine—here with me"—was appealing, a different Romney. Obama looked at his wife and said, "I just want to wish, Sweetie, you happy anniversary and let you know that a year from now we will not be celebrating it in front of 40 million people." The line was scripted but was nonetheless a tip-off that the president would rather be somewhere, anywhere, else. Romney was crisp, confident, and well-informed. He pushed around the moderator, Jim Lehrer, but most critics blamed Lehrer for not having better control. Obama was vague, halting. His team, huddled backstage, thought the president held his own in the first fifteen minutes, slipped behind in the next fifteen, and the wheels came off after that. The low point was when he brought up IPAB, the Obamacare advisory board charged with reviewing health care costs, three times in three consecutive answers.

Chicago had been perhaps too effective in making Romney look like a rich and untrustworthy twit. Now, when he seemed presidential and decent, it undercut everything the Obama campaign had been trying to build or destroy. But Romney didn't just beat the expectations spread. He won outright with a mixture of energy and fluency on policy. The joke afterward was that he had violated Mormon dietary strictures and downed three cups of coffee beforehand. That many of his statements (such as "I will not reduce the taxes paid by high-income Americans") were at odds with his stated program didn't seem to matter.

Obama embodied the late Israeli foreign minister Abba Eban's description of the Palestinians: They never miss an opportunity to miss an opportunity. The president muffed chances to bring up the 47 percent, the auto rescue (mentioned only in passing), and the jobs bill that could have created a million jobs had Romney's party approved it. And he confirmed liberal suspicions about his fundamental aversion to conflict when he tried to find common ground with Romney even on Social Security, thereby tossing away one of the party's trustiest weapons and sending up a cheer in Boston.

Chicago wasn't surprised that Romney ditched his past positions, but he "did it more shamelessly than we expected," Benenson said. "We should have called bullshit on him right from the start." Romney seemed flexible on his plans to shrink government ("Regulation is essential"); he vowed not to cut education and, in a move he had earlier rejected when Paul Ryan proposed it, accused the president of "kissing up to banks" in the Dodd-Frank financial reform. When in reference to Obamacare he said that "preexisting conditions are covered under my plan"—as if the high-risk pools that had been failing for years were an answer—Obama seemed at a loss for words.

Jake Tapper, who covered Obama on a daily basis for ABC News, thought that what happened in Denver was predictable. The president, he said, had no one around every day to tell him to straighten up. And because he hadn't held a press conference since June, he had had no sparring partners. Obama advisers rejected that argument, insisting that even the most contentious press conferences weren't preparation for a challenger given ninety minutes to insult you to your face.

A transcript of the debate shows a closer contest than many recalled. Obama worked in most of his major points and was more accurate than Romney.* On camera, Obama looked "logy," as Sheehan put it, listless, lacking in mental energy. It was, he said, like seeing someone run in a swimming pool. Romney is "about a minute away from holding Obama down and cutting his hair," the comedian Bill Maher tweeted, a reference to Romney's bullying a gay student when he was in prep school. The dominant impression was of a passive president receding from view. Afterward the *New Yorker* ran a cover that depicted Romney debating an empty chair.

It wasn't the first time Obama had shrunk from a fight or failed to finish someone off. After beating Hillary Clinton in a string of 2008 primaries and caucuses that took him to the threshold of the nomination, he let her back into the race until the end. Once in office, he failed to nail down his signature health care plan until it was almost too late and never sharply called out the Republicans for taking the country

---

* That was like saying that Nixon won his first debate with Kennedy in 1960 because he sounded better on the radio.

to the brink of default. Could it be that he wanted the game to be a little more challenging, like Michael Jordan sitting on the bench in the early fourth quarter? Obama's basketball buddies knew that he always wanted the ball for the final shot in a close game. It was left to those with less confidence to worry that, more times than not, the buzzer shot goes off the rim.

More to the point, Obama didn't trust himself to tangle with Romney. He thought Romney was a liar and an empty suit and would reverse everything worthy he had done as president. Even if the Democrats hung on to the Senate 52–48, he figured, Romney would be able to win over a couple of Democrats and push through some version of the Ryan Plan. That would be a disaster for the country. Obama had long worried that his attitude would spill out. Suppressing that was part of what threw him off his game.

The prospect of a Romney administration was what propelled him. According to one senior staffer, Obama would have been ready to move on if he had lost to Hillary Clinton, or someone else he respected. For his whole life, he had been restless and impatient in whatever he was doing, always looking to the next chapter. Being president was no different. He still liked the policy challenges and the chance to bend history, but he could do without the political part. This was his last campaign, and he was damn glad to be almost done with it. For those ninety minutes in Denver, it showed.

———

AS THEY HAD in 2008, the Obama high command held a conference call with ten minutes remaining in the debate to decide on spin. This one was full of lame rationalizations—the president kept Romney on the defensive; Romney was bullying Jim Lehrer—but everyone knew that convincing anyone he had won was out of the question. Plouffe, Axelrod, Messina, Cutter, and Psaki plunged into the crowd, determined to say it wasn't as bad as the initial reaction indicated. The spin room ritual has long ago descended into self-parody, with both sides always claiming a victory. But on this night it was more like the locker room after a lopsided playoff game.

In 2012 Twitter put the spin room on steroids. Chicago's entire social media plan depended on getting out the message that Obama was winning (fifteen minutes into the debate) to hundreds of "validators," prominent Democrats who could retweet positive coverage. As the first debate ended, the plan collapsed. "We had nothing," Adam Fetcher of the Comm staff recalled. For an hour Chicago couldn't credibly tweet anything. The instant CNN poll showed more than 70 percent of viewers thought Romney won. The coverage on MSNBC was brutal, with Obama supporters like Chris Matthews and Al Sharpton mincing no words, and blogger Andrew Sullivan's attack on a president "too arrogant to take a core campaign responsibility seriously" not far behind. The old metric for measuring debates was how they affected undecided voters. But this was a base election, with ideological cable news and ubiquitous social media. That meant that the new measure of success was whether a debate performance energized supporters.

Klain told the president that he had lost 60–40, but the press would make it 80–20. Obama told Klain, Axelrod, and Plouffe, "I didn't think it was so bad." Back at the hotel, he told Messina the same thing. A few hours later, after he saw the scorching reviews on his iPad, he told Axelrod, "I guess I lost." "That's the consensus," Axelrod replied.

The good news was that there was no killer exchange that could be played on an endless loop and burned into the mind of the public. The only thing anyone remembered was that Obama lost and Big Bird got a shout-out when Romney called for cutting federal funding for PBS.

A couple days later the president called Messina to apologize: "I didn't bring my A game. I was a little rusty." To others he admitted, "Message received." He was frustrated that he had to wait thirteen days before getting a chance to redeem himself. The staff found him gracious and humble in blaming his performance, not the preparation.

Obama told Patrick Gaspard of the DNC that he had seen an amusing viral video of the actor Samuel L. Jackson appearing in a family's home and telling them to "wake the fuck up" and recognize the stakes in the election. "I didn't realize he was talking to me," the president chuckled.

––––––

IN CHICAGO THE debate, like other big TV events, was projected onto the white walls. Dan Wagner stuck his head out of the Cave and said that the silence was so overwhelming he thought he heard a pin drop on the Floor. Young staffers were angry and disoriented. The president had let them down. They had thought if Obama lost it would be because of something they did wrong, some poorly executed decision or organizational lapse. It never occurred to them that the man they worshiped could be so, well, disrespectful of all of their work and personal sacrifice. "Why am I here until two in the morning night after night and the president can't even show up for the debate?" one senior staffer complained before his fury turned to sadness. "The idea that we could be looking back and saying this was all *his* fault—it's heartbreaking."

The first forty-eight hours were brutal. Chicago worried that the spin would feed on itself and turn the debacle into a nosedive. The only question was "Where's the floor?," and it was all hands on deck to figure it out. Dan Wagner shut the door of the Cave and told his people that nobody could leave until they found out exactly what was going on. He was exaggerating, but only slightly. After increasing the Cave's sample size from nine thousand to twelve thousand a night—eight to ten times the sample size of everyone else's *weekly* polls—Elan Kriegel, the thirty-one-year-old director of battleground state analytics, finally got to go home. His last email was logged at 4:02 a.m.

The next night, before all the numbers were crunched, Kriegel listened in remotely on call center interviews and heard voters answering the short survey with "Yes, I thought the president was crushed in the debate. No, it doesn't change my decision to vote for him." It settled his stomach.

Joel Benenson's fresh polls showed the race going from 51–44 to 50–47, but with Romney's momentum stopping. The president hadn't lost much ground. Romney had simply picked up Republican-leaning independents he had lost since the Democratic Convention and the 47 percent remark. Had the famous videotape not provided Obama with a cushion, he would be in much bigger trouble now, maybe even behind.

The next day Kriegel delivered a twenty-page PowerPoint to the high command that echoed Benenson's numbers and argued that the campaign should do the hardest thing in a tough situation: nothing. There was no movement in Ohio and no need to drop out of Florida or drop into Pennsylvania, though both options would be discussed at length. Even better, early voting had started in Iowa on September 27, a week before Denver, and the debate had no impact on Obama's turnout, which was almost precisely what the Cave's models predicted.

When public polls and Nate Silver's model showed Obama in trouble, Chicago continued to fret. Then, less than a week after Denver, David Shor, the former child prodigy in the Cave, dove into the latest numbers and told Kriegel, "Tomorrow, Nate Silver goes up." Sure enough, the *New York Times* polling analyst, a security blanket for millions of Obama supporters, reported the next day what Chicago had already heard from the Cave and from Benenson: No big change.

The Golden Reports from Analytics found the race stable, with one exception: Numbers coming out of the Green Bay area showed Romney expanding his lead there from 2 points to between 6 and 9. This didn't sound right, but the Cave's models couldn't be dismissed. The campaign bought more ad time and eventually sent both Obama and Bill Clinton into the region, even though it may not have been necessary.*

The numbers from battleground states relaxed the president. After he had apologized to his staff and told major supporters, "This one's on me," Obama himself was cool about the whole thing. Talking with Marty Nesbitt, he took on the tone of a basketball star in the NBA finals: "Look, we were up 2 to 0 and Game 3 was the first debate. They beat us on our home court. We win Game 4, people will say it's over."

Chicago didn't want people saying that. As long as the media narrative of a close race didn't spin too far out of control, it helped immensely with fundraising and volunteer recruitment. On the day after the debate, Bill Burton's pro-Obama super PAC had his biggest day, $7 million, as Plouffe's Democratic bedwetters drenched the sheets. Small fry went on donating binges on their mobile phones. And the big donors turned out. On October 7 the Hollywood mogul Jeffrey Katzenberg hosted a late lunch at his home on Loma Vista Drive in Beverly Hills that may have been the priciest political fundraiser ever held, though the public learned only that it was a thank-you event. The meeting featured two presidents, Obama and Clinton, and the dozen or so guests (including Eric Schmidt and David Geffen) each paid $1 million apiece for the privilege, with the money going to the super PAC. Clinton was deferential to Obama, but the donors were not. They peppered him with questions about the first debate and other topics. The lunch made him late for a splashy public fundraiser with George Clooney, Jennifer Hudson, and Stevie Wonder. "They just perform flawlessly night after night," he said of the stars. "I can't always say the same."

THE EIGHT DAYS between Denver and the vice presidential debate in Danville, Kentucky, felt like an eternity to hard-core Democrats. Had they been inside Joe Biden's prep sessions, they would have rested easier. The format for the debate was Biden and Ryan sitting around a table with Martha Raddatz of ABC News. Once the vice president was reminded that he shouldn't confuse the setting with a Sunday show, debate prep went well, with Congressman Chris Van Hollen channeling Ryan perfectly. Because the aim was to revive and rally the base, Biden was told it was "literally" (his favorite word) impossible for him to go too far. He needed to raise the flag high and rip Ryan, buying Obama time for a comeback in Round 2.

---

* Romney ended up winning there by 2 points.

After the vice president landed in Kentucky, he took a call from Obama on the tarmac. "I know we're in trouble now," he told aides moments later. "The president just said, 'Joe, be yourself.' In four years, he has never said that before."

Biden took grief for smiling too much in the debate, but he was only trying to show his fangs. From the start, he hammered Ryan's budget and called his numbers "malarkey." Ryan hit hard on Benghazi, but it didn't stick. While instant polls rated the contest a draw and some voters thought Biden had shown bad manners, Obama World was ecstatic. Biden had done just what he needed to do to stop the bleeding and rally the Democrats. When Boston attacked him for appearing "unhinged," Chicago knew he had won. Style points are the last refuge of debate losers.

———

THE OCTOBER 16 debate at Hofstra University on Long Island was a nerve-racking experience for Obama supporters. A second consecutive lopsided loss would have put Obama in a deep hole. He told his debate prep team, gathered in the Roosevelt Room, "I think this whole thing is fake, a TV show performance. I'm not good at it. But I will do whatever it takes to win the next ones, and I *will* win them." This time the prep team would feed him no lines. The advice was to avoid getting caught up in Romney's distortions, just say "That's not true," and pivot to message.

Ron Klain thought the key statistic from Denver was that Obama spoke for a full four minutes more than Romney, but Romney got out seven hundred more words. As a theater major in college, Benenson had learned to recite *Hamlet* at top speed. En route to Delaware for a meeting with the president, he entertained other senior advisers in the car with his rapid-fire *Hamlet* monologues. During prep, Michael Sheehan would hold up a sign saying "FASTER." This time, Obama listened.

At the Hilton Hotel in Suffolk County, where the president and his team gathered for a final run-through before heading to the debate venue nearby, Ben Rhodes of the National Security Council put the president through one last rehearsal on Benghazi. Romney had made it part of his stump speech that Obama had never called the attacks terrorism. But the transcript of Obama's remarks in the Rose Garden on September 12, the day after the Benghazi attacks, clearly showed that Obama's words "acts of terror" applied to Benghazi as well as other terrorist attacks. Now Obama prepared to spring his trap.

Hofstra's town hall format favored the president, who had done well in that setting in 2008. His movements across the stage were graceful, while Romney walked in baby steps like Hercule Poirot. From the start, Obama was crisp, quick, and aggressive, everything that was missing in Denver. Romney's decision to repeat many of the lines that had worked so well two weeks before was the wrong strategy. He was facing a different opponent. Obama was ready for each thrust, and he counterpunched effectively. Bill Clinton was listening to the debate on the radio in a car, en route from an event in Baltimore. When Obama hit Romney on his math, as Clinton had at the Democratic Convention, the former president knew the current president had his mojo back.

The same for auto bailouts, where Obama showed that Romney would have let the car companies go out of business; on immigration, where the president nailed Romney for threatening to veto the DREAM Act and favoring "self-deportation"; and on contraception, where the president mentioned three times that Romney wanted to get rid of Planned Parenthood. In each case, Romney paid the price for pandering during the GOP primaries.

Polls after the first debate showed a narrowing in the gender gap, an ominous sign for Obama if the trend continued. So it was a stroke of fortune for Obama at Hofstra that a questioner raised women's issues. While Obama used the Lily Ledbetter Fair Pay Act to drive his message, Romney tried to tout his record hiring women in Massachusetts. Once again, he let words tumble out of his mouth that would haunt him. His description of résumés for cabinet positions during his time as governor of Massachusetts as "binders full of women" would likely have been downplayed or ignored by the (mostly male) pundits of the past. This time, when the reference surged to number one on Twitter's trending topics, the press and the Obama campaign leaped on it.

The climax came when Romney began to describe how the president had failed to respond properly to the September 11 attack on the U.S. consulate in Benghazi. Obama, with the steely gaze of an executioner, said coolly, "Please proceed, Governor." Romney may have sensed he was falling into a trap, but he plowed ahead, wondering why it took the president fourteen days before he called the attack in Benghazi an act of terror. Moderator Candy Crowley confirmed: "He—he did call it an act of terror." The theatricality that Obama disdained now worked to his advantage. "Can you say that a little louder, Candy?" he said. The debate was effectively over.

The spin room was a perfect reflection of the order of battle in a divided America. While polls and all independent pundits said Obama won overwhelmingly, Sean Hannity on Fox claimed it was a "big night, a big win" for Romney, more proof that Fox was not the mirror image of MSNBC, which had reported Obama's loss honestly in Denver. Republicans reacted bitterly to Obama's new combativeness. Tagg Romney said that he wanted to take a swing at Obama for calling his father a liar. But it was Romney who was seen as out of line by undecided voters, who gave the debate to the president by several points.

———

IN 2000 GOVERNOR George W. Bush neutralized Vice President Al Gore in their foreign policy debate by agreeing with him all the time. Romney tried the same strategy at the final debate, in Boca Raton. Obama's foreign policy was popular, and Boston figured there was no sense getting too hawkish. Chicago anticipated this. "If he's agreeing with you, you need to punch him in the nose," Karen Dunn, a member of the debate prep team, told the president.

Onstage in Boca, Obama once more came out aggressively. In every reaction shot, he looked like a cat about to pounce. Romney was sweaty and flat, Etch-A-Sketching away his old hawkishness just well enough to justify the spin room talking points that he had cleared the bar as a competent commander in chief.

With the CIA releasing documents showing that no one in the administration was told until a week afterward that the attacks in Benghazi were premeditated, the air went out of the story. The Obama team expected it to be a major theme anyway, but Romney gave up on Benghazi after the opening exchange. He felt Obama had won the foreign policy argument by killing bin Laden and that less than 30 percent of the public thought foreign policy was even relevant to the campaign. So the best strategy was to just get through the final debate. Romney was convinced he would win the election and was trying to avoid a mistake, almost like Obama in Denver. "They were drinking the polling Kool-Aid, not the Benghazi Kool-Aid," Klain said later.*

Obama had been cautious in earlier debates about bringing up bin Laden, but now, closing in for the kill, he mentioned Romney's old comment that he "wouldn't move heaven and earth" to get the Al Qaeda leader and wouldn't go into Pakistan without permission to do so. Then he even made Joe Biden take one for the team. "Those decisions generally are not poll-tested," the president said. "And even some in my own party, including my current vice president, had the same critique as you did." Biden had been tipped off beforehand and was fine with it.

———

* This didn't stop Sarah Palin, who stepped boldly over the racial line the day after the last debate with a Facebook post entitled "Obama's Shuck and Jive Ends with Benghazi Lies."

About the only compelling moment in Boca came when Obama's attitude toward Romney showed through. "You mention the navy, for example, and the fact that we have fewer ships than we did in 1916," Obama said. "Well, governor, we also have fewer *horses and bayonets*." In prep the line ended there, but the president couldn't contain himself. "We have these things called aircraft carriers and planes land on them," he added. "It's not a game of Battleship." A line dripped with sarcasm that would have backfired as recently as the Denver debate—and been viewed as far out of bounds in earlier elections—was now toasted as clever on Twitter.

It was a new day, and only one presidential campaign was ready to seize it.

25

The Homestretch

Two days after the Denver debate, the Bureau of Labor Statistics released its much-awaited September jobs numbers. The survey of thousands of employers and households showed 114,000 new jobs and, much more significantly, that the unemployment rate dropped from 8.1 to 7.8 percent, which was where it was when Obama became president. This was serendipitous news for the Obama campaign. The margin of error in the BLS numbers was 100,000 jobs and half a point. Had unemployment spiked to 8.6 percent and job growth fallen below zero—both possible within the margin of error—Obama would most likely have lost the 2012 election right there.

Within an hour of the happier numbers, Jack Welch, the legendary former CEO of General Electric, tweeted, "Unbelievable jobs numbers . . . These Chicago guys will do anything. . . . Can't debate so change numbers." When confronted by Chris Matthews on MSNBC that evening, Welch, apparently suffering from Obama Derangement Syndrome, admitted he had no evidence that nonpartisan civil servants at the BLS had cooked the books in cahoots with Chicago to bring unemployment below 8 percent. But he refused to back off his charge, which was echoed by the onetime presidential candidate Steve Forbes. The arrival of "BLS truthers" marked a milestone in the radicalization of the right. This wasn't Donald Trump or Michelle Bachmann or Jerome Corsi. Upstanding members of the American financial elite were now peddling outlandish conspiracy theories and sliming innocent federal employees in order to drive an American president from power.

Of course, Trump himself was still onstage, but his transition from role model of crass success to national joke was almost complete. For weeks he had hyped an upcoming "October Surprise" that Fox took seriously as a potentially pivotal event. Finally, on October 24, Trump announced with great fanfare that he was offering $5 million to the charity of the president's choice if he would agree to release his college transcripts, college applications, and passport applications to Trump's satisfaction by October 31. Trump apparently believed that young Obama had been too stupid to be admitted to college except as an affirmative action case and was simultaneously covering up that he was born abroad or, in another racist conspiracy fantasy, had traveled to Pakistan to hang with terrorists.

That evening Stephen Colbert said on his show that he was so moved by Trump's offer that he would give the $1 million collected by his Colbert super PAC ("Making a better tomorrow, tomorrow") to a charity of Trump's choice if he met certain conditions by October 31. "One million actual dollars, if you will let me dip my balls in your mouth. One million," Colbert said, in a comedy bit that went viral and was eventually seen at the highest levels of the government. "Nothing would make me happier than to write this check. And nothing would make America happier than to have something going into your mouth instead of coming out of it."

John Sununu, who had been forced to resign in 1991 as George H. W. Bush's chief of staff after he used a government limo to pursue his stamp-collecting hobby, proved to be almost as divisive a surrogate as Trump.* In July he said he wished "this president would learn to be an American." Now, not long before the election, he called Obama "lazy" and said that Colin Powell only supported him because they both were black, a remark Powell found so offensive that he vowed to call Sununu out on it every chance he got. The "lazy" line, long a racist stereotype, circulated widely on the right. "How often does he play basketball and golf? I wish I had that kind of time," Roger Ailes told a biographer. "He's lazy, but the media won't report that."† The media didn't report that because it wasn't true; despite the golf outings, Obama was, by the accounts of officials who had served in prior administrations of both parties, better prepared in meetings and more attentive to his job than most of his recent predecessors.

The final weeks of the campaign saw a mountain of other lies. Billboards in Florida depicted Obama bowing to a Saudi king and charged

---

* Sununu ran up $615,000 between 1989 and 1991 in government-paid travel to ski holidays, golf outings, GOP events, and trips to Boston to see his dentist and to New York for a rare stamp auction.

† Ailes's excuse for using the line was an ABC News Obama interview with Barbara Walters after the election in which he said, "There is a deep down, underneath all the work that I do, I think there's a laziness in me. It's probably from, you know, growing up in Hawaii and it's sunny outside, and sitting on the beach." Right-wing accounts failed to include the full context, in which Obama said he also deplores laziness in others, noting, "Nothing frustrates me more than when people aren't doing their jobs." And when he sees himself getting lazy, "then I get mad at myself." Sununu's "lazy" comments came before this interview.

that he intentionally raised gas prices. An email went viral claiming that the inside of the president's wedding ring bore the inscription "There is no god but Allah." More than 2.5 million voters in battleground states received a free DVD in the mail of a scurrilous movie alleging, with no evidence, that the president was the love child of Stanley Ann Dunham and Frank Marshall Davis, a onetime communist who befriended Obama when he was a teenager in Honolulu. The film, *Dreams from My Real Father*, directed by Joel Gilbert, speculated that Obama and Davis had the same freckles. In an especially disgusting touch, the film showed nude pictures from a bondage magazine and falsely claimed the woman depicted in them was the president's mother. Jerome Corsi, who did so much to spread the "birther" story, now put his energy behind this alternative conspiracy theory, while the conservative commentator Monica Crowley gave Gilbert a platform to promote his film on Fox News. A group of well-funded conservative activists had been planning over the summer to distribute the film even more widely until Frank Luntz's focus groups found that audiences were "revolted" by it.

———

MITT ROMNEY THOUGHT he had Florida in the bag. On September 20, still reeling from the release of the 47 percent video, he had answered questions at a candidate forum at the University of Miami from Univision anchor Jorge Ramos. With the help of a university official on the local Romney steering committee, he packed the hall with supporters (in violation of the rules) and held his own with Ramos before a huge Latino TV audience.* The next night, Ramos grilled the president on why he hadn't delivered on comprehensive immigration reform. The comparison played to Romney's advantage. He didn't have to win the Latino vote outright, just get close to 40 percent, which seemed doable. Then his edge along the I-4 corridor in Florida would take him across the finish line.

Boston figured that with Florida safely in hand, it could concentrate on an aerial assault in Ohio, where Romney's approach seemed to have been borrowed from Curtis LeMay, the air force general who believed in carpet bombing. The combination of Republican super PACs and Romney's own ads meant that viewers sometimes saw as many as seven or eight ads in a row. It was overkill. After World War II the Stra-

---

* At the beginning of the show, Ramos announced that Romney would answer questions for only thirty-five minutes, while the president the next night would stay for an hour. Infuriated, Romney refused to take the stage until the introduction was retaped without reference to the time discrepancy.

tegic Bombing Survey found that air campaigns don't work in combat without coordinated ground forces. The same went for politics.

Boston kept saying it was not about the numbers of offices in states. But that metric was a good indication of the reach of OFA, which had built an intricate "snowflake" of paid organizers and volunteers to take advantage of Chicago's microtargeting. In Ohio Obama had 121 offices, three times as many as Romney. In Florida the president's campaign had 104 offices, twice as many as four years earlier and twice as many as Romney. OFA registered an astonishing nearly half a million new voters in Florida, including 50,000 in a four-day period just before the October 9 deadline, which Jeremy Bird said may have been the most extraordinary organizing effort he had ever seen.

Among the other factors that Romney didn't foresee was the passion of the uncontested blue states. California, nicknamed "the Death Star" for its potency in 2008, this time outdid itself, placing 16 million calls into battleground areas. Mary Jane Stevenson's crew boasted fourteen huge phone banks (including seven hundred people assembled on a soundstage in Culver City) and tens of thousands of volunteers calling from home, where "predictive caller" software that automatically teed up calls let them work eight times faster. After Analytics found that California's out-of-state calls were just as effective as in-state calls in generating absentee ballot returns and early voting, it freed up battleground state directors to direct more resources to "knock and drag," knocking on doors and dragging people out to vote early, as 70 percent did in Colorado. When early voting there was going only 51–49 for Obama, closer than the models predicted, Chicago had time to reallocate money to the state to target early voters who hadn't yet turned in their ballots.

The story was much the same on fundraising. Romney did well, but Obama did better, and he did it in a small "d" democratic way. The contrast on fundraising spoke to the class issues at the center of the campaign.

Romney raised nearly $950 million, 70 percent of which came from its "high dollar program," run by Spencer Zwick, the campaign's talented finance director. With few small donors (the average donation was $1,000), Boston relied on "bundlers" who competed with each other to raise enough to gain access to special briefings on policy areas that might affect their industries and, if they were successful enough, to the candidate himself. Worried about carried interest? Give to Romney. Clean air rules? Give to Romney. Raising $100,000 entitled the bundler to certain privileges, $200,000 to more perks, and so on. The innermost group consisted of a hundred hard-chargers who raised $1 million each, all, as required by law, in increments of only a few thousand dollars. The program was run like a business, with even volunteer fundraisers being fired if they missed their goals.

Obama also attended scores of major donor events, especially at the beginning, when campaigns are like start-up businesses seeking seed capital. But even as Obama solidified his record as the president who killed public financing, he was setting a new standard in how to convince average people that they owned a piece of the campaign. All told, Obama attracted 4.5 million donors, 2.9 million of them new since 2008. OFA became the first-ever billion-dollar campaign, ending with $1.1 billion, about a third more than expected in early summer. Although wealthy donors still accounted for nearly half of the total raised, they no longer dominated Democratic politics the way they once did. Of the last $200 million in donations to Obama, only $22 million came from big donors. An amazing 97 percent of Obama contributors gave less than $250, with the average donation being $66. They couldn't buy access with that, only a T-shirt or bumper sticker.

Chicago was thrilled with the $181 million raised in September, a one-month record that wouldn't have been possible without Digital's email tests. But the biggest draw was still the Obamas. Michelle attended about a fundraiser a day in October and charmed everyone. The money machine was humming so well that the president and vice president could stop attending fundraisers on October 15, while Romney and Ryan had to soldier on to Election Day.

The bed-wetting on the Democratic side continued nonetheless. In October Obama supporters outside the campaign grew worried about the movement of independents toward Romney. Chicago reasoned that many of these voters weren't truly independents; they were Republicans who got fed up with the party in 2011 and stopped self-identifying as Republicans, which led to a precipitous drop in party membership. Now they were coming home to Romney, which brought his standing back to where it had been in midsummer.

Plouffe thought all the fevered talk about national polls was pointless. The election, he said, amounted to "governors' races on steroids" and everything else was noise. For months he had been convinced that Romney's best shot "was to attack our economy and Bush's economy and offer something really new," but he never separated himself from the Bush years and never recovered from all of the incoming fire.

Now, just weeks before the election, Plouffe and Messina had their metrics and they were sticking to them. The excitable Benenson could always be relied on to tell the morning conference call why the latest AP or Gallup or *Washington Post*–ABC News poll showing Romney surging was "complete shit," with the wrong methodology for determining likely voters. He fervently believed the race had been remarkably stable for months, that Romney was simply returning to where they expected him to be all along. The Benenson analysis, confirmed in the Cave, was compelling enough to convince the high command to believe its own spin, which is always helpful in making the case to the outside world.

For all the talk of airpower (Romney) versus a ground game (Obama), it turned out the president had air superiority as well. Obama bought a staggering 503,000 TV spots, more than twice as many as Romney, but for $135 million less, mostly because Chicago purchased them earlier, when they were cheaper. Inside the political industry, Boston took heat for overpaying for ads and for exceeding saturation levels. By the last week of the campaign, pro-Romney forces bought 7,000 gross ratings points, which meant that the targeted viewers could see the ads as many as seventy times—ten times a day. Obama bought about 4,500 points, which was also over the top. Jim Margolis, responsible for OFA's ads, had to wonder, "So at what point do people say, 'Fuck all of this'?"*

All of the firepower was directed at about 0.5 percent of the electorate: the 700,000 voters in battleground states who were up for grabs. It came out to about $1,000 per undecided voter. With a month to go, Sheldon Adelson put another $33 million into pro-Romney and pro-business PACs, bringing his total over the staggering $100 million he pledged. While most of his money went to holding the House for the GOP, by the end he was funding half of the super PAC ads from the pro-Romney side. But even Adelson had his limits. He said no to the Chamber of Commerce when it appealed for even more in the closing days. The Kochs also pulled back a bit at the end. They disliked Karl Rove, were lukewarm about Romney, and decided to pour money into grassroots organizing in state and local races, where they bolstered the Republican ticket.

ROMNEY HAD THE misfortune to be running in the same cycle as two Republican senatorial candidates who self-immolated by discussing rape in ways that made them look like creepy fringe candidates. When

---

* Federal regulations required that local stations charge the lowest possible ad rates to candidates and that their ads had first dibs on good time slots. Super PACs and dark money advertisers didn't get those privileges, which meant that their ads were far more expensive and often relegated to the middle of the night.

Todd Akin, the Tea Party Republican Senate candidate in Missouri, blew up his campaign in August over a comment about "legitimate rape," it didn't seem at first to be close enough to the election to do Romney much harm. But Richard Mourdock, the Tea Party candidate who had unseated Senator Richard Lugar in Indiana's GOP primary, made his comment about pregnancies resulting from rape being "something God intended to happen" only a fortnight before November 6. Worse for Boston, Mourdock was one of only two candidates for whom Romney had cut ads on which he spoke into the camera endorsing their candidacies.

Boston's initial internal reaction was that Mourdock's comment hadn't been as bad as Akin's and therefore it had no reason to pull the ad and denounce him. The story, Republicans assured themselves, would fade. This wishful thinking was based on a determination to hold the Senate seat in Indiana and not antagonize the evangelical base. Boston, knowing Romney would carry Indiana in any event, didn't monitor events there closely enough. Stevens didn't even notice at first that John McCain went off script and criticized Mourdock, giving the story more air. And no one in Boston bothered to check in with Governor Mitch Daniels, who was saying privately that Mourdock was "dead" and Romney should cut him loose. Once Romney publicly declined to pull his ad for Mourdock, he was trapped. Obama weighed in on the controversy ("Rape is rape") in front of Jay Leno's large audience, and Stephanie Cutter rushed out the message that Paul Ryan shared Mourdock's opposition to abortion even in cases of rape and incest. All the talk of rape helped Obama solidify his strong edge among women.

————

IN OHIO RIGHT-WINGERS turned on Jon Husted, long the symbol of voter suppression in the state. Judicial Watch, True the Vote, and other conservative groups accused him of not moving fast enough to purge voter rolls of ineligible voters (Democrats, not surprisingly, thought the opposite) and for failing to get a much tougher voter ID bill enacted. On the Friday before the election, Husted made one last attempt to prove his devotion to the voter-suppression cause, issuing a directive—after the courts had closed—requiring that provisional ballots (those cast when voters have no driver's license, only something like a utility bill) be disqualified if the voter improperly filled out the ID portion of the form, though Ohio law stated that this was the poll workers' responsibility.

This new rule on provisional ballots was a great worry for the Obama Ohio team going into Election Day. It didn't help that the conservative billionaire Steve Einhorn put up posters in inner-city Cleveland announcing "VOTER FRAUD IS A FELONY!" punishable by up to three and a half years in prison and a $10,000 fine. The obvious aim was to scare blacks into thinking that if they didn't have the right identification, they might be arrested.

Last-ditch voter-suppression efforts were under way in other states too. In Iowa Romney field organizers distributed instructions to poll watchers explaining that they should make sure all voters had photo ID, though Iowa state law didn't require it. In Pennsylvania state-sponsored ads saying voters must show their IDs were still up after the law was overturned. In Florida thousands of voters received bogus letters from an unknown source saying that their citizenship was under investigation. And in Wisconsin Governor Scott Walker's organization instructed volunteer Romney poll watchers in some areas to lie at polling stations by registering as "concerned citizens" rather than Republicans. They were then to tell voters they couldn't vote without a photo ID or if they had ever been convicted of a crime, neither of which was true under Wisconsin law.

Despite the talk on the right of Chicago "thuggery," there were no significant reports of dirty tricks on the Democratic side. When the Obama team played rough, it was on the theme of Romney as rich and out of touch. The tagline of one Obama attack ad, "He's not one of us," would have caused a huge outcry had it been directed toward the president, as Stuart Stevens pointed out. But that's because it would have been seen as race-baiting. The news media took a more benign view of populist arguments. The Obama campaign sent out a mailer with a picture of Romney on his yacht and the line "Mitt Romney's Plan Cuts Taxes for Families Like His—But Raises Taxes on Ours." It occasioned little comment, in part because nonpartisan fact-checkers deemed it to be true.

Populist sentiment fused with outrage over racial injustice as black voters came to believe that, like their parents and grandparents, they were facing a genuine threat to their most basic civil rights. "We got so much stronger as an organization because of voter suppression," Jeremy Bird said later. "Souls to the Polls" and other organized early voting efforts in the black community would be even bigger than in 2008.

Suddenly Al Sharpton was drawing thousands of people when he appeared in Ohio, Florida, or Virginia—the biggest crowds of his career. "Black people vote when they're proud or angry," Sharpton said. "They were proud in 2008 and angry in 2012." He recalled the civil rights leader Wyatt Walker telling him that activists combed the South in the early 1960s looking for a symbol, and they finally found one in Bull Connor, the Birmingham police chief who turned fire hoses and dogs on black children. "Voter suppression was our Bull Connor," Sharpton said.

─────────

WITH EIGHT DAYS to go before the election and Romney holding a slight lead in several national polls, experts agreed that the race was too close to call. With Obama's advantage in the Electoral College and on the ground (early voting by Democrats was already exceeding that in 2008), Romney was still the slight underdog. And yet seasoned political professionals were beginning to conclude that Boston's supreme confidence was more than just spin. Despite important endorsements from Michael Bloomberg and Colin Powell, self-described independents seemed to be moving to Romney. Even savvy political analysts didn't understand at the time that a large proportion of them were actually Republicans disgusted by the primaries coming back into the fold. True independents were splitting more evenly, though this was hard to discern amid all the noise. With Florida close again and polls tightening in Ohio, Wisconsin, and Pennsylvania, fears arose that the country might face another contested election like 2000.

For months Bob Bauer had organized a huge voter-protection effort that included hundreds of lawyers across nine states and hundreds more available by phone. Six days before the election, he held a conference call for senior staff to review contingency plans for a possible recount. "It was nauseating to contemplate," Dan Pfeiffer recalled.

In Florida, scene of the 2000 fiasco, it looked as if history might be repeating itself. On the Friday before the election, voters in Miami-Dade County waited in line as long as nine hours to vote early. When officials at polling places tried to end the early voting, hundreds still in line chanted, "Let us vote!" The same day, Orange County closed an early voting site for four hours to contend with a bomb threat, leaving hundreds without the chance to vote when they planned.

At 1 a.m. on Saturday, Bauer, pulling an all-nighter in the Legal Brain Trust office in Chicago, directed that a suit be immediately filed in federal court against three Florida counties to compel them to keep their polls open over the weekend for early voting. This was a huge piece of business for OFA; at least 100,000 Obama voters were being prevented from voting on the last weekend in a state that was too close to call. After OFA's suit, Miami-Dade and Palm Beach counties quickly agreed to restore early voting. Orange County, facing a state court suit, argued tough luck: Those voters thwarted by the bomb scare could come back and wait in line on Election Day if they wanted to vote so badly. First thing Saturday morning, a state court judge ordered the Orange County polls reopened immediately. The judge asked, in essence, Why should those four hours come out of the hides of voters? Broward County held out until a federal judge, angry at the resistance, beat up the county in court. This was only the latest judicial shot at those who didn't understand that election officials were duty-bound to help voters, not restrict the franchise. "The courts had had enough. They kept asking, 'Why are you making it harder to vote?'" Bauer remembered.

SANDY DEVELOPED LATE for a hurricane. Until recent years, when the end of the hurricane season was pushed back a month (likely by climate change), it was rare to see hurricanes at the end of October and even rarer to see them hitting as far north as the New York area. On October 24 a tropical cyclone was upgraded to a hurricane shortly before making landfall in Jamaica, then gained strength as it headed out to sea again. By the time the storm hit Cape May, New Jersey, at 5:46 p.m. on Monday, October 29, Hurricane Sandy was the largest hurricane (in diameter) on record.

The president left Andrews Air Force Base for Orlando on Sunday evening, hoping to squeeze in a rally before the storm hit. But by midnight *Air Force One* pilots indicated that Monday afternoon might be too late to get back to Washington in time. This conjured memories of President Bush being out of town and off the case during Hurricane Katrina in 2005, the kind of mistake that could blow the election. So at 6:30 a.m. the White House scrapped Obama's 10 a.m. campus rally and flew back to Washington Monday morning under threatening skies, leaving the less airworthy press plane behind. At 2:15 p.m. the president called New Jersey Governor Chris Christie, the beginning of a beautiful friendship. The Federal Emergency Management Agency (FEMA) and other federal agencies had already positioned resources to respond quickly to the storm, and the president and governor had a good discussion about the preparations. They spoke again at midnight, after much of the New Jersey that Christie knew as a kid, the Jersey Shore, lay in ruins.

From the Situation Room, Obama declared a predisaster state of emergency in several states and signed edicts that speeded aid for New Jersey and New York by forgoing the usual paperwork. Just as he had during the BP oil spill, he gave the governors and big-city mayors his cell phone number and insisted they call him directly anytime red tape held something up. He instructed his agency heads not to tell him why something couldn't be done but to figure out how it could.

The grim totals for the United States and the Caribbean—138 dead, $75 billion in property damage, 81 million people without power— were worse than expected. But like so much else in his presidency, Obama had undertaken careful preparation. As a senator, he won notice for his close analysis of Katrina and FEMA's poor response. After becoming president, he promptly asked Craig Fugate, who managed Florida's emergency preparedness under Republican Governor Jeb Bush, to run FEMA, and Fugate accepted. When congressional Republicans tried to starve FEMA's budget, the Obama White House fought back hard and won.

Christie was impressed by the president's attentiveness. On Wednesday, October 31, after postponing Halloween in New Jersey, he hosted Obama on a tour of hurricane damage in his state. Later he told the press about the goose bumps he felt riding on *Air Force One*. The image of a Democratic president and a Republican governor working well together sent a powerful bipartisan message.

For three days in a row, Christie went out of his way to heap accolades on Obama. "The president has been outstanding in this," he told the *Today* show. "I have to give the president great credit," he gushed to Fox. Rush Limbaugh was so upset about the remarks that he suggested a gay subtext to the Christie-Obama relationship by describing their "man loving man" tour of hurricane damage.

Fox's Steve Doocy asked Christie whether Romney would visit New Jersey with him. Christie was dismissive: "I have no idea, nor am I the least bit concerned or interested." Republicans were sure that Christie was just sore over not being selected for the ticket, or perhaps figured that he would have a better chance to win the presidency in 2016, at the end of Obama's second term, than in 2020, at the end of Romney's. In truth, Romney had nothing to add to managing the crisis, and it would have looked like a campaign stunt for him to jump into the story.

Tuesday, October 30, a week before the election, was the day Romney appeared to lose his footing. At a campaign event billed as "storm relief" in Kettering, Ohio, Romney asked for donations of supplies and possessions—just what professional relief workers don't want from the public. (They have trouble sorting them, and many of the intended recipients don't need what donors provide from their closets.) McKay Coppins of BuzzFeed revealed that Romney staffers spent $5,000 at a local Walmart on granola bars, canned food, and diapers to make the photo-op look good. It had the opposite effect.

Worse, Romney was on record in the GOP primaries pandering to Republicans who viewed FEMA as just more big government. During a June 2011 CNN debate, moderator John King asked him whether disaster relief money should be on the chopping block. Romney said, "Absolutely. Every time you have an occasion to take something from the federal government and send it back to the states, that's the right direction. And if you can go even further and send it back to the private sector, that's even better." At a press conference on the day after the storm, reporters tried seven times to get Romney to talk about FEMA and he refused. It had been more than three weeks since he had subjected himself to any questions at all, even from Fox or ESPN, an unprecedented degree of inaccessibility at the end of a presidential campaign. With his embrace of antigovernment ideology catching up to him, he looked like a man with something to hide.

Chris Christie was sleeping about two hours a night. He was stressed by the crisis and still shaken by the destruction of the Jersey Shore. Finally, he realized he had to attend to political business, especially after Rupert Murdoch tweeted that Christie "must re-declare for Romney or take blame for the next dire four years." On November 4 the Christie team planted a question about Romney with Fox News reporter Rick Leventhal. Christie began his answer with fake pique ("This is the kind of silliness that really drives me crazy") before explaining that he was the first governor to endorse Romney, had raised millions for him, and of course would be voting for him. He then finished with a typical Christie-esque riff on how the media was stupid for even asking the question he had just planted.

For months Bill Clinton's gut had told him that Romney would win. It wasn't until the Obama-Christie moment during Hurricane Sandy that he changed his mind. After that, he was confident. Obama was acting like a president, while Romney lost a precious ten days just before the election. In Boston Stuart Stevens thought for the first time that maybe his man might lose. In the end, the election wasn't close enough for Sandy to be decisive, but it clearly helped Obama.

ON NOVEMBER 1 Romney held a conference call with big donors. After an upbeat presentation by pollster Neil Newhouse, Romney said, "Neil's giving you the straight scoop. I feel very positive. The energy flow is tremendous. You should see the crowds!" He explained that the campaign was expanding the battlefield to Minnesota and Pennsylvania. "Dick Morris is predicting a landslide," he added. "I don't think that. It's very close, but I'm in good shape to win."

The logic was that Romney had closed the gap in states where he had trailed a month earlier. Obama had won independents by 8 points in 2008 but trailed with them now by an average of 11 points in the Newhouse polls. Obama had outspent McCain by 4 to 1 in 2008, but now there was rough parity. The money was flowing in, with several hundred Romney donors giving more than $50,000 apiece.

Newhouse's polls showed Romney ahead in Ohio, Florida, Iowa, and North Carolina and tied in Virginia, Wisconsin, and New Hampshire. He had Romney within the margin of error in Colorado, Nevada, and, incredibly, Minnesota. Newhouse, until then a well-regarded pollster, was certain that the white vote would make up at least 74 percent of the electorate, as it had in 2008. But that percentage had been falling by 2 or 3 points every four years in every election cycle since 1988, as whites aged and had fewer children and minority populations grew. Joe Trippi, who had run Howard Dean's campaign in 2004 and was now an analyst for Fox News, kept telling viewers that white turnout would be 72 percent of the electorate. You could set your watch to it.

Newhouse argued his numbers vigorously and benefited from the group-think that had taken over the Romney campaign and much of the Republican Party. Their working assumption was that this was 1980, when voters had broken sharply at the end for Reagan against the incumbent Carter.

———

VOTER SUPPRESSION TURNED out to be one big boomerang. On the day before the election, Mayor Michael Nutter of Philadelphia called Jim Messina. All the talk of a "white wave" washing Romney into office amused him. There was a wave in Philadelphia, all right—a huge wave of angry black voters headed to the polls not out of joy but because, as many African Americans told the mayor, "they're fucking with our president." The Obama camp had never worried much about Pennsylvania, but this was a good sign nonetheless, and the same news was coming out of Ohio, Virginia, and Florida.

The black ministers who had been so upset about Obama's support for same-sex marriage discovered that they were more upset by the threatened cancellation of voting on the Sunday before the election. "Souls to the Polls" was their chance to show their communities how much clout they had compared to other congregations. The number of buses lined up in the church parking lot became a way of keeping score. They had the president's back, of course, but their own as well.

As the backlash gathered strength, Republicans were about to get the worst of both worlds: no suppression efforts upheld by the courts but the full force of the reaction against them. OFA had two hundred paid staffers on the ground in Pennsylvania, and no one there doubted the outcome. The Cave thought the white Republican legislators in Pennsylvania who admitted trying to suppress the vote in order to elect Romney had been too stupid to do proper research. If they had, they would have found that large numbers of those with expired driver's licenses were rural white seniors—the core of Romney's support.

The Romney high command blithely assumed that a combination of devastating black unemployment and disappointment with Obama would inevitably dampen turnout in urban areas. It was wishful thinking.

———

WHILE FOX NEWS had a financial incentive to see Obama reelected (the network generally enjoyed higher ratings under Democrats), it was still trying to help Romney until the end. Roger Ailes covered the Benghazi story as if it were Watergate just before Nixon's resignation, with almost wall-to-wall coverage. Only one Fox anchor was allowed to offer a dissenting view, and even that had its limits. On November 2 Geraldo Rivera appeared on *Fox & Friends* and said that "it broke [his] heart" that Charles Woods, the father of one of the contractors killed in Benghazi, "has been led to believe that the president of the United States went gambling in Las Vegas instead of saving our kids in Benghazi, and that's a lie." When another Fox host, Eric Bolling, began attacking Obama's negligence, Rivera shouted, "That's a lie! You are a politician trying to make a political point."

After the argument continued for several minutes, Ailes called the control room and told the producers to cut Rivera's mic. Just after Rivera said, "It makes it seem as if bureaucrats were sitting there scratching their bellies and that's not what happened," his next words—"I'm sorry, ladies and gentlemen, it's very frustrating"—were picked up, though faintly, on the microphone of Steve Doocy, who had placed his hand on Rivera's shoulder. As host Gretchen Carlson previewed an upcoming story, Rivera could be heard on her mic saying, almost inaudibly, "Oh, great, great, now I'm gonna get lynched." The video was available from YouTube for several weeks before being mysteriously taken down. Ailes was happy to employ Rivera on his network; he was a flamboyant reporter who attracted viewers. But when Rivera used facts to destroy Fox's bogus narrative on Benghazi, it was time to pull the plug.

———

OBAMA FIGURED RACE was playing less of a role than in 2008, when voters didn't know him. This time the election was more about class.

"The folks at the very top—they'll always have a champion," Obama
said in his new combative stump speech. "The people who need a
champion never have lobbyists in Washington working for them. They
need a president fighting for them." These were Democratic Party
themes going back to Andrew Jackson, and he seemed exhilarated to
express them. "This is coming from his loins," Axelrod said after a rally
in Linn, Ohio, as the traveling press corps snickered.

With unemployment below 8 percent in the final jobs report before
the election, the president could afford to brag a bit about his fore-
sight on the economy ("The auto rescue wasn't even popular in Ohio
and Michigan, but I knew it was the right thing to do") and even his
own integrity ("You may be frustrated with the pace of change, but
you know where I stand. You know I tell the truth"). When he warned
about the opposition trying "to buy an election" and the booing began,
he always said the same thing: "Don't boo. Vote."

As Obama found his groove, all the talk about his not communicating seemed in the past. By the end of the campaign, he was conveying
his message so well that voters on the street were regurgitating "make-
or-break moment for the middle class" and other arguments back to
reporters and pollsters. And Obama communicated the one quality that
matters most in politics: trust. For all of the disappointments in their
own lives, the people still felt that the president of the United States
was honest and even a little cool.

On the road Obama enjoyed spending time with the campaign's
state directors. They all had the same playoff beards and the same
approach—humble, hardworking, smart, and almost always willing to
give credit first to their troops. The president would say, "Take a picture," and usually the state director would reply, "No, take one with
my team." Finally, Marty Nesbitt said to Obama, "Everywhere we go,
that's the same dude." The president agreed and he loved it. He had
created a self-reinforcing subculture of young leaders much less self-
absorbed than the activists of an earlier era. "They're better than we
were—much better," he liked to say.

Obama was not just self-aware; he was a bit detached from his own
experiences, as if he were focused on collecting novelistic string for his
memoirs. Some of his comments along the way were merely nostalgic
("This is my last debate prep" or "This is my last walk-through"), but
others seemed ripped from a Walker Percy novel. "I'm sort of a prop
in the campaign," he said onstage two days before the election. But
in Des Moines at the end, he felt the full force of what everyone had
done for him. Out in the crowd he saw so many people who had been
with him from the beginning, still working their hearts out for him five

years later. The standoffishness of those dutiful occasions in the East Room evaporated. "He was feeling the love," Nesbitt remembered. In Virginia in 2008 Obama had wept at his final event in part because his grandmother had just died. This time, without grief, his face once again glistened with tears. It had been a long road, and this was his last event ever as a candidate, back where it all began.

STYMIED ON THE auto rescue, Romney was still unwilling to give up on cars. His campaign saw a squib in *Bloomberg News* suggesting that Jeep might move its production to China. In fact Jeep was merely building a Chinese plant for the sale of cars in China, the kind of local production that all automakers have undertaken for years. It had no plans to lay off Jeep workers in Ohio, as Romney's comment implied. Undeterred by denials from the car companies, Romney cut ads saying, "Obama says he saved the auto industry. But for who? Obama or China?" The ads were not just false and inflammatory; they traded on a cynical assumption that Ohio voters were too dumb to sort out the truth about their own livelihoods. The ads were denounced in editorials across the state and didn't seem to move the numbers.

Six days before the election, Dan Centinello, the director of voter contact for the Romney campaign, held a conference call with organizers in key states. The subject was "Project ORCA," a secret smartphone system for communicating with thirty thousand fieldworkers stationed at polling places on Election Day. For weeks Centinello had been working overtime responding personally to hundreds of emails from low-level organizers inquiring about ORCA, which had yet to be unveiled. The name of the custom-built system was an inside joke. An orca whale is the only known predator of the narwhal whale, though Boston didn't know that Chicago had long since given up on the Narwhal software. On the ORCA training call, Centinello was brimming with confidence. The young operative with no computer-related experience on his résumé told the troops, "There's nothing that the Obama data team, there's nothing that the Obama campaign, there's nothing that President Obama himself can do to even come close to what we are putting together here."

Centinello didn't know it, but his doomed tracking system was a secret even inside his own campaign. Stuart Stevens and Spencer Zwick later said that the first they ever heard of ORCA was on Election Day.

FOSTER FRIESS HAD pumped millions of dollars into the campaigns of Rick Santorum, Mitt Romney, and other Republicans. Exactly how much was unknown because he had no problem contributing to (c)4 entities that were not required to disclose the source of their donations. But Friess thought that the days of money controlling politics were over. In the new era, he said, information controlled politics. And he was beginning to think that the Obama ground game, with its sophisticated information systems, would be too powerful for Romney to prevail. He found himself in Reno, Nevada, on the night before the election volunteering on a phone bank: "I was dialing up people whose name I wasn't quite sure I was going to pronounce correctly, when it dawned on me that the same person was being invited to dinners and barbecues in his neighborhood by paid staff that Obama had kept on after the 2008 elections."

The Romney forces felt no such trepidation. Driving to a Romney speech in Virginia late in the campaign, senior staffers down from Boston hit a huge traffic jam. They thought there had been an accident and were thrilled to learn that it was all the people going to their event. Big crowds were good for morale, but anyone with experience in politics knew they were deceptive (Goldwater and Mondale had them at the end of their disastrous campaigns), not to mention being unscientific in a campaign whose candidate had insisted he wanted to be "data-driven."

On November 3 Romney drew a crowd of thirty thousand in West Chester, Ohio, home of John Boehner. It was an enthusiastic rally, but the "feeling" it generated said nothing about the outcome of the election. Obama's rallies were smaller because his team reasoned that in the closing days it was more important to organize early voting than to run up the size of the crowd at campaign events.

Romney closed on moochers. "We're not promising to hand out checks," he said. Obama closed by mocking the challenger's "Romnesia" on his previous positions and concluded, "This is about trust."

On the day before the election, the Romney campaign in Ohio proudly tweeted that it had knocked on 75,000 doors on Sunday, an impressive number. Obama's Ohio state directors immediately reported that OFA had knocked on 376,000—five times as many. The word went up the chain to Plouffe, who told the president. "That's my team," he responded. On the weekend before the election, 700,000 Obama volunteers in nine battleground states knocked on 5.2 million doors. It gave the president a lot of confidence going into Election Day.

With less than twenty-four hours to go, Joel Benenson ran into Rahm Emanuel at the Chicago headquarters. "You better fucking be right," the mayor told the pollster, only half-joking. "See these guys?" he said, pointing to his security detail. "If you're not fucking right they will hunt you down and bring you back to me and I'll fucking take care of you myself."

Romney's running mate joined him in assuming that victory was near. On the evening before the election, Paul Ryan was campaigning in Des Moines and so confident of victory that he asked two of his advisers, "Do you think I have to give up my congressional seat during the transition?" He was concerned that if he didn't resign from Congress it might create the impression that he was serving in the executive branch and the legislative branch at the same time. It apparently didn't occur to him that he might not have to worry about it.

26

Shell-shocked

After the election, it was hard to believe that Romney and his campaign hadn't seen it coming. The signs were there all along, from the forbidding math of the Electoral College, which required Romney to run the table, to polling in media markets showing that $100 million in late ad buys by super PACs had not moved the needle even slightly. Early voting—more than a third of the total ballots cast across the country—appeared to be overwhelmingly for Obama in every battleground state except Colorado. But the whole Romney team—and much of conservative America—seemed to be swimming in a sea of denial.

Ever since the first debate, Fox News had covered Romney's supposed "momentum" as if it would inevitably carry him into the White House. Conservatives avidly followed a website called "Unskewed Polls" that purported to show why any polls showing Obama ahead were faulty. In truth, it was the Romney polls that used the wrong turnout models. The normally sober Neil Newhouse was projecting a win. "IN EVERY SINGLE STATE WE HAVE A SIGNIFICANT MOMENTUM LEAD," Newhouse wrote in one of his last emails to supporters. The all-caps message was clear: Only clueless skeptics who weren't in touch with the numbers—up by 20 points with white women! up by 28 with white men!—could not see the victory ahead.

Romney, determined to leave everything on the (reality distortion) field, campaigned in Florida, Virginia, and New Hampshire on the day before the election, ending with a relaxed halftime appearance on *Monday Night Football*. The crowds at the end were large and often ecstatic, chanting "One more day! One more day!" On Tuesday, Romney got up and voted at home in Belmont, Massachusetts, before heading out on a final trip to Ohio and Pennsylvania, where 96 percent of voters cast their ballots on Election Day. Obama had harvested most of his votes early, Boston reasoned, and Romney would rule when it counted.

Blessed by good health and great business success, Romney had suffered few setbacks in his life. In politics, his loss to Ted Kennedy in the

1994 Senate race was hardly devastating; he had beaten expectations and given Kennedy his toughest race ever. Now the man groomed and conditioned for great success landed at Boston's Logan Airport more than merely confident of what the evening's returns held in store for him. He fully expected to be elected president of the United States.

———

STARTING AT 6 A.M. on Election Day, Dan Wagner came up from the Cave every half-hour to brief the high command, gathered on the seventh floor in what was known (in homage to an earlier political era) as "the Boiler Room." Axelrod said to Wagner, only half-joking, "If we lose, there are two people who can never go outside again: you and Nate Silver." Wagner said he had a hara-kiri knife ready downstairs for ritual suicide.

By 11 a.m. the joke didn't seem so funny in the Cave. Most areas looked good, but some Ohio numbers were throwing the models out of whack. When Wagner stepped out of the Cave for a moment, two analysts approached Elan Kriegel, who ran battleground state analytics, with troubling numbers. Gordon, the Election Day voter tracking system named for the man who killed Houdini, was producing data with disturbing anomalies. All of the subgroups most supportive of the president were down roughly 5 percent. Kriegel said the numbers must be wrong and asked the statisticians to run them again. When they did, they came back the same. He asked David Shor, the twenty-year-old onetime prodigy who helped him prepare the Golden Reports, what it meant. Shor said it meant that Obama was losing Ohio.

Kriegel walked into the bathroom and stared at the toilet. Because he was the kind of person who counted everything, he knew that he had vomited exactly six times in his life. Now he prepared for a seventh. "I thought I was going to be living in Mitt Romney Land," he remembered. But the seventh didn't come. Gathering control, he returned to the Cave and made an executive decision: He would not tell Wagner or other higher-ups. He lived with the news for an excruciating hour until his team recognized that because poll watchers in black precincts used fewer handhelds to file their reports identifying which Obama supporters voted, the data flow had been "chunky" and thus wrongly modeled. The president was winning after all, though only by 1 percent, a smaller margin than expected.

For much of the day, Obama's GOTV operations went smoothly. Harper Reed's October dry runs, code-named "Game Day," had made sure the servers and other Election Day systems could handle any data load. But local election officials in many states had not made proper preparations for the volume of voters, in some cases withholding additional voting booths from Democratic precincts while Republican areas had plenty. In midafternoon reports began filtering in of long lines at polling places in urban regions of battleground states. Thousands of Obama volunteers were mobilized to remind those in line that all of them would get to vote—no matter how long it took—and to provide food, water, and any other assistance needed, in some cases even picking up their neighbors' kids at school and babysitting them until their parents had a chance to vote.

———

IF GORDON HAD glitches, ORCA was a fiasco. Romney's poll watcher tracking system launched with no significant user testing and little more than a prayer that the system wouldn't crash. The sixty-page ORCA packets for poll workers had been emailed from Boston at 4 p.m. on the day before the election—much too late, considering the possibility of error and the difficulty that poll watchers (many of them elderly) would have printing out and absorbing such a long document. Sure enough, large numbers of packets contained a crucial typo: A duplicate reminder to bring a folding chair to the polling site for a long day of sitting accidentally replaced essential information on where to obtain the poll watching certificate that most states required. This meant that thousands of would-be Romney poll watchers wouldn't be using those folding chairs because they wouldn't be allowed to sit at the polling sites in the first place. They went home angry and called headquarters.

By midmorning on Election Day, Boston and the regional Romney "victory centers" were besieged by calls, few of which were answered by anything but a useless recording. Volunteers at the polls were supposed to report voter information on their mobile phones, but the instructions described the designated website as an app by mistake, causing further frustration. By midday the ORCA system automatically interpreted the high traffic on its server as an attack by hackers, and by midafternoon it crashed. Thousands of Romney poll watchers—an important link in the campaign's GOTV operations and its internal source of reporting returns—spent the day in a state of confusion. No one thought the failure of ORCA cost Romney the election, but Dan Centinello became Boston's favorite punching bag and ORCA the symbol of a campaign badly outgunned on every front of the new digital politics.

Romney was disturbed to learn that one of his computer systems had crashed, but he remained confident of victory—so confident that he didn't bother to prepare a concession speech (a contingency plan undertaken by Obama in both 2008 and 2012). The only pessimist

in the high command was Dan Senor, who was also, not coincidentally, the only one forced to leave the bubble and deal with Hurricane
Sandy. The week before, after evacuating his young family from their
Tribeca apartment, he looked out his window at flooded lower Manhattan and it hit him: The president was acting like a president and they
were going to lose. He kept his feelings mostly to himself.

Most of the Romney team was confident, even optimistic, with some
already measuring the drapes in the West Wing. Major party nominees
almost always prepare for a transition to the presidency in secret, but
over the summer Romney had decided to be open about it. He told
former Utah governor Mike Leavitt to begin collecting résumés. The
campaign invited dozens of candidates for jobs in a Romney administration to Boston for Election Night, where they joined donors and
hung around the TD Garden convention center waiting for the victory
party.

OBAMA HAD A ritual of playing basketball every Election Day. The one
time he didn't play, on the day of the 2008 New Hampshire primary,
he lost to Hillary Clinton. This time the game, at the Attack Gym on
Chicago's West Side, included retired Chicago Bulls stars Scottie Pippin,
Jeff Sanders, and Randy Brown. The president sank a couple of shots
early on, and his team, which conveniently included Pippin, won easily. All players on both sides wore the same number and words on their
blue-and-white jerseys: 4 More Years.

The exit polls looked good, but when the early votes, which were
counted first, were tallied in Hamilton County, Ohio (the Cincinnati
area), just after 8 p.m., the Boiler Room knew for sure that Obama
would be reelected. The model that Analytics built said that Obama
would carry 56.4 percent of the early votes there. He ended up with
57 percent, a remarkably close projection. The Cave had overestimated
the number of undecided voters and predicted Colorado to be a point
closer than it turned out to be. Otherwise, its track record was impressive. In Florida the statewide early voting model would be off by a
mere 0.3 percent out of 4.4 million early votes cast.

The election was over before anyone expected. At 11:12, when NBC
News was the first to project Obama the winner, the president and his
family were watching the returns in his suite at the Fairmont Hotel. Valerie Jarrett exclaimed, "You won!"

Obama still wasn't smiling. "I'll believe it when Fox calls it," the president said. Four and a half minutes later Fox did.

Obama was happier than in 2008. He felt the stakes had been higher this time than when he ran against McCain and the affirmation more satisfying. His close friends liked to think of it as the ultimate positive job evaluation—a validation of what he was doing for the country.

Over at the Prudential Building, a brief silence descended on the seventh floor when NBC News called the race. Then the place erupted, with people crying and hugging and jumping around in their special blue Obama-Biden Boiler Room T-shirts. Almost the entire group had been with Obama four years earlier, and everyone agreed that the mood was different this time. In 2008 they felt euphoria; in 2012, release. Afterward several remembered that someone came in playing bagpipes. The sound was appropriate—celebratory but deeper and more resonant than blasting rock and roll. Teddy Goff's people tweeted a Pete Souza shot of the president and first lady hugging on an airport tarmac. It was retweeted 817,159 times, beating the all-time record set by Justin Bieber.

By the time Axelrod, Plouffe, Messina, Pfeiffer, and others arrived at the Fairmont a boisterous celebration was under way. Marty Nesbitt and Anita Blanchard's young kids made so much noise that Obama had to hold his hand over one ear to talk on the phone, but he was loving every minute of it. He hugged each key member of the team, thanked them effusively, and told several, "This one actually means more to me than 2008." It meant more, he said, because the public had made what he considered an educated judgment of him and what he had done.

In 2008 the victory celebration was in Grant Park. This time the crowds gathered at McCormick Place, the Chicago convention center not far from Obama's home. Stevie Wonder's "Signed, Sealed, Delivered, I'm Yours" played on the sound track as the president strode to the stage and told the world, "We are an American family, and we rise and fall together as one nation."

————

WITHOUT ORCA, its internal system for reporting voting patterns, Romney and his team were flying blind, reduced to watching CNN and relying on leaks of network exit polls. When those polls in the early afternoon showed a close race in Florida, a state Romney expected to carry comfortably, Stuart Stevens and company knew things were worse than they had anticipated, though they didn't know how much worse. Hope died hard. It wasn't until 5 p.m., when exit polls showed Virginia trending for Obama, that Spencer Zwick began to think his boss might lose. North Carolina, which Romney officials thought an easy win, was close, and Pennsylvania, where they had hoped to catch Obama at the tape, wasn't. The donors and hangers-on didn't believe the rumors. Stanley Tate, who headed Florida's finance committee, remembered that supporters gathered in Romney's suite at the Westin remained optimistic until well past 10 p.m. Paul Ryan even went over to the donor suites at the TD Garden and gave a couple of pep talks.

As battleground states began to come in for Obama, the suites grew silent. Long before Romney conceded, donors left for Logan Airport, where they faced traffic jams on the tarmac as their private planes waited to take off. On the way out of town, Donald Trump tweeted that the election returns were "a travesty, a total sham, a disgusting injustice." Later, when he learned that the election had not been stolen by the Democrats, he tweeted, "Congrats to @KarlRove on blowing $400 million this cycle."

BEFORE THE ELECTION, Joe Trippi tried to tell his Fox colleagues that they were living in a fantasyland. "You guys think Barack Obama created all the change. He's the *result* of the change," Trippi told Rove. "The Republicans are the party of old white guys, and old white guys die." But Trippi and Juan Williams and anyone else who made such arguments were immediately dismissed as "in the tank" for Obama. Fox wasn't the only network with pundits out on a limb. George Will, usually a clear-eyed conservative columnist and ABC News analyst, predicted that Romney would carry Minnesota en route to an easy victory with more than three hundred electoral votes. On Election Day even liberal Fox News employees, conditioned by what they heard all day, went to work thinking Romney had it. Roger Ailes saw which way things were moving earlier than many of his people. In the morning he told his on-air talent, "If things don't go well, don't look like your dog died on the air."

After all the networks, including Fox, called the election for Obama, Rich Beeson, Romney's political director, began emailing complaints to Fox anchor Chris Wallace. Boston claimed "real doubts," as Wallace told viewers at 11:25 p.m., that Ohio was in the Obama column. Rove, also receiving emails from the Romney high command, echoed the caution. During a commercial break, producers in the Fox control room asked him, "Karl, what do you know?" Rove invoked the disputed election of 2000 but otherwise offered no new information.

When live coverage resumed, viewers were treated to nearly twenty minutes of indelible political television as Rove stood athwart history shouting "No!" In the calm voice of an analyst, he told the anchors, "We've got to be careful about calling this when we have 991 votes separating the candidates." Given the reversed network calls of 2000 and 2004, Rove might have had reason to be cautious, but the part about "991 votes separating the candidates" signaled that he was desperately grasping at straws. Even casual observers of politics know that the raw vote total is irrelevant when teams of statisticians across five networks use sample precincts for projections.

As Rove patronized the anchors—"I'd be very cautious about intruding into this process"—and continued his odd and fact-free analysis of Ohio counties, a huge cheer went up at the Boston convention center, where the Romney throng watching Fox on the monitors saw hope from a celebrated Republican strategist. Fox didn't air the cheer, keeping its cameras on the anchors and analysts in New York. After Rove finished and a brief silence settled over the set, anchor Megyn Kelly said, "That's awkward."

Calling in from home, Ailes told his news chief, Mike Clemente, to have Kelly stay on-camera and stroll down the hall to the Fox decision desk to find out what was going on, another sign of Ailes's instinctive talent as a TV producer. When she arrived, Arnon Mishkin and Chris Stirewalt of the decision desk told her they were "quite comfortable with the call in Ohio" and "99.9 percent" certain that the president had been reelected.

Back on the set, Rove continued to contest the call. "They know the science!" Kelly responded, with the exasperation she usually reserved for Democrats. As Fox cameras cut to another roar from the crowd at McCormick Place in Chicago, Kelly inadvertently captured the mood of Obama supporters everywhere. "They are not listening to Karl," she said. "They don't care what Karl said."

Next to the president's reelection, Rove's odd appearance was the main topic of conversation in millions of homes and workplaces the next day. Here was a man responsible for investing hundreds of millions of super PAC dollars into the campaign helplessly watching it all disappear. Liberals thought it was outrageous that Fox would have the quarterback of their team deciding who won, but they relished a different metaphor: the Wicked Witch of the West melting before Dorothy's eyes. Embarrassed conservatives praised Fox for standing up to Rove, who would face their wrath for wasting so much money with so little to show for it.

———

EVERY ELECTION DAY assumption of the Romney campaign was mistaken. It assumed the Democratic turnout would end up somewhere between that in 2004 and 2010 when it was much closer to that in 2008. It failed to recognize that the independents moving their way (the much heralded "momentum") were just former Republicans returning to their natural home. And it wrongly predicted that undecided voters would break for Romney in the end.

But even after Fox projected that Obama won, the Romney high command wouldn't give up for nearly an hour. Campaign lawyers had planes ready to fly to Florida, Virginia, and Ohio, where Scott Jennings, the Ohio state director, and his colleagues were still saying it was too close to call. Visions of 2000, when the networks late in the evening moved Florida from Gore's column to Bush's, danced in their heads. Romney's friend and campaign chairman, Bob White, was game to reprise Don Evans's role in 2000 and go into the convention hall and tell the world that the governor wasn't ready to concede. But now Colorado and Virginia were definitely gone, and Florida much closer than expected. Romney was "shell shocked," as one aide put it. "It's not going to happen."

All night Paul Ryan had clung to the example of the June 2012 Wisconsin recall election that Governor Scott Walker survived: "I heard the same thing before the recall: 'Walker's not gonna win.' And then he blew it out." He paced the living room of his hotel suite as the returns flowed in. Finally, Dan Senor, hearing on the phone that Romney was preparing to concede, pulled Ryan into the bedroom of the suite, sat him down, and told him it was over. Ryan was stunned. "What are we in for?" he said, worrying aloud about the country with four more years of Obama.

By the time the running mates and their families came together at the Westin, Ann Romney and Janna Ryan were weeping. As staff filtered in, Romney wrapped his people in warm hugs. They had always seen a humanity and decency in him that many voters never glimpsed. Romney's personal assistant, Garrett Jackson, called Marvin Nicholson to arrange the concession call. The rivals had a short polite conversation that the president, with a hand over one ear, couldn't hear well because of the noise in his suite. Romney's impromptu five-minute concession speech, delivered an hour and forty minutes after the networks called the election, was gracious, but the strain showed.

———

THE 2012 PRESIDENTIAL election wasn't close. Obama crushed Romney in the Electoral College, 332–206, and carried every original battleground state except North Carolina. He could have lost both Ohio and Florida and still prevailed. When the popular vote was fully counted a week later, he had won 51 to 47 percent (a fitting number for Romney), with a margin of around five million votes out of 126 million ballots cast. The Obama coalition consisted of women, young people, labor, blacks, Latinos, Asian Americans, gays, and those with advanced degrees. A collection of Democratic Party constituency groups that had managed to carry only one state for George McGovern in 1972 (Massachusetts) and one state for Walter Mondale in 1984 (Minnesota) now constituted a majority. Romney won 59 percent of the white vote and carried seniors by 12 points, but it wasn't nearly enough.

The gender gap remained, with Obama carrying 55 percent of women and Romney 52 percent of men. But all of the stories about "the enthusiasm gap" turned out to be wrong. While young voters may not have swooned for Obama this time, they voted for him by 20 points. That was down from his unprecedented margin of 35 points in 2008 but still a large part of his victory, especially as the youth vote grew to one-fifth of the electorate. While Romney narrowly carried the white youth vote, it didn't help him much. More than 40 percent of eighteen- to twenty-nine-year-old voters were nonwhite, a sign of America's new face. Young voters were now a dependable part of the Democratic coalition and less likely than in the past to find an excuse not to vote.

African Americans, 93 percent for Obama, remained constant from 2008 at 13 percent of the electorate. Boston had few contacts in the black community, and its assumptions (and those of much of the press) of dampened enthusiasm were inaccurate. To the surprise of everyone except African American politicians and local leaders, black turnout was actually up in battleground states over 2008. In Ohio, where 200,000 more blacks voted than the last time, their percentage of the electorate increased by nearly a third (to 15 percent), in part because many whites stayed home. In Virginia eleven predominantly black counties in the southeastern part of the state increased their turnout over 2008, more than compensating for rural white counties that voted heavily for Romney.

Latinos were the big demographic story. They went 71 percent for Obama nationwide, up 4 points from 2008, and made the difference in Nevada, Colorado, and Florida, where the president won an astonishing 83 percent of the Puerto Rican vote, up 20 points over 2008. (The Sotomayor ad was crucial.) Obama was especially pleased to carry nearly half of Florida's Cuban Americans, who had been overwhelmingly Republican for half a century. The Latino vote in Florida helped compensate for a 10-point drop in white support there and gave Obama a state that even some of his top aides doubted he would win. Asian Americans, favoring a larger role for government, went 73 percent for Obama nationwide, an increase of 11 points over 2008. The president also won 73 percent of the LGBT vote, up 6 points, in part because of his support for gay marriage.*

---

* Exit polls are unreliable on the LGBT vote because they record only those who self-identify.

Throughout the campaign, Romney and his team had always taken comfort in the otherwise disturbing right track/wrong track figures. As long as most voters thought the country was headed in the wrong direction, they figured, Romney had a good chance. No president had ever been reelected with negative numbers on this question. When the exit polls came out, Obama was the first. More than half the country, 52 percent, thought the United States was still on the wrong track.

But on the critical question of which candidate "cares more about people like me," Obama won overwhelmingly. He also prevailed among those who felt he better represented the middle class. And Obama won on the issues: Only 25 percent wanted Obamacare repealed and 60 percent favored an increase in taxes for the wealthy. A majority of self-described moderates backed the president.

The president had coattails in 2012, though not long enough to change control of the House of Representatives. Democratic candidates for the House won 1.1 million more votes than Republican candidates, but Republicans ended up with 55 percent of the House seats, which gave them a comfortable margin of thirty-three seats. The explanation was gerrymandering in state capitals after the 2010 midterms. For instance, Obama prevailed in Ohio by 2 points, but Republicans carried twelve of the state's sixteen seats. In Pennsylvania, which Obama won by 5 points, Republicans took thirteen of eighteen seats. The Senate was a different story. Todd Akin in Missouri and Richard Mourdock in Indiana were defeated over rape gaffes, but Republicans also lost contested races in Massachusetts, Connecticut, Virginia, Ohio, North Dakota, and Montana. Six months after most experts predicted that they would lose control of the upper chamber, Democrats expanded their majority from fifty-three to fifty-five seats.

At least the prognosticators who miscalled the Senate months earlier could plead that conditions had changed and that their predictions were mostly accurate at the end. Many pollsters didn't have that excuse. As Joel Benenson and Dan Wagner had been saying all year, the polling profession in the United States was in deep trouble. It wasn't just the discrediting of Neil Newhouse, the Romney pollster whose descent from math into spin was captured in his infamous comment, "We're not going to let our campaign be dictated by fact-checkers." Unreliable polls with shoddy methodology (including the granddaddy of pollsters, Gallup) had infected the entire process. Their "likely voter" models, based partly on such outdated questions as whether voters knew where their polling places were (younger voters just looked up the location on their iPhones that morning) and whether they had voted in 2010, were often worthless. Even on the day before the election, when polls are usually spot-on, Gallup had Obama up by only 1 point, and the much-read RCP Average of polls had Obama winning nationally by only 0.7 percent—more than 3 points less than the actual result.

————

THE BACKLASH AGAINST voter suppression had helped to power the president's victory. In Ohio more than 100,000 Obama voters cast their ballots early in the last three days in a state the president won by only 166,000 votes. In Virginia thousands of blacks waited patiently in line for more than five hours to vote. In Florida 150 pastors organized "Operation Lemonade"—named for the "lemon" that Governor Rick Scott handed them—and nearly matched their "Souls to the Polls" turnout in 2008 despite six fewer early voting days. Florida would have been out of reach for Obama without the pushback against suppression. The president carried the state by only seventy-four thousand votes, far fewer than the numbers who voted early in Miami-Dade, Palm Beach, and Broward counties, all three of which were initially barred from opening their polling places longer to relieve long lines. In Pennsylvania several all-black precincts in Philadelphia reported no votes for Romney. Not less than 1 percent, not 0.1 percent: not a single vote.

It sounded suspicious to conservatives, but they had no indication of fraud. True the Vote, the right-wing organization that promised one million poll watchers, fizzled on Election Day. The group's Internet training was focused on harassing lightly documented voters in African American communities by photographing and videotaping them and threatening to report them to authorities. But the training instructions were slipshod, and many would-be poll watchers were turned away by county election officials after they failed to complete the requirements for certification.

Overall the Tea Party wasn't much of a presence on the ground. Dick Armey's FreedomWorks spent $40 million on Senate races and lost them all; two House stalwarts, Allen West of Florida and Joe Walsh of Illinois, went down.* Local Tea Party organizations helped bring evangelicals to the polls who might not have otherwise voted for a Mormon, and they turned out their hard-core voters, many of them older. But 46 million more people voted in 2012 than in 2010, their year of

————

* After management turmoil, Armey walked away from FreedomWorks with $8 million. The group lost more credibility when it was revealed that staffers shot an obscene video featuring a man in a panda bear suit appearing to perform oral sex on a woman in a Hillary Clinton mask.

glory. That meant that more than one-third of the electorate was voting only once every four years. While Tea Party members wanted the world to believe they were the "true" Americans, the 2012 returns exposed this as a nostalgic fantasy. They were what European and other multiparty states called a "remnant party," still powerful in midterm and other low-turnout elections but hardly the wave of the future.

——————

WITHIN MINUTES OF the outcome, the conservative rationalizations began: Romney was too moderate; the liberal media was to blame; Obama stole the election. Late on Election Night, Bill O'Reilly set the pace for the "moocher" analysis. He pointed to exit polls saying the president's response to Hurricane Sandy was important and noted, "There are 50 percent of the voting public who want stuff. They want things. And who is going to give them things? President Obama."

This was the makers-versus-takers argument all over again, but it was at odds with the facts of what are known in budget circles as "transfer payments." In truth, the age group receiving the most "stuff" from Washington is the elderly, who voted overwhelmingly for Romney. And most of the biggest "takers" among the states—the places that receive far more money from Washington than they send in taxes—are red states in the South and West. And then there are the hedge fund managers who, as Warren Buffett said, pay at a lower tax rate than their secretaries, not to mention $500 billion in additional tax breaks that the wealthy expected from a Romney administration, all of which might fairly be called "gifts."

Two days after the election, Romney held a closed-door postmortem. He was once again the clinical Bain analyst of the 1980s, assessing a deal gone sour: Beating an incumbent who has no primary opponent is tough. Beating an incumbent when you have a prolonged primary is even tougher. Beating an incumbent who has not lost his popularity with the American people—who is not hated—is toughest of all.

In later conference calls with donors, he moved toward O'Reilly's "stuff" analysis. After praising his "no drama" campaign team and criticizing the GOP primary system ("We had twenty Republican primary debates—that was absolutely nuts"), Romney zeroed in on the "gifts" that Obama handed out. He mentioned forgiveness of college loan debt, free contraceptives, and especially Obamacare. "For any lower-income Hispanic family, Obamacare was massive," Romney said. "For a home earning let's say thirty thousand a year, free health care, which is worth about ten thousand dollars a year, I mean is massive, it's huge."

News of the conference call offended Democrats. "It all came full circle, back to the 47 percent," Senator Al Franken told a friend. "It's like he was saying, 'See, I told you that you didn't want to vote for me.'"

Many conservatives thought "gifts" were only part of the explanation for minority turnout they claimed was suspiciously high. Right-wing blogs cried fraud based on comparing voter turnout to census figures. They failed to factor in student voting and seniors who still voted in the North but were often counted for the census in the South, or vice versa. A September story in the *Columbus Dispatch* saying that a few Ohio counties had more registered voters than eligible voters got a lot of attention after the election. But as the story pointed out, there was nothing unusual about voter rolls that hadn't been updated after people died or moved. Despite the best efforts of Obama haters, no credible evidence of vote fraud surfaced in 2012, and even the sketchy accounts amounted to a minuscule number of irregularities— not enough to affect the outcome in a single precinct, much less to justify harsh new restrictions on voting. That didn't stop many Republicans from challenging the validity of the election. Public Policy Polling, a mischievous liberal pollster, later asked Republicans if they believed ACORN, a community action group, stole the 2012 election for Obama, and 49 percent said yes, even though ACORN went out of business in 2010, which suggested that close to half of the GOP was still prepared to believe the worst about the president regardless of the facts.*

The reactionary spasm after the election took different forms. Hundreds of students rioted at the University of Mississippi, burning Obama posters and, in some cases, hurling racial epithets. Reuters reported financial advisers around the country having to talk "inconsolable" small business owners "off the ledge." Robert Murray of Murray Energy, a coal company, read a prayer and laid off fifty employees. Writing in WorldNetDaily, Larry Klayman, who had hounded Bill Clinton during impeachment, argued that the United States was headed toward Egyptian-like bondage "thanks to our 'Mullah in Chief' and his growing voter hoards of socialists, communists, anti-Semites, anti-Christians, atheists, radical gays and lesbians, feminists, illegal immigrants, Muslims, anti-Anglo whites and others who last Tuesday cemented his destructive hold on the White House and our country."

---

* In March 2013 the House Republican leadership introduced a budget bill to de-fund ACORN, even though an earlier law had already done so and the organization had been defunct for three years.

THE BIG DONORS were shocked at first but quickly concluded that Romney had run a poor campaign and the super PAC ads had failed to resonate. Several regretted that in September, when Romney was tanking in the polls, they had considered shifting their money into Senate races but stuck with Romney when he won the first debate. Now they were hardly impressed by the logic of Carl Forti, head of Restore Our Future, the pro-Romney super PAC, who claimed, "We accomplished our goals. Barack Obama got five million fewer votes than in 2008." *Accomplished our goals?* If the goals were just to lose less badly than John McCain had, one GOP donor said, "it would have been nice to know that beforehand."

Americans for Prosperity, the Koch brothers' super PAC, claimed to have 1.9 million members in thirty-five states, but the campaign workers who went door-to-door were paid, which made them less effective. It turned out that voters want to hear from sincere representatives of candidates, not paid callers or canvassers reading material provided by organizations the voters had never heard of. Super PACs were learning that they couldn't buy a ground game. And even in the air they were largely impotent, in part because their Wall Street donors shied away from hot-button issues like gay marriage and China-bashing that might break through the clutter.

David Koch called the election results "bitterly disappointing," and his brother Charles vowed, "We're going to fight the battle as long as we breathe." They set about on a "deep-dive" analysis of what went wrong in 2012, with plans to report back to donors in the summer of 2013. At the top of their list of culprits was Karl Rove. After the election, the tension between Americans for Prosperity and Crossroads had descended into the usual finger-pointing that follows a big loss. Donors to both super PACs thought the bad blood would be a huge headache for the party in the years ahead, though Rove, humiliated by 2012 and not independently wealthy, was in no position to win the struggle.

Many Republicans analyzing Romney's loss concluded that the critical period was June and July 2012, just as the graphs on media coverage in Alex Gage's National Dialogue Monitor had indicated. The debate at the time in Boston over whether to defend Bain and Romney's honor or go on the offensive against Obama had been resolved in favor of the latter strategy. Now the Kochs and other Monday-morning quarterbacks concluded that this was the pivotal error. Had they rebutted better on Bain and Romney's character, they might have dampened Gage's "kindling," and the 47 percent fiasco would have been a two-day story instead of a defining event.

Stuart Stevens wasn't buying it. While he took public responsibility for what went wrong ("Blame me for everything," he said repeatedly), he never regretted his basic strategy. He called the decision in early summer on whether to defend and humanize Romney or to stick with the economic theme "a kind of Sophie's choice." He recalled that when focus groups were shown warm and fuzzy ads about Romney, their reaction was, "That's nice, but I'm not looking for a friend. What's he going to do as president?" Stevens would have liked to stress both themes but said that after the bruising primaries, the Romney campaign had only $4.2 million in the bank on May 1, not enough to repel the Obama onslaught. He argued persuasively that Obama had not taken enough grief for opting out of public financing of his fall campaigns in both 2008 and 2012, breaking a limitation on money in politics that had been observed through the previous eight presidential elections. "When public financing was passed [in 1974], it was said that without it, no incumbent president would ever be beaten," Stevens concluded. "There was a lot of truth to that."

AFTER THE ELECTION Jim Messina had one favor to ask the president, which was easily granted. In mid-November he walked into the Oval Office, where Obama presented him with a signed and framed cover of the *New York Times Magazine* with Nate Silver's "Is Obama Toast?" story.

The president was feeling liberated and free to express himself a little more now. About a month after the election, the Obamas hosted a small party for close friends and a few people from the administration and the campaign. The president was standing in a small group and said he was the only president since Roosevelt to have won twice with more than 51 percent of the vote. It was true that Nixon, Reagan, and Clinton all had three-way races that kept them under 51 percent. Eisenhower was in fact the last such president, but that was more than a half-century ago, so the boast was still impressive enough.

One of his African American friends, switching to street vernacular, said, "Well, I guess that makes it perfectly clear: youse a bad motherfucker."

"That's my point," the president replied, without missing a beat.

ON DECEMBER 2 the Obamas greeted Stephen Colbert and his wife, Evie, as they made their way through the receiving line after a reception for the winners of Kennedy Center Honors. (Colbert had toasted David Letterman, one of the winners.) "Congratulations, Mr. President,"

Colbert said, referring to the election. "I'm sure it was due in part to the efforts of your super PAC," Obama responded, showing familiarity with the comedian's yearlong efforts to lampoon big money in politics. Colbert joked that they couldn't talk about it: "That would be coordination—a federal offense." "Fair enough," the president replied. "So it must have been the offer you made Donald Trump." The comedian was surprised the president was so familiar with the joke, which was causing some embarrassment in Colbert's own family. The first lady chimed in that they had watched that Colbert bit "over and over."

———

AS HE PROCESSED his victory, the president's emotions sometimes caught him by surprise, most famously on a visit to his Chicago campaign headquarters on the day after the election. After the cheers, he began his remarks casually, chewing Nicorette gum and discussing his arrival in Chicago in the 1980s, determined to make a difference when "Ronald Reagan was president and incredibly popular." Within a couple of minutes the enormity of what had happened in the years since seemed to wash over him, and with it an appreciation of how much better as organizers "you guys" were than he had ever been. This was his greatest hope made real: inspiring people to accomplish something larger than themselves. It was the organizer in him, the truest part of him, laid before the world.

"I'm just looking around the room and I'm thinking, wherever you guys end up . . . you're just going to do great things," he said, tears now visible. "And that's why, even before last night's results, I felt that the work that I had done in running for office had come full circle, because what you guys have done means that the work that I'm doing is approved. I'm really proud of that. I'm really proud of all of you."

Then the president of the United States wiped away his tears and waded onto the Floor for an hour of hugs and funny pictures and memories of what they had done together.

Afterword

After the shock of the 2012 election wore off, many prominent Republicans acknowledged that they had become "the stupid party," as Bobby Jindal, the Republican governor of Louisiana, put it. Senators took positions in support of comprehensive immigration reform that would have led them to be ostracized from the GOP a year earlier. Governors who had supported repeal of Obamacare changed their minds and accepted it for their states. A long list of prominent conservatives signed a letter supporting same-sex marriage. But on taxes and spending, the only issues that united the party, conservatives dug in.

At the end of the year, the president and Congress began negotiating to avoid the so-called fiscal cliff, an expression coined in early 2012 by Federal Reserve Chairman Ben Bernanke, a man not otherwise known for memorable phrases. The result was a return to what the White House felt had become a Washington version of *Groundhog Day*, the Bill Murray movie in which every frustrating day is like the day before.

But Obama's end-of-the-year talks with John Boehner went badly. In their six one-on-one meetings in the president's first term (a small fraction of the times President Reagan and House Speaker Tip O'Neill got together in the 1980s), the two men talked past each other. Boehner, who feared not being reelected speaker in January, claimed that 2012 was a "status quo election," resulting in a Democratic presidency and Senate and a Republican House, just like before. Obama replied at a meeting on December 4, "Let me get this straight. I won the election and you want Mitt Romney's tax cuts? Let's get serious." After their next one-on-one meeting, on December 13, Boehner complained to reporters that Obama talked "nearly the entire time," lecturing him for more than thirty minutes on his mandate and what the Republican caucus might swallow. Boehner much preferred negotiating with Nancy Pelosi. "I'm not trying to make her a Republican," Boehner said, "and she's not trying to make me a Democrat."

The Republicans acted as if accepting the expiration of the Bush tax cuts for the wealthy constituted a major concession. When the president repeated his long-standing proposal for a "balanced approach" that would include $1.6 trillion in new tax revenues over ten years as well as spending cuts and entitlement reform, Mitch McConnell dismissed it as "laughable." In late December, Boehner once again walked away from the negotiations. The speaker's "Plan B"—letting taxes rise for those earning more than $1 million but offering no other suggestions for increasing revenue—failed with his own caucus.

Obama and Boehner were annoyed with each other; their staffs even quarreled over the speaker's disrespecting the president by not accepting his invitation for a screening of the movie *Lincoln*, which depicts Abraham Lincoln and a resistant House of Representatives coming together to enact the Thirteenth Amendment. (Boehner claimed the invitation came too late.) Obama decided to let Joe Biden and Mitch McConnell hammer out the deal, as they had at the time of the debt-ceiling crisis in 2011. Just before January 1, they settled on extending the Bush tax cuts for everyone except individuals making more than $400,000 a year, resolving the estate tax and other high-end tax breaks, ending the payroll tax holiday, and kicking the $1.2 trillion in "sequestration" budget cuts down the road. Boehner's caucus balked; he needed Pelosi's Democrats to get the compromise through the House and avoid the cliff.

In retrospect, it was a mistake for Obama to give up the leverage offered by the January 1 expiration of the Bush tax cuts. Doing so left him with no bargaining power to prevent what he called "the idiotic" sequestration cuts that began in March, when everything from critical scientific research to White House tours faced indiscriminate cuts. Republicans trying to eliminate the $600 billion in crude cuts scheduled over ten years for the Pentagon made the peculiar economic argument that building aircraft carriers helped create jobs and a strong economy, but building roads and bridges did not. Democrats were unhappy about the $600 billion in domestic cuts being phased in more quickly under the sequester. Many felt the Republicans were acting as if there had never been an election.

That was certainly Paul Ryan's approach. As a vice presidential candidate he had spoken constantly about how the 2012 election would "determine the path forward" for the country. But in March 2013 Ryan introduced a draconian budget that was almost identical to those he proposed in 2011 and 2012. (The only major difference was that the 2013 version balanced the budget in ten years instead of twenty-five, based on implausibly high growth figures that existed only in the dot-com bubble of the late 1990s.) Ryan's budget, which once again easily passed the House and fell seven votes short in the Democratic-controlled Senate, would have cut trillions from social programs (three times as much as the sequester in the short-term alone) and rewritten the social contract.

Had Romney been elected, some version of Ryan's budget likely would have become law.* Now, contrary to the disingenuous pleas of fundraising emails from Democrats, that radical vision had no chance. Nor did any of the rest of the conservative agenda. Obama still held the veto pen. The center would hold.

BY EARLY 2013 the reactionary forces that would have been emboldened by a Romney victory were divided and in retreat. RNC Chairman Reince Priebus commissioned a report that concluded the Republican Party's message was "weak" and the party was behind in digital innovation and field organizing. Priebus reported that focus groups "said that the party is 'scary,' 'narrow-minded,' and 'out of touch' and that we were a party of 'stuffy old men.'" But it would take more than rebranding the GOP the "Growth and Opportunity Party" and Roger Ailes starting a Spanish-language cable news network to bring Republicans back to power. "You can't just put a sombrero on the elephant," said Michael Steele, the former RNC chairman.

A split on foreign policy seemed inevitable. At the CPAC in March 2013, Senator Rand Paul of Kentucky won the straw poll for president after a neo-isolationist speech that pleased some liberal Democrats but led John McCain to call Rand and freshman senator Ted Cruz of Texas (who charged that Obama administration nominees were in cahoots with terrorists) "wacko birds." Cruz decided to wear McCain's moniker as a badge of honor.

Obama Derangement Syndrome remained at epidemic proportions, though now it was often just another way of monetizing political ideology. Sarah Palin, still raking in big money on the lecture circuit, delighted right-wing audiences with her riff about applying "background checks" to Obama, not gun owners. Palin routinely attacked Obama's use of a teleprompter in a speech she read from a teleprompter. Tens of thousands of southerners, who apparently hated the president more than they loved the United States, signed petitions calling for secession. In the popular History Channel series *The Bible*, the actor playing Satan was made up to look almost exactly like Obama, a decision

---

* Under the "Byrd Rule," named for the late Senator Robert C. Byrd, budget and tax bills need only fifty-one votes in the Senate, which was how Obamacare was enacted in 2010.

that the publicity-savvy executive producer, Mark Burnett, claimed was
unintentional.

Capitol Hill remained a zoo of exotic species. Representative Paul
Broun of Georgia said that "the only constitution that Barack Obama
upholds is the Soviet constitution," while Representative James Lank-
ford of Oklahoma blamed gun violence on "welfare moms." Senate Republicans ignored the pleading of a wheelchair-bound Bob Dole, the
former Republican majority leader, and refused to ratify a nonbinding
UN treaty that offered people around the world with disabilities some
of the same respect they receive in the United States.

Obama decided he would no longer let his frustrations with Congress prevent him from talking to more people outside his orbit. In January he said he would have more time for schmoozing: "The nice thing
is that now that my girls are getting older, they don't want to spend that
much time with me anyway. So I'll probably be calling around, looking for somebody to play cards with or something, because I'm getting
kind of lonely in this big house." After the Inauguration he launched a
charm offensive, wining and dining senators he had neglected in the
past. The president and first lady finally hosted Bill and Hillary Clinton
for dinner in the family residence and it went well. Obama made sure
the world knew how grateful he was for Hillary's service.

Valerie Jarrett began what she called a "do-over" with business. The
Chamber of Commerce, once a sworn enemy of the president, now
joined with the White House to push for immigration reform. Even Stephen Schwarzman, who had compared Obama's position on carried
interest to Hitler invading Poland, went on a conference call with the
president, though it would be a while before Obama knew whether
schmoozing with his enemies was worth his time.

Jarrett said that after the election the president was even more confident than he had been in the past, which was saying something considering his level of confidence all along: "Having juggled a thousand
balls and made life-and-death decisions, he felt tested." During the first
two years he focused so much on the inside game that "he lost that
connection to the American people." In the second term he would
leave Washington regularly and work on his outside game.

———

WHEN NEWS REACHED the president on the morning of December 14
of a mass shooting at the Sandy Hook Elementary School in Newtown,
Connecticut, it shook him to the core. The killing of twenty children
and six adults took the event to a level of devastation unmatched by the
other gun violence that occurred on his watch. He wasn't proud of the

fact that after the shooting at a movie theater in Aurora, Colorado, which took place in the middle of the campaign, he had shied away from any talk of guns. This time would be different. By noon he was already telling Governor Dan Malloy of Connecticut that this was the worst day of his presidency and that much would change in the aftermath.

On Sunday, two days after the shootings, the president followed the governor through five rooms in the local high school where the families of the surviving children had gathered. In each room, he stopped to hear survivors' memories of the children and teachers who died and shared the raw grief of the moment, crying and praying with the parents and other family members. After an hour of personal visits, he spoke at length about the loss. As in Tucson, he was an eloquent mourner in chief, but this time he made it clear that he would be launching a new effort to stem gun violence. "Can we honestly say that we're doing enough to keep our children—all of them—safe from harm?" the president asked, before concluding that the answer was no.

OBAMA'S SECOND INAUGURAL fell on Martin Luther King Day, lending symmetry and resonance to the festivities.* His Inaugural Address was crisp and inspiring, though it characteristically contained no memorable lines that would fit easily onto memorabilia. While the speech would likely be remembered for the first mention of gay rights in an Inaugural Address, it was mostly an idealistic defense of the twentieth-century consensus on the role of government. Widely covered as an ode to liberalism, its celebration of Social Security, Medicare, infrastructure, science, education, and the nation's openness to immigrants was in fact a testament to the postwar bipartisan consensus ratified in the election. Obama wasn't turning left but driving right down the median strip of U.S. politics, as Newt Gingrich understood when he called it "a great speech about fundamental American values." The president wrapped those values in progressive rhetoric to be true to himself and his liberal ideas and, more pragmatically, to give himself cover with the left for the painful budget and entitlement compromises to come. On the MLK holiday he was, as usual, playing a longer game, pledging to bend the arc of King's moral universe toward justice, a little at a time.

---

* January 20, the official beginning of his new term, fell on a Sunday, a day not allowed for Inaugural ceremonies. So the president took the formal oath that day in private and repeated the swearing-in on Monday before the world. Because he and Chief Justice Roberts had stumbled over the oath in the 2009 Inauguration and repeated it the next day in private, Obama in 2013 became the only president other than Franklin Roosevelt to be sworn-in four times.

On the morning of the Inauguration no one in Obama's circle was sure the Mall would be filled with people, as it had been in 2009. It was. As he exited the platform, a wistful president turned around for several seconds to view the throng. "I'm going to look one more time. I'll never see this again," he said, in a moment caught on television. Watching the tape, Jarrett said that in twenty-two years she had never seen that expression on his face. The combination of exhilaration and nostalgia, the sense that all of those people had once more come there for him, left her in tears.

At the staff inaugural ball, the president paid tribute again to his young staffers and volunteers. Referring to himself in the third person as "kind of old and gray-haired," he credited his team with "carrying him across the finish line" for larger reasons: "Because this is not about him; this is about us. This is about America. This is about what we believe. This is about what our values are. This is what our ideals are all about. We are going to go out there and change America."

Scott Prouty, the man who taped Romney's "47 percent" speech, had come to the Inauguration, thrilled to be there on his first trip to Washington. Leo Gerard, president of the Steelworkers Union, knew his identity by then and found him and his girlfriend tickets to the swearing-in and one of the Inaugural Balls, where they were introduced—without any last names—to Teddy Goff and his family, who almost fell over when they heard who he was. "You changed history," Goff's mother gushed. Two months later Gerard arranged for Prouty, who needed a job, to get work investigating international labor abuses. But to do so, he would need to surface publicly, which he did on Ed Schultz's show on MSNBC. The reaction from the right was less than Prouty feared.

The squabbling among black leaders continued even at the Inauguration. When the leaders of half a dozen civil rights organizations were granted honored seats on the inaugural platform, Jesse Jackson complained that they had grown too close to Obama and needed to be fighting from the outside. Al Sharpton, who still talked regularly to Jackson despite their differences, reminded him that Jackson's daughter, Santita, had sung at Bill Clinton's Second Inaugural. When Jackson spoke at Hugo Chávez's funeral, Sharpton upbraided him for it: "Do you think Dr. King would have spoken at Ho Chi Minh's funeral? Of course not."

In early March, Sharpton and seven other African American leaders met with the president in the Roosevelt Room. The issue of whether Obama was pursuing a pro-black agenda came up again. Sharpton told the story of a friend who converted to Islam, then ate a ham sandwich and claimed it wasn't pork. Sharpton told the president, "I said to my friend that day, 'Just because it's not called pork doesn't mean it isn't.' And just because your agenda isn't called pro-black doesn't mean it isn't." Obama was happy to embrace the pork metaphor.

FOX NEWS CHANNEL'S ratings were down sharply after the election. Conservative media had stormed the liberal barricades over the previous twenty years and become an insular establishment of their own. The belittling of the president continued. One day in November a missive came down from Ailes saying that when Obama was speaking, producers should feel free to use a "big/little," TV-speak for a smaller window on the bottom of the screen that shows something different from the main image. Under previous presidents, big/littles were barred as disrespectful of the office. According to one producer, "This was Roger saying of Obama, 'I'm just going to minimize this man as much as I can.'"

Ailes recognized that the predictions of a Romney victory made Fox look bad. The week after the election he decreed that Karl Rove and Dick Morris no longer be booked on Fox without special approval. Rove's Fox contract was eventually renewed, but Morris's wasn't. "I was wrong at the top of my lungs," Morris later explained. Rove went on to found a new organization, the Conservative Victory Group, devoted to fighting Obama's agenda and to helping mainstream Republicans who found themselves "primaried" by Tea Party extremists.

Grover Norquist was still putting antitax starch in the shirts of Republican House members. But he was also doing all he could to get the GOP on the side of comprehensive immigration reform. He was comforted by his certainty that the GOP had a lock on the House at least through 2022, when the next census would bring redistricting.

Alan Simpson and Erskine Bowles seemed to have missed that there was an election. Ceding ground to conservative critics, they issued a new version of their plan in February that eliminated much of the tax revenue in their original proposal in favor of deeper cuts in social welfare programs. "Kicking the can down the road is bad," said retiring congressman Barney Frank, summarizing the liberal view of the budget and the new Simpson-Bowles proposal. "But kicking the ass of the poor is even worse."

To protect programs for the poor, the president would need to cut elsewhere. That meant not just reductions in Pentagon spending but tackling entitlements. In April, Obama finally released a budget. In exchange for tax increases on the wealthy and his other spending priorities, it offered to change the way the Consumer Price Index calcu-lated inflation, which would result in lower cost-of-living increases for wealthier seniors under Social Security. Contrary to the claims of some liberals, Obama was not tampering with the social contract (the origi-nal Social Security contained no COLAs at all), merely acknowledging that social insurance programs were unsustainable if they remained un-amended amid the retirement of the baby boomers. On three big issues of 2013—entitlements, guns, and immigration—Obama would have to find the right balance between rallying public support and working the Washington levers of power.

THE BATTLE OVER voting rights would continue. While fourteen state laws restricting voting were weakened or delayed by court decisions, vetoes, referenda, and Department of Justice probes, dozens more re-mained on the books, a testament to the Republican Party's efforts to change the playing field. Many judges hadn't fully overturned these bills, merely ruled that they didn't apply in the 2012 election. This set up the potential for significant losses at the polls for Democrats if they didn't organize better for the 2014 midterm elections than they had in 2010.

But some of their adversaries were in weaker positions. Governor Rick Scott of Florida, recognizing the power of the backlash against voter suppression, opposed reviving the legislation he once champi-oned. In Colorado, Secretary of State Scott Gessler was on the defen-sive. The Colorado state ethics commission and the Denver district attorney both launched probes into Gessler's decision to bill taxpayers for his trips to Republican Party conferences, as well as his depositing the year-end balance from his office's discretionary account into his own pocket. Gessler's legal troubles did nothing to dissuade him from joining with Attorney General Kris Kobach of Kansas and Hans von Spakovsky of the Heritage Foundation to denounce the plan by the Brennan Center for Justice to modernize polling places and computer-ize voter registration systems so that people don't lose the right to vote when they move. They falsely claimed the modernization plan consti-tuted "mandatory voter registration."

OBAMA ADMINISTRATION OFFICIALS generally stayed in their jobs longer than their predecessors had, but the end of the first term brought big personnel changes. Hillary Clinton, exhausted after hundreds of thousands of miles of travel, resigned as secretary of state in favor of

John Kerry. The inside choice for secretary of state had been the U.S. ambassador to the United Nations, Susan Rice, but she withdrew from consideration after intense opposition led by Senators John McCain and Lindsey Graham, who got it into their heads that Rice should have somehow known better than to use the CIA's wrong assessment of who was behind the Benghazi attacks. Treasury Secretary Tim Geithner was replaced by White House Chief of Staff Jack Lew, who in turn was succeeded by Denis McDonough, a former deputy director of the National Security Council and another example of the president's preference for comfortable choices. David Plouffe gave way as senior political adviser to Dan Pfeiffer, who had been the communications director from the start. This led to head-scratching because Obama had said repeatedly that communications failures were at the top of his list of shortcomings in his first term. He apparently didn't blame Pfeiffer.

Jon Favreau, Obama's chief speechwriter, quit to try his hand at political consulting and writing TV scripts. Before he left, he looked back at old speeches and concluded that Obama's rhetoric had been amazingly consistent throughout—same voice, same policy ideas. And he thought there was already plenty that he and the president wrote that could be chipped into marble someday, when history decided which lines or even paragraphs had stood the test of time. By then, he figured, no one would be complaining about a lack of sound bites.

Few campaign veterans went back into the White House. David Axelrod founded the University of Chicago's Institute of Politics, and Jim Messina became chair of the successor to Obama for America, which was renamed Organizing for Action. The new OFA, with more than 20 million email addresses in its database, would try to make the 2012 Chicago machine a permanent force in American politics, applying money, analytics, door-knocking, and the rest of the magic formula to advancing the president's agenda. At first the new OFA planned to accept dark money from undisclosed donors, an idea that stank of the old politics and was quickly abandoned. Jeremy Bird, Mitch Stewart, Teddy Goff, and many of Dan Wagner's Cave dwellers took their skills into the private sector, though they still worked on long-term political projects, like turning Texas blue.

Even if future campaigns didn't have eighteen months to prepare, as Chicago did, the Obama team's innovative tools set a new standard. Wagner envisioned a "culture of data" extending to the lowest volunteer. His favorite moment of the whole campaign came at an OFA conference after the election, when a volunteer approached him and said, "I like your persuasion models, but I think the messaging was too chunky." He figured that if a volunteer from Ohio was thinking like an analyst, the use of data in politics would soon extend all the way down to the local level.

But campaigns trying to reverse-engineer the Obama machine would quickly learn that it wasn't technology that made the difference in 2012. "If Dan [Wagner] gave us support scores and we didn't have hundreds of thousands of volunteers, they would have meant nothing," Bird said after the election. The same was true for TV ads. While aerial bombard-ment on television can work for a while, most wars eventually require boots on the ground. Obama's weaponry was superior, but only be-cause his soldiers knew how to use it.

———

FROM THE FIRST news of the Newtown killings, the president had re-solved to devote significant political capital to pushing gun control, though he was careful not to call it that or otherwise offend law-abiding gun owners.* His aim was to highlight his commitment to doing some-thing about gun violence while keeping expectations reasonable. He asked Biden to supervise the process of preparing legislation. When it was complete, he used his State of the Union Address for dramatic effect.

Obama described the shooting death, only a mile from his home in Chicago, of Hadiya Pendleton, who just three weeks earlier had per-formed as a drum majorette in his inaugural parade. The president pointed to Hadiya's parents in the gallery and said, "They deserve a vote." Then, as he acknowledged former congresswoman Gabrielle Gif-fords, herself a survivor of the Tucson shooting, and the families of other shooting victims, "They deserve a vote" became a powerful re-frain, which he recited seven more times to rising applause and tears.

It was impossible to predict how Obama's agenda would fare; fights over the debt ceiling and a hundred other issues lay down the road. The president would inevitably be subjected to the external events that have had a way of upending the best-laid plans of second-term presidents. He would likely join his two-term predecessors in stressing foreign affairs, which have historically allowed presidents more auton-omy from Congress. Even so, he would almost certainly be judged dur-ing and after leaving office on whether the American economy finally shook off its torpor and began to thrive again. If the economy revived more quickly, Democrats would likely do better than expected in the 2014 midterms, which would allow the president to make more prog-

---

* When skeptics doubted his claim that he enjoyed shooting skeet at Camp David, the White House released a photograph of him firing a gun.

ress on his agenda. If economic growth stalled, he would be seen as more of a lame duck.

Should Hillary Clinton become the Democratic nominee in 2016, her success in the election would be tied in part to the strength of the Obama record that she would be forced to defend. If she won, it would enhance the chances of Obama's policies being validated, much as Harry Truman built on the New Deal and the Bushes extended the conservative trajectory begun by Ronald Reagan. In that sense, the often bitter rivals from the 2008 Democratic primaries—brought closer when Clinton became secretary of state—would find themselves not just dependent on one another but bound together by history.

In the meantime, the conservative agenda of dramatically shrinking government that seemed achievable in 2011 and 2012 was now little more than a fantasy. Whatever changes Obama agreed to in the programs originated by FDR and LBJ would be at the margins. A set of values that had been part of the American consensus since at least the New Deal would remain in place. The country's defense of that social contract had been tested and it held, and the consequences of the voters' decision in 2012 would play out for years. For all the struggles to come, nothing radical would occur in government until 2017 at the earliest, and, given the demographic changes at hand, probably not even then. The United States would remain a highly partisan and often gridlocked nation, but a centrist one.

The personal dimension was no less significant. Whatever his mistakes in his second term, Obama was no longer in danger of being seen as a historical fluke. Voters didn't rehire him just because they felt good about voting for a black president. As the face of a changing country, he had integrated not just the presidency but the political future. Barack Obama was in the American grain now, a symbol for all time of democracy at work.

Acknowledgments

Books are both solo enterprises and collective projects, and I got a lot of help on this one. As with *The Promise*, I interviewed more than two hundred people, this time in 2011 and 2012. Once again many of the interviews, especially those below the top, were conducted on background. Unfortunately this is the only way to learn certain things nowadays. It also means that I cannot properly thank all of the people who helped me. So while some readers might be tempted to play a guessing game on who told me what, it would be a mistake to assume any sourcing based on those who are identified or quoted in the book or named below. To all of those in government and politics who lent a hand, but whom I cannot acknowledge, my sincerest thanks.

For sourcing, I've mostly used the endnotes to credit people who broke stories or otherwise came up with something new. Quotations not cited in an endnote generally come from my reporting or from easily accessible public statements.

Despite plenty of frustrations along the way, I received the access I needed. Special thanks at the White House to Pete Rouse, Valerie Jarrett, David Plouffe, Dan Pfeiffer, Jon Favreau, and many of those below them whom I don't identify. I couldn't have written the book without a lot of help from "Chicago" and "Boston." David Axelrod and Stuart Stevens, chief strategists for the Obama and Romney campaigns, respectively, were exceptionally cooperative over a two-year period. I'd also like to single out Scott Prouty, who spent many hours helping me detail his motivation for famously videotaping Mitt Romney's comments at a Boca Raton fundraiser.

I began reporting for this book in early 2011 and wrote most of it in late 2012 and early 2013. I received research help from Anna Pelluchia and Rob Grabow at the beginning, transcription help from Jonathan Aronoff in the middle, and photo and editorial help from Amanda Hameline at the end. All were assets in a difficult process.

At Simon & Schuster, thanks to Jonathan Karp, Jonathan Cox, Julia

Prosser, Lisa Healy, Judith Hoover, Martin P. Karlow, Susan Gamer, Jackie Seow, Carol Shapiro, and Elisa Rivlin, among others. They offered uniformly first-rate suggestions and helped me turn this around under an extremely tight deadline. This is my third book in seven years with S&S's legendary Alice Mayhew, who once again kept me on track with her peerless editorial judgment.

Cliff Sloan, my college roommate and lawyer, helped birth this project and saved me from more than one mishap. I'm also indebted to Dan Klaidman, Ed Kosner, and Jodi Kantor for reading portions of the manuscript. Keith Ulrich went above and beyond what friendship required in carefully reading the manuscript. Once again, Joan and Ev Shorey provided hospitality nonpareil in Washington, D.C.

I want to thank all of my colleagues at *Bloomberg View*, MSNBC, *Alpha House*, and the nonprofit boards on which I serve for putting up with the demands of book writing.

Among those outside of the Obama administration and the 2012 campaign who offered time, insight, stories, advice, friendship, or otherwise helped out were, in no particular order, Jerry Groopman, Michael Waldman, Austan Goolsbee, Bob Shapiro, Alan Brinkley, Charlie Peters, Phil Griffin, David Shipley, Grover Norquist, David Corn, Tom Coburn, Craig Shirley, David McKean, Chris Ruddy, Ed Rendell, Hugh Hewitt, Doug Band, Marty Nesbitt, Christi Parsons, Don Katz, Ed Rollins, Yitzchok Itkin, E. J. Dionne, Elizabeth Warren, Evan Thomas, Evie Colbert, Stephen Colbert, Bill Broyles, Foster Friess, Martin Bashir, Frank Luntz, Michael Bennet, Gene Robinson, Shannah Goldner, Bill Daley, Dan Gross, Al Franken, Gregg Cockrell, George Haywood, Jim Fallows, Byron Dorgan, Eric Lesser, Al Sharpton, Alex Gage, Rahm Emanuel, Mark Whitaker, Calvin Trillin, Cornel West, Justin Cooper, David Lane, Cary Chevat, Michael Hastings, Mark McKenna, Michael Burgess, Alex Castellanos, Jared Bernstein, Luis Guitierrez, Doug Band, Michael Kinsley, Rob Warden, Tom Burrell, Steve Clemons, Hunter Owens, Jeff Toobin, Andy Borowitz, Nancy Pelosi, Lamar Alexander, Katie Johnson, the late Harry McPherson, Rick Hertzberg, Howard Fineman, Jane Hartley, Ralph Schlosstein, Ed Shultz, Chris Matthews, Pete Dominick, Jacob Weisberg, Michael Scherer, Roger Altman, Jurate Kazickas, Jessica Yellin, Arne Duncan, Ray LaHood, Jake Tapper, Jim Manley, Steve Engelberg, John Harwood, Will Eger, Caroline Kennedy, Judy McGee, Ken Baer, Ken Duberstein, Sal Russo, Amy Kremer, John Rogers, Josh Marshall, Lynn Sweet, Maria Teresa Kumar, Fernand Amandi, Mark Landler, Mark Leibovich, Tom Hamburger, Mickey Kaus, Mike Allen, Glenn Thrush, Jonathan Martin, Michael Eric Dyson, Garry Trudeau, Elliot Webb, Rachel Shorey, Jamie Smith, Ken Duberstein, Paul Begala, Paul Glastris,

Peter Orszag, Max Berley, James Gibney, Newt Minow, Rita Hauser, Simon Rosenberg, Stanley Tate, Robert Wolf, Rob Stein, Mark McKinnon, Nina Easton, Walter Isaacson, Todd Harris, and Wendy Weiser.

In my family, special thanks to my nephew, Graham Lazar, and my siblings, Jennifer Alter Warden, Jamie Alter Lynton, and Harrison Alter. My father, Jim Alter, now ninety-one, cheered me on from Chicago. He and my late mother, Joanne Alter, gave me my love of politics.

Closer to Montclair, I'm grateful to my son, Tommy, for help chronicling Obama's enemies, and to my daughter Charlotte for the title and some editing suggestions. My daughter Molly provided much-needed comic relief before decamping for college, and my lovely and wise wife, Emily Lazar, kept me sane during an insane seven-days-a-week process. This one is for all of them.

Notes

AUTHOR'S NOTE

ix "There's class warfare, all right: Warren Buffett quoted in *New York Times*, November 26, 2006.

xiii "At the heart of the American idea: E. J. Dionne, *Our Divided Political Heart: The Battle for the American Idea in an Age of Discontent* (Bloomsbury: New York, 2013), 6.

1. THE SHELLACKING

3 "When you say the word 'compromise': *60 Minutes*, CBS News, December 12, 2010.

4 Even in heavily blue New York City: Gail Sheehy, *Daily Beast,* September 23, 2010.

5 "best-case scenario": Charlie Cook, *National Journal*, November 17, 2011.

6 He rarely went to the Oval Office: John Harris, *The Survivor: Bill Clinton in the White House* (New York: Random House, 2005), 155.

7 "We were so busy and so focused: *60 Minutes*, CBS News, November 7, 2010.

7 "The single most important thing: interview with Mitch McConnell, Major Garrett, *National Journal,* October 29, 2010.

9 social dysfunction in white working-class areas: Don Peck, *The Atlantic Magazine,* March 2010.

9 "The hardest thing to do: James Carville quoted in Sam Stein, *The Huffington Post*, May 31, 2010.

15 Gibbs had also run afoul of Jarrett: see Jodi Kantor, *The Obamas* (New York: Back Bay Books, 2012).

2. TEA PARTY TEMPEST

20 inadvertently called them "tea-baggers": Jonathan Alter, *The Promise: President Obama, Year One* (New York: Simon & Schuster, 2010), 129.

20 Only about a quarter of the small Tea Party websites: see William Eger, "Hanging Together: Overcoming Dissent in the Tea Party Movement," senior thesis, Harvard University, 2012.

21 Between 600,000 and 1.2 million people: TalkingPointsMemo.com, December 28, 2011.

21 Tea Party made up 20 percent of the American population: see Pew Forum on Religion and Public Life.

22 "the Incredible HOLC": Alan Blinder, *New York Times,* February 4, 2008.

3. OBAMA DERANGEMENT SYNDROME

31 Nearly 25 percent of Republicans: *Newsweek* poll. See Jonathan Alter, "The Illustrated Man," *Newsweek,* September 6, 2010; CNN poll, Politico, August 14, 2010.

31 16 percent of the people she talked to: Sabrina Tavernise and Jeff Zeleny, *New York Times*, April 18, 2012.

32 "the paranoid style: Richard Hofstadter, *The Paranoid Style in American Politics and Other Essays* (Cambridge: Harvard University Press, 1963)

33 "All of these articles: Mark Penn quoted in Joshua Green, *Atlantic,* May 30, 2012.

36 Weissberg wrote that "countless conservatives despised: Robert Weissberg, "A Stranger in Our Midst," *American Thinker,* April 29, 2010.

38 "those days when we were in different classes: Sarah Palin on *Hannity*, Fox News Channel, March 8, 2012.

39 "the collapse of conservatism: Brian Stelter and Bill Carter, *New York Times*, March 29, 2009.

43 "We're Not Perfect. But They're Nuts": Jason Zengerle, interview with Barney Frank, *New York,* April 15, 2012.

4. STRANGLED IN THE BATHTUB

44 "Seeing Purple": Jonathan Alter, "Barack Obama: Seeing Purple," *Newsweek,* December 27, 2004.

46 The combined effect of the Bush and Clinton budget deals: Eduardo Porter, *New York Times*, March 28, 2012; Peter Diamond and Emmanuel Saez, *Wall Street Journal*, April 24, 2012.

46 Shortly before the 2012 election: Jonathan Weisman, *New York Times,* November 1, 2012.

47 "We are using Communist military: Jonas Savimbi (with Grover Norquist), *The Policy Review*, January 1986.

48 By this time Norquist had emerged as a right-wing antihero: see Nina Easton, *Gang of Five: Five Leaders at the Center of the Conservative Ascendency* (New York: Touchstone, 2002).

48 "We are trying to change the tones: Grover Norquist quoted in John Aloysius Farrell, *Boston Globe*, May 26, 2003.

48 "*after* the Cold War was over: Matthew Continetti, *The K Street Gang: The Rise and Fall of the Republican Machine* (New York: Doubleday, 2006).

50 But another adviser, Roger Ailes: Richard Darman, *Who's in Control? Polar Politics and the Sensible Center* (New York: Simon & Schuster, 1996), 193.

51 "The only way we'll succeed: Robert Draper, *Do Not Ask What Good We Do* (New York: Free Press, 2012), xviii.

56 "Who the hell is Grover Norquist, anyway?": Mark K. Updegrove, *Parade,* July 15, 2012.

5. FOX NATION

62 "I hired Sarah Palin: Roger Ailes to Associated Press, October 5, 2011.

64 Ailes confirmed the story to Woodward: Bob Woodward, *Washington Post*, December 4, 2012.

64 McFarland was right: Alter, *The Promise,* 365.

65 build a White House–run TV network: John Cook, *Business Insider*, June 30, 2011.

65 when he demanded that security: Tim Dickinson, *Rolling Stone,* May 25, 2011.

69 "Take that bone out of your nose: see http://www.esquire.com/blogs/politics/rush -limbaugh-racist-quotes-070710; http://newsone.com/16051/top-10-racist-limbaugh-quotes/.

6. THE VOTER-SUPPRESSION PROJECT

73 "I don't want everyone to vote: see Josh Glasstetter, RightWingWatch.org, November 5, 2012.

73 ALEC sponsored forums: See ALECEXPOSED.org.

74 The improperly purged names: David Margolick, Evangelina Peretz, and Michael Shnayerson, *Vanity Fair*, October 2004.

75 the Bush Justice Department acknowledged in 2007: Eric Lipton and Ian Urbina, *New York Times,* April 12, 2007.

75 Because Franken's race against Norm Coleman: Steven Rosenfeld, AlterNet.com, August 8, 2012.

77 GOP state legislators introduced 140 bills: see Brennan Center for Justice.
78 three other former GOP officials: Dara Kam and John Lantigua, *Palm Beach Post,* November 25, 2012; Lucy Morgan, *Tampa Bay Times,* July 26, 2012.
79 The racial disparities: *Obama for America v Husted,* 2012.
80 "Voting as a liberal, that's what kids do": Peter Wallsten, *Washington Post,* March 8, 2011.
81 "driving and seeing the police following [them]": Brentin Mock, ColorLines.com, August 23, 2012.

7. THE NEW CHICAGO MACHINE
84 new statistics: For a statistical look at OFA's technology efforts, see Engage Research, *Inside the Cave,* 2012.
88 let OFA wither: For an independent take on OFA after 2008, see Ari Melber, "Year One of Organizing for America," Techpresident Special Report, January 14, 2010.

8. THE CAVE
99 In 2012 Chicago sought to extend the modeling: see Sasha Issenberg, *The Victory Lab: The Secret Science of Winning Campaigns* (New York: Crown, 2012); Sasha Issenberg, "A More Perfect Union," *Technology Review,* December 19, 2012.
100 politics as done by Martians: Peggy Noonan, *Wall Street Journal,* July 30, 2011.

9. NOT SO GREAT COMMUNICATOR?
111 Obama was also much taken with an article: Ezra Klein, *New Yorker,* March 19, 2012.
111 "It's as if Superman stepped out of a phone booth: Associated Press, January 20, 2009.
116 "In this country, there's no reason why: *The O'Reilly Factor,* Fox News, February 6, 2011.
120 "the American people were hungry for the truth: Douglas Brinkley, *Cronkite* (New York: HarperCollins, 2012), 664.
120 "The mistake of my first couple of years: Interview with Charlie Rose, CBS News, July 13, 2012.

10. MISSING THE SCHMOOZE GENE
123 "When I'm over here at the congressional picnic: White House News Conference, January 14, 2013
125 During a scene in *By the People*: see *By the People: The Election of Barack Obama,* HBO Documentary Films, 2009.
129 "a bit of a wall—the veil: Genevieve Cook quoted in David Maraniss, *Barack Obama: The Story* (New York: Simon & Schuster, 2012), 481.
130 to read classic American novels together: Jodi Kantor, *New York Times,* January 21, 2013.

11. THE KEEPER OF THE ESSENCE
138 "We got a lot of Barack Obama's Wall Street money: see Institute of Politics, University of Chicago, conversation with Spencer Zwick and Julianna Smoot, March 5, 2013.
143 Then came an interview Daley gave: Bill Daley interview with Roger Simon, Politico, October 28, 2011.

12. "WE GOT HIM!"
Much of this chapter is based on background interviews with four officials who were in the room with the president for key meetings related to the bin Laden raid.

145 This meant that use of the word *assassination*: see Daniel Klaidman, *Kill or Capture: The War on Terror and the Soul of the Obama Presidency* (New York: Houghton Mifflin Harcourt, 2012).
146 "Oh, absolutely: Obama interview with Jessica Yellin, "Obama Revealed: The Man, the President," CNN, September 3, 2012.
147 "about as active as any project: *60 Minutes,* CBS News, May 8, 2011.

149   Obama later told the author: Mark Bowden, *The Finish: The Killing of Osama bin Laden* (New York: Atlantic Monthly Press, 2012), 252.
150   "And you do a little prayin' ": *Rock Center with Brian Williams,* NBC News, May 2, 2012.
151   "That was a little bit of acting: Ibid.
152   "This was the longest forty minutes: Ibid.
155   bin Laden's being buried at sea: Brian Whitaker, *Guardian,* May 2, 2011.
155   "Shut the fuck up": David E. Sanger, *Confront and Conceal: Obama's Secret Wars and the Surprising Use of American Power* (New York: Crown, 2012), 107.
155   "give those SEALs a big hug: author interview with Virginia Bauer.
155   "most important single day of my presidency": *Rock Center with Brian Williams,* NBC News, May 2, 2012.
156   Karl Rove wrote in his *Wall Street Journal* column: Karl Rove, *Wall Street Journal,* May 2, 2012.
157   "I'm not a political guy: Interview with Admiral McRaven, *The Situation Room,* CNN, July 26, 2012.
157   expansion to so-called signature strikes: Scott Shane, *New York Times,* November 24, 2012; Bowden, *The Finish*; *The Daily Show with Jon Stewart,* Comedy Central, October 18, 2012.

13. OBAMA'S LOW POINT
165   "A tax increase now: *Wall Street Journal* editorial staff, *The Wall Street Journal,* July 9, 2011.
165   "I'm going to have to walk away: Bob Woodward, *Obama's Wars* (New York: Simon & Schuster, 2010), 182.
166   "Ooh, he was hot: Ibid., 299.
168   Goolsbee estimated that default: see Bipartisan Policy Center.
168   "It's reasonable," said Bruce Bartlett: Bruce Bartlett, *Financial Times,* May 6, 2011.
170   Obama denied that account to Bob Woodward: Woodward, *Obama's Wars,* 312.
172   "I felt like I died and went to black heaven: Chris Rock stand-up routine, The Comedy Store, Los Angeles, March 3, 2012.
174   "Is Obama Toast?": Nate Silver, *New York Times Magazine,* November 3, 2011.

14. THE CLOWN CAR
177   "People will look back at these Republican candidates: Joe Scarborough, *Morning Joe,* MSNBC, October 24, 2011.
178   Those people in the Republican primary: Pat Robertson, *700 Club,* Christian Broadcasting Network, October 24, 2011.
178   Federal Judge Richard Posner, a barometer: Nina Totenberg, *Morning Edition,* National Public Radio, July 5, 2012.
178   Columnist Charles Krauthammer referred to the field: *Daily Beast,* August 9, 2012.
178   The News Corp. founder was eager for: Rupert Murdoch to author, April 30, 2012.
185   "We could have beaten Perry: Matt Rhoades, Harvard Campaign Managers Conference, Institute of Politics, Harvard University, December 4, 2012.
186   He was a serial adulterer: Neil King Jr., *Wall Street Journal,* December 5, 2011.
188   "What the hell are you doing, Newt?": Rudy Giuliani, *Fox and Friends,* Fox News, January 12, 2012.

15. PLAYGROUND OF THE SUPERRICH
191   In a CNN poll: CNN/ORC International poll, November 26, 2012.
193   Cyrus McCormick sent 7,500 field agents: see Jack Beatty, *Age of Betrayal: The Triumph of Money in America, 1865–1900* (New York: Knopf, 2007).
193   "The secrecy seems hypocritical": Daniel Fisher, *Forbes,* December 24, 2012.
194   According to a surreptitious taping of his speech: Brad Friedman, *Mother Jones,* September 6, 2011.

195 Their family fortune grew from $50 billion to $62 billion: *Forbes,* September 20, 2012.

196 "Look, I'm basically a social liberal": Alicia Mundy, *Wall Street Journal,* December 5, 2012.

197 "If I'm fortunate enough to be invited to another: Maggie Haberman, Politico, September 23, 2012.

199 Through much of the twentieth century, class rhetoric: Beatty, *Age of Betrayal,* 164; *New York Times,* April 23, 1962.

200 His mother, Ann, wrote to a friend: Maraniss, *Barack Obama,* 488.

200 "like a spy beyond enemy lines": Barack Obama, *Dreams from My Father: A Story of Race and Inheritance* (New York: Random House, 1995), 200.

201 They spent more than $30 million a year: private report by Robert G. Wilmers, chairman, M&T Bank Corp.

203 In January of 2012, Priorities USA spent almost as much on salaries: Peter Nicholas and Carol E. Lee, *Wall Street Journal,* April 5, 2012.

205 "It's a war: Jonathan Alter, *Newsweek,* August 15, 2010.

205 "The metrosexual black Abe Lincoln: Jeff Zeleny and Jim Rutenberg, *New York Times,* May 17, 2012.

16. THE BOOK OF MITT

207 The most common indictment of Romney: see www.RomneyFlop.com.

208 "[My father] wanted to be president less than anyone: Michael Kranish, "The Story behind Mitt Romney's Loss in the Presidential Campaign to Barack Obama," *Boston Globe,* December 12, 2012. See also Michael Kranish and Scott Helman, *The Real Romney* (New York: HarperCollins, 2012).

208 Theodore White found him almost embarrassingly sincere: Theodore H. White, *The Making of the President 1968* (New York: Atheneum, 1969), 36.

210 "because his supporters are convinced that he's a liar": Michael Kinsley, *Bloomberg View,* October 6, 2011.

17. BOSTON MAD MEN

229 The *Wall Street Journal* editorialized that a "coasting" Romney campaign: *Wall Street Journal,* July 6, 2012.

229 "the campaign's monomaniacal belief: Bill Kristol, *Weekly Standard,* July 5, 2012.

18. A MESSAGE BUILT TO LAST?

234 "Stop Coddling the Super-Rich: Warren E. Buffett, *New York Times,* August 14, 2011.

238 When informed that Romney supported: Robert Draper, *New York Times Magazine,* July 5, 2012.

239 The *New York Times* described the rally: Mark Landler, *New York Times,* May 5, 2011.

242 "The First Gay President": Andrew Sullivan, *Newsweek,* May 21, 2012.

19. OBAMACARE'S CLOSE SHAVE

249 "The taxing power of the federal government, my dear: Jonathan Alter, *The Defining Moment: FDR's 100 Days and the Triumph of Hope* (New York: Simon & Schuster, 2006), 313.

253 "with specific knowledge: Jan Crawford, "Roberts Switched Vote to Uphold Health Care Law," *CBSnews.com,* July 1, 2012.

255 Romney needed to make Obamacare a big issue: editorial, *Wall Street Journal,* July 6, 2012.

20. THE MACHINE HUMS

256 He warned them that if "a couple billionaires": Lloyd Grove, *Daily Beast,* June 30, 2012.

256 By mid-2012 the Obama campaign had burned through: Nicholas Confessore and Jo Craven McGinty, *New York Times,* August 4, 2012.

262 "Do you remember any phrase or sentence: Peggy Noonan, *Wall Street Journal*, June 22, 2012.

21. DEMOGRAPHY AS DESTINY
271 "I think my dear brother Barack: Chris Hedges, truthdig.com, May 16, 2011.

22. IN THE SCRUM
288 Obama was acting "un-American": Charles Murray, "Ideas Blog," American Enterprise Institute, July 18, 2012.
291 A reporter for *Bloomberg Businessweek*: Sheelah Kolhatkar, "Exclusive: Inside Karl Rove's Billionaire Fundraiser," *Bloomberg Businessweek*, August 31, 2012.
292 sought explicit business favors from the government in a Romney administration: Alison Fitzgerald and Julie Bykowicz, *Bloomberg News*, August 29, 2012.
292 Harold Simmons, who would give nearly $27 million: see Opensecrets.com.
293 "You need to actually convince voters: Bill Kristol, *Fox News Sunday*, Fox News, September 2, 2012.
296 "Where Clinton entertains: Joseph Lelyveld, *New York Review of Books*, October 11, 2012.
300 "I guess I really actually feel: Darrel Rowland, *Columbus Dispatch*, August 19, 2012.

23. MAKERS VERSUS TAKERS
303 Then he repeated the number: Brian Beutler, TalkingPointsMemo.com, September 19, 2012.
309 He was especially interested when: see David Corn, *47 Percent: Uncovering the Romney Video That Rocked the 2012 Election* (New York: William Morrow, 2012).
313 "Lucky duckies": *The Wall Street Journal*, "The Non-Taxpayer Class," November 20, 2002.
313 Academic research showed that if the calculations included "submerged" government benefits: Suzanne Mettler and John Sides, *New York Times*, October 25, 2012.
316 "Between 60 and 70 percent of Americans: see Nick Baumann, *Mother Jones*, January 22, 2013.
317 "government closest to the people: Paul Ryan, Christian Broadcasting Network, April 10, 2012.
317 The Church must stand with the poor and forsaken: see CatholicMoralPhilosophy.com.
317 spoke at length with FDR about Pope Leo: Alter, *The Defining Moment*, 98.
317 Romney resembled Thurston Howell: David Brooks, *The New York Times*, September 18, 2012.
317 "arrogant and stupid": Bill Kristol, *The Weekly Standard*, September 18, 2012.
318 *Washington Post* poll: *The Washington Post*, September 26, 2012.

24. THE FIRST DEBATE
320 "We had this inflated lead: Harvard Campaign Managers Conference, December 4, 2012. For more on the fall campaign, see Glenn Thrush and Jonathan Martin, *The End of the Line* (New York: Random House, 2013); Michael Hastings, *Panic 2012: The Sublime and Terrifying Inside Story of Obama's Final Campaign* (New York: BuzzFeed/Blue Rider Press Book, 2013).

25. THE HOMESTRETCH
335 "How often does he play basketball: Zev Chafets, "Roger Ailes—Off Camera," *Vanity Fair*, April, 2013.
336 focus groups found that audiences were "revolted" by it: *New York Times*, October 24, 2012; *Media Matters*, October 25, 2012.
339 Chicago purchased them earlier, when they were cheaper: see Wesleyan Media Project, Wesleyan University.
339 But even Adelson had his limits: Alicia Mundy, *Wall Street Journal*, December 7, 2012.

341 In Iowa Romney field organizers distributed instructions: *Think Progress*, November 1, 2012.

344 Romney staffers spent $5,000: McKay Coppins, BuzzFeed, October 31, 2012.

26. SHELL-SHOCKED

352 "IN EVERY SINGLE STATE: See Thrush and Martin, *The End of the Line*, p. 209.

359 Romney was "shell shocked": Jan Crawford, "Adviser: Romney 'Shellshocked' by Loss," CBSNews.com, November 8, 2012.

362 panda bear suit: David Corn, *Mother Jones*, February 14, 2013.

363 the conservative rationalizations began: Ben Adler, *Nation*, November 13, 2012.

363 Romney zeroed in on the "gifts": Ashley Parker, "Romney Blames Loss on Gifts," *New York Times*, November 14, 2012.

364 more registered voters than eligible voters: *Columbus Dispatch*, September 13, 2012.

364 The reactionary spasm after the election: Tom Kludt, TalkingPointsMemo.com, November 14, 2012.

364 Reuters reported financial advisers: Jennifer Hoyt Cummings, *Reuters*, November 10, 2012.

365 "bitterly disappointing": Daniel Fisher, "Inside the Koch Empire," *Forbes*, December 24, 2012.

AFTERWORD

375 "Kicking the can down the road: *Bloomberg Businessweek*, March 10, 2013.

Photo Credits

1: Twitter
2: Bob Kreisel/Alamy
3: Will White/Wikimedia Commons
4: Fred Prouser/Reuters/Corbis
5: The *Washington Post*/Getty
6: Andrew Welsh-Huggins/AP
7: The League of Women Voters of Florida
8: Christopher Dilts
9: Elan Kriegel
10: Christopher Dilts
11: Official White House Photo/Pete Souza
12: Official White House Photo/Pete Souza
13: C-Span via YouTube
14: Official White House Photo/Pete Souza
15: Official White House Photo/Pete Souza
16: Official White House Photo/Pete Souza
17: Fox News via YouTube
18: Bectrigger/Wikimedia Commons
19: Courtesy of Romney Family/Brooks Kraft/Corbis
20: *Washington Post*/Getty Images
21: Christopher Dilts
22: Obama for America
23: Christopher Dilts
24: Pablo Martinez Monsivais/AP
25: Official White House Photo/Pete Souza
26: Obama for America via YouTubetube
27: *Mother Jones* via YouTube
28: Scott Prouty
29: Institute for Global Labour and Human Rights
30: Institute for Global Labour and Human Rights
31: Official White House Photo/ Pete Souza

32: Official White House Photo/Pete Souza
33: J. Pat Carter/AP
34: Lawrence Jackson
35: Official White House Photo/Pete Souza
36: Official White House Photo/Pete Souza
37: Elise Amendola/AP
38: Twitter
39: Official White House Photo/Pete Souza

Index

About the Author

Jonathan Alter is a columnist for *Bloomberg View* and an analyst and contributing correspondent for NBC News and MSNBC. He is a former senior editor and columnist for *Newsweek*, where he worked for twenty-eight years, writing more than fifty cover stories. He has also written for the *New York Times*, the *Washington Post*, the *Washington Monthly*, the *Atlantic*, *Vanity Fair*, the *New Republic,* and other publications. He is the author of *The Promise: President Obama, Year One* and *The Defining Moment: FDR's Hundred Days and the Triumph of Hope*, both *New York Times* bestsellers and Notable Books of the Year, and *Between the Lines*, a collection of his *Newsweek* columns. Alter lives in Montclair, New Jersey, with his wife, Emily Lazar. They have three children, Charlotte, Tommy, and Molly.